National Security

DEFENSE POLICY IN A CHANGED INTERNATIONAL ORDER

Fourth Edition

Donald M. Snow

University of Alabama

St. Martin's Press   **New York**

Sponsoring editor: Beth A. Gillett
Manager, Publishing services: Emily Berleth
Senior editor, Publishing services: Douglas Bell
Project management: Pine Tree Composition
Production supervisor: Joe Ford
Cover design: Patricia McFadden
Cover photo: Copyright © Brian R. Wolff/IIPI

Library of Congress Catalog Card Number: 97–065172

For information, write:

St. Martin's Press, Inc.
175 Fifth Avenue
New York, NY 10010

ISBN: 0-312-14828-3

Contents

Preface

The history of this book has reflected the enormous changes that have occurred in the international environment since the first edition was published in 1987. The first edition was written entirely in the context of the Cold War. Any thaw in that environment was only a distant possibility, as leaders speculated leerily about the new Soviet leadership under Mikhail S. Gorbachev. By the time the second edition was produced in 1991, the Cold War structure and its most obvious artifacts had crumbled: the Berlin Wall had fallen in November 1989, and the Warsaw Pact had voted itself out of existence effective July 1, 1991. The Soviet Union still existed as a formidable unit, however, and the failed coup against Gorbachev in August 1991 left observers on edge about the future.

The scene is far different now. Not only is the Warsaw Pact a bit of history, but all its members are now participants in the North Atlantic Treaty Organization (NATO) through the Partnership for Peace (PfP) program, as are most of the Soviet successor states. The Soviet Union is now fifteen independent countries, most of which share a wary view of Russia.

Because international relations generally, and national security policy specifically, were dominated for over forty years by the Cold War, the end of that competition left a notable void that has affected both policymakers and analysts. The national security problem, so focused and clear in the Cold War, became blurred. Had American interests changed? What are the new threats, and how important are they to the United States? What are the roles and missions of American armed forces for the future? How many and what kinds of forces will be needed to face a changed international order?

These are some of the questions addressed in the third edition, which appeared in 1995. Because of the amount of change that was necessary to incorporate, that edition bore scant resemblance to the earlier ones. Eight of the chapters were entirely new; others had to be updated to include the transition to the Clinton presidency.

ORGANIZATION OF THE FOURTH EDITION. A new Chapter 1 suggests an altered direction in the national security debate, conditioned both by a changed environment and a transition in national leadership. The changed environment is described as an international system of two distinct tiers, each with different characteristics and each posing different national security problems and challenges. The chapters in Part I are carry overs from the earlier editions, with updates and some added material.

Part II deals with how the world has been changing. Chapter 6 recounts the end of the Cold War and its residues. Chapter 7 takes a detailed look at the problem of security, national interests in an altered environment, and the array of instruments of national power available to deal with threats. Chapter 8 looks at the structure of threats in what I call the "Second Tier," (in contrast to the "First Tier" composed of the most advanced states) a category of countries that is fundamentally similar to the old Third World of the Cold War, and examines such topics as violence within countries, regional conflicts, and nuclear proliferation. Chapter 9 deals with nontraditional problems such as terrorism, transnational problems, economic security, and a phenomenon called "new internal war."

Part III examines the implications of these changes for the U.S. national security system. Chapter 10 looks at the whole concept of collective action in the form of peacekeeping and what I call "peace imposition" (but what the United Nations calls "peace enforcement"), with specific application to Bosnia, Somalia, and elsewhere. Chapter 11 then examines American forces, both nuclear and conventional, and discusses how they relate to future roles and missions. Chapter 12 looks again at the world of tiers as a way to project defense policy into the future.

ACKNOWLEDGMENTS.   This edition, like its predecessors, was noticeably enhanced by the helpful suggestions of a number of reviewers. These include: Delane E. Clark, U.S. Air Force Academy; Mark Clark, California State University at San Bernadino; Edward B. Davis, The Citadel; Larry Elowitz, Georgia College; Valerie Schwebach, University of Nebraska at Lincoln; and Chris Van Aller, Winthrop University. In addition, I extend my thanks to my sponsoring editor at St. Martin's Press, Beth Gillett, and her assistant editor, Jayme Heffler.

Donald M. Snow

About the Author

Donald M. Snow is professor of political science at the University of Alabama and has held visiting faculty positions at the U.S. Air Command and Staff College, the U.S. Naval War College (where he was the first Secretary of the Navy Senior Research Fellow), and the U.S. Army War College. He is currently a visiting professor at the U.S. Air War College. His most recent books include *Distant Thunder: Third World Conflict and the New International Order* (St. Martin's Press, 1993); *From Lexington to Desert Storm: War and Politics in the American Experience*, with Dennis Drew (M.E. Sharpe, 1994); *The Shape of the Future: The Post–Cold War World*, second edition (M.E. Sharpe, 1995); *Beyond the Water's Edge: An Introduction to U.S. Foreign Policy*, with Eugene Brown (St. Martin's Press, 1997); and *Uncivil Wars: International Security and the New Internal Conflicts* (Lynne Ritnner, 1996). He holds the B.A. and M.A. degrees from the University of Colorado and the Ph.D. from Indiana University.

Chapter 1

Introduction: National Security in a World of Tiers

The major convulsions in the international system that accompanied the end of the Cold War are now over five years old. The patterns that formed the context for national security during that era have washed away; a new, if more ambiguous, structure is emerging in its place.

The changes have been profound. Think of the international system as it was at the beginning of summer 1991, and compare it to what it is now. In June 1991 the structure of the Cold War system that had evolved after World War II was still largely intact. Granted, the rule of Mikhail S. Gorbachev had reduced tensions between East and West greatly: most of eastern Europe had peacefully decommunized, pieces of the fallen Berlin Wall (or facsimiles thereof) were hot souvenirs in a united Germany, and much of the harsh U.S.-Soviet rhetoric had evaporated.

Still, the old structure remained. Both the United States and the Soviet Union remained heavily armed, with both nuclear and conventional arms still aimed at one another. The Warsaw Pact and the North Atlantic Treaty Organization (NATO) still faced one another in Germany and elsewhere. Change was in the air, but it was not yet developed reality.

And then everything started to unravel. On July 1, 1991, the Warsaw Pact members assembled in Prague and formally dissolved the alliance. On August 19, the world watched—literally, thanks to global television—the last death throes of Soviet communism. On that day, an amazingly inept group of eight Soviet communist functionaries, "led" by Soviet vice president Gennadi Yenayev, launched a coup to overthrow Gorbachev and, presumably, to reinstate the communist dictatorship he had been systematically dismantling for over five years.

At first, there were dire fears that the counterrevolution many had predicted was upon us, and that the "bad old days" of competition and confrontation would come back. The conspirators called out the armed forces; early clashes resulted in three civilian deaths. Forces loyal to Russian President Boris Yeltsin confronted Soviet forces as the fiery Yeltsin stood astride a Russian tank in photographs eerily reminiscent of similar pictures from the Hungarian Revolution of 1956, crushed ruthlessly by Soviet tanks. Gorbachev remained incognito in the Crimea.

Then the pathos and comedy began. The inheritors of Joseph Stalin felt the need to call a live televised *press conference* to explain that there really had not been a coup at all. Visibly nervous, Yanayev and his co-conspirators explained that Gorbachev had taken ill and that the State Committee for the State of Emergency, as they called themselves, was merely assuming power until he was well enough to return. Two days later, the coup collapsed, Gorbachev returned to Moscow, and the conspirators were arrested.

The performance of the conspirators was pathetic, showing the depths to which the leadership of Soviet communism had fallen. Yanayev and his comrades lacked the "iron teeth" Andrei Gromyko once attributed to Gorbachev. More importantly, their action lacked support anywhere within Soviet society. Had there been any previous question about the demise of communism in the Soviet Union, it was laid to rest by the coup.

The coup accelerated Soviet disintegration. Emboldened by the surrounding chaos, Estonia and Latvia declared their independence as the coup unravelled, and Lithuania reaffirmed its intention to secede. Within a week, the Ukraine, Byelorussia (now Belarus), and Moldavia (now Moldova) had followed suit. By the end of the summer, most of the central Asian republics had done the same. On December 9, the leaders of Russia, Ukraine, and Belarus declared that the Soviet Union had ceased to exist and would be replaced by a Commonwealth of Independent States (CIS), which all former Soviet republics were invited to join. On December 17, Gorbachev made it official, stating that all central governmental institutions would cease to exist at year's end. With the last second of 1991, the Union of Soviet Socialist Republics passed into history.

The systemic and national security implications were profound. The system shock was all the greater because essentially no one anticipated what would happen. The collapse of the Soviet Union both deflated what was left of the Cold War structure *and* the military confrontation that was its central feature. The prophecy uttered tongue-in-cheek a year or so earlier by Georgi Arbatov, a leading Soviet spokesman and Director of the USA and Canada Institute, had come true: "We have done a terrible thing to you; we have deprived you of an enemy."

Now, the general contours of the new system are beginning to take shape, if the details are not yet entirely in focus. It is clear that the evolving environment is different—even profoundly so. What does this mean for the international system? And, more specifically, what does it mean for the conduct of American national security policy?

In the pages that follow, I will lay out some of the changes as an introduction to the subsequent chapters. For now, however, I will look at four aspects of change emerging from the decline of the Cold War: the transition in leadership in the United States and its orientation toward national security; the national security debate about the size and kind of armed forces America will require in the new environment; the evolving international system in a world of tiers, and the evolving and unique role of the United States in the system.

THE TRANSITION IN LEADERSHIP

A whole generation of leaders and analysts was raised, educated, and conditioned to a set of assumptions about the world based on the immutability of the "protracted conflict" (to borrow the Yugoslav dissident Milovan Djilas's phrase) of the Cold War. The central political reality of that construct was a world permanently divided between communist and anticommunist opponents locked in a competition from which there was no apparent escape or end—other than the fiery Armageddon of nuclear holocaust.

The enormous nuclear arsenals possessed by the United States and the Soviet Union and aimed at one another were capable of destroying both countries as functional societies—to say nothing of the world at large—and their confrontation provided the central military facet of the system. The nature of the adversarial relationship overwhelmed all other foreign and defense considerations: if either side could not successfully protect itself from the other, nothing else mattered. The confrontation defined defense policy and, in a neat deductive exercise, military strategy, tactics, and force size and competition. The Soviet threat was the bellwether for the United States, and vice versa.

This set of assumptions, especially the belief in the endurance of the competition, blinded analysts and policymakers alike to the possibility of change—the possibility that the Cold War could end with a whimper, not a bang. The idea of peace was utopian, unrealistic, a knee-jerk reaction without base for the "realists" who controlled the intellectual agenda of national security. The Cold War may have been cold, but it was also war.

When change began in the Soviet Union under Gorbachev in the middle 1980s, these Cold Warriors were still clearly in the ascendancy at all levels of government. Indeed, Ronald W. Reagan, probably the leading symbol of the Cold War mentality, occupied the White House and presided over the largest peacetime military buildup in American history during the first half of the decade to counter and overwhelm the "evil empire" he had proclaimed in a 1994 speech.

As the momentum of Soviet implosion grew, Reagan gave way to his former vice president, George Bush. In important ways, Bush was the quintessential Cold Warrior, having been honed in a variety of positions under Gerald Ford (Ambassador to the United Nations, Director of Central Intelligence) and as the number two man under Reagan. Bush understood the nature of the Cold War, the nature of the Soviet opponent, and the machinery of U.S. government to combat that enemy.

It is arguable that Bush and those around him understood the Cold War too well. All his principal advisors (Secretary of State James Baker, Vice President Dan Quayle, Secretary of Defense Dick Cheney, National Security Advisor Brent Scowcroft, and Chairman of the Joint Chiefs of Staff General Colin Powell) were, like the president himself, products of the Cold War. Their collective strength was their common devotion to conducting the Cold War; their common weakness was their apparent inability either to anticipate the possibility of the end of the Cold War or to adapt to it. In the end, the "vision thing" betrayed Bush; that the tenure of this last resolute Cold Warrior and the Cold War itself would end at more or less the same time may be symbolically appropriate.

Bush was replaced, of course, by President Bill Clinton, part of whose job is to figure out the nature of the new international system and the American national security response to it. Clinton entered the national security playing field with some disadvantages. Since states lack foreign policies and military forces (other than National Guardsmen), the former Arkansas governor's direct experience was minimal. Although he was an international relations major at Georgetown University and is an avid reader, his knowledge base was circumscribed. As the first post–World War II president without military service of any kind, his grasp of military affairs and military life was similarly suspect. All these traits made the professional national security community wary of Clinton and concerned about how he would handle this crucial aspect of his job.

Because the Democrats had been out of power for twelve years, Clinton had to dip back into a pool of people who had last served in government under Jimmy Carter. His Secretary of State, Warren Christopher, had returned to practicing corporate law, and National Security Advisor Anthony Lake was teaching at a New England college. His original Secretary of Defense, Les Aspin, was chair of the House Armed Services Committee; Aspin's successor, William Perry, had directed Pentagon research under Carter; and Vice President Al Gore was a member of the Senate Armed Services Committee. General Powell was a holdover in the early going, thereby providing some continuity. The very slow pace at which sub-cabinet-level appointments were made in the Defense Department and elsewhere suggested, as well, the difficulty of finding experienced hands.

The Clinton administration's relative inexperience meant he was less encumbered by the Cold War mindest and thus offered a hope of sorts in thinking about the new dictates of national security policy. There has been less of that mindset, which could only be detrimental to reorganizing and reconceptualizing the national security orientation of the United States. The administration's relative inexperience and a whole new set of problems has meant a good many hit-and-run approaches in the early going as well.

What this situation may suggest is that the Clinton contribution will be to act as a transition between the old system and that which replaces it. An obvious outcome of the end of the Cold War has been to relieve some of the pressure for large defense spending of the kind that marked the 1980s and was part of the cause of Soviet collapse (see Chapter 6 for a more detailed argument). Questions now emerge about the kind of post–Cold War military the United States requires and the purposes that military should serve.

THE NATIONAL SECURITY DEBATE

The end of the Cold War was obviously accompanied by the collapse of the intellectual framework that had long dominated thinking about national security in the United States. With the passage of time, a remarkable consensus had evolved about the nature of the threat and proper strategy for dealing with it that was shared by most within the national security community. The consensus among so-called "defense intellectuals" and the uniformed services occasionally frayed at the edges on particular items, such as whether the United States needed a particular weapons system or a certain number of troops or carrier battle groups, but the central problem was not a matter of disagreement. From outside the defense community came calls for reductions, for nuclear disarmament, and the like, but these were generally ignorable as howlings from the fringes.

That consensus is gone, the victim of three related phenomena. First, the disappearance of the threat and the absence of an obvious successor threat has unfocused attention, leaving a much more disorderly intellectual landscape. There is currently no organizing concept on which to agree. Second, the threat ended at a time of growing concern about domestic priorities, especially deficit reduction and infrastructural investment. Politicians turned a hungry eye on a defense budget, the size of which now appeared to overshadow the size of the threat. Third, the happy twelve-year consensus between conservative Republicans and an equally conservative professional military ended with the advent of an apparently more liberal Democratic regime of which the professional military was inherently suspicious. Civilian-military relations, always somewhat strained, rapidly approached the adversarial.

Any of these three elements by itself would have created a debate about the future of national security policy. Their conjunction both widened and deepened the extent to which it would be argued. The Clinton administration came to office riding the banner of deficit reduction and new domestic priorities at a time when the defense community was feeling reactive and vulnerable. Rightly or wrongly, the military felt itself more at risk with the Arkansan who had avoided military service in Vietnam than it would have had the Republicans been returned to office. The new administration, in turn, contributed to its own problems early in its tenure with clumsy handling of issues such as homosexuality in the military.

The point is clear: there would have been profound debate about the future of American national security policy regardless of who emerged triumphant in the 1992 election because of the confluence of factors listed earlier. The Cold War orientation of the Bush administration and the synergism between the professional military and the Bush team might have changed the tone and pace of debate, but ultimately the debate had to go on.

The debate is about what kind of policy and what kinds of military capability the United States will have in the future. One aspect is the changed world environment, which is the subject of the next section. For present purposes, we will examine two other factors that exemplify the debate: the defense contribution to deficit reduction and the role of the armed forces in American society in the future.

Defense and the Deficit

No one inside or outside the defense community disagrees either that deficit reduction is needed to produce the balanced budget the advocacy of which dominates domestic concerns or that defense should absorb some of the cuts that reduction requires. The defense budget is the largest *controllable* element of the overall federal budget, which means that about two-thirds of all defense appropriations require annual positive legislative actions (as opposed to *uncontrollable* elements such as interest payments on the deficit and entitlements, which are appropriated automatically in the absence of contrary legislation). This status makes the defense budget apparently vulnerable. In combination with the vulnerability of a new era in which a looming threat cannot dissuade budget cutters, it makes many in the defense community nervous about the future, even though the conservative Republican congressional majorities elected in 1994 protected the budget from noticeable reductions.

Cuts in spending, of course, equate to a diminished force capability. Some cuts can be absorbed by pulling forward-deployed American troops out of expensive overseas billets; some can be absorbed by decreasing the size of the force; and some can be absorbed by cutting back on training exercises, reducing stockpiles of weapons and equipment, or by decreasing new weapons research, development, and procurement. All such measures have the common effect, of course, of reducing readiness and the ability to project certain kinds of forces in certain areas in a timely manner.

The situation is not without irony. As the Cold War ended, the United States emerged as the remaining "superpower"—the only country on earth with adequate power to provide global leadership in a time of transition. Whenever crisis arose almost anywhere (violence in the former Soviet Union being a notable exception), the other major states turned to the United States for leadership, a phenomenon examined later in the chapter. Where it was not forthcoming or contradicted what the other major powers were inclined to do, the result was inaction. Bosnia was the prototype: the

Clinton administration was blamed when it wanted to do nothing and equally pilloried when it proposed military action with which the others disagreed. Still, U.S. leadership was critical to energizing the peace process that resulted in the Paris peace accords (negotiated in Dayton, Ohio) in December 1995 the ongoing deployment of U.S. and other NATO forces in Bosnia, and their scheduled withdrawal in 1998.

The irony here is that the new definition of superpower status contained contradictory elements. During the Cold War, the possession of large arsenals of nuclear weapons largely distinguished the superpowers; nuclear weapons possession was the initiation fee for membership in the major power club. In the new order, nuclear weapons have lost some importance, although they remain part of the calculation because of their feared proliferation in the old Third World, a problem discussed in Chapter 8.

Because of the changing nature of power, the term superpower means something different. The United States *is* the remaining superpower because of its unique combination of military and economic power that can be used to influence events. Other countries possess one form of power or the other: Japan, for instance, has great economic power, but essentially no military power. Russia maintains large—if arguably impotent outside its borders—military forces, but is an economic basket case. China has large armed forces but limited ability to project them beyond its borders, and its economic power is only *emerging*. Only the United States presently has both, and, as we shall see in Chapters 2 and 7, both are useful and necessary to maintain America's place in the world.

The irony, of course, is that one builds one kind of power at the sacrifice of the other. Spending on defense often comes at the expense of expanding and making robust the economic base on which economic power is predicated. Likewise, investment in the domestic economy (for example, jobs programs, support for education, federal support for research and development) requires cutbacks in defense spending if deficit reduction is also to be pursued. The only other source of significant potential cuts in the federal budget is the entitlement programs that, along with servicing the interest on the federal debt, make up the vast majority of the budget. Rhetoric aside, elimination of "welfare baby" abuses will not reduce the debt; only cuts in defense or what amounts to middle-class welfare (including social security and medicare) can make a dent. All these elements have been prominent parts of the 1996 presidential campaign plans to balance the federal budget and have emerged as prominent during the second Clinton term.

We are only at the front end of this debate. The Clinton defense plan announced on September 1, 1993, would reduce the active duty armed forces to 1.4 million, a sizable cutback from the 2.1 million serving during the salad days of the Reagan buildup. Clearly, a force this size cannot do the number of things—especially, simultaneously—that the old force could do. That is the bad news. The somewhat better news is that the structure of threats for which the larger numbers were mobilized has diminished. The debate will be about how much is too little and how much is enough. It is a debate with strategic, economic, and political aspects, with ample room for disagreement along each of those dimensions.

The Armed Forces in Society

The relative regard in which military matters are held by the body politic has also become a matter of some scrutiny. The professional military force that is one of the proudest artifacts of the past fifteen years views this matter with great anxiety. As it arose from the ashes of Vietnam, the most humiliating experience in the history of the American military, it was committed to producing the most highly sophisticated, professional, and competent military force in the world. Aided by new attitudes about recruiting, training, motivating, and retaining armed forces in the absence of conscription, the American military worked diligently to improve both its competence and its image.

These efforts have largely succeeded. Although the United States suffered a humiliating incident in Beirut in 1983 (the truck bombing that killed 241 Marines in their barracks) and a dubious victory in Grenada later that year, by the latter half of the decade the trend seemed reversed. Operation Just Cause—despite its euphemistic name—in Panama seemed a smashing success, and Operation Desert Storm, the first fully televised war, provided a worldwide showcase for U.S. military genius against the world's fourth largest army (Iraq's). The American military's prestige skyrocketed, apparently reversing traditional American negative attitudes toward peacetime soldiers and sailors (see Chapter 3).

But much of the euphoria exploded like a pricked balloon, and the American military once again found itself on the defensive. The reasons are cumulative, including a changed environment, the souring of apparent successes, misdeeds within the services themselves, initial Clinton mishandling of the military, and a general feeling that the military is no longer so important in a post–Cold War system.

The environmental factor of greatest importance, of course, is the essential disappearance of the major threat that had defined the Cold War: a nuclear-armed Soviet Union with huge and apparently impressive conventional capabilities. That is utterly gone. Russian (and other successor Soviet states) officers attend the American war colleges, pretensively learning the strategies and tactics developed to defeat them, and American businesspeople swarm about the former Soviet Union, seeking not to conquer but to profit. The scramble to identify a successor threat that can prove the firm base for defense investment has remained nebulous and unconvincing.

A second problem relates to the "successes" of the past few years. Operation Just Cause succeeded (although with considerable operational difficulty) in capturing Panamanian dictator Manuel Noriega, but the drugs still flow freely through Panama toward the United States, and only the most charitable interpretation allows one to talk about the restoration of Panamanian democracy (the other goal of the invasion). Iraq's Saddam Hussein remains defiantly in power, and the U.S. commitment is ongoing through protection of the Kurds in the north and the Shiite rebels in the south of Iraq (Operations Provide Comfort and Southern Watch). Operation Restore Hope in Somalia turned predictably sour with the American initial withdrawal, and the return of Americans to capture General Mohammed Farah Aidid, the Somali clan leader and warlord, had an almost Gilbert and Sullivan air about it that aroused angry public demands for total withdrawal from a country where we had initially been hailed as saviors. Somalia remains in chaos, ostensibly led by Aidid's son, the self-declared president who, as a U.S. Marine reservist, was part of Restore Hope. (For a detailed discussion, see Chapter 10.) Our impotence in Bosnia before the end of 1995 closed the loop.

A third problem came from some miscues by the military itself that appeared to reflect a dangerous arrogance and elitism that left segments of the public ill at ease. Two incidents, both involving the Department of the Navy, stood out initially. The first was the Tailhook scandal. At the 1991 convention of the Tailhook Association (the name comes from the fact that airplanes landing on aircraft carriers come to a halt when a hook on the tail of the craft engages a tether that stops them) in Las Vegas, there was apparent sexual misconduct by a large number of naval aviators toward women attending the convention, including fellow aviators. Until public revelations impelled civilian authorities to force the Navy to conduct a real investigation, it was evident that the service had no intention of punishing its own most elite flyers; "boys will be boys" was the apparent attitude. Top-level Navy officials, including Chief of Naval Operations Admiral Frank B. Kelso II, were implicated in the cover-up. In late 1996, revelations of sexual harassment and even rape involving Army recruits further tarnished the military's self-image as a moral exemplar within society; centering on the Aberdeen (Md.) Testing Ground, these problems careened out of control into mid-1997, refusing to disappear.

The other incident occurred in the summer of 1993 when the Marines announced, without consulting its civilian authorities (which it technically was not required to do), that it would institute a ban on recruiting married enlisted personnel. The reasons (not without military merit) were reduced Marine efficiency, high divorce rates among this class of enlistees, and low reenlistment rates caused by long separations due to field training. The Marines argued that military service is not like civilian life, and the detriment of having young married personnel is one of those differences. The problem was not the substance of the message, which the Marines could document. The problem lay in the way it was presented. Politically, the message left the administration looking antifamily at a time it was pushing for "family values." Seeing a potential political embarrassment, Secretary Aspin ordered the policy reversed; the Marines saluted briskly and sulked away muttering. It was not a seemly performance.

These instances of "foot shooting" by the military simply reinforced the gulf between the professional military and its commander in chief, Bill Clinton. That gap was probably inevitable to some degree: Clinton had essentially no experience with the military and apparently little interest in it, and few military professionals knew much about him or his defense policy preferences. What they did know was that Clinton had used legally prescribed procedures to avoid induction into the military service during Vietnam. Since most of the senior leaders of the services had seen active duty during the Vietnam conflict, they were suspicious of this "draft dodger," as some termed the new president.

Clinton initially made matters worse by serving notice almost immediately upon assuming office of his intention to end service discrimination against gays in the military. The decision, especially its timing, was unfortunate. It was unfortunate because it appeared to constitute pandering to a constituency that had been influential in his election. The timing could hardly have been worse. First, the notice of intention was issued without consulting the senior military leadership (the Joint Chiefs of Staff) and listening to their objections; thus, their opposition was guaranteed.

Second, the issue would obviously be highly divisive at a time when the new president should have been enjoying the "honeymoon" normally accorded new chief executives. It was probably also unnecessary, as litigation was moving forward that may eventually resolve the issue constitutionally and, hence, with less partisan rancor. In the end, the compromise solution of "don't ask, don't tell, don't pursue" (recruits cannot be asked about sexual preference and, in turn, do not need to disclose that preference—a policy of neither confirming nor denying preference) pleased no one, but certainly left a highly homophobic professional military suspicious about how good a friend they have in the White House.

All these things have congealed to fray civilian-military relations. As noted, some tension was inevitable as the military was predictably scaled back in a post–Cold War environment and was exacerbated by a round of legislatively prescribed base closings in 1993 and 1995 that threatened to undermine the economies of many communities while making boom towns out of a few selected others (for example, Fort Hood, Texas, and neighboring Killeen). As reaction to the unravelling of the situations in places such as Somalia and Bosnia left the military with apparently less to do, the question, "What have you done for us lately?" inevitably arose. In this charged atmosphere, an assessment of the new international situation and the military's place in it seems inevitable.

TIERS AND THE SECURITY EQUATION: A FIRST BRUSH

It is now reasonably clear what the general nature of the international system that is succeeding the Cold War system will be. We lack general agreement on the terminology with which to describe the new arrangements. Referring to the new environment as a post–Cold War world describes what the system is *not*, but not what it is. For lack of a better set of terms, I will refer to it as a "world of tiers."

The basic idea is simple: as the post–Cold War world evolves, the international system is clearly divided into two distinct groups (or tiers) of states. The first tier, composed basically of the membership of the Organization of Economic Cooperation and Development (OECD), represents the most prosperous countries in the world. The second tier, representing the rest of humankind (about six-sevenths of the world's population, according to Max Singer and the late Aaron Wildavksy), is composed of those countries materially and politically less prosperous and content.

This division suggests that the system consists of two separate components, each with a different set of governing rules and dynamics such that no single set of descriptions can encompass them both. Rather, each has its own distinct set of relationships and problems. The national security equation, in turn, will largely be the result of where the two tiers intersect.

The First Tier

The defining characteristic of the countries of the First Tier is their political and economic similarity: all have well-established, stable democratic political systems, and they all share a commitment to market-based capitalist economics. Moreover, they are all part of the interlocking global international economy in which the distinctly national basis of economic activity is decreasingly possible.

These countries thus have much more in common than they have that divides them. The central relationship among them is probably most dramatically symbolized by the ongoing concert of summit meetings between their leaders, such as the Group of Seven (G-7) biannual meetings. Certainly they are not in accord on all matters. They disagree, for instance, on the terms of trade among themselves and on the amount and pace of assistance that should be given to rehabilitate Russia and other parts of the former Soviet Union.

Their disagreements are, however, marginal, not central. The leadership has progressed into the third industrial revolution that has globalized economic activity; their economic differences can hardly deteriorate except beyond the peripheries of the central relationship. Cultural differences may create a different view on democratic politics (say American versus Japanese variants), but the core common commitment remains the same among the most consequential members of the international system.

This commonality leads to a striking, if intuitively obvious, national security consequence: *it is essentially impossible to think of war among any of the members of the First Tier.* Singer and Wildavsky, indeed, refer to the First Tier as the "zone of peace." This means that among the most technologically advanced countries—those with the prospects of raising the most sophisticated and formidable threats—there is basically no national security problem, and military power is basically irrelevant to the relations among First Tier states.

Why is this so? For one thing, it has become a generally (although not universally) accepted tenet that modern political democracies do not go to war with one another: free people do not willingly choose to attack other free people. (The limited exceptions may be countries like Ecuador and Peru, who are in the transition to democracy but have differences that predate democracy—in their case, a major land dispute over parts of the upper Amazon basin.) At the same time, there is little reason for any of the countries of the First Tier to fight; the economic and political ideological differences that marked the Cold War have simply disappeared. It should be noted that this assertion is controversial among some academic critics, whose analysis of the evidence leads them to the conclusion that the "democratic peace" is overly optimistic and not well grounded in fact.

Because the countries of the First Tier compose the heart of the international system, this also means the absence of conflicts that could basically threaten the viability of the system as a whole, as did the confrontation between the United States–led North Atlantic Treaty Organization coalition and the Soviet-led Warsaw Pact. Rather than being divided, the First Tier stands together. Our principal disagreements arise over how to deal with the problems of the Second Tier and with instances where the problems of the Second Tier offer the prospects of disruption within the general tranquillity of the First Tier.

The Second Tier

The basic tranquillity and unity of the First Tier stands in stark contrast to the roughly six-sevenths of the world's population that comprises the Second Tier. Roughly speaking, the Second Tier is made up of most of what used to be called the Third World—the developing countries of Africa, Asia, and Latin America—and the former Second (or communist/socialist) World.

The most obvious characteristic of the Second Tier is its diversity. What distinguishes the Second Tier from the First is that its countries lack either or both a commitment to, or attainment of, political democracy or advanced market-based capitalism, defined as entrance into the high-technology revolution. Those countries that most closely resemble the First Tier approximate it on one dimension or the other. The so-called Four Tigers of East Asia (Republic of Korea, Hong Kong, Taiwan, and Singapore) have economies that look much akin to those of the First Tier, but they have not evolved the politically democratic forms of the First Tier. In the former Second World, a number of states (Poland and the Baltic states, for example) have made political progress, but still lag behind economically.

Second Tier states differ from one another on both the political and economic dimensions. There are very wealthy Second Tier states—the oil-rich states of the Middle East come to mind—that have highly un-democratic political systems, and there are extremely poor countries such as Bangladesh and Mali. Similarly, India is the world's largest democracy, but various forms of despotism are the rule in many areas.

Although there are exceptions, the Second Tier is marked by instability and the potential or actuality of violence that is quite absent in the First Tier. Some of this instability is a concomitant of the developmental process itself, as economic and political forces adjust to modernization. At the same time, what Samuel Huntington has called democracy's "third wave" has spawned a form of revived, exclusionary nationalism that is tearing apart some states and is forcing a redrawing of political maps in many places.

The instability and violence has both internal and international roots. Domestically, the post–Cold War world has watched in increasing horror a surge of national self-assertion by ethnic and national groups within states seeking power at the expense of other groups. Primordial nationalism—an attachment to ethnic and other roots not overcome by socialization into a broader national identity—has torn the fabric of states as diverse as Yugoslavia, Iraq, a number of the successor states of the Soviet Union (such as Armenia, Azerbaijan, and Georgia), and much of Africa (Somalia, Sudan, Mozambique, Rwanda, and Angola, for example).

The worst of these conflicts involve countries divided on religious and/or ethnic grounds, where attempts to suppress differences in the past have failed and where the hints of freedom have been expressed not in a desire for inclusionary democracy but in a mean and spiteful exclusionary self-determination that pits neighbors against one another in frenzies of hatred and violence with incredible passion. The communal bloodletting in Bosnia is the most visible instance of this for most Americans; it is, unfortunately, by no means rare, as we shall see in Chapter 8. In an increasing number of states, criminal and narcotics insurgencies are replacing more "traditional" forms of civil wars in ways that older modes of thinking about insurgency do not readily encompass. These "new internal wars" are discussed in depth in Chapter 9.

International violence may also increase in the Second Tier. Regional conflicts—disagreements between neighboring countries in geographic regions—have long festered in places such as the Asian subcontinent and Southeast Asia. During the Cold War, a certain control was imposed by the superpowers, which generally supported opposite sides (the Soviets aiding India, the United States helping Pakistan, for instance) in regional conflicts. Motivated by a desire to avoid being drawn physically into shooting conflicts with escalatory potential, the superpowers sought to contain those conflicts within reasonable bounds that did not risk direct confrontation. Progress, however unsteady, in ending the Arab-Israeli conflict offers some hope for peaceful resolution of these conflicts.

As the Soviet Union dissolved and its successor Russia retreated from this competition, so too did the United States; consequently, many of the constraints have disappeared as well. As we shall see in Chapter 8, these conflicts are now enlivened by the introduction of weapons of mass destruction—notably nuclear, biological, or chemical (NBC) munitions—and ballistic missile means of delivery that potentially raise notably the stakes and deadliness of already volatile situations.

Three of the world's largest and most important states, China, India, and Russia, reside in the Second Tier, and each has some or all of these problems. China continues its economic miracle as one of the world's most vibrant economies, but within a system of political repressiveness that the *New York Times* called "market Leninism" in 1993. The sharp contrast between the extremely economically vibrant special economic zones (SEZs) and the rest of the country is increasingly evident. China's future raises questions of inevitable demands for political liberalization and the possibility of political breakup at the peripheries—for instance, in Tibet.

India, the world's second most populous country after China, faces severe challenges. Internally, the possibility of secessionary demands that could break apart the Indian state are clear and compelling. These are especially evident in the northern states such as Kashmir, but they could occur also in the south (the Tamil region, for instance) as well. India is also locked in a long international conflict with Pakistan that is made more tense by the mutual possession—or near possession—of nuclear weapons.

The breakup of the former Soviet Union has also unleashed violence and instability with two bases. First, Soviet policy consciously encouraged the migration of national groups across the boundaries of the internal republics (states) that are now independent states. Most notably, over 25 million ethnic Russians live outside Russia and are potentially subject to repression that Russia is unlikely to ignore. Second, Stalinist policy drew arbitrary boundaries between the republics that now manifest themselves in international violence. The most obvious case in point is the Armenian-Azerbaijani conflict over the Armenian enclave of Nagorno-Karabakh within Azerbaijan and the Azeri enclave of Nakichevan within Armenia. These conflicts are especially lively in those parts of the former Soviet Union where Islam and Christianity collide—a general source of problems in those parts of the world where it occurs. As exploitation of the Azeri-controlled oil fields off the coast in the Caspian Sea (the world's second largest known reserves after those of the Persian Gulf—although their actual size is contested) begins and secure access to those fields becomes an issue, the area will increase in geopolitical importance.

First Tier Second Tier Intersection and the National Security Problem

Violence and instability in the Second Tier is not a new phenomenon; both internal and international wars were waged regularly throughout the Cold War period. Three factors, however, have raised Second Tier conflict to a position on the national security agenda that it formerly did not occupy.

The first and most obvious factor is that Second Tier violence is the *major, even sole,* source of violence in the system. If one is to see where the general tranquillity is being upset, it is in the Second Tier. Second, the mechanisms that used to serve to moderate that violence have largely disappeared. The superpowers have reduced their commitments in most Second Tier areas, and most of the regions lack regional organizations that can readily restore or enforce the peace.

Third, and possibly most importantly, Second Tier violence is much more public than it used to be, courtesy of global television outlets such as Cable News Network (CNN) and the Independent Television Network (ITN). Violence and its accompanying atrocities and gore are an everyday part of television news, impossible to ignore. The visual images that television produces are far more evocative than written accounts of violence: it is one thing to read that 100 civilians were killed in fighting somewhere; it is quite another to see images of the maimed bodies, filmed on the scene and in color, that were broadcast from Rwanda in 1994.

Television may, in an indirect and largely unintended way, be setting the national security agenda, what some call the "CNN effect." People see an atrocity and are horrified by it. The result is clamor for redress, the "do something syndrome." Would the United States have come to the aid of the Iraqi Kurds huddled on Turkish mountainsides had CNN not publicized their suffering? Would there have been such a public outpouring had televised pictures not shown us Somali starvation? Would we have been so embarassed by our apparent impotence had the siege of Sarajevo not been a nightly reality? Slaughter of innocents and acts of barbarity are nothing new; unrelenting coverage of them is. On the other side of the coin, the relentless exposure to atrocity may instead breed an insensitivity to these acts that is much the same as our almost routine acceptance of inner-city violence, such as drive-by shootings.

Because of the general peace in the First Tier, the way we think about national security changes. We no longer need to devote considerable resources to preventing a general war that could threaten to destroy the system, as we once did. The violence and instability to be dealt with now is at the periphery of the central system defined as the First Tier. The traditional military base of national security now lies at the intersection of the First and Second Tiers.

What should be our attitude toward violence in the Second Tier? To begin answering that question requires confronting two realities about the pattern. First, it is difficult—maybe impossible—to think of any conflict in the Second Tier that has the escalatory potential to engulf the entire system in general war—that is, World War III or its equivalent. Probably the worst case that one can conjure is a general war on the Asian subcontinent between India and Pakistan that escalated to nuclear exchange. Such a prospect would be gruesome and awful, and the literal fallout would pose a health hazard for those downwind. Such a war would *not*, however, necessarily draw in the major countries, except possibly as mediaries to end the violence. Although it can only be viewed as a hypothesis, there is no conflict that could occur in the Second Tier that would compel First Tier (including American) involvement. We could, quite literally, ignore such conflicts and, by any objective manner, be hardly worse off.

This leads to the second reality: *with the possible exception of areas where there are large amounts of petroleum, First Tier (including American) important interests are nowhere threatened by Second Tier military conflict.* The traditional use of military force has been grounded in so-called *vital interests*, conditions a state would not willingly tolerate and which it would use armed force to prevent. (This concept is elaborated in Chapter 7.) A European continent forcibly communized would represent a vital threat to the United States; a militantly anti-American, nuclear-armed Mexico would also. In a similar vein, the proliferation of weapons of mass destruction (WMD) to areas not otherwise of U.S. vital interest could, of course, increase their importance.

With the exception of the Persian Gulf, from which the oil necessary to satisfy First Tier petroleum addiction comes, there are no equivalents in the Second Tier. When one combines this realization with the assertion that none of these conflicts threatens the central system, the calculation of national security also must change.

First, the changed conditions mean that, at least for the foreseeable future, the United States will employ armed forces *where it chooses to do so, not where it has to fight.* A realpolitik analysis will not send us to war in any but the most unforeseen situations. Unforeseen things do, of course, happen, and one must be prepared for uncertainty. Who would have thought in early 1990, for example, that we would mount a huge military expedition against Iraq? The offshoot of the "optional use of force" is not that we do not need force, but that the calculation of when we may use it is different. Our basic orientation toward the use of armed force, noted in the Cold War calculation of vital interests, may simply be inadequate for understanding and calculating force in the new system, an idea introduced in the next section and developed throughout the book.

This leads to a second conditioning observation: the way we view national security will be increasingly nontraditional. Responses to events in places such as Iraq and Somalia suggested to many (most notably, former United Nations Secretary-General Boutros Boutros-Ghali) a new category of occasions to use force. Called "humanitarian vital interests," this category calls for employing force—probably under UN auspices—in situations where the atrocious behavior of states against their own people or other states violates basic humanitarian standards. This idea had broad currency as the vestiges of the Cold War dissipated; the souring of the most glowing application of the principle in Somalia has cooled the ardor. The idea is unlikely to go away, however, and it is treated in some depth in Chapter 10.

Other nontraditional roles will also likely emerge. One way in which Second Tier states can affect the First Tier is through the promotion of terrorism or the production of narcotics. These kinds of acts do not threaten the First Tier, but they are annoyances with which we may decide to deal. At the same time, it has become fashionable to think of so-called *transstate issues* such as environmental degradation and the population explosion in something like national security terms.

THE U.S. ROLE IN THE NEW INTERNATIONAL SYSTEM

It is clear that the United States occupies a special place in the post–Cold War international system, especially in those aspects of the system dealing with national and international security. Despite the fact, already noted, that the United States has physically reduced the size of its armed forces, it remains the preeminent military force in the world. This apparent anomaly can be explained in at least three ways.

First, traditional adversaries, such as the successor states of the Soviet Union, have reduced the size and especially the quality of their forces even more than has the United States. The performance of the Russian army in Chechnya is vivid evidence of this decline. Second, the application of high technology to military matters has produced a so-called revolution in military affairs (RMA) that has made U.S. (and other First Tier) forces qualitatively much superior to those forces outside the RMA. Third, other major countries have cut their force sizes even more than has the United States, and those countries that have not cut their forces—such as Iraq and North Korea—are outside the RMA. As noted later, there is no consensus about how much or what effect the RMA will have in the future.

The result is to help define the role of the United States as the remaining superpower. The United States is unquestionably the militarily most powerful country in the contemporary system. This does not mean that the United States has hegemonic power to the extent that it could, if it wished, impose its military will wherever it chose. A land war in Asia, for instance, would be as inadvisable now as it has been in the past. It does, however, mean that the United States possesses the most capable and flexible forces in the world, especially in critical areas such as airlift and sealift, which can carry forces (American or other) to trouble spots around the globe.

U.S. superpower status is by no means confined to the military dimension. In addition, the United States still has the largest economy in the world and, as a result, is a world leader in the global economy that marks the First Tier. At the same time, the combination of market-based economies and political democracies is largely an American construct, and the global trend toward emulation of that combination represents the power of American political, economic, and social ideas (what Joseph S. Nye Jr. calls soft power). This combination, in turn, drives the political and military strategy of "engagement and enlargement" that has become the lynchpin of U.S. foreign and national security policy.

AMPLIFICATION:

Clausewitzian and Non-Clausewitzian War

The most basic contribution of the Prussian strategist Carl von Clausewitz comes from his famous dictum that "war is the continuation of politics by other means." The heart of this statement is that war is a political act that gains its meaning to the extent that it serves the political ends of the state. This results in the firm idea that the military aspects of warfare must always be subjugated to the political objectives that give rise to war.

The Clausewitzian understanding was definitely appropriate to the Cold War period and especially to the military's adjustment to the results of the Vietnam War. For one thing, the Soviets were, if anything, more Clausewitzian than the U.S. leadership, making adoption of the paradigm a useful exercise in mirror imaging. At the same time, the Vietnam War was fought against an opponent who employed a variant of the Maoist mobile-guerrilla strategy, and Mao's understanding of the purpose of war was heavily influenced by his reading of Clausewitz. Also, the Clausewitzian paradigm fit nicely into the realist analysis that dominated governmental decision-making: the relationship between vital interests and the possible use of military force, for instance.

The problem is that not all war follows the Clausewitzian pattern. As the historian John Keegan reminds us, there was *pre*-Clausewitzian warfare fought before the Napoleonic wars (on which Clausewitz based his observations) in which war was an autonomous activity fought for its own sake and deliberately divorced from politics. At the same time (and as discussed in more detail in Chapter 9), we may be witnessing a series of *post*-Clausewitzian wars in the forms of narco-insurgencies and criminal insurgencies. In these wars, the sides have no discernible political purposes beyond destabilizing government in order to assist their commission of illegal acts. In places such as Liberia or Colombia, it is not clear that a Clausewitzian framework is especially helpful in understanding these wars. It may even be that the nineteenth century ideas of Jomini, Clausewitz's primary rival who emphasized the divorce of war from politics, may become relevant.

The significance of this new role will, of course, occupy our concern throughout this book, but it is possible to suggest at least one of its results by means of illustration: the emergence of the United States, notably the Clinton administration, as a global peacemaker. Progress toward a comprehensive Middle East peace accord is the centerpiece of this effort, but it also extends to Northern Ireland and even to Angola. Although the dynamics behind this phenomenon are not clearly understood, they include the positive effect of American diplomacy, the inability of parties to turn to alternate sources of support if they are unhappy with the content of U.S. initiatives, and the ability of the United States to guarantee physically the outcome of an accord. This dynamic is no better exemplified than in the Bosnian accords, where closure was possible only because the United States was willing to commit ground forces to enforce the agreement.

This new status and the changes in the international system that surround it, suggest as well the need to rethink some of the basic concepts about the national security paradigm that guided U.S. Cold War defense policy. The framework was based very much on realist assumptions about what was important in the world. Particularly in the post–Vietnam War context, this has meant framing questions and answers in an especially Clausewitzian framework about the relationships between politics and military activity and about the legitimate uses of military force (see Amplification box "Clausewitzian and Non-Clausewitzian War"). It is not clear that this paradigm matches as well the circumstances of a post–Cold War world and, hence, whether some modification is appropriate.

CONCLUSIONS

Are the kinds of trends and changes suggested here permanent or transitory? If they are permanent, they can be extrapolated into some very real and profound changes in the way we look at, organize, and employ military forces, the bulwark of national security policy. The answer, of course, is that we cannot know for certain the permanency of change. Uncertainty will always be an important element of the national security equation that militates for conservancy and caution in how we adapt to the winds of change.

That change is upon us is undeniable. In subsequent chapters we elaborate on the national security condition. The next four chapters (Part I) lay out the basic context of the system: basic concepts, the American tradition in thinking about force, and the bones of the decision process. In Part II (Chapters 6 to 9), we review the evolution of defense policy from the Cold War to the present. In Part III (Chapters 10 to 12), we look at the challenges currently facing the national security community. In those two final chapters, we speculate on the likely shape of the future and how we might respond to it.

Suggested Reading

Dessouki, Ali E. Hilial. "Globalization and the Two Spheres of Security," *Washington Quarterly* 16, 4 (Autumn 1993): 107–117.

Djilas, Milovan. *The New Class: An Analysis of the Communist System.* New York: Praeger, 1957.

Halperin, Morton. "Guaranteeing Democracy," *Foreign Policy* 91 (Summer 1993): 105–123.

Huntington, Samuel P. *The Third Wave: Democratization in the Late Twentieth Century.* Norman, Okla.: University of Oklahoma Press, 1991.

Kaplan, Robert D. "The Coming Anarchy," *Atlantic Monthly* (February 1994): 44–76.

Keegan, John. *A History of Warfare.* London: Hutchison, 1991.

Luttwak, Edward N. "Toward Post-Heroic Warfare," *Foreign Affairs* 74, 3 (May/June 1995): 109–122.

Nye, Joseph S., Jr. *Bound to Lead: The Changing Nature of American Power.* New York: Basic Books, 1990.

———. "What New World Order?" *Foreign Affairs* 71, 2 (Spring 1992): 83–96.

Rosecrance, Richard. "A New Concert of Powers," *Foreign Affairs* 71, 2 (Spring 1992): 64–82.

Singer, Max, and Aaron Wildavsky. *The Real World Order: Zones of Peace, Zones of Turmoil.* Chatham, N.J.: Chatham House, 1993.

Smith, Tony. "Making the World Safe for Democracy," *Washington Quarterly* 16, 4 (Autumn 1993): 197–218.

Snow, Donald M. *The Shape of the Future: The Post–Cold War World,* 2nd ed. Armonk, N.Y.: M E Sharpe Publishers, 1995.

———. *Third World Conflict and American Response in the Post–Cold War World.* Carlisle Barracks, Pa.: Strategic Studies Institute, 1991.

Chapter 2

Security and Politics

The kinds of changes in the international environment suggested in Chapter 1 have refocused the quality of attention we now place on national security concerns. This attention stands in marked contrast to the mood in the years immediately following the end of U.S. military involvement in the Vietnam war. As the memories of America's worst military experience have faded, both growth and change have taken place in the area of national security studies. Because the field has emerged recently and is evolving rapidly, there is widespread agreement neither on exactly what constitutes national security studies nor on what its basic thrust and orientation are.

Any generalization runs the risk of oversimplification, but two basic orientations — which may be described as the extremes in the discussion — have emerged on what national security is about. At one end of the spectrum are those approaches that describe national security primarily or exclusively in military terms. In this construction, national security and military defense are viewed as more or less the same thing. The emphasis is on how the threat or use of military force can accomplish the security goals of the state. The orientation of those holding this view is geopolitical and deeply rooted in the theoretical approach known as realism. Looking at the international system, they emphasize the role of force in a system where supranational authority is absent and where traditional concepts of interest drive policy.

At the other extreme—and more contemporary in its origin—is the position that this traditional approach is too restricted in concept. In this view, security extends both above the state to something called international security, and below it to individual security. Pointing to the enormous destructive capability of modern (especially thermonuclear) weaponry, contemporary thinkers stress the frequent incompatibility of national with international or individual security; the need for a broader concept of security that encompasses the individual and international dimensions; and the need to harness through arms control, internationalization, and other mechanisms the enormous destructive capacities humankind has devised. These thinkers also extend the notion of security beyond a narrow focus on the military element alone to areas such as economic security, the environment, and other nontraditional areas. Moreover, a growing number of analysts believe that the realist paradigm that is at the base of traditional national security constructs may be inappropriate to framing and resolving questions in a post–Cold War environment.

Any contemporary view of national security must incorporate elements of both views. On the one hand, the continuing organization of the international system as a group of sovereign states means that national concerns—some with military implications—remain of primary importance. On the other hand, the international system is changing radically, and its problems and their solutions can decreasingly be framed in military terms and the kinds of interests that have historically activated military force. The third industrial revolution, with its emphasis on information and generation and diffusion of knowledge, is making the world a far different place; at a minimum, the economic aspect of security is becoming vital to national health and well-being. The end of the Cold War and the emergence of new problems outside the Cold War model challenges our basic framework for viewing national security.

The purpose of this chapter is to provide a framework of concepts and relationships to assist in understanding defense policy issues. It begins with a brief discussion of what makes up national security, followed by descriptions of the relationship between national security and politics, the nature of the international system that requires states to possess military force, the relative role of the various "instruments of national power" in dealing with national problems, and the role of risk in the policy and strategy context. The bulk of the discussion is framed in terms of the realist approach to the national security problem; challenges to that approach are noted.

NATIONAL SECURITY AS A CONCEPT

To begin to understand what constitutes national security, it is useful to look individually at the two words that compose the concept. This is particularly helpful in the case of the first word, *national*, because it is on this point that the traditional and contemporary schools of thought on the subject disagree most.

National security has traditionally emphasized the security of the state as its primary concern, hence the adjectival use of the term *national*. Technically, use of the term *national* is incorrect, since the units of the international system are states; hence, the proper term is *state*, rather than national, security. The concept of national security is used so commonly, however, that it will be used here as a synonym for state security. Legally and politically, the world is divided into jurisdictions defined by state boundaries, and the highest form of authority is that of the state. Moreover, the primary political loyalty that most people (certainly Americans and most inhabitants of the "developed" countries, or First Tier) have is to the state, and the state is the basic unit, or building block, of the global system. If there is a political unit whose security needs to be guaranteed, it is the state. This has been true since the emergence of the state system in the Treaty of Westphalia of 1648.

From this perspective, anything that enhances the security of the state is beneficial, and anything that detracts from its security is harmful. The emphasis tends to be particularistic, focusing on individual problems and threats that face the state and, thus, particularly on short-range problems that states experience. Moreover, this viewpoint suggests that if the good of the individual state and the benefit of the international system as a whole or of other members of that system are incompatible, it is the interest of the state that must be served. This emphasis is fundamental to the realist explanation of security.

The particularistic emphasis draws the fire of the contemporary school of thought, both because of its exclusive attention to state problems and because of the tendency to look at the shorter- rather than the longer-range consequences of actions. Since what could promote state security (for instance, a global monopoly on access to petroleum) would come at the expense of other members of the international system and of the system itself, the national emphasis is viewed as short-sighted and ultimately self-defeating.

According to these critics, problems of security are increasingly akin to other global issues in that they transcend state boundaries; state solutions may thus be counterproductive. During the Cold War, for instance, the possibility of global ecological disaster (the "nuclear winter") caused by nuclear war between the United States and the former Soviet Union was not a national but a global security problem that could be dealt with only at the global level. To treat the problem of nuclear deterrence as national in nature would be to court disaster. Moreover, one country's security, maintained by a large military force, may well be its neighbor's insecurity and, thus, in the long run be destabilizing (this problem is known as the security dilemma).

The second word of the concept is *security*. What contributes to a sense of security, and, conversely, what makes one insecure? The primary dictionary definition of the term captures both the meaning and dimensions of security: "the state or feeling of being free from fear, care, danger, etc.; safety or a sense of safety." Here two aspects of security arise: security as a physical condition, and security as a psychological state. Each sense is present in the debate about what constitutes state security.

The traditional view of state security based in realism emphasizes the physical aspect. From the traditional perspective, the most obvious component of national security is protection of state boundaries from encroachment by other states; this is a physical value so basic that no other goals can be pursued in its absence. Other physical forms of security, such as guaranteed access to natural resources, can be pursued only after hearth and home have been secured. Such concrete symbols represent the bedrock of the physical sense of security.

But security is more than the objective physical state of being free from physical threat. It is also psychological: we are free from fear to the extent that we lack a feeling of fear. Different people have contrasting notions about what makes them feel safe or secure; security will thus always, to some extent, be subjective. We may all agree on certain core conditions, primarily physical in nature, that define security, but there will also be areas where we disagree on what enhances or diminishes security. It is largely these disagreements that divide the traditionalists from the contemporary school.

This problem is part of the security dilemma, and it is best described by example. In the 1950s, when the perception of the menace posed by the then Soviet Union was at its zenith in the United States, there was widespread disagreement on what the United States should do in the face of a gigantic and aggressive Soviet military machine. The debate was framed mainly in terms of the growing thermonuclear threat and the terrible consequences of a nuclear war. Nuclear weapons were thought to provide the primary means of coping with the Soviet threat, yet their existence, proliferation, and potential usage threatened the most basic security value, physical survival.

The security debate can be reduced to those two dimensions. Those who argued for security based on nuclear weapons were saying that the most basic requisites of security are protection of the integrity of state boundaries and of the national political form. Those who opposed this formulation maintained that individual survival is a more important concern than the state's political identity, and that if one or the other must be sacrificed, it should be the state rather than the individual aspect of security. Moreover, the possibility existed that war could now devastate the globe. (This was the period when the doomsday book by Nevil Shute and motion picture *On the Beach* was popular.) As a result, national and international security were incompatible, because defending the state could result in international devastation.

Questions about what contributes to or detracts from national security are often phrased in terms of national interests (an issue to be discussed later in this chapter) and often reflect policy preferences. Thus, for instance, the question of what, if anything, the United States should do about periodic political turmoil in Central America is placed in these kinds of terms. Are U.S. interests, whatever they may be, best served by military intervention, a political and economic approach, or a hands-off policy? For that matter, are those interests primarily military, political, or economic? And what sense of security (if any) is affected? Which outcomes are likely to occur as a result of following each approach? At the bottom line, which outcomes will affect U.S. security, and how? Since it is difficult to argue that the physical boundaries of the United States will be threatened by any particular outcome, the matter falls within the psychological realm of security and is therefore highly debatable. Where there is debate, there is inevitably politics, which is the next element in the puzzle.

POLITICS, THE NATURE OF THE INTERNATIONAL SYSTEM, AND POWER

Deciding what is and is not a matter of national security is a political matter. The word *politics* is defined in various ways, but they all tend to focus on how authoritative decisions are reached. Thus, for our purposes, *politics* will be defined as "the ways in which conflicts of interest over scarce resources are resolved."

This definition suggests two distinct attributes of a political situation, one substantive and the other procedural. Substantively, the phrase "conflicts of interest over scarce resources" suggests the kinds of situations where a political solution is necessary. A potential political situation exists whenever scarcity (the circumstance in which all claimants to a resource cannot simultaneously have all the resource they desire) is present. Scarcity becomes a political problem in need of resolution when those who have claims seek to exercise them and, hence, demand more of the resource than can be provided.

This sounds like an economic definition, but it need not be. Almost anything can be scarce. Economic riches are an obvious example: not everyone can be rich simultaneously. Access to natural resources (such as Persian Gulf oil), social status (being part of the "upper class"), or political power (holding office) are also scarce in this definition. Only one person at a time can possess the U.S. presidency, after all, and there is always more than one aspirant to the office, especially in an election year.

When a condition of scarcity exists, ways to resolve the differences among claimants are needed; this is the procedural aspect of politics. Differences may be resolved in many ways, ranging from the highly orderly and cooperative to the disorderly and conflictual. This variety of means of conflict resolution, in turn, points to basic differences between domestic (national) society and the international system.

In domestic society, there are orderly, predictable ways to go about resolving differences between individuals and between individuals and the state. In the United States, the formal and legal bases of order are stated most fundamentally in the Constitution and federal law, in the state constitutions and laws, and in local criminal and civil codes. The cumulative effect of these statements and more informal social conventions and rules is to produce a set of ways to resolve conflicts over scarce resources.

The system works because it has *legitimacy* and *authority*. Legitimacy means that the majority of people living in the system believe it produces justice for its members; this is a particularly important concern in Western democracies. Were that not the case, it would be silly in some cases to remain loyal to the system (assuming one had a choice). Whenever one puts a dispute over scarcity before the system, after all, there is always the possibility of losing. If one is going to take that chance, it is probably because one trusts that the system will produce an equitable outcome.

The domestic system also works because it has authority to enforce its rules. If you or I break a rule of society regulating our mutual interaction or our interaction with the state, there is a regulatory body to enforce our compliance. There is, in other words, a police force that makes certain the law is obeyed—at least, most of the time. Authority is thus the ability to enforce society's rules of conflict resolution. A society whose members have endowed it with both legitimacy and authority will normally be a stable entity capable of solving most of its problems. Unfortunately, this condition does not exist in much of the Second Tier.

Contrast this situation to that in the international arena, in which the interactions between states take place. International politics, as distinct from domestic politics, is characterized by a lower degree of regularity and predictability. The rules and regulations for resolving conflicts among states are neither as extensive nor as explicit as the rules in domestic society, although most states conform to basic international rules most of the time. Those rules, however, lack both legitimacy and authority, partly because there are fewer legal norms and partly because of the relative absence of mutual values on which social conventions are based.

Role of Sovereignty

The reason for this difference is both straightforward and absolutely fundamental. International politics operates from the first premise of *sovereignty*, from which all else flows. *Sovereignty* is defined as "supreme and independent authority." In domestic politics, the state possesses sovereignty, which allows the government of the state to enforce its policies on its individual members. In international politics, each state maintains sovereignty; the consequences are very different.

In domestic society, sovereignty normally is the source of order because the supreme value it enforces is the maintenance of the society itself. (This is, in fact, the purpose for which Jean Bodin, who desired a strong, unified France, invented the concept in the sixteenth century.) In international politics, the consequence is the opposite; because each member of the system retains that same control, no superior mechanism has the authority to resolve differences between the sovereign members.

Sovereignty—that ultimate and independent authority—thus makes politics in the international and domestic arenas fundamentally different. Because each member of the international system (each country or state) has sovereign control over its own territory, no authority is superior to the state in territorial matters. Should more than one state have claims on, for instance, a piece of territory over which one presently exercises sovereignty, there is no other authority to which the nonpossessing claimant can turn.

States not only possess sovereignty but are very jealous about keeping it. To relinquish sovereignty—to give away power over national territory—is to diminish control, and no state will voluntarily do so. The reason sovereignty is so jealously guarded is the "vital national interests" of states. Traditionally, individuals and groups within states do not always have vital interests, but states do. As we shall see in Chapter 10, this rigid conception is being challenged. The existence of these interests makes the maintenance of sovereignty necessary.

Vital national interests are defined in various ways by different analysts, but a vital interest normally has two characteristics. First, it is a condition so overwhelmingly important to the state that it is unwilling to compromise on it. Second, a state normally will go to war over it.

The concept of vital interests is the lynchpin of the traditional study of security based in realism. To the realist, state sovereignty is the basic reality, and the protection of sovereign interests is the state's most important order of business. Because that protection includes the determination of those circumstances in which armed force will be contemplated, defining vital interests is the key to understanding security policy.

In other words, vital interests are matters of the most extreme importance to the state, justifying extreme measures in their defense. The most obvious example of a vital interest is the territorial integrity of the state itself. No state will relinquish a part of its sovereign territory if it can avoid doing so, nor will it willingly allow any other authority to be placed in a position where state territory might be compromised. Moreover, when conflict over claims on territory between two contenders becomes ineluctable, the resort to war is one means to settle the political problem of scarce territory.

As an illustration of what sovereignty and vital interests imply, contrast an international boundary dispute with the same kind of phenomenon within society. If, for instance, my neighbor and I have a disagreement over where our common lot line runs—that is, a boundary dispute—we have means to determine whose property is whose. If we cannot compromise, we can take the matter into litigation, where a court will decide the issue. We will either willingly accept or be compelled to accept the decision. That one or the other of us must ultimately lose in the judgment does not keep us from pursuing the matter in court, because the domestic legal process has both legitimacy and authority.

In an international boundary dispute (if it is a matter of vital importance to both sides) such an outcome will not normally occur unless the states in question agree to submit to such a ruling. A basic hindrance here is the lack of a "court" with superior authority that could adjudicate the problem. This is so because of sovereignty, and because the states insist that no such intrusion on their sovereign rights should be allowed to occur. If both parties define the property as constituting a vital interest, neither is willing to compromise—that is, to accept defeat. The best way to avoid defeat is to be sure that nobody is in a position to enforce a compromise.

The notion of vital interest must be qualified. Because it marks the boundary in the hierarchy of national interests between where military force will and will not be used, the concept appears very militaristic, and it tends to drive discussion toward military means of resolving differences. But there are mitigating factors. First, there is great debate about what are and are not vital interests. Is there, for instance, any U.S. interest in Central America worth going to war over? Many would argue that the heart of the national security policy debate is about where the boundary between vital and lesser interests should be located, a discussion expanded in Chapter 7.

Second, the applicability and suitability of using military force (and, hence, applying the vital interest standard) is changing. In a world where the major powers possess the ability to destroy one another and, arguably, the world, the question of what is worth going to war over takes on a more restricted meaning. In the process, the definition of what composes national security must be broadened to include concerns such as economic security, the environment, and the like. At the same time, instruments other than military force become central means to pursue national interests.

Third, it is not clear that the realist paradigm and its propensity to activate the national security mechanisms to protect vital interests applies as well in the post–Cold War world as it did before. The idea that vital interests must be involved before national security mechanisms are engaged can easily lead to paralysis in situations where vital interests are not clearly involved. U.S. participation in the limited-objective military effort in Bosnia is a case in point.

If there are no formal, authoritative mechanisms to resolve political differences in the international system, how are the conflicts that inevitably arise between states resolved? The answer is that one gets situations resolved in one's favor to the extent that one has the ability to do so. The means of conflict resolution in international politics is the recourse to self-help. The instrument of self-help is *power*. Unlike domestic politics, in which the force of influence or power is lessened by the existence of authoritative, legitimate systems for resolving differences, international politics is, at heart, power politics.

Power

The most basic instrument for resolving international political conflicts is the exercise of power. Without going into the numerous theoretical debates over the concept, we can use a common and simple definition. *Power* is "the ability to get people to do something they might not otherwise do." In a political situation, all claimants to a resource cannot simultaneously have all they want; as a result, some or all of the contenders will have to accept less. Those forced to accept less will thus have to do something they do not want to do. Why they will do so depends on a variety of things, such as how important the matter is to them and, thus, their ability to compromise, and the existence of mechanisms to settle differences. One way in which resolution may occur is through the exercise of power by one party over the other(s).

Two characteristics of power need to be pointed out. First, power is a relationship; it gains its meaning not from some objective possession or measure but in a relationship between two or more parties. For instance, we often refer to countries as superpowers, major powers, and minor powers, and we assume that, other things being equal, a superpower will be able to exercise power over a lesser power.

Other things are, however, rarely ever equal, which brings us to the second characteristic of power: it is situation-specific. This means that the ability to exercise power is bounded by the specific situations where its exercise might occur. Simply knowing who, in a general sense, has more power will not allow you to predict for all instances whether its exercise will be successful. That depends on the situation, the usability of power, and the willingness to employ power (see the Amplification box "Measuring Power").

How is power applied? Generally, the answer is that it is exercised, where persuasion has failed, through threats or promises to do either harmful or helpful things to the party at which it is aimed, in return for something that party would not otherwise do. Thus, one way to gain compliance with a policy is to threaten harm for noncompliance; another is to offer rewards for compliance. Given the nature of military force, the threat to do harm is the more common means of exercising power.

Threats are "promises to do something harmful if the target does not comply with some demand." They can be categorized in several ways. One way is to distinguish between good threats and bad threats. The difference is simple: a good threat is one that gains compliance without having to be carried out; a bad threat is one you have to carry out. A good threat will be believed and achieve compliance; a bad threat must not have been believed, or it would not have been challenged. Moreover, carrying out almost any threat—especially, those involving military force—means engaging in actions that harm the threatener as well as the threatened. Thus, it is better not to have to carry them out.

A second and related way to categorize threats is as meaningful threats and hollow threats. A meaningful threat is one the threatener is both able and willing to carry out. As such, meaningful threats are said to possess both capability (the physical wherewithal to carry them out) and credibility (the perceived will to carry them out). For someone being threatened, it is often possible to determine fairly precisely whether capability is present. The willingness to carry out a threat resides in the mind of the threatener, but the threatened party must believe it for it to exist. The need for these mental acts in a situation of imperfect information—for one cannot "see" will—makes credibility the less precise element of a

AMPLIFICATION

Measuring Power

Although the concept of power is so pervasive and attractive for describing the operation of the international system, its precise measurement remains elusive. The difficulty has two bases.

The first is finding physical measures that adequately describe the abilities of states to influence one another. A common effort has been to try to find concrete, physical measures, such as the size or sophistication of the armed forces or the productivity of states' industrial bases that should indicate which is the more powerful country in any head-to-head confrontation. The problem is that such measures work only part of the time; there is, for instance, no physical measurement to compare national capacities that would have led to the conclusion that North Vietnam had any chance of defeating the United States in a war, but they certainly did.

The second problem is that measures cannot get at the psychological dimension of will and commitment. How can an outside observer determine, for instance, when a clash of interests is clearly more important to one party to a dispute than it is to the adversary (at least before the fact)? Once again, the Vietnam War is illustrative; the outcome of that conflict (unification of the country) was clearly more important to the North Vietnamese and its southern allies than its avoidance was to the United States. That is clear in retrospect; it was not at all clear before and even during the conduct of hostilities. Being able to see clearly in retrospect is of very little comfort to the policymaker.

meaningful threat. A hollow threat is one that, for lack of credibility or capability, or both, the threatener has no intention of carrying out.

These notions of capability and credibility relate back to the situation-specific nature of applying power. The United States, for instance, is the world's most powerful state by almost all measures of capability—the world's remaining superpower—but that does not mean we can work our will in all situations over all others who are, by definition, less powerful. An example may help clarify the point. During much of the 1970s, the East African state of Uganda was ruled by a dictator named Idi Amin Dada. Amin was a particularly cruel and barbaric ruler who reportedly engaged in genocidal activities against minority tribes in his country, drove Europeans and Indians (who made up Uganda's professional and commercial classes) out of the country, and generally wreaked havoc with the economy. In addition, Amin was fond of giving gratuitous political advice to world leaders, including advice to President Nixon about how to handle his Watergate-related difficulties.

Amin was seen by most as a disgrace to the world community and was at least a minor irritant to the U.S. government. Clearly, the United States would have preferred that he change his racial and economic policies and adopt a more responsible attitude in international relations, or that he be replaced with a more responsible leader. What, however, could the United States do to accomplish those ends? The desired changes would have forced Amin to do things he apparently did not want to do, and there was no court or tribunal before which to drag him to make him change. Resolving the question was thus a matter of power.

Obviously, the United States is more powerful than Uganda, by any measure one might choose. The problem was that U.S. power was not relevant to the situation of dealing with the African strongman. The United States clearly has military power superior to that of Uganda, but were military threats against the Ugandan regime believable? They clearly were not. As annoying as Amin might be, overthrowing or coercing his regime was not worth the expenditure of American blood. Our economic leverage was equally weak; there was minor U.S. trade in Ugandan coffee, but even its suspension did not help in the situation, particularly since American coffee companies ignored the sanctions until compelled to honor them. Try as it might, the government of the United States had essentially no leverage over Idi Amin Dada, unless it were to adopt clandestine means, such as assassination, that are illegal under American law. Amin was, in fact, overthrown several years later by a combination of rebels within Uganda and the army of neighboring Tanzania, both forces with less absolute but more relevant, situation-specific power than the United States.

Power and Self-Help

International politics as an exercise in power implies that one's interests are served to the extent one can engage in self-help. This is another way of saying that the international system is anarchical; and, in a literal sense, it is. If anarchy is the condition where no political authority can enforce rules on society, then the international system is anarchical: everyone is, to the extent of his abilities, the policeman who enforces the law. It therefore should not be surprising that states, since they are not protected by anybody else, feel the need to have armed forces.

This stark description overstates the operational degree of anarchy in international relations. Members of the contemporary school of thought, while admitting that the concept of sovereignty undergirds the system, argue that there are additional dynamics at work. Sovereignty suggests that only limits on amounts of power constrain states, but there are clearly other constraints as well. States are, for instance, bound by many conventions and treaties that limit the things they can and cannot do, and matters of self-interest (for example, the fear of retaliation) keep states from engaging in acts they might otherwise undertake. Put another way, the result of anarchy is not chaos; it is the absence of government and, hence, a weak order.

Moreover, the world is increasingly one in which all states are forced to rely upon one another for a variety of goods and services. This phenomenon is known as *interdependence,* the mutual dependence of all countries on one another for their well-being and, in some cases, survival. The First Tier states rely on the Second Tier for energy and mineral resources necessary to run their industrial plants, and the Second Tier depends on the developed countries for industrial and agricultural goods. Proponents of the interdependence school maintain that this mutual dependence is increasing and that, in the future, the states of the world will come to depend on one another to such an extent that it will not be possible for them to come into violent conflict.

The crux of the contemporary school's analysis is that the state is becoming less central in international politics, that sovereignty in fact is a good deal less absolute than sovereignty in theory, and that factors eroding national sovereignty are gradually transforming the international system into something different from what it is now, a process accelerated by the end of the Cold War. One of the major consequences of these trends is to downgrade the importance of military power, or at least to rethink its utility. As anarchy recedes and a more cooperative international system emerges, the role of power will also decline, and force may come to occupy a different place in the dynamics of international relations.

A changing international environment forces us to expand our notions about power and security. As will be argued in the next chapter, the exercise of power and military force have historically been viewed as nearly synonymous. Such an equation is no longer adequate in an international economy marked by multinational corporations doing business in many countries, internationalization of scientific effort, and the emergence of an internationalized production system. (Hardly any sophisticated product is now made exclusively from components manufactured in a single country.) Likewise, the tremendous increase in weapons lethality initiated by nuclear weapons and extended to biological and chemical agents makes regional and global survival a global security concern.

How the world is evolving can be—and often heatedly is—debated. What is not debatable is that those forces acting to move us beyond an international system based on usable power have not yet taken over. There are, in fact, times when power—including military power—must be exerted to achieve state goals. In those situations, governments continue to feel they have the duty and responsibility to develop and maintain state power that can be effectively applied to guarantee vital state interests. The question, then, is the kinds of power a state must develop and maintain. This leads to a discussion of the so-called instruments of power.

EVOLUTION OF STATE POWER

Historically, the primary—but certainly not the only—measure of a country's power has been its military capability. Such a typification fit in a different and earlier time, when military power played a different role in international relations than it does today. In the contemporary world, the exercise of power is more complex: we now consider more elements, including economic, geographic, demographic, and moral dimensions. To understand the nature of usable power and the so-called instruments of national power now available to states requires contrasting the modern world and its model of war with what it succeeded, notably, the model of war developed and seen in practice during the eighteenth century.

The Eighteenth-Century International System

The eighteenth century, and especially the model of war it adopted, were very unlike the contemporary world in several ways. First and most important, the ordinary citizen's involvement in the domestic politics of states and in the relations between states was absent. Before the success of the American Revolution, rule was uniformly monarchical: kings and queens exercising more or less absolute power, in physical isolation from their subjects. Rulers were, themselves, called sovereigns, and the role of sovereignty was pronounced.

The relationship between rulers and ruled had particular consequences. On the one hand, it meant that the average citizen was apolitical: he had little stake or interest in political matters, both because he did not affect them and, for the most part, because they did not affect him. Feeling as he did about politics and government, he was unwilling to participate in the affairs of state, particularly in the wars the monarch waged against other monarchs. They simply were not his affair. The average man was unwilling to be pressed into service if he could avoid it, and he certainly would not volunteer to fight wars in which he had no stake. Moreover, he was reluctant to be taxed to support the king's wars. Reinforcing this set of attitudes, the ruling elites of most European countries were quite divorced from the rest of the citizenry by rank, education, and wealth. Most members of ruling families, in fact, had more in common with their counterparts in other countries than with the lower classes in their own countries.

This latter phenomenon underlay a second salient characteristic of the eighteenth century: it was a remarkably cosmopolitan system. Its cosmopolitanism was based on the free flow of members of the upper classes from country to country. It was common for royal families to marry across state boundaries; royal civil services were generally composed of nationals from several states, and those armed forces contained individuals—occasionally, whole units—from other countries.

This cosmopolitanism was reinforced by a third major characteristic of the system; there was little political division among the rulers of Europe. Since all states had more or less absolute monarchies as their forms of government, no competing political systems or ideologies that could become the source of conflict, even of war, divided them, a condition of ideological tranquility that is basically replicated within the contemporary First Tier.

This world produced its own style and model of war and warfare. Citizen noninvolvement in the affairs of state meant a limited tax base for the monarch and the absence of any large number of citizens willing to serve in the military. The cosmopolitanism of the system and the absence of ideological cleavage among rulers meant that their disagreements were comparatively mild. The result was that war tended to be limited both in its political purposes and in the means of its conduct.

It was limited for obvious reasons. Relatively poor monarchs who could not recruit soldiers through patriotic pleas had, instead, to raise mercenary armies that were expensive to recruit, train, and maintain. Because of limited resources, the armies the monarch could afford were comparatively small and could, hence, only be used in support of limited purposes. Moreover, the style of physical combat emphasized linear formations crashing against one another and engaging in brutal hand-to-hand fighting that produced very high casualty rates. Given the difficulty and expense of recruiting and preparing soldiers, placing them into combat was avoided whenever possible.

At the same time, the purposes of war were limited by the nature of the system. There were no great moral crusades to impose one political ideology on another, because there was general ideological agreement about how the system should operate. Indeed, the intimate relationships between the political purposes of war and its military conduct (the Clausewitzian influence) was mostly absent when talk of war arose. Moreover, since monarchs either knew one another or were related by marriage, their conflicts tended to be more muted than those we have become accustomed to in the twentieth century.

This comparatively tranquil situation ended with the French Revolution and Napoleonic empire, which began the evolution to a model of total warfare exemplified most dramatically in the twentieth century by the two world wars. With the military applications of the Industrial Revolution available, both the political purposes and the means of war could now be total.

The French Revolution and Beyond

The French Revolution and the following Napoleonic era introduced modern political ideology into international relations, with major domestic and international repercussions. Domestically, the Revolution democratized politics, creating a sense of citizen involvement previously missing in the masses of the population. The fervent cries of "Liberty,

Equality, Fraternity!" activated common French people and made them willing both to serve in the military and to be taxed to support France's military adventures, at least during the Revolution's early years. Internationally, the Revolution introduced political ideology as the basis on which states would fight for the first time in centuries. This Napoleonic influence was, of course, chronicled by Clausewitz, in the process of normalizing the expanded purposes of war and the politics-war connection.

Application of the fruits of the Industrial Revolution to warfare and its subsequent mechanization was the other great change of the period. Previously, hand-held, single-firing muskets and unwieldy artillery had produced a style of war in which the musket used as a club or spear was the most common means of killing on the battlefield. The products of industrialization changed all that. Killing efficiency (sometimes called, antiseptically, the "lethality index") was increased. The old smooth-bore, muzzle-loading musket gave way to the breech-loading repeating rifle, which would be followed in time by the gatling gun, the machine gun, the submarine, the tank, the airplane, and the intercontinental nuclear missile.

Total war, while not unknown to history, was the exception and not the rule. War became the clash of societies, as competing ideological systems sought to destroy and supplant one another by fielding enormous armed forces with great physical capabilities. War became a life-and-death matter for whole societies, not only for its combatants. Ultimately, with nuclear weapons, the means of war surpassed any sensible ends to which they might be put.

In the eighteenth century, military power was the standard by which a country's greatness was normally measured, but no state's military capability was very great, nor were the political differences that occasionally brought war. In the Cold War, the issues that divided societies were framed in ideological terms that could have led to conflicts of total political purpose. New forms of power allowed a greater range of means of warfare. Yet it was difficult or impossible to imagine how the use of the most powerful means available, nuclear weapons, for other than passive deterrence could accomplish any rational purpose of state. Ideological similarity among First Tier states has moderated ideological differences— at least among the major powers.

The result of this evolution is a remarkable change in the utility of force. As the modern state system took its roots in the seventeenth and eighteenth centuries, the usability of military force was quite high, for the paradoxical reasons that there were modest reasons for which force might be used and there were equally modest amounts of force available. Limited political purposes and limited military means coincided. After a century and a half between the French Revolution and World War II, when war's purposes and means became total, the ultimate means, nuclear power, forced a reversion to limited wars, at least as fought by nuclear weapons possessors. Total nuclear means are excessive to any imaginable political purpose, so that the means now force the possessors to limit the ends. The ripple effects this situation has on security issues more broadly defined will recur throughout the following analysis. Moreover, the virtual collapse of communism has removed ideological division as a reason for the major powers to fight, at least for the time being.

Where political division is profound but unresolvable by the application of maximum military force, other means now must be found to exercise power. The means available are the so-called instruments of national power.

Instruments of National Power

Conventionally, the means are divided into three basic categories, the so-called economic, political (or diplomatic), and military instruments of power. Some analysts add other instruments, such as geographic, demographic, or moral (national will), to the sources of power, and such things as clandestine tools like covert action to the means of its exercise. The three-part designation will, however, serve for analytical purposes. In practice, the three forms of power are related, and applications are rarely discrete.

The economic instrument of power refers to the use of economic rewards or penalties (often called sanctions) to compel people or states to comply with policies. Rewards—"carrots," in the familiar analogy—are economic payments for doing what we would like done. The United States, for instance, might offer to increase the level of economic aid to a country in return for allowing port-of-call rights for U.S. naval vessels. A penalty—a "stick"—might consist of a threat to withdraw a loan offer if the country failed to comply. As an example, the Carter administration often threatened to withhold economic and military assistance to countries charged with human rights violations. In cases where violations did not cease, such as Turkey and Argentina, programs were suspended.

The political, or diplomatic, instrument of power consists of the skilled activities of one's diplomats to try to convince another party to comply with policy preferences. The successful use of this instrument in its pure form, not backed by economic or military instruments, is difficult. One can think of instances such as then Secretary of State Henry Kissinger's shuttle diplomacy in the early 1970s to settle the Arab-Israeli conflict as an example, but even these efforts were backed by the secret promise of economic and military rewards if the parties could reach agreement. More recently, successful peace negotiations between Israel and its adversaries have been brokered by the Clinton administration, with economic and even military guarantees in the background.

Military force, either in threat or in use, is the third and final instrument of power. In the American culture, we think of the use of force as a last resort, something to which we turn when all else fails. In other cultures, such as the former Soviet Union, this is not necessarily the case;

military force may be contemplated or used in circumstances where U.S. citizens would not find its use appropriate.

Any state's array of instruments of power will be limited by its resources, which are never unlimited. The result is a policy choice among instruments. The former Soviet Union, for instance, emphasized the military instrument at the expense of economic strength during the Cold War; Japan did just the opposite. With more resources than anyone else, the United States emphasized both; that mix is now being adjusted away from the military instrument.

Once the policy process produces a set of instruments for dealing with perceived threats, the process turns to devising strategy—means to apply power to achieve political ends—to meet challenges. In the military sector, the process extends to defining potential missions—that is, specific ways and places in which military force may have to be employed to achieve national interests—and to building forces to implement those missions. The end of the Cold War requires reassessing strategies and missions, as we will discuss in Chapter 11.

Which individual instrument or combination of instruments of power are used in any circumstance will, of course, be situation-specific. Economic strength, for instance, is clearly the basis of modern military power in a world where war is a contest between societies (total war) and where military power can help ensure access to the vital resources on which economic strength relies. Diplomats sound more convincing if their arguments are backed by economic or military power, or both. Similarly, the state of health of a country's military forces depends heavily on the health of its economic structure. In some cases, economic power may be the most applicable and, thus, the most effective instrument of power, while at other times military or diplomatic power may be most appropriate. A situation may evolve so that the appropriate combination of instruments changes over time. Moreover, some conditions—for instance, revolutionary or terrorist situations—may arise where no instrument is effective. The attempts to free the U.S. embassy personnel held by Iranian militants in Teheran illustrates this dynamic relationship.

The Iranian Hostage Crisis

During the fourteen long months of the siege of the U.S. embassy and the holding of its staff between 1979 and 1981, attempts were made at one time or another to use each instrument of power. The first to be employed was the economic instrument: Iranian assets (estimated by various sources at between $5 and $8 billion) in U.S. banks were seized, so that they were unavailable to the Iranian government controlled by the Ayatollah Ruhollah Khomeini. At the same time, shipments of economic goods and military equipment were suspended pending the release of the hostages.

Initially, at least, the economic instrument did not provide sufficient leverage to secure the release of the hostages. The Carter administration then turned to the military instrument. Planning for a forceful takeover of the embassy had been authorized the day after the initial seizure, and in April 1980, the president authorized the ill-fated hostage raid known as Desert One. When the mission was aborted in the Iranian desert for logistical reasons, the emphasis of activity shifted once again.

The third attempt was to use the diplomatic instrument. Along with clandestine efforts by administration personnel, such as White House Chief of Staff Hamilton Jordan's secret meetings with Iranian personnel in Paris, the administration used Algerian go-betweens to negotiate a release.

In the end, it was probably a combination of the economic and diplomatic instruments that proved decisive. Economically, the Iranians were in difficult straits because of their war with Iraq, which broke out in September 1980; they needed their funds unfrozen so that they could buy weapons to continue that effort. Politically, the Reagan administration was about to come into office; it appeared likely to be more intransigent on the hostage issue than the Carter administration, making a settlement before the change in power in Washington attractive. As a result, the hostages were released on January 20, 1981, the day the oath of office was administered to President Ronald Reagan, and they arrived in Germany hours before the new president took office.

Coordinating the instruments of power and deciding which is appropriate in any given situation is, of course, at the heart of conducting a state's foreign policy. To some extent, the nature of the situation will dictate which instrument or combination of instruments is employed. At the same time, the choice depends on the availability of various instruments of power and on national predilections to use one form or another.

This latter point deserves some attention. If some power situations inevitably require the use of threats, then it is clear that those threats must be credible; this requirement, in turn, means that whatever kind of power is involved must be available. In the case of military power, for instance, it is idle and often dangerous to make threats one appears unable or unwilling to carry out to gain compliance. Canada cannot, for example, issue military threats against the United States that would be believable, and what President Clinton calls the "circle of market democracies" (the First Tier) cannot and do not issue what would be incredible military threats against one another.

At the same time, different states have predispositions to use various instruments of power. Reflecting American economic and industrial might, the United States has traditionally preferred to rely heavily on the economic instrument; doing so allowed us to act from strength. During the period from the end of World War II until the mid-1960s, for instance, the strength of the American economy and, particularly, the paramount position of the American dollar as the standard for international trade allowed the United States tremendous leverage in international politics. The promise to give or the threat to withhold the dollar provided power that made the use of other instruments unnecessary. As the dollar has declined relative to other currencies and as the economies of Western Europe and Japan have become rivals of the U.S. economy, that preeminence has diminished; the ability to employ the economic instrument in a wide variety of situations has thus declined.

The debate in this country about the way the international system is evolving relates to this question about the instruments of national power. The contemporary school argues that the role and relevance of the military instrument of power is receding rapidly and is being replaced in prominence by the economic instrument. The very destructiveness of the military instruments now available (nuclear weapons) causes this new security dilemma. The military instrument has, in this construction, become so muscle-bound that the threat of its use is no longer credible. In this void, other means of settling differences must emerge—chiefly, it would appear, the economic instrument—because of the growing interdependence of the world. It is arguable that the evolving system is creating a situation wherein the United States will be able to threaten or use force only in parts of the Second Tier where traditional U.S. interests may be insufficient to justify using that force.

More traditional analysts disagree with this assessment. While agreeing that the role of military force in international politics is changing, they maintain that the military instrument is not becoming anachronistic. Rather, the existence of nuclear weapons restricts the kinds of circumstances in which it may be employed and the way in which force may be used. From this vantage point, the question is not whether force is relevant but how that relevance has changed and in what circumstances it continues to exist.

RISK AND RISK ASSESSMENT

In a world where national security depends on the exercise of one kind of power or another, the individual and cumulative instruments of power define the state's capability to deal with threats to its interests. As indicated, threats and the power to negate them has a broader meaning than simply military power, although that form of power may be the ultimate resort.

The problem, broadly speaking, is that threats to national interests generally exceed total national resources to negate them. The difference between perceived threats and the ability (capabilities) to negate those threats is defined as risk: those threats for which resources are unavailable. Where capabilities are inadequate and risk must be accepted, the heart of policy is determining which risks are most and least tolerable (risk assessment), and the basis of strategy is taking action that maximizes the use of resources to minimize those risks.

Risk and risk assessment (what is called "net assessment" in official U.S. governmental circles) are crucial in national security policy for at least two reasons. First, in the contemporary world there is no shortage of national security challenges, some of them military, some not. While the United States no longer faces serious technological challenges in military technologies from the former Soviet Union, Japan and the countries of the European Union (EU) challenge U.S. technological advantage in a whole spectrum of goods and services. The receded Russian challenge makes military balance and national security defined strictly in military terms archaic; military expenditures negatively affect American commercial competitiveness in world markets and national security is defined as economic security and well-being. Assuming that the United States has neither the financial nor labor power resources simultaneously to negate both economic and military threats, where does it choose to concentrate its efforts and where does it accept risk?

Second, the assessment of risk occurs at a time of declining resources available for national security. The reason, of course, is the need to deal with the so-called "double deficits": the federal budget deficit that requires decreased federal spending, and the trade deficit between the United States and the rest of the world. The result is that smaller amounts of federal dollars will be available in the future to deal with all problems, including those associated with national security.

If one finds the acceptance of risk intolerable, then there are two broad policy options one may follow, independently or in tandem. The first is to increase capability to negate threat; as the immediately preceding discussion suggests, this is unlikely to work. If anything, capability is likely to decrease as the federal budget axe continues to fall. The second option is to reduce the threat. The rapidly changing political situation in Europe that witnessed the dissolution of the Warsaw Pact and the Soviet Union, combined with progress in conventional arms reduction negotiations (the Conventional Forces in Europe, or CFE, talks), have all but eliminated the perceived risk of war in Europe and, hence, the level of necessary commitment. At the same time, new threats are emerging in the Second Tier.

CONCLUSIONS

The purpose of this chapter has been to introduce the context that creates the need for a concern with national security. The heart of the need for national security is the international system and its organization around the idea of sovereignty. As long as the members of the system retain supreme and independent authority, anarchy will be the prevailing form of organization. In this situation, the resolution of differences cannot be assigned to a superior authority, and the exercise of power will be the means by which states engage in conflict resolution. Self-help, in other words, will continue to rule.

Traditionally, the means by which power is exercised is through the threat or application of military force. In that context, national defense policy and security policy are more or less synonymous. As has been suggested, that focus clearly has not disappeared, although it has come increasingly under question as an adequate framework for organizing an understanding of the evolving system. The nature of the system has demanded the possession and occasional use of military force in the past, and it is likely to continue to do so in the future. Military force remains, after all, one way in which risk is reduced in international relations.

These are, however, dynamic times, in which the nature of the international system is rapidly changing. The breakdown of the traditional East-West Cold War as the focus of international relations is one source of change, as is the emergence of a new economic set of rivalries focused around the United States, Japan, and the EU. At the same time, the Second Tier poses continuing challenges.

These new foci have an impact on American national security that is not always, or necessarily, heavily military in character. National security now means more than military policy and strategy, and both the student and the policymaker need to look at matters affecting the well-being of the country in a more comprehensive manner, recognizing that traditional ways of thinking remain a part, but not the only part, of the equation.

Suggested Reading

Brodie, Bernard. *Strategy in the Missile Age*. Princeton, N.J.: Princeton University Press, 1959.

Brodie, Bernard. *War and Politics*. New York: Macmillan, 1973.

Brown, Harold. *Thinking about National Security*. Boulder, Colo.: Westview Press, 1983.

Clausewitz, Carl von. *On War*, rev. ed. Translated and edited by Michael Howard and Peter Paret. Princeton, N.J.: Princeton University Press, 1984.

Collins, John M. *Grand Strategy: Practices and Principles*. Annapolis, Md.: Naval Institute Press, 1973.

Fromkin, David. *The Independence of Nations*. New York: Praeger Special Studies, 1981.

Keegan, John. *A History of Warfare*. London: Hutchison, 1991.

Knorr, Klaus. *On the Uses of Military Power in the Nuclear Age*. Princeton, N.J.: Princeton University Press, 1966.

Mandelbaum, Michael. *The Fate of Nations: The Search for National Security in the Nineteenth and Twentieth Centuries*. Cambridge, U.K.: Cambridge University Press, 1988.

Morgenthau, Hans J., and Kenneth W. Thompson. *Politics among Nations: The Struggle for Power and Peace*, 6th ed. New York: Knopf, 1985.

Nye, Joseph S., Jr., and Robert O. Keohane. *Power and Interdependence: World Politics in Transition*. Boston: Little, Brown, 1977.

Schelling, Thomas C. *Arms and Influence*. New Haven, Conn.: Yale University Press, 1966.

Smoke, Richard. *National Security and the Nuclear Dilemma*. New York: Random House, 1984.

Waltz, Kenneth. *Man, the State, and War: A Theoretical Analysis*. New York: Columbia University Press, 1959.

Chapter 3

The American Experience

Although military force is not the entirety of national security, its role remains central. Americans have historically had a unique and essentially naive view of the role of military force. For most of us, a constant concern with matters of national defense and security is a post–World War II phenomenon. Questions of war and peace and the political purposes for which military force is employed are alien to the average American, who has never had to come seriously to grips with the power-politics aspects of the world in which we live.

Our atypical experience and the perceptions it has generated are worth exploring. To that end, let us begin by looking at three broad conditioning factors that have helped shape the American self-image. From these we will proceed to discuss the accumulation of a series of attitudes that frame the American military tradition and popular feelings toward the role of military force.

CONDITIONING FACTORS

At least three factors stand out as important influences on how Americans have come to view the role of defense and national security. These (doubtless, alternative lists could be constructed) are the essential American lack of a sense of history, the unique American geographical endowment, and the country's Anglo-Saxon heritage.

American Ahistoricism

It is not too strong an assertion to say that Americans are an ahistorical people. This characteristic is particularly evident in their view of military history. In large measure, the brevity of American history helps explain it; the record is, after all, fewer than 400 years long, and even this history is not shared in its entirety by large parts of the population. The history of the United States is punctuated by the successive waves of immigration that produced its population. Only a relatively few Americans can trace their own heritage in this country to the nation's birth. That there are no Vietnamese-Americans in the Daughters of the American Revolution is a result of how the United States was populated; that fact explains why sizable parts of American history do not conjure up a personal sense of identification for many Americans.

If Americans lack a detailed and specific sense of common history, we do have a general impression of how history has treated the United States, and it is a positive image. The result is an essential optimism—an expectation that the future will hold more of the same success—that has only recently been challenged by changes in the international environment.

This general orientation toward history spills over to the American sense of military experience in a couple of ways. On the most general level, a sense that we are a successful country extends to a belief in a positive experience whenever the call to arms is sounded. Americans think of themselves as winners at war and at peace; when the United States is forced to fight, it prevails. That this image is not entirely accurate (portraying the War of 1812 as anything even vaguely resembling a military success requires a considerable convolution of fact) is almost beside the point. The myth persists. Acceptance of the failure to prevail militarily in Vietnam was, thus, all the more difficult—indeed, nationally traumatic.

Americans are also portrayed as an essentially pacific people, slow to anger but, once aroused, capable of vanquishing any foe. The notion of our peacefulness would, of course, be disputed by most American Indians, as would the implication that Americans fight only when provoked. War was declared on Spain, for instance, in 1898, even though Spain had agreed to all American demands. In fact, of course, the United States has fought six major wars (the Revolution, the Civil War, World Wars I and II, Korea, and Vietnam), three minor wars (the War of 1812, the Mexican War, and the war with Spain in 1898), as well as numerous Indian campaigns and skirmishes from that with the Barbary pirates to the sideshow in Panama in 1990 and the Persian Gulf War—all packed into a 200-year history. Still, most Americans think that war is an aberration, an unusual occurrence representing an interruption in the peace that is the normal condition.

Accident of Geography

Geography has blessed the United States in at least two distinct ways. First, the accident of geography has made the United States virtually an island country. Broad oceans buffer the North American continent on both the east and the west, and weak or friendly neighbors to both the north and south present no military threat. With its isolation and sheer size, the United States has been immune from significant military threats for most of its history. Its distance from both Europe and Asia has meant that invading the territorial United States is virtually impossible. At the same time, its territorial expanse has made it, like China and Russia, too large to effectively conquer and hold.

The second geographic blessing is resource abundance. The North American continent is blessed with a wide variety of mineral and energy resources and with fertile soil. For most of its history, the United States has been, to the extent it wanted to be, virtually independent of the rest of the world in the resources necessary for prosperity. It has been only in recent years—primarily since World War II—that depletion of some resources, such as copper; exhaustion of cheap, economically profitable reserves of others, such as petroleum; or the emergence of a need for exotic resources, such as titanium, has created a dependence on foreign sources of supply.

This experience stands in sharp contrast to that of most of the rest of the world. Geography made the United States impregnable to foreign invasion or military action from 1815 until the continent fell under the shadow of Soviet nuclear missiles after 1957, when *Sputnik* and the first Soviet ballistic missiles were first launched. Geography has not been so kind to the countries on the northern European plain: the former Soviet Union, Poland, and Germany have known numerous invasions through history. Similarly, resource-poor countries such as Japan have known the need for secure access to all sorts of natural resources for a long time, and they have had to take measures to defend that access.

Our geographic legacy teaches Americans two things for the present and future. On the one hand, for most of American history, the United States has not had to worry much about military force. There has been no need to maintain and pay for national military forces in times of peace. Since the War of 1812, after all, military force has been used on American territory only in acts of self-infliction—the Civil War—or territorial expansion—the various Indian campaigns. Maintaining military forces to deter or repel foreign invaders (the raids of Pancho Villa against settlements in the Southwest during the 1910s notwithstanding) has simply never been much of an American problem. Also, the United States has not needed to participate in the geopolitical game of access to overseas resources because of its own natural riches.

These natural protections have, however, prejudiced the American view of military force. Since we have not had to defend ourselves, our military involvements have been expeditionary in nature, with forces being sent to far-flung shores. Besides creating the somewhat cynical feeling that we have had to "snatch someone else's chestnuts from the fire," expeditionary uses of force have rarely engendered or sustained the levels of support that a defense of national territory would have. At the same time, knowing that the fight would be elsewhere has taken some of the urgency out of American military adventures and has allowed for a more or less leisurely preparation for war behind the safety of broad oceans.

Cultural Heritage

The third factor is America's Anglo-Saxon heritage. Although most Americans are not Anglo-Saxon in ancestry (the largest single group of Americans, at least as measured by surnames, is German), people of English background were heavily represented in the colonies before American independence. Our institutions and the attitudes present at the birth of the country reflect that background.

This heritage can be seen as relevant to questions of national defense in a couple of ways. First, there has been an aversion to, and suspicion of, the military—especially the army—during peacetime. This comes in large measure from the British experience, particularly from the reaction to the Cromwellian period of the 1640s, when the Commonwealth's army was used to suppress opposition to the regime. A provision of the settlement of the Glorious Revolution that restored the monarchy in 1688 forbade a standing British army during peacetime.

This preference was clearly present in the American colonies. One of the major causes underlying the American Revolution was the stationing of British troops on American soil after the French and Indian Wars. The colonials objected that such an intrusion would not have been tolerated in the mother country, and when the British government levied a series of taxes and duties on the colonists to help pay to maintain those troops, the process that led to the Revolution was accelerated.

This same attitude remained prominent during the Revolution itself. In his attempts to get the Continental Congress to authorize and provision the Continental Army, General Washington had to assure the Congress constantly that he had no intention of using the army to usurp their authority. In one fit of exasperation, he was overheard to observe that he could understand why the Congress objected to the idea of any army during peacetime, but had difficulty understanding their objection to an army in time of war.

The second relevant aspect of the Anglo-Saxon heritage is a strong commitment to constitutional rule, especially to the guarantee of individual rights and liberties. Military service, especially when it is compulsory through conscription or draft, obviously represents an infringement on and compromise of individual liberties and, as such, becomes somewhat objectionable. It is not coincidental, in this regard, that only four of the sixteen members of the North Atlantic Treaty Organization (NATO) did not have conscription during the Cold War. Besides Luxembourg (which has a total armed force of 300), those countries were Great Britain, Canada, and the United States, all of which share that common heritage.

These three factors are not, of course, entirely independent of one another. The accident of geography, for instance, made an ahistoricism about military power possible; there were few important lessons to learn. At the same time, the legacies of the Anglo-Saxon heritage are much easier to sustain for what is, in essence, an island country. Not maintaining a standing army in peacetime is a luxury that a country protected from invasion by broad oceans can afford; a continental state with hostile neighbors cannot. It is significant to note that the prejudice against standing armies in both the United States and Britain has never extended to a standing navy. Navies are rarely large enough to pose a threat to the regime. They can be kept at sea and out of sight, and their existence provides whatever protection is needed for the country.

These conditioning factors help create the environment in which a distinctly American tradition of looking at military matters has evolved. In the next section, we examine components of that tradition and discuss how it contributes to the shape of contemporary defense policy.

THE AMERICAN MILITARY TRADITION

The way a country's citizens view the role of defense and military power is the result of the kinds of forces discussed in the previous section. This military tradition, or what some scholars call "strategic culture," consists of a number of elements that, in combination, give one a good idea of a country's orientations.

All countries evolve different strategic cultures because of variations in historical experience, geography, culture, and a variety of other factors. This fact should seem obvious enough, but sometimes it is not. When one does not know much about an opponent, one tends to transpose one's own attitudes and beliefs onto that adversary and to anticipate actions like those one would take oneself in certain situations. Such a transposition can lead to mistakes with serious consequences.

The Vietnam War illustrates this point. When American involvement in that tragic episode began, relatively few Americans inside or outside of government had much expertise about Southeast Asia. Knowing little of Vietnamese history, culture, and—especially—nationalism, American decision makers had a difficult time understanding the enormous physical sacrifices the North Vietnamese were willing to endure to reunify the country. Rather, the Johnson administration gradually escalated the violence—notably through the aerial bombardment campaign against the Democratic Republic of Vietnam (DRV) known as "Rolling Thunder." The idea was that, at some point, the amount of suffering the North Vietnamese people were willing to endure would be exceeded and they would stop their actions against South Vietnam. This approach failed to appreciate that the North Vietnamese, and many South Vietnamese, viewed the struggle as a total effort aimed at removing the last vestiges of French colonialism. In a word, it was nationalistic, and its appeal was firmly embedded in Vietnamese history and culture. It would not be as easily abandoned as the American cost-benefit approach suggested.

The American strategic culture, or military tradition, is also distinctive, reflecting American history and culture. While any list of elements is bound to be somewhat arbitrary, seven factors can be identified as playing a part in forming that tradition:

1. An underlying antimilitarism and suspicion of things military.
2. Belief in the efficacy of the citizen-soldier.
3. The legend of American military invincibility.
4. The tradition of mobilization and demobilization.
5. The impact of America's democratic institutions.
6. A preference for total rather than limited war.
7. The impact of the media on the conduct of war.

Clearly, these factors are related to one another; examining each helps explain why Americans view military activity the way they do.

Antimilitary Bias

Suspicion of the military and of military solutions to problems is as old as the Republic, and it is a major legacy of the Anglo-Saxon heritage. From the time the United States was founded, a standing professional military has been looked on with suspicion and even disdain as something not entirely to be trusted or respected.

Antimilitarism has manifested itself in several ways. One response to the distrust of a standing military has been to keep it as small as possible during peacetime. Throughout American history, up to the 1950s, the professional military (mainly the army) was quite small, comprising a compact professional officer corps and a noncommissioned officer corps. Moreover, it was kept physically isolated, where people did not have to look at it closely—for example, by posting it on the frontier to deal with the Indians in the nineteenth century. In the eighteenth and nineteenth centuries, reliance on the military for protection aganst naval threats to coastal forts also reflected this feeling: most of the time the forts were unmanned, and personnel were called up only in response to an imminent threat.

A second way of responding to antimilitarism was to make the professional military, such as it was, as nonpolitical and, hence, as nonthreatening as possible. To this end, the professional military establishment—especially its officer corps—has been strictly separated from the political arena. The military academies at West Point and Annapolis have traditionally been engineering schools in their academic orientation, with little emphasis on training in the political aspects of military activity. Thus Clausewitz's On War, the seminal work on the relationship between politics and military activity originally published in 1832, was not even translated into English and introduced at the U.S. Military Academy until 1873, more than forty years after its original appearance in German. Moreover, for a long time military officers effectively had to forfeit the vote: until absentee balloting became law in 1944, the only military personnel who could vote were those stationed close enough to their hometowns to cast ballots. And their political activity was (and to some extent still is) restricted to the act of voting.

This antimilitarism and its manifestations have had serious consequences for the American view of military affairs. Having a very small and generally underpaid military establishment has been, among other things, fairly inexpensive. It is really only in the period since the Korean War that the United States has made a large and continuous economic commitment to national defense. An apolitical military, at the same time, has certainly meant that fear of the "Seven Days in May" phenomenon (from the book and film about an attempted military takeover of the government) is farfetched. It has also meant a politically ignorant military establishment with limited ability to advise the political authority on matters beyond the battlefield.

Antimilitarism and a small commitment to a military establishment could be sustained for most of American history because the accident of geography meant that the military was not needed most of the time. Further reinforcing this predilection was the belief, which really died only after World War II, that the national defense could basically be entrusted to the citizen-soldier, the militia member who was more citizen than soldier. During the Cold War, the population embraced a large, highly professionalized military as a hedge against aggression and accorded the military heightened status. Whether that attitude or the more traditional view will hold with the Cold War over remains to be seen.

The Citizen-Soldier

The myth of the efficacy of the citizen-soldier is as old as the Revolution. When the Revolution broke out in April 1775 at Lexington and Concord, regular British units confronted various colonial militia groups that had collected at the scene. When the British retreated into Boston, shifting bands of militia laid siege to the city. From those bands of what we would now call reserves or national guardsmen, General Washington tried to fashion an army.

The problem with the militia myth is the belief that militia units, which were about the only military forces the United States entered wars with until well into the twentieth century, are effective fighting forces. The facts, sadly, do not bear out this contention. Certainly the colonial militia had some successes in the Revolution, but that was largely because their experience with the Indians had taught them a style of fighting, now termed guerrilla warfare, with which the British were unfamiliar and to which they could never adapt tactically. But when it has come to serious, conventional warfare, those same militia units have generally not fared well.

The development and sustenance of the belief in the citizen-soldier suited national predilections. The militia member was more citizen than soldier and thus did not pose any potential threat to the political system. His lack of prowess as a fighting man was almost beside the point, since there were only minor threats to be dealt with, anyway.

The reserves in all services and the National Guard are the lineal descendents of the militia tradition—part-time warriors who are more citizens than soldiers. Their role, as we shall see in Chapter 11, remains controversial. The professional, active-duty military tends to view them with some disdain as erstwhile amateurs with little combat utility, even if they provide valuable support services. The Congress, on the other hand, places great value on the resources and support that reserve elements bring to individual congressional constituencies.

Two other elements of the American strategic culture are closely related to the mythology surrounding the citizen-soldier. These are the legend of invincibility and the tradition of mobilization and demobilization.

Invincibility

The notion of American invincibility has at least two corollaries. One is the tradition of "can do," the idea that no military task is too difficult to overcome if Americans truly apply themselves to overcoming it. It is an image out of a John Wayne World War II movie, where American fighting men face insuperable odds but somehow manage always to overcome them.

The other corollary is the idea that Americans prevail because of the skill and brilliance with which they fight. The American fighting man prevails because he is resourceful and determined and because his leaders show foresight and skill in managing military tasks. The traits that make Americans successful in civilian affairs also make them successful at war—another manifestation of the belief in the militia tradition. Moreover, Yankee ingenuity produces a military leadership that overcomes any adversity.

The problem is that these traditions are not entirely true; they create a false, inflated view of what the U.S. military can accomplish. This distortion can be seen by looking at each corollary historically.

The "can do" idea suggests that the military will do whatever is necessary in the future, just as it has in the past. The problem with this premise is that it does not entirely hold up under the light of past experience. Americans have generally prevailed in their military undertakings, but that has not always been the case. The War of 1812 can hardly be considered a military success; the American army won only one battle decisively, at New Orleans, and that encounter was fought over two weeks after the peace treaty ending the war had been signed. Otherwise, there was very little military glory in that war, and the invasion of Canada stands as one of the least glorious exploits in American military history.

What Americans have shown they can do is prevail eventually in long, total wars, where superior U.S. resources can be used to fight wars of attrition. The prototypical war in the American mind is World War II, where the United States played a large and critical role in the defeat of the Axis powers. That war, however, was the exception rather than the rule, both because it was a war of total political purpose and military means and because of the role Americans played in it. In the only other world war, for instance, the U.S. role was limited to the last six months of combat.

What the myth of invincibility and the idea of can do masks is the kinds of circumstances in which the U.S. military has historically not done well. Americans have not been especially adept at what is generally called "unconventional warfare," fighting against an enemy that does not employ standard military methods. Whether it was the subjugation of the Seminole Indians in the Florida swamps (which took the U.S. Army two years, against about 1,000 Indians who lacked firearms), the Filipino insurrection of 1899–1902, General Pershing's largely futile pursuit of Pancho Villa in Mexico just before World War I, or campaigns against the Apache Indians, the regular army has never displayed any particular talent or relish for fighting an unconventional war. Only a few Americans, such as Francis ("the Swamp Fox") Marion in the Revolution, have excelled as guerrilla fighters.

The notion of American military brilliance is similarly flawed. The United States has, by and large, produced competent military leadership, but the idea that it has been systematically brilliant and superior to its adversaries is difficult to sustain. American military leaders have sometimes been plainly outgeneraled, as when General Hull surrendered an entire army to a smaller British force at Detroit, without a shot having been fired, during the War of 1812. Although that is an admittedly extreme example, there is also President Lincoln's inability to find a competent general to lead the Army of the Potomac before Grant was placed in charge of all Union armies. The lack of sound leadership undoubtedly lengthened the Civil War. Moreover, there are very few instances in which the United States has produced military strategists and thinkers of note. The most distinguished American strategist is probably Alfred Thayer Mahan, whose *Influence of Sea Power upon History* (1890) is a classic, but similarly important strategies of land or air warfare produced by Americans are difficult to find.

The myth of invincibility has made the recent American lack of military success all the more difficult to accept. To many, World War II was the last real victory for American arms until Operation Desert Storm (the Persian Gulf War). World War II was followed by a string of partial successes in Korea and Panama and failures in Vietnam, the unsuccessful Iranian hostage rescue raid (Desert One), and the truck bombing of American marines in Beirut. How could these things happen to a country with a military tradition of untrammeled success? The answer, as examination of a couple of examples in this light shows, is found in measuring the incidents by the legends and not the realities.

The Vietnam War is the recurring nightmare and symbol of failure. Vietnam is the first war America lost, so the story goes; to make matters worse, it was lost to a third-rate, undeveloped country. Why?

Part of the answer lies in examining the concept of invincibility. Despite a spate of revisionist literature trying to depict the conflict in conventional terms, Vietnam was an unconventional war, the kind Americans have traditionally not fought well. If the American military leaders, when asked if they could prevail in Vietnam, answered with a hearty "can do" (and the evidence certainly does not, at a minimum, suggest they ever said "can't do"), their judgment flew in the face of past experience. Certainly, the failure of the military to assess critically its abilities and disabilities to fight in Southeast Asia was partly the result of not understanding the true nature of the war. That failure left American forces fighting a style of war for which they had little positive experience.

The image of invincibility arising from the brilliance of tactical leadership took a similar beating in Vietnam. Not only did the political and military leaders not understand what kind of war they were getting into, they also did not know how to fight it, once engaged. Reflecting historical experience, their predisposition was to fight it as a conventional war, matching large units with overwhelming firepower against conventional enemy units. In this way, American technical prowess would win out. Where the enemy stood and fought in classic conventional style, as in the 1965 campaign in the Ia Drang valley and in the Tet offensive and counteroffensive of 1968, American forces did defeat the enemy decisively.

The problem was that, most of the time, the enemy would not fight conventionally. Instead, the Vietnamese fought guerrilla-style, emphasizing mobile warfare, ambushes, and the avoidance of combat when the odds were not overwhelmingly in their favor. It was a tactical and strategic concept that dates from antiquity, but one with which the American military has never dealt well. A closer historical self-examination would have made the failure in Vietnam less surprising than it obviously was. This observation is relevant for future involvements in Second Tier conflicts, as discussed in Chapter 9.

The bomb attack on the American Marines in Beirut in 1983 offers another, slightly more positive example. The episode involved the successful penetration of the security of the American occupation zone protecting the Beirut International Airport by a terrorist driving a truck loaded with explosives in a suicide attack. The result was the death of 241 marines asleep in a dormitory. On the surface, it was a shocking, even humiliating, experience.

Most of the problems connected with the entire Lebanese mission were anticipated by the military, which opposed sending American forces into Beirut in the first place. The first and most obvious difficulty was the political purpose of the mission. The Marines originally went in to shield the withdrawal of the Palestine Liberation Organization, then left. When they were brought back into Lebanon, along with soldiers of three other members of the international peacekeeping force (Italy, France, and Great Britain), after Lebanese Christian militiamen attacked the Sabra and Shetila Palestinian refugee camps within Beirut, their mission was vague: they were there to "help reestablish peace and security."

The problem was how 1,800 marines were to accomplish that end in a country that had been torn by periodic violence since 1975 and that was in a state of almost total military and political chaos resembling that in contemporary Bosnia and Herzegovina. It was a mission that was clearly not possible to accomplish with the forces authorized. In other words, it was a situation where "can do" was clearly impossible, and apparently many of the president's military advisers said as much.

The other problem was with the kinds of troops involved. Sending the U.S. Marines in for the very limited mission of shielding the evacuation of the Palestine Liberation Organization (PLO) and its leader Yasir Arafat was probably appropriate; the marines are designed for quick insertion into troubled situations. Even sending them in the second time may initially have been the right thing to do, for the same reason. The problem came in leaving them there to do what amounted to garrison duty.

Apparently overlooked was the experience of World War II in the Pacific. In that war, the marines were used as crack amphibious assault troops whose job was to establish the beachhead, secure it, and begin to break the enemy. Once the Japanese garrisons were basically broken, however, the army was brought in to mop up remaining resistance and establish control. The army, in other words, has historically been much better equipped to do the kind of garrison duty that was required in the Beirut situation. One can only speculate whether the army would have done a better job of securing its base than the marines, whose stationary garrison experience is limited. The tragedy of that situation is that economic constraints dictated their use. The marines were closer by, and it was thus less costly to get them to and from the scene. This negative experience has contributed to the military's reluctance to being inserted into similar situations.

Mobilization

The fourth element in the American strategic culture is the tradition of mobilization and demobilization. Since the time of the American Revolution, it has been the practice of the United States to maintain a very small standing armed force during peacetime, to mobilize only when war was thrust upon the country, and then to demobilize the troops as quickly as possible once the war was concluded.

A number of factors have allowed this practice and made it appealing. Most obvious has been America's geographic blessing. Since geography provides a shield for the continental United States, there has always been the luxury of being unprepared for war; no one could attack American shores; thus, war could be prepared for at leisure, with no immediate threat while mobilization occurred.

A second reason is philosophical, and goes back to the Anglo-Saxon heritage. A standing armed force is a potential threat to civilian government. Besides this, military service, for large numbers of Americans, is an infringement on freedom and on the ability to live as one wishes. Third, of course, the need for such forces has rarely been felt; a belief in the efficacy of the militia to handle any emergency has made a professional standing force in peacetime seem unnecessary. Fourth, such a defense structure was relatively cheap. When a standing army consists of only 10,000 to 20,000 men, as it did during most of the nineteenth century, there is no great physical investment in national defense or consequent drain of resources away from other priorities.

The mobilization-demobilization tradition has been a constant in American military history, ending only after the Korean War in the 1950s and, especially, with the emphasis on military preparedness by the Kennedy administration in the 1960s. Earlier, the pattern was inviolate, and it has had consequences for how the United States views military force and for America's military performance.

First, the United States has entered every war it fought before Vietnam unprepared to fight. As a result, it has always taken a long time to mobilize and train an army. The effect has been twofold: Americans have entered wars late and have not begun to fight for some time after being technically at war, with the probable result of making the wars last longer than they otherwise would have. Also, this long mobilization period has, on occasion, made for a relatively inefficient war effort.

A look at American wars illustrates the point. The Civil War lasted officially from April 1861 to April 1865, but the actual fighting was a good bit shorter than that. After the abortive first battle at Manassas, in May 1861, both sides retired to organize, train, and equip armies. The first real campaigns did not begin until the winter and spring of 1861–1862. The war with Spain, that "splendid little war," was fought in a little over two months. The United States recruited an army of 275,000 to fight it, but the war was over so fast that only about 37,000 ever left the territorial United States. In World War I, the United States declared war on Germany in April 1917, but it took over a year to forge an American Expeditionary Force of 1.75 million. The force had to be equipped with weaponry purchased from Britain and France, since the United States never did mobilize a defense industry. Americans were engaged in combat for only about five months, from June to November 1918. Similarly, although war was declared on the Axis powers in December 1941, American land operations in World War II had to be delayed for almost a year. In the disastrous North African campaign of late 1942, green American troops were decimated by seasoned German regulars, and the first major land campaigns were not conducted until 1943. Korea is a partial exception, only because it occurred five years after the end of World War II, when the reserves were still largely manned by veterans of that war.

Second, the luxury of being able to follow the mobilization-demobilization pattern prejudiced Americans against the expenditure of large amounts of money for defense in peacetime—a problem that plagues administrations to this day. The United States has traditionally been able to engage in defense without maintaining large standing armies, and people like it that way. It means less personal and economic sacrifice for a defense commitment and, therefore, lower taxes and more attention to the so-called social net of benefit programs that began to appear during the 1930s New Deal. This preference is being revisited with the end of the Cold War.

A third and more arguable consequence is that the contemporary emergence of a real threat against the United States—one that requires constant attention and vigilance—is more traumatizing. The United States may have been immune from physical threat for over 140 years after the War of 1812, but that perception came to a sudden end with the first Soviet test of an intercontinental ballistic missile and the more publicized launching of *Sputnik* (the satellite) into space in 1957. The ICBM put the United States under threat of direct attack at all times and in a way to which Americans were profoundly unaccustomed. This situation helped justify the large and permanent peacetime military establishment that emerged from the Korean War—a phenomenon unprecedented in American history.

The recent commitment to a large standing military force is the primary change in the American defense situation. Americans are still adjusting to the radical departure from their traditional relationship to security matters. They chafe at defense budgets that amount to hundreds of billions of dollars, and this contributes greatly to the tensions between the advocates of defense and nondefense budgets, particularly as the country faces the problem of erasing the federal deficit. The "military-industrial complex" of defense and defense-related industry is scrutinized microscopically for excesses—alleged waste, fraud, and abuse that became a well-publicized and politicized issue during the Reagan years and resurfaced in 1994—and the urge to shy away from ongoing defense commitments is demonstrated by a vibrant movement toward nuclear disarmament and nonintervention in the affairs of others. With the nuclear threat ended and the need for large standing forces less obvious, there may be a retreat toward tradition.

The Impact of America's Democratic Institutions

The strategic culture's existence within the fabric of uniquely American democratic institutions leads to many complexities. Those institutions regulate the relationship between the military and civilian authorities, and they clearly rest on the principle of civilian decision of when, where, and how American military forces will be maintained and employed.

The "rules of the game" within which military forces exist are clearly set out. By constitutional provision, the Congress is entrusted with the responsibility for raising and maintaining armed forces. In peacetime, this means Congress must approve that part of the federal budget allocated for defense and must set manpower levels. At the same time, the power to declare war (and thus, historically, to use the armed forces) is a responsibility of the Congress. Under the checks-and-balances principle, the president is designated as commander-in-chief of those armed forces, at the top of a military chain of command designed to guarantee that political decision-making power in military matters is not usurped by the military.

The foundation of the constitutional provisions is that the democratic heritage demands popular support of whatever the government does in the area of national security. This is hardly a shocking observation, but it is particularly important in the area of national defense. Partly, the reason is the historical American aversion to and suspicion of the military and military solutions to problems. Whenever a military situation arises, some initial resistance must be overcome before policy can be pursued. At the same time, the use of military force entails greater sacrifices, up to and including those of lives and national treasure, than other policy choices. This creates an arguably greater need for acquiescence than in less-demanding policy areas.

The need for popular support for governmental actions creates pressures that cut both ways. On the positive side, the need to rationalize intended military actions constrains military action in situations where it cannot be adequately justified. A governmental planner, in addition to geopolitical determinations about using American forces in a given situation, must also consider if the proposed action will gain public support. If not, it will probably have to be modified or abandoned.

Much of the constraint on military action has, until recently, been exercised through the War Powers Act of 1973. That legislation, passed over the veto of then President Nixon, was intended to check the president's ability to place American military forces into combat without prior agreement by the Congress.

The perceived need for the War Powers Act came from the Vietnam and Korean wars. Neither of those military actions was technically a war in the sense of having been preceded by a congressional declaration of war. Rather, the Korean conflict was an American participation in a "police action" sponsored by the United Nations; American participation in the Vietnam "conflict" was always under the guise of assistance to the South Vietnamese government. (The American military command was designated the Military Assistance Command Vietnam, or MACV, throughout the war.) Since neither war was declared, the constitutional requirement that the Congress declare wars (which, in the minds of the framers of the Constitution, included virtually any military action) was bypassed, and so was a check on presidential power. The only constraining power left to the Congress was the power of the purse; but Congress was unwilling to cut off funds to American servicemen in combat.

The War Powers Act appeared to Congress a necessary means to reassert popular control over the use of American forces. More important than the act's formal powers are the informal pressures it exerts on the executive branch to consider popular sentiment before engaging in a military action.

The provisions of the act are straightforward. Whenever the president contemplates placing Americans into a potential combat situation, he has forty-eight hours after the commitment to inform the Congress of his action. Congress then has thirty days to approve or disapprove the action. If it disapproves, then the president has an additional thirty days to remove the forces. Thus, the act does not prohibit the president from using American forces without explicit congressional authority; it simply limits the length of time such a commitment can continue without that permission.

It is at the informal level that the act provides real constraint. Knowing that there is a possibility it could be invoked forces the president to consider, first, whether the Congress and the people will sustain an action. If the answer is clearly no, as it was in the case of a proposed intervention by American forces in the Angolan civil war in 1975, then the proposed action will probably be nipped in the bud. (Former Secretary of State Henry Kissinger complained bitterly of the constraint in the Angolan situation in his memoirs.) If the popular appeal of the action is questionable, there will probably be prior, informal consultation with key congressional leaders before it is taken. The American military reaction to the seizure of the merchant ship *Mayaguez* by Cambodia in 1975 involved this kind of informal consultation.

The War Powers Act has been controversial. Detractors have argued that it unnecessarily and unduly restricts presidential ability to conduct foreign policy and, especially, to respond rapidly in situations where military force might be effective. All presidents in office since its passage have opposed it on Constitutional grounds. Supporters find a virtue in this vice: they believe that in the absence of some constraint, the president might employ American forces in situations where the interests of the United States, as agreed upon by most Americans, would not be served. In the early 1980s, the situation most often cited as an example of the useful constraint provided by the act was that in Central America. Many Americans believed that President Reagan would have sought an overtly military solution to the situation in El Salvador and possibly to that in Nicaragua had he not been limited by almost certain congressional disapproval, as the controversy over military assistance to antigovernment Nicaraguan rebels (the Contras) demonstrated before the election of Violetta Chamorro and relinquishing of power by the Sandinistas in March 1990.

Interestingly, this latter judgment is shared by some within the professional military, a position most eloquently argued by retired Colonel Harry Summers in his work *On Strategy*. He argues that a major flaw of our involvement in Vietnam was that it was not preceded by some overt act of popular commitment, such as a declaration of war or at least a formal mobilization such as the calling up of reserves, as had been done in Korea. In the absence of such acts, the American people were not forced either to agree to the commitment or to say that they would not back the action. In Summers's view, this failure fatally undercut long-term support for the war effort. His conclusion is that the military should never allow itself to be committed to major action without the explicit blessing of the American people. The War Powers Act provides an instrument for the American people, through their elected representatives, to either bless or condemn any proposed action. The need to call up reserves for the Persian Gulf War reflected such an implicit grant of support by the American people.

The continuing controversy over the War Powers Act symbolizes the important role public opinion plays in the military actions proposed or undertaken by any political democracy. Democratic institutions emphasize the responsibility and accountability of those in power to the governed. Very few would argue against a public veto on policy actions.

If one looks at the sweep of the American military experience, one is struck by anomalies in the kinds of wars the American people are most and least likely to support. Long wars have failed to generate or sustain support, especially if limited or inconclusive. The prime example is, of course, Vietnam; the War of 1812 and the Korean conflict roughly meet this description as well. If war is limited in its purposes and is to be sustained by popular opinion, it must be over quickly (the Spanish-American War, the excursion against Panama) or at least produce minimal casualties (only 237 Americans died in combat during the war with Spain, and less than 150 died in the Persian Gulf War).

Total War Preference

At the same time, Americans have been willing to support total wars. The most popular wars in the American experience have been wars of total political purpose and, in the twentieth century, of total means. It was, after all, the American Civil War that served as the transition from eighteenth- to twentieth-century warfare: the total political purposes that were introduced by the American and French revolutions were wedded in the "brothers' war" to total means. The Civil War was the first "war of factories," in which the total resources of two societies were mobilized for military purposes. Given its superior industrial base, the Union could hardly have failed to prevail in the end. Moreover, Ulysses S. Grant and his lieutenant, William Tecumseh Sherman, were the first apostles of modern war. The 1864 and 1865 campaigns of Grant to destroy Lee's

Army of Northern Virginia and Sherman's campaign to bring the "hard hand of war" directly to the Southern people and to destroy their will and ability to continue were the precursors of the strategy of the twentieth-century global wars.

The trend toward total war reached its zenith in World War II. It is estimated that 80 million people saw uniformed service in that conflict and that around 20 million combatants and about an equal number of civilians were killed. The war raged for nearly six years, beginning with the German invasion of Poland and ending with the Japanese surrender to the United States. It was truly a global war; no continent was completely exempt from its ravages.

It was also a war of total purposes, a battle of survival between fascist authoritarianism, on one side, and political democracy and communism, on the other. Its purpose was cast in highly moralistic terms. The absolute evil represented by Nazi and imperial Japanese fascism had to be expunged from the earth, and the American people shared in the sacrifices that the war's conduct entailed. A moral crusade of an even greater dimension than World War I had been twenty years earlier, it was the kind of war the American people could and did support.

The impact of democratic institutions and the preference of Americans either for short and decisive limited wars or wars of total political purpose are of considerable importance in the current and future context. With general tranquillity prevailing in the First Tier, the probability of total war has virtually disappeared. What is left are the smaller, more limited (at least from an American viewpoint) wars within and between Second Tier states. Of these, the larger number are likely to be protracted, complex, internal affairs without decisive outcomes—the very kind of wars the American people have been least likely to support in the past.

If there are no total wars that we can afford to fight, then by definition the possible future military engagements of the United States are going to be limited in political purpose and probably in means. The likely battlefields are Second Tier areas in Latin America, Africa, and Asia, where the United States has limited interests.

The question is whether the American people will support these kinds of actions. Any time American action in the Second Tier has been suggested, the first reaction has been that such activity would constitute another Vietnam. Thus, "Is El Salvador another Vietnam?" was almost the first question raised about American involvement in that situation and about the recently concluded U.S. involvement in Somalia. History, as represented by the strategic culture, suggests that these kinds of actions are the most problematical in terms of public support, especially if they are at all protracted. Given the leadership role that the United States has inherited in the post–Cold War world, the willingness of the American people to be involved at times and in places where traditionally defined national interests are not engaged will go a long way toward determining systemic responses.

The Media

The seventh and final element having an impact on how military force and defense are viewed is the influence of the media. Although there has been a relationship between those who conduct and those who report America's military exploits since the Revolution, the role of the media as a major shaper of our thoughts about force—especially about war—is relatively new. On-the-scene, same-day coverage of warfare goes back to the Civil War and extensive use of telegraphy, and in World War I the military for the first time transported journalists to war zones.

But the introduction of the electronic media—specifically, global television—has appeared to make a difference. The extent of that difference was first seen in the Vietnam War. America's first "living-room war" was covered in excruciating, occasionally bloody, detail by the media and was relentlessly beamed into American homes on network nightly news. The result was not only a war that could not be ignored but a war whose nastiness and inhumanity became part of daily lives. The image of war was changed drastically for those who had never experienced it and did not know what it truly is like. At that, the coverage of carnage was pale by current standards.

Because its principal contribution is its visual impact, television has a particular effect, one that is undoubtedly somewhat distorting. The distortion arises at least partly out of the nature of what makes good television as opposed to print news. War has been described as consisting of long periods of utter boredom punctuated by brief periods of total terror when one is in combat. Those long periods when troops are marching unmolested down a trail or resting under a tree do not make good television; brief moments of mayhem that can be captured in a film clip do. War is unquestionably dirty, nasty business; electronic coverage is best at capturing it at its nastiest.

Television also tends to be myopic. It can capture what its lenses can see, but it does not do well at encompassing the broader context of the events it covers. Individual instances of violence in war are dramatic, sometimes horrible, but they occur within a context of purposes difficult to portray in a one- or two-minute news report. One of the most dramatic, revolting images from Vietnam was a wirephoto picture of a South Vietnamese military official executing a suspected Vietcong on the streets of Saigon with a pistol. People remember that incident and are disgusted by it. What neither the picture nor the memory recall is the broader campaign of Vietcong infiltration and terrorism of which this incident was only a part; there was active fighting going on around the corner from where the picture was taken.

These problems are not so great for the print media, partly because the written word is not as evocative as a picture and does not relay the same emotional content. The written reports of the slaughter of twenty-one people at a McDonald's restaurant in California in 1984 did not have the same emotional impact, for instance, as a single picture of a dead eleven-year-old boy lying in a pool of blood beside his bicycle. On the other hand, a newspaper or magazine article is generally longer and more complete than an electronic report and, thus, stands a better chance of putting matters into their broader context.

We are still learning about the impact of the media as it affects the use of force and, more specifically, people's support or aversion to the use of force. The phenomenon is certainly not limited to the United States. Two non-American events and the way they were covered illustrate this: the 1982 Falkland Islands war between Great Britain and Argentina, and Israel's siege of West Beirut during its 1982 campaign against the Palestine Liberation Organization in Lebanon.

Media coverage did not affect the way the British public viewed the actual fighting in the short Falkland Islands conflict. Because Argentina had seized the islands (known to Argentinians as the Malvinas) militarily, there was great patriotic support for action to wrest them back from the invader. Electronic coverage of the assembly of a naval flotilla and amphibious troops was extensive and added to the fervor. But as the British neared the islands, all electronic coverage stopped.

Many people initially attributed the absence of "real time" coverage to clever, efficient censorship by the British employing the Official Secrets Act. In fact, the reason media coverage was delayed was idiosyncratic and situation-specific. As it turns out, electronic journalists did not transmit their stories because they were on the decks of rolling ships and hence could not focus their images to overhead satellites for transmission. Moreover, there was not a single satellite station on the main Falkland Island; thus, the only way tape could be sent home was by flying it several thousand miles to the nearest transmission site, located on Ascension Island.

This idiosyncrasy points to the extreme difficulty governments have and increasingly will have regulating the flow of electronic news in the future. In a world of hand-held "camcorders" and satellite dishes, there is no governmental mediation between journalistic coverage and transmission, which results in instant news coverage from all corners of the globe. The operation of organizations such as Cable News Network (CNN) are the prototype of the future and place real limits on the future conduct of military operations. The military will not always be able to control coverage as it did in Kuwait, as the accompanying Amplification box "The Media and Desert Storm" discusses.

The siege of Beirut provided a striking contrast. Sieges, among the oldest of all military tactics, are inherently nasty, inhumane experiences, as the world has come to learn only too vividly watching the lengthy siege of Sarajevo, Bosnia. The purpose, of course, is to force an adversary to surrender by denying access to the necessities of life, such as food and water, while at the same time applying military pressure. The civilian population and the military are equally affected by siege operations.

AMPLIFICATION

The Media and Desert Storm

Coverage of the Persian Gulf War illustrates vividly the ever-changing relationship between the media and the U.S. military. In the decades before the war and, most noticeably, during coverage of the Vietnam War, the relationship had become highly adversarial: the media were unwilling to accept official pronouncements about military actions without witnessing the actions themselves. The fact that American journalists were not even allowed to accompany the first combat forces that invaded Grenada in 1983 had further soured relations; it is not unfair to say that the media and the military had come to view one another as virtual adversaries in the years leading to the Persian Gulf War.

The major issue is, and has always been, whether the military has the right to exclude reporters from the battlefield or whether it has an obligation to assist reporters in informing the U.S. population. In earlier wars, the military was able to censor reporting because it controlled access to the telephone and telegraph lines that were necessary to get stories to press. This ability has been negated by hand-held camcorders and small satellite dishes that can instantaneously relay electronic images from the source to receiving units. In that circumstance, the only method of control left to the military is to restrict access by reporters to battle areas—in effect, censoring what the reporters can learn. This was done in the Persian Gulf War, as only a handful of reporters from a pool were actually allowed to accompany military units; after they returned from the front, these pool reporters shared the information with their colleagues. Most reporters resented this practice (which pleased the military) as an unnecessary intrusion on their right to know, and this experience will undoubtedly vex future American battles and wars.

The other interesting aspect of media-military relations in Desert Storm was the extent to which the military had learned to use the media to dramatize the side of the war they wanted emphasized. It was certainly no coincidence, for instance, that the bombing campaign against Iraq began with raids against Baghdad at precisely 6:55 P.M. eastern standard time on January 16, 1991—during the evening news on the major networks. By making available to the press highly selective but dramatic film footage, such as a cruise missile following an Iraqi soldier through a door into a building and another rocket tracking through an air vent in another Iraqi building, the military was quite successful in portraying the technological superiority of U.S. forces.

Television coverage reported the Beirut siege in the most graphic and revolting detail up to that time. During the weeks it lasted, nightly news coverage often began with the scream of Israeli fighter-bombers (American-made, as was invariably pointed out) overhead dropping their deadly payloads on the Muslim section of the city; this would be followed by pictures of bombed-out buildings and an occasional dead or maimed victim.

The effect was to repel the viewing public; given what was being done, this may or may not have been a bad thing. How much impact that coverage had on the public is impossible to know precisely, but the campaign marked the first time that Americans, including American Jews, rose in large numbers to condemn an Israeli action. The Palestine Liberation Organization, objects of the siege, were hardly criticized for hiding within the civilian areas of West Beirut.

The central questions are what difference this relatively new phenomenon makes in how Americans view the use of military force, and how support for future military actions will be affected by unrestricted television coverage. In the early post–Cold War period, global television images of massive Kurdish and Somali suffering helped impel hastily conceived military responses. How will television affect the military agenda of the future?

This question evokes passion in both military and journalistic circles, but produces more emotion than enlightenment. Rightly or wrongly, large segments of the military still believe that the nature and quality of press coverage of the Vietnam War, especially after the 1968 Tet offensive, was responsible for forcing the United States out of the war; they hold the media in some contempt as a result. Journalists counter that the military lied and withheld critical information about Vietnam and that it was the facts that forced us out. When the military speaks wistfully about the Official Secrets Act, the press reacts to what it believes are assaults on the First Amendment's guarantee of freedom of the press. Emotions of the press were heightened by their exclusion, on national security grounds, from accompanying the invasion force to Grenada in 1983; the first reports of that event available to Americans came, ironically, from Radio Havana.

The impact of the media on military affairs, especially on war, is clearly controversial and difficult to specify, but we can say that it is there and that it may dilute rather than increase public support. Whatever the exact impact is, future military planning needs to take it into account.

There seem to be two possible impacts of television coverage. In reporting on conflicts and atrocities, it may force action where the camera's eye can roam (Somalia, for instance) but be ineffective where the same kinds of atrocity are not so visibly reported (the Sudan). In this way, television may become the primary agenda setter for the national security community—a role the military fears. At the other extreme, television coverage of conflict and atrocity may simply desensitize the public to the point that it is no longer affected by the physical horrors. Certainly, television coverage of domestic murder scenes, much more vivid than a decade ago, elicits little response these days from most people, and there was no American outrage at the slaughter in Rwanda in April 1994.

At a minimum, the media—especially, the electronic forms—place another constraint on the use of military power. A question that must be asked whenever the use of force is contemplated is whether the public will sustain support for it. The emergence of the media as an element in the strategic culture requires an additional question: how likely, if at all, will coverage of the way military force is used contribute to public support or disillusionment?

CONCLUSIONS

Taken in combination, these loosely connected elements help explain why Americans view military force and its role as they do. The elements are obviously diverse, comprising tendencies and predilections (such as the militia tradition) that go back to the founding of the United States, as well as elements as recent as the invention of the communications satellite.

The elements vary in how directly they affect current issues. The militia tradition and its concomitant mobilization-demobilization pattern have practically disappeared as direct influences on policy, as we have accustomed ourselves in the past quarter-century to a large standing military. Even recent conventional arms reductions do not question the need for a robust residual force. The "can do" spirit emerging from the legend of invincibility was dealt a serious blow by the Vietnam experience, where Americans "couldn't do," but more recent successes like the Persian Gulf War have repaired that image.

If some parts of the tradition have faded, it would be incorrect to say they have disappeared altogether. Antimilitarism, the militia tradition, the invincibility myth, and mobilization-demobilization remain nostalgic reminders of older, simpler, and cheaper days when the military played a much smaller, less conspicuous part in national life. They represent the way Americans liked the world to be and the way many would prefer it to be again if someone could figure out how to make it that way.

The problem, of course, is that the world in which the United States exists has become much more complicated and dangerous since the end of World War II. Geography and history no longer provide protective shields, facilitating a nostalgic world view. Instead, the final three elements of the American tradition—democratic institutions, the preference for total war, and the media—have risen to the fore, but with ambivalent effect.

The key element, probably, is the democratic tradition, with the consequent need to obtain popular support for military activity. That need, in turn, manifests itself in at least two ways that form common and recurring threads. The first is the question of military spending. Because American history and traditions have depreciated the need for much costly military preparedness, Americans have more difficulty dealing with constant, on-going, and sizable expenditures on military force than does a country that has been under the gun throughout its national existence.

Second, there is the question of what kinds of wars the American people are and are not willing to support. Our lack of historical perspective allows Americans to remember the two world conflicts—total wars—as the most glorious and, hence, the preferable military experience, when in fact, they represented aberrations. Wars of limited political purpose and limited means have been the rule and not the exception in both the American and world experiences. The preference for total wars reflects an American crusader's zeal, but in today's world this is anachronistic.

The kinds of places where the United States still can fight are on the peripheries. These are conflicts in the volatile areas of the Second Tier, where good and bad are not clearly seen and where the objectives are both limited and not obviously glorious—such as protection of access to energy or mineral resources. The Persian Gulf War, where American forces were dropped into Kuwait to reinstall a sheikh who, in Western moral terms, is not much of an improvement on his adversary, is a caricature of that reality.

This situation is a new experience for the United States. Certainly, Americans are primarily accustomed to the expeditionary use of force, not having fought on home soil since 1865. Other countries, either because they lack natural resources or are geographically vulnerable, have been forced into this role for centuries. For the United States, current circumstances test the national will, requiring willingness to engage in military matters with which Americans are unaccustomed and which, in most cases, lack moral force.

The evolving role of the media, especially the electronic media, will be important in the outcome of this debate. Television and its adjuncts are the source of a great deal of most people's information about the world and can serve to educate and sophisticate the electorate. At the same time, the way the media portray American actions can vitally affect the way not only the American people but even their leaders view American actions. President Reagan, for instance, was apparently very moved by initial television accounts of slaughter in the Beirut refugee camps after the assassination of Bashir Gemayel in 1982, and this reaction was partly why he ordered the marines back into Lebanon. When George Bush discovered the Iraqi Kurds (who had fled Saddam Hussein's revenge after the Persian Gulf War) huddled and dying on Turkish mountainsides, Operation Provide Comfort was born. At the same time, an adversarial, sensationalistic approach to military action will almost certainly help undermine support to some extent. A proper balance between blatant promotion of the military and undiluted skepticism has yet to evolve, but such a balance will be critical in the future.

This mixture of influences suggests the evolutionary nature of American defense policy. For much of our history, the kinds of influences and issues raised in these pages were not prominent parts of the national debate. They have gained prominence since 1945, as the United States has gradually—if fitfully—accepted the role of a world power. Because the post–World War II period has been so important in the evolution of our policy, Chapter 4 will offer an overview of how that policy has developed and changed.

Suggested Reading

Booth, Ken, and Moorhead Wright. *American Thinking about War and Peace: New Essays on American Thought and Attitudes*. New York: Harvester Press, 1978.

Dupuy, R. Ernest, and Trevor N. Dupuy. *Military Heritage of America*. Fairfax, Va.: Hero Books, 1984.

Hassler, Warren W., Jr. *With Shield and Sword: American Military Affairs, Colonial Times to the Present*. Ames, Iowa: Iowa State University Press, 1982.

Huntington, Samuel P. *The Soldier and the State: The Theory and Politics of Civil-Military Relations*. Cambridge, Mass.: Harvard University Press, 1957.

Koenig, William J. *Americans at War: From the Colonial Wars to Vietnam*. New York: Putnam, 1980.

Leckie, Robert. *The Wars of America*, rev. ed. New York: Harper and Row, 1981.

Millett, Allan R., and Peter Maslowski. *For the Common Defense: A Military History of the United States of America*, rev. and exp. ed. New York: Free Press, 1994.

Millis, Walter. *Arms and Men: A Study of American Military History*. New York: Putnam, 1956.

Snow, Donald M., and Dennis M. Drew. *From Lexington to Desert Storm: The American Experience at War*. Armonk, N.Y.: M E Sharpe, 1994.

Summers, Harry. *On Strategy: A Critical Assessment of the Vietnam War*. Novato, Calif.: Presidio Press, 1982.

Weigley, Russell O. *The American Way of War: A History of United States Military Strategy and Policy*. Bloomington, Ind.: Indiana University Press, 1977.

Williams, T. Harry. *Americans at War: The Development of the American Military System*. Baton Rouge, La.: Louisiana State University Press, 1960.

Chapter 4

An Overview of Defense Policy

Before World War II, the United States never had an explicit national defense or security policy expressed in coherent statements on where external U.S. military interests lay, what kinds of threats and military actions the United States was willing to undertake to protect those interests, and how those policies related to broader American foreign policy goals. There had, of course, been general or partial statements with defense implications. The Monroe Doctrine, for example, asserted American opposition to recolonization of the Western Hemisphere, but it was actually enforced militarily by Great Britain until a sizable American navy was built at the end of the nineteenth century. The Roosevelt Corollary to the doctrine asserted the American "right" to interfere in Latin American affairs. These were not, however, broad statements of overall policy translated into articulated defense plans and postures.

The question of American security was a matter not of policies but of themes, such as mobilization and demobilization. A national security policy was lacking, of course, because there was little need for one. U.S. involvement in the international system before the twentieth century was minimal; there were few threats to American interests that required a coherent response, at least after the War of 1812. At the same time, ongoing American commitments to defense were generally small enough that they did not require a detailed justification or organization.

After World War II, the world was radically different. Most saliently, it was a shrunken globe on which the United States had no choice but to play a major role. It was also a world for which Americans were, characteristically, not well prepared to assume a new and expanded role.

American security policy has been in a state of evolution ever since. To understand how it has changed over time requires first looking at the kinds of influences that lead a country to develop and to alter defense policy. With those categories established, the discussion can move on to how American policies have developed and changed from 1945 to the present and to provide some analytical perspective to help examine how policy might change in the future.

INFLUENCES ON DEFENSE POLICY

Any analytic device will, to some extent, oversimplify the reality it seeks to depict. The milieu in which foreign and defense policies are made is, indeed, one of the most difficult and complicated of all policy areas to comprehend. With that warning in mind, I shall propose a framework that identifies three categories of influences upon defense policy that are, in turn, influenced by the shape of that policy. These are the international setting, domestic political concerns, and military technology.

International Setting

All those events and actions outside the territorial United States that affect the United States compose the international setting of defense policy. More specifically, those trends, events, and problems that may directly or indirectly influence American security, and to which the United States must respond through military action or threat, form the relevant international setting.

Defense policies focus on adversaries, since they, by definition, pose threats to national security. In a world where today's friend may be tomorrow's enemy and where sometimes the enemy of my enemy is my friend, it is not always clear who are adversaries and who are not. Moreover, as policies and actions change, so does the list of friends and foes.

After World War II, the Soviet Union provided a consistent and important adversary. It is no coincidence that most of American defense policy has been directed at the Soviet Union and its allies over time, although the exact nature of the adversarial relationship has varied. At the same time, the international setting does change as the situations and policies of states change. In 1946 the government on the Chinese mainland was a staunch ally of the United States. After the communists won the Chinese civil war and subsequently intervened in the Korean War, that same mainland government became an implacable enemy for over twenty years, until the opening of China by Henry Kissinger and Richard Nixon in 1972. In the early 1980s, the still-communist government of that same mainland talked openly of a joint American-Chinese military relationship against the Soviet Union and began to adopt Western economic practices. In the aftermath of the Chinese government's brutal suppression of student-led demonstrators in Tiananmen Square in Beijing in June 1989, relations cooled again, only to be rekindled in 1993. The relationship continues to ebb and flow. Today's friends are indeed tomorrow's enemies, and vice versa.

Neither the actors in nor the content of national security problems remain constant. The warming of East-West relations by Mikhail S. Gorbachev, as well as the unraveling of the Soviet bloc that began in 1989 and, ultimately, the demise of the Soviet Union itself, serve as examples of how the power map—and, thus, the list of allies, friends, and adversaries—can change. The end of the Cold War completes the forty-plus years of military confrontation in Europe.

At the same time, situations that constitute threats to security change as well. Security is more than the absence of hostile military force, after all, and increasingly global issues and the conditions underlying citizen well-being are finding their way onto the national security agenda, especially in the spate of hideous new internal wars in central Africa and elsewhere.

Domestic Political Concerns

Those internal American factors that shape the way defense policies are viewed and the kinds of defense policies Americans are willing or unwilling to consider make up domestic political concerns. The military tradition forms a backdrop for much of this consideration, as do such things as the national mood toward defense, activities of other states, and actions adverse to U.S. interests. At the same time, factors apparently unrelated to defense concerns, such as the condition of the national economy, also influence the political process. In determining the general domestic attitude toward defense and security issues, the president, as political leader and commander-in-chief of the armed forces, has particular influence. The increasingly international nature of the global economy and the rise of transstate issues such as environment—problems that cannot be solved by individual states—progressively blur the distinction between purely domestic and purely international concerns.

Technology

The current and projected state of military and military-related technology forms a third area of consideration. Technology should not really be considered an independent category, because the state of the adversary's military technology is actually part of the international setting and the state of American technology is part of the domestic milieu.

Technology is equated with the other factors because of the extraordinary influence it has had in the setting of policy. Moreover, the pace of technology has been so great that, in some areas, it has nearly outstripped the purposes for which it has been developed. The impact is most dramatically seen by contrasting military capability up to 1945, when the first atomic bomb was made, with the current situation, in which nuclear-tipped ballistic missiles could radically alter civilization in a matter of hours. The impact of technology has not been limited to nuclear weapons, however, but has extended to virtually all forms of warfare. In particular, the most advanced states, and notably the United States, are in the midst of what is called the *revolution in military affairs* (RMA), which involves applying the most advanced technologies to warfare, thus creating an enormous qualitative gap between those who do and those who do not have the RMA-driven capability. (See the Amplification box "The Nature of the RMA.")

AMPLIFICATION

The Nature of the RMA

The idea of the revolution in military affairs is that occasionally a group of advances, such as those associated with technology, come together at a point in time and can be applied to military weapons and associated strategies in such a way as to alter warfare fundamentally, primarily by giving the possessor enormous, usually decisive, advantage over the nonpossessor. This was clearly the case in nineteenth- and early twentieth-century Europe, where a series of technologies deriving from such inventions as the internal combustion engine (for cars, trucks, tanks, heavier-than-air airplanes, and the like) and batteries (for submarines) removed the decisive advantage that earlier advances in warfare, notably firepower, had given to the defense.

The current RMA is, arguably, of the same order of magnitude as that which occurred at the beginning of the century. Its base is in high technology, notably advances in the rapidly unifying areas of computation and telecommunications. When these technologies are weaponized, the results can be the dramatic effects seen selectively in the Persian Gulf War: long-range munitions delivered precisely on target, monopolies in information and intelligence, and considerable advantages in locating and targeting an enemy beyond that enemy's firing range. Although the implications of this RMA are still being discovered, one hears talk about such things as disengaged warfare (campaigns are organized and executed from computer terminals far from the battlefield) and information warfare (superior information about the enemy is gathered and manipulated to gain advantage—and a decisive victory).

Policy

The interaction of these factors shapes defense policy. That policy has traditionally been divided into two categories: conventional policy and thermonuclear policy. Conventional policy traditionally comprised plans for employing the non-nuclear forces of the United States, or at least those forces whose purpose is not a direct attack against the Soviet homeland. (So-called theater or tactical weapons, intended for battlefield use in Europe rather than for direct attacks on Soviet soil, were termed conventional—but the designation is highly controversial.)

The other policy area is thermonuclear weapons policy. Nuclear policy, synonymous with strategic weapons policy, concerns those nuclear weapons designated for direct use against the former Soviet Union. Their existence sought to deter the Soviets from a nuclear attack against the

United States. Because a failure of deterrence leading to a nuclear exchange is potentially devastating, nuclear policy was the "glamour" area, receiving great attention although expenditures on these forces generally approximated only one-tenth of the defense budget. Most defense issues were framed in terms of the nuclear balance and deterrence.

In strictly defense terms, these imperatives were translated into three "planning cases," or war-fighting scenarios, for which the United States must prepare as a means of deterring war and, if necessary, fighting it. The three scenarios, from most to least stressful and significant, were strategic nuclear war (SNW) with the Soviet Union, conventional war between NATO and the Warsaw Pact that could become nuclear, and low-intensity conflict (LIC), or unconventional war, somewhere in the Third World.

There are at least two traditional problems attaching to this formulation. First, the number of threats falling under these categories has always exceeded the resources necessary to deal with them, since each case represents a different problem requiring different kinds of forces. The result is risk. Second, although the three cases were normally presented as above because of the consequences of each, they were actually listed in reverse order of likelihood—that is to say, for example, there are far more Third World conflicts that involve U.S. interests than there are wars in Europe. The consequences and likelihood of different kinds of war are thus in reverse order, making the assessment of risk all the more difficult for policymakers. Indeed, now LIC is the "normal" form, and both strategic nuclear and large-scale conventional war have virtually disappeared as planning problems.

In addition, there are other sources of threat to American security that do not fall into the planning cases, yet they are becoming increasingly obvious and important. The economic challenge, pitting American interests in some conflict with military allies Japan and the European Union (EU), is one dimension of this problem, as are the economic, demographic, environmental, and other sets of problems issuing from the Second Tier. There is also the drug problem, which has both international and domestic elements and which will require the infusion of massive resources if there is to be any chance of "winning the war on drugs." The contemporary scourge of drugs clearly threatens basic American values and can be viewed as a challenge to U.S. national security. The question is where to allocate resources to deal with this problem and, hence concomitantly, from what other area does one transfer resources, thereby increasing risk somewhere else. The problems of terrorism and the proliferation of weapons of mass destruction in the Second Tier also appear on most lists of contemporary threats.

The emphasis in national security policy, in other words, is shifting dramatically. One can be blinded by the moment and overstate change, but it is there nonetheless. At the same time, the shape and extent of change gain their meaning by comparing present policy with how policy has developed through the postwar period.

THE EVOLUTION OF POLICY

American conventional and thermonuclear policy have evolved together. The earliest period, from the end of World War II to the Korean conflict, saw rapid change, from which the first outlines of policy emerged in a way not dissimilar to the changes occurring today. Dwight D. Eisenhower articulated our first formal, comprehensive defense policy, the New Look, when he entered the White House in 1953. John F. Kennedy altered that policy when he became president in 1961, and Richard M. Nixon's concept of realistic deterrence changed the Kennedy/Lyndon Johnson formula. Jimmy Carter moved to place his own distinctive imprint on policy, as did Ronald Reagan and George Bush. Bill Clinton is continuing the process of adapting defense policy to the post-Cold War environment.

Before examining these policies, two conditioning factors should be noted. The first is that distinctive changes—or, at least, what seem like basic alterations—tend to accompany changes in party control of the White House. This is true because, within the intellectual defense community (the group of scholars, retired military officers, and professional advisers who seek to influence policy), ideologies vary. When one party comes into power, a group of advisers with sympathetic viewpoints and party identifications is assembled, replacing a group with (at least partially) contrary ideas. Also, defense and foreign policy are high-visibility, glamorous areas of policy, and modern presidents have generally wanted to establish a distinctive position in these areas.

The result is often change that appears more dramatic than it actually is. The movement from Eisenhower's New Look to Kennedy's flexible response sounded radical, but it contained significant elements of continuity as well as change. Most of the strategic force elements and plans adopted by the Kennedy administration had their birth in the latter part of the Eisenhower administration.

The second conditioning factor is that change is normally associated with some basic alteration in one of the three environments that affect policy: the international setting, domestic political considerations, and technology. Such changes are natural; how a particular president reacts to any given change affects the shape of policy.

The Early Years (1945–1953)

The period from the end of World War II to the inauguration of Dwight Eisenhower was one of the most turbulent, fertile periods in American history. As the war ended, the United States had no particular defense or foreign posture with which to confront a radically altered world. Technology had produced the Damoclean majesty of atomic weapons, and their impact would require ongoing assessment.

The central international fact was that the old European-centered order was effectively destroyed. The old international system had been dominated by France, Germany, Great Britain, and Russia (whether tsarist or Soviet); those powers also dominated most of the rest of the world (outside the Western Hemisphere) through their extensive empires. European politics and world politics were virtually synonymous. World War II, which many historians saw as the final act in the drama of whether Germany or France would dominate the European continent, ended with neither triumphant and both prostrate. The war exhausted the major European powers economically, politically, and morally. From its ashes, it was clear that France, Germany, and Britain would have to reduce their roles and become regional, rather than world, powers. The experience, especially liquidating their far-flung empires, would be wrenching but necessary.

Only the United States and the Soviet Union emerged as significant powers capable of global reach. Of the two, the United States was clearly stronger; the American economy was actually strengthened by the war, American casualties were comparatively light, and the United States had a monopoly on the atomic bomb. By contrast, the Soviets had suffered enormously, although they retained a very large army as a source of power.

The question was how the two giants, soon to be called "superpowers," would organize the postwar peace. If they could continue the cooperation of the wartime alliance, the new United Nations provided a mechanism for peace. If their cooperation were to disintegrate into conflict, some other relationship would have to give rise to policy.

The signs that conflict would dominate did not take long to emerge. A civil war between communist insurgents apparently supported by the Soviets and pro-Western forces broke out in 1946 in Greece, the Soviets refused to leave their occupation zone in the Iranian province of Azerbaijan, and Soviet pressures mounted against Turkey. In the Soviet-occupied countries of eastern Europe, communist regimes were installed, a process most dramatically highlighted by the brutal overthrow of the democratically elected government of Czechoslovakia. In 1948 a disagreement over currency reforms in occupied Germany led to the blockade of the West's land access to Berlin and, thus, to the Berlin airlift. Finally, North Korea invaded South Korea in 1950, an aggression widely and probably correctly assumed to have had Soviet authorization. In this country, however, the first American reaction to war's end was predictable: a call for rapid demobilization. An army of slightly over eight million when Japan surrendered shrank to fewer than two million a year later. That the Soviets did not follow suit hardly caused a ripple.

Mounting evidence of Soviet-American conflict changed those attitudes, and a spirit of anticommunism arose that crested in the excesses of Senator Joseph McCarthy's attempts to rid the government of communists. The need to respond to perceived Soviet threats and the belief that

American security hung in the balance produced both major organizational and policy change.

One major organizational change was the National Security Act of 1947. Given America's historical experience, the title of the act is remarkable in itself. The act created a permanent peacetime defense establishment. More specifically, it created the Department of Defense (which unified the armed services under one cabinet-level official), the Central Intelligence Agency (the first peacetime civilian intelligence institution in U.S. history), the National Security Council (a body consisting of the president and relevant cabinet members, to coordinate national security policy), and an independent U.S. Air Force. Symbolically, the act admitted that foreign affairs in the future would likely have a significant national security content.

Policy development was even more dynamic and creative. International tensions and communist expansionism required a coherent policy response. The policy, articulated by George F. Kennan, then charge d'affaires to the Soviet Union, in a diplomatic telegram later released in the July 1947 edition of *Foreign Affairs* as "The Sources of Soviet Conduct" (under the authorship of X), was *containment*.

Containment became the basic postwar American foreign and defense policy. Kennan's major points help in understanding it. First, he argued that the Soviet regime, for reasons of both Russian history and current ideology, was expansionist and would seek to spread communism worldwide. Second, however, that ideology set no timetable for expansion, the Soviets arguing that it was historically inevitable. Thus, they could always rationalize temporary setbacks. Third, the regime itself was inherently unstable, having produced no predictable mechanism of succession. Thus, no Soviet regime could accept an embarrassment grievous enough to topple it from power. Finally and prophetically, he argued that the system was inherently flawed and that a vigilant policy of containment could cause it to self-destruct.

Containment followed from these observations. The basic idea was to draw a line dividing the communist and noncommunist worlds, beyond which communist expansion was intolerable and would be resisted. The West would not, however, actively seek to diminish communist hegemony for fear of backing the Soviet leadership into a corner and forcing them to go to war. The Soviets could accept being contained because they believed in a historical dialectic that told them the triumph of communism was inevitable in the long run.

Once containment was established as the core of American policy, the question was how to implement it. At the simply military level, the answer was not immediately obvious. Demobilization had left the United States militarily weak, except for the unilateral possession of the atomic bomb. At that, the United States had a very small nuclear arsenal (about thirty bombs in 1946) and a modest intercontinental bomber capability to deliver the weapons. Such utility as the bomb had was further diminished when the Soviets tested their own atomic device in 1949.

Three related policy acts implemented containment. The first was the *Truman Doctrine.* This was a response to the civil war in Greece—specifically, to the British-announced intention to withdraw financial assistance to the anticommunist government—and to communist pressures on Turkey. The Truman Doctrine provided economic and military assistance to the governments of the two countries. The rationale was that it was an American duty to assist victims of totalitarian (communist) aggression; it provided the precedent for both economic and military assistance programs worldwide under the guise of anticommunism.

The second major act was the *Marshall Plan.* It was also a response to a specific problem: the very slow rate at which European economies were recovering from World War II. The heart of the difficulty was lack of capital to rebuild war-torn industrial bases, and the failure to recover was causing serious political problems. In 1947 the communists emerged as the largest electoral party in France, and the harsh winter of 1947–1948 suggested that worse was to come.

The Marshall Plan provided American dollars to underwrite European recovery. Its rationale was that recovery was necessary to produce strong European governments capable of resisting communist blandishments. Moreover, the money was administered by the recipients through the Organization of European Economic Cooperation, thereby avoiding charges of favoritism that would have accompanied direct American administration and putting pressure on the Europeans to cooperate.

The third element was the *North Atlantic Treaty Organization* (NATO). The first major peacetime military alliance in American history, NATO responded to the need for a united, powerful military front in the face of an expansionist Soviet Union in eastern and southern Europe. In 1949 the original twelve signatories (there were sixteen members in early 1997, pending actions on membership expansion) pledged to engage in mutual self-defense. The alliance provided the precedent for other American multilateral and bilateral defense arrangements during the 1950s and 1960s. The Partnership for Peace program of 1994 extended association with NATO to former communist countries in Europe, the Soviet successor states, and former European neutral states, many of which seek full membership.

These actions formed the outline of an American foreign policy whose central feature was the containment of Soviet communism. Since military might was the primary, if not the sole, basis of the Soviet challenge, the need for a coordinated defense policy was obvious. Formulation of such a policy began with an extensive internal study by the National Security Council staff, known as NSC-68. That document outlined the military problems the United States faced and the deficiencies in American capabilities to deal with those problems, and it suggested remedial efforts on which the first comprehensive American defense policy could have been based.

The formation of such a policy was, however, delayed by the North Korean aggression against South Korea, to which the United States responded with force. In the heat of that ultimately frustrating conflict, the debate over broad policy was submerged. It would return upon the election of Dwight Eisenhower to the presidency in 1952 and on the subsequent conclusion of the Korean conflict in 1953.

The Eisenhower Years (1953–1961)

The physical and intellectual turbulence of the early postwar years began to subside with the inauguration of Dwight Eisenhower. A military leader who had commanded Allied forces in Europe during World War II, Eisenhower entered office with strong feelings about the requirements for national security, ideas to which his background lent credibility. Elected by a landslide over the Democratic candidate, Governor Adlai Stevenson of Illinois, he promised to end the war in Korea. Fulfilling his promise that "I will go to Korea" was, however, but one factor that contributed to the first comprehensive peacetime defense policy.

Two important domestic political considerations stand out as influences on American policy in this period. The first and most pressing was public reaction to the Korean War, one of revulsion combined with a continuing virulent anticommunism that complicated policy formulation.

Public opinion on the Korean War varied. When the North Koreans invaded on June 25, 1950, and President Truman announced, two days later, his intent to send troops under United Nations auspices to defend the Republic of Korea (ROK), the decision was very popular. During the first nine months or so, as the UN forces moved north, were pushed back by the North Koreans and Chinese "volunteers," and then counterattacked, public support never wavered. Then the war stalemated around the 38th parallel, which divided the two Koreas, and public opinion gradually soured. (This period of stalemate is the part of the war depicted on the popular television series "M*A*S*H.")

This growing unpopularity had at least two sources. One was the perception that the United States was not trying to win the war, that it was a purposeless endeavor. The reason for this belief was the war's limited purpose; its goal was to remove the North Koreans and their allies from the ROK and to ensure that they did not return. (For a short period, the liberation of all Korea had been the object, but it was dashed by Chinese intervention.) This goal required neither overthrowing the North Korean government nor causing the unconditional surrender of its armed forces. To Americans conditioned by the two world wars, a limited political objective did not seem as worthy as MacArthur's famous phrase, "There is no substitute for victory." A return to the status quo before the invasion did not look like victory.

The second basis was that the absence of a total victory was incompatible with the mood of anticommunism in this country. In the years before and during the Korean War, the communists had a string of successes: the communization of eastern Europe was completed, North Korea fell under the communist "yoke," China fell to Mao Tse-tung's communist forces in what was widely described as a shameless sellout of Chiang Kai-shek's Nationalists, and a communist-inspired insurgency raged in French Indochina (Vietnam).

These communist victories seemed to represent an ominous and unacceptable trend. The competition with "godless" communism defined in containment theory required more; the evil should be expunged where it spread, and that was clearly not American policy in Korea. If a total, and morally redeeming, victory over communism was not the goal in Korea, then the enterprise was not worth the effort and the boys should come home. That, of course, was Eisenhower's pledge, but it did have a policy price.

The other internal domestic factor was Eisenhower's conviction that national security rested upon and required a healthy economy. To him, a healthy economy required a balanced budget, which meant a decrease in federal spending. A main cause of the deficit that the Republican leader inherited was the money being spent on the Korean conflict (just as American deficit financing had underwritten much of the Allied effort in World War II). Cuts had to come from somewhere.

The international situation, for most Americans, was dominated by fears of the communist menace. How, Americans asked, could this flood be stopped or, even better, reversed?

American concern had by now focused on the Soviet Union as the culprit in all this mischief. Long forgotten were the wartime depictions of Soviet leader Josef Stalin as "Uncle Joe." That rosy image was replaced by a dark and sinister picture of evil men emitting antagonistic directives from the Kremlin's dark recesses.

The symbol of this new perception was the "international communist conspiracy." In this framework, the worldwide rash of communist activities was viewed not as resulting from the rise of indigenous communist movements but rather as a conspiracy activated, orchestrated, and controlled by Moscow. When communists were active anywhere, the source of mischief was the Kremlin. Thus, the problem of containing communism everywhere came down to influencing Moscow not to authorize communist actions anywhere.

There was another aspect of the Soviet problem troubling the public and policymakers: the impressive Soviet military machine backing the regime and its expansionism. The Soviets did not demobilize their huge armed forces after World War II, but instead kept large numbers under arms to enforce their policies in eastern Europe and to face western Europe. As time went by, it became increasingly clear that the military instrument of power played a very important part in Soviet foreign policy. When the Soviets became a nuclear power, the United States would be physically menaced for the first time in over 140 years.

The Eisenhower years also saw rapid technological change, particularly in the evolution of nuclear forces. In 1949 the Soviets broke the American nuclear monopoly by exploding an atomic (fission) bomb; in 1953 they trailed the Americans by only a year in testing the first hydrogen (thermonuclear or fission-fusion) device, a weapon of truly awesome destructive power. In 1957 the Soviets in fast succession launched the first intercontinental ballistic missile and put into orbit the first manmade satellite, *Sputnik*. By the end of the decade, both land-based and submarine-based nuclear-tipped ballistic missiles would begin entering strategic inventories.

All these factors influenced President Eisenhower's formulation of a defense policy. Internal factors suggested the United States must steadfastly oppose communism, but that opposition must be accomplished within economic constraints that would not undermine the very national security they were designed to serve. The international setting suggested the key to containment was to deter the Soviet Union, and American nuclear superiority was crucial in this regard. The result was the overall policy known as the New Look and its centerpiece, the nuclear strategy of massive retaliation.

The strategy had both a conventional and a nuclear component. In its conventional aspect, it sought to create a sense of priority and limitation on those places the United States would defend with military and, especially, ground forces. In essence, the policy said the United States should be willing to use American ground forces where U.S. vital interests existed, notably in western Europe and Japan. Other areas under communist attack would receive American material assistance and training for their forces, but not American ground combat forces.

This policy, revived by Richard Nixon as the Nixon Doctrine in 1969, rested on several assumptions. The first was the belief that the United States could not afford anything more. Defense spending had grown since 1950, and in 1955 it represented almost half of the federal budget. Because of personnel costs, ground forces are expensive; cutting down when and where they would be committed allowed trimming their size. A second assumption was that maintaining large ground forces in peacetime was repulsive to the American public and thus not sustainable politically. Finally, cutting back on ground commitments minimized the danger of a future land war in Asia with China.

The means chosen to maintain a credible defense while cutting back conventional force was to place greatly increased emphasis on nuclear weapons and to create a series of alliances making nuclear threats believable. Thus, theater nuclear weapons (TNWs) were integrated into NATO defense plans for western Europe as early as 1955 to compensate for inferior NATO manpower levels. At the same time, the administration signed a series of multilateral (for instance, the Southeast Asia Treaty Organization, or SEATO) and bilateral (for instance, with Nationalist China) defense treaties to convince adversaries not to test American will.

The massive retaliation strategy was first announced in a speech by Eisenhower's secretary of state, John Foster Dulles. Speaking before the New York Council on Foreign Relations, Dulles announced that the United States, by policy and capability, had the power to retaliate massively with nuclear weapons against any communist aggression "at times and in places of our choosing." This pronouncement was a threat to the Soviets not to initiate or authorize probes anywhere along the containment line, because the United States might devastate the Soviet Union with nuclear weapons in response.

This threat had two notable aspects. The first was the broad range of communist provocations that might bring about an American retaliation. By not specifying what times or places would activate the policy and by constraining conventional capability, the administration assigned a very broad deterring role (sometimes called "spectrum defense") to nuclear weapons. The second characteristic was the policy's vagueness. It did not specify what might bring on a massive nuclear retaliation, and there were no great efforts to produce clarification. Rather, the Soviets had to guess what would trigger the response; their uncertainty would paralyze hostile action.

The policy was reasonable for the time. First, it was comparatively cheap. By placing considerable responsibility on the Strategic Air Command (SAC) to deliver nuclear weapons, a relatively small investment (especially in manpower) could be achieved. As then Secretary of Defense Charles ("Engine Charlie") Wilson said, nuclear weapons produced "more bang for the buck." Economy appealed to a balanced-budget-conscious administration. Second, it directly threatened the Soviet Union, which was the clear object of massive retaliation. If one accepted the international communist conspiracy as the basis of all hostile communist action, the threat was aimed at the proper party.

In the contemporary world of mutual nuclear balance and beyond, the strategy seems foolhardy. In the early 1950s, however, both the Soviets and the United States had nuclear weapons, but only the United States had a strategic bomber force capable of attacking the other's homeland. The Soviet Union had no equivalent of SAC and thus had no real retaliatory capability against an American first launch of nuclear weapons (which massive retaliation did not rule out). The American threat was credible because carrying it out did not entail a devastating response.

Credibility lies at the heart of any threat. Massive retaliation was credible when it was announced as policy, but that credibility came under attack in the latter 1950s. The criticism had two basic thrusts and resulted in a major revision in defense policy when John F. Kennedy entered the White House in 1961.

The first criticism, voiced by such analysts as Henry Kissinger, was directed at the spectrum defense role assigned to nuclear weapons. Since the use of nuclear weapons was clearly a dire act, one would hardly carry it out unless the threat to American interests was severe. The United

States might well invoke massive retaliation in the event of an aggression against NATO or Japan, but what about probes against less important points along the containment line? Would we really attack the Soviet Union with nuclear weapons in response to an uprising in Africa or Asia? The critics answered, "No."

The second criticism amplified the first and ultimately was more telling. After the Soviet Union tested its ICBM and launched *Sputnik*, the credibility of massive retaliation came into question. The reason was simple: Soviet intercontinental missile capability meant they could now counterattack after an American massive retaliatory attack. The United States would henceforth suffer real and devastating physical consequences if it activated massive retaliation. The kinds of circumstances important enough to take that risk were once again raised. One could argue one way or the other whether the United States would still accept massive damage in defense of NATO; to most, however, it was not credible that we would risk such consequences over areas of lesser importance to our interests. The Soviet ICBM destroyed the credibility of massive retaliation and started a debate that led to a new policy direction for Eisenhower's Democratic successor.

The Kennedy-Johnson Years (1961–1969)

When the country's youngest elected president assumed office in January 1961, a new era in American politics and in notions about national defense began. As had been the case in 1952, national defense issues—notably, the "missile gap" discussed below and the debate over massive retaliation—helped propel John Kennedy past Richard M. Nixon in an extremely close election.

The period initiated by President Kennedy, of course, encompassed Lyndon B. Johnson as well. In examining national security issues, the two presidencies can be combined, because both were Democrats and because one figure, Secretary of Defense Robert S. McNamara, served both men and dominated national defense considerations. In many ways, McNamara and his "whiz kids," and their systems-analysis approach to managing Pentagon problems, still dominate the way policy is made.

It was a particularly important time for policy development and debate. Political concerns included a growing consensus about the conceptual inadequacy of the New Look, the question of nuclear—particularly, missile—balance between the United States and the Soviet Union, a more aggressive attitude by the new administration on defense issues, and a growing popular and scholarly dialogue on nuclear weapons.

By the time John Kennedy was elected, there was general agreement that the New Look, especially massive retaliation, needed scrapping. The Eisenhower administration had tacitly admitted this inadequacy by moving toward increased emphasis on conventional weaponry in its second term. It required a new president to complete the transformation.

The missile gap issue had been an important part of the 1960 campaign. It had been raised by candidate Kennedy, who suggested the United States had lagged behind the Soviet Union in producing nuclear-tipped missiles since *Sputnik*'s launch. He charged that the Soviets had considerably more of these missiles and that a U.S. crash program to re-establish nuclear superiority was needed.

There was, in fact, a missile gap, but in the direction opposite to that portrayed by Kennedy. He had seized upon the issue because a Central Intelligence Agency study had projected Soviet missile superiority based on maximum production capability. In that age, prior to satellite reconnaissance that allows reliable monitoring of such production, the report assumed that the Soviets were building at their maximum rate and extrapolated their force size from that assumption. In fact, the Soviets had built very few missiles, and American missiles outnumbered their Soviet counterparts by about a 4 to 1 ratio, a fact Kennedy learned only after making the charge.

The young president had his own distinct ideas. Convinced that a primary flaw in the New Look was its de-emphasis of conventional forces, Kennedy also did not fear the prospect of an unbalanced budget. Among the things he asked people to do for their country was to spend more on national defense, even if those increases would eventually contribute to a substantial national debt.

His other major idea dealt with the problem of unconventional warfare—an area that had been given little attention within the armed forces, especially within the army. Having read widely on guerrilla warfare, Kennedy was convinced that the United States must have an unconventional warfare capability to meet the challenges of the future. The result of his concern, embraced reluctantly by the Army, was to expand greatly the so-called Special Forces or Green Berets, who were to be prominent in the early stages of American involvement in Vietnam.

Finally, there was a very active public examination of nuclear weapons and the possibilities for nuclear war. The popular side of this phenomenon closely paralleled a similar movement in the early 1980s. In the aftermath of the *Sputnik* shock, a kind of fatalistic popular culture about nuclear weapons and the "inevitability" of nuclear war appeared. The movie *Dr. Strangelove,* with its subtitle *How I Learned to Love the Bomb,* captured this mood. Herman Kahn's studies *On Thermonuclear War* and *Thinking about the Unthinkable* graced drugstore book displays. When John Kennedy suggested the efficacy of civil defense, a fallout shelter industry quickly was born, and thousands of backyards were dug up to install shelters.

The ICBM also produced a spate of scholarly concerns. Before Soviet acquisition of a delivery capability against the United States, nuclear deterrence was no more than U.S. self-restraint. The weapons even seemed to be useful for purposes of coercive diplomacy, to gain Soviet compliance with American demands. American vulnerability to nuclear attack changed all that, and resulted in the emergence of a large, sophisticated body of thought on nuclear deterrence, often referred to as the golden age of thinking about nuclear weapons and deterrence. Most of the ideas and constructs that dominate contemporary discussions are extrapolations from concerns first elaborated at that time.

Of all the international forces affecting American security in the Kennedy/Johnson era, three stand out. They are the Cuban missile crisis, the Vietnam War, and the growth in Soviet conventional and nuclear power.

The Cuban missile crisis of September and October 1962 was the first of these. It followed the Berlin crisis of 1961, when the Berlin Wall was erected, and a summit between Kennedy and Soviet Premier Khrushchev in Vienna, where the Soviet leader perceived Kennedy to be irresolute and indecisive. In that belief, Khrushchev authorized placing offensive missiles in Cuba capable of attacking much of the eastern and southeastern United States. When American U-2 reconnaissance overflights of Cuba revealed construction of these missile sites, Kennedy demanded they be dismantled, and the confrontation began.

The details of the Cuban crisis need not concern us here. What does matter is the result of that extremely tense two-week period, when the world appeared to be teetering on the brink of nuclear war. Aside from beginning the process that led to Khrushchev's fall from power, the crisis was universally agreed to have been the closest humankind had come to nuclear holocaust. (Some would argue that the Yom Kippur War of 1973 approached Cuba in that dubious regard.) Both sides were sobered by what almost happened. The result was that the first real progress in arms control came in the following years. The "Missiles of October," to borrow the motion picture title, helped convince the superpowers that they at least had a common interest in avoiding mutual incineration.

The second major event was the Vietnam War. American involvement in that tragedy was gradual. Some date the beginning to World War II collaboration between the American Office of Strategic Services (OSS, the predecessor of the CIA) and communist leader Ho Chi Minh; some date involvement to the 1950 decision to aid the French attempt to maintain colonial power; and others choose 1955 or 1956, when decisions were made to ignore the Geneva Accords of 1954 and to support South Vietnam's Ngo Dinh Diem.

Regardless of when involvement began, about 600 American "advisers" were in South Vietnam when Kennedy took office. When an assassin's bullet felled him in November 1963, that figure had risen to around 17,000, and American combat casualties had been incurred. Lyndon Johnson increased the commitment, introducing American combat troops into the country until they peaked at 541,500 early in 1969.

Vietnam had three important policy impacts. First, it was terribly expensive. The entire cost of American involvement, about $150 billion, made it the second most expensive conflict in U.S. history, after World

War II. Investment in other defense areas was stunted. In combination with the series of welfare and entitlement programs known as the Great Society, it helped begin a spiral of inflation and government deficits. The war virtually preempted other defense concerns. Attention focused first on trying to prevail, then failing in that, on extrication with some sense of grace. Finally, Vietnam was politically divisive. In its "Vietnam hangover," the country was simply unwilling to concentrate on questions of national security for the balance of the 1970s.

Growing Soviet military capability was the final major influence on American security considerations in the Kennedy-Johnson years. Decisions made by the Soviets in the early 1960s and evidenced as the decade went on greatly increased the military threat to American interests. On the one hand, the Soviets' ability to project global power expanded, largely because their navy burgeoned from little more than a coastal protecting force to a true "blue water" navy that could intrude into all the world's oceans. On the other hand, the Russians began a massive expansion of their thermonuclear forces that continued through the 1970s and into the 1980s. Measured in numbers of launchers, Soviet forces surpassed American totals by the end of the 1960s.

The Kennedy-Johnson years were also technologically interesting. The computer began to have a sizable impact. Computerized weapons systems made arsenals more sophisticated and deadly, as items as diverse as "smart bombs" (bombs with some form of terminal guidance) and electronic sensors capable of monitoring enemy troop movements entered the inventory. Computerized management allowed a more detailed accounting for defense activities than had previously been possible.

At the strategic level, the most important technological factor was a limitation on the accuracy of guidance systems for the ballistic missiles that were entering strategic inventories. Compared with their modern counterparts, these systems were quite crude. Today the accuracy of a missile launched over a several-thousand-mile flight is a few hundred feet, but in the early and middle 1960s it was in the range of several miles.

These factors combined to influence policy during the two Democratic administrations of the 1960s. John Kennedy organized his defense policy around the concept of flexible response. This organizing concept was translated into a strategy of expanding the size of general forces and the kinds of military missions they were prepared to undertake. At the strategic level, the strategy was "controlled response," modified to "assured destruction" during Lyndon Johnson's tenure in office.

The debate over conventional force strategy went back to the reaction to demobilization after Korea. The cutback sustained at that time left the United States with a "force in being," arguably capable of carrying out its commitment to defend NATO Europe but with questionable capacity to engage simultaneously in another military action elsewhere. The question was whether this "one-war" capability was adequate; the

Eisenhower administration had begun to move slowly toward expanding it before leaving office.

Kennedy preferred expansion to a "two-and-a-half-war" footing to allow simultaneous engagement in NATO Europe and northeast Asia, while also waging a minor war somewhere in the Third World. This latter capability was designed to deal with communist probes along the containment line in such places as Asia, called "brushfire wars," so named by an analyst at the RAND Corporation in southern California, where real brushfires are common. The analogy was that these minor problems might be ignited unpredictably but could be "put out" as one does a wildfire.

Kennedy was particularly interested in the brushfire war problem, especially because such wars were often unconventional, guerrilla conflicts. Support for or opposition to such a capability reflects differing views of containment. The negative side supports the original Eisenhower position of indirect involvement in such conflicts limited to equipping and training indigenous forces in their own self-defense, because direct intervention is simply too expensive to sustain. Proponents argue that these are the really dangerous situations the United States faces, that the nuclear threat is not credible to deter them, and that only an unconventional capability can stop this form of communist aggression.

The two-and-a-half-war strategy required increasing U.S. capabilities. The size of the armed forces had to be expanded, as did their capabilities to handle new and diversified missions. It was clearly a more expensive policy than the New Look, but, as mentioned earlier, Kennedy was undaunted by the additional costs. As a result, the United States was reasonably well prepared militarily for the Vietnam War when the decision to escalate was made. Especially in retrospect, many critics of the Vietnam experience have maintained that had the expanded capability not been developed, the United States might never have become involved in that morass.

Meanwhile, nuclear strategy evolved. The golden age debate had created a reasonable consensus that the major, if not the sole, future utility of nuclear weapons was deterrence of nuclear attack against the United States. The question was how best to dissuade the Soviet Union from launching such an attack. The answer largely depended on how one thought a nuclear war would be conducted.

Very little prior thought had gone into the subject. Such speculation as there had been centered on the idea of a "salvo" or "spasm" war, where both sides would more or less simultaneously launch all their missiles at each other. The result would be a very brief, cataclysmic exchange.

Secretary of Defense Robert McNamara challenged this conceptualization, largely because such an exchange made absolutely no military sense. Nuclear war, he maintained, might instead be a gradual affair, where each side engaged in measured nuclear attacks against the other. At each level of violence, there might be negotiations to decide whether or not to escalate. Terminating the war short of a general exchange might be negotiated. The idea that nuclear war might be limited was announced by McNamara as the strategy of controlled response.

Over time, McNamara came to doubt the ability to limit a nuclear conflict once engaged. He reasoned that the enormous destruction the weapons would cause would so enrage the victims that vindictiveness, if not sheer irrationality, would reign, leading inevitably to all-out hostilities. The result was a change in strategy to something called assured destruction.

Assured destruction was a description raised to the status of a strategy. As a description, it was a very accurate statement of the consequences of a United States retaliation against the Soviet Union after a Soviet attack. It said that even after such an attack, the United States could retaliate with its surviving forces and inflict unacceptable damage—assuredly destroy—such a large part of the Soviet Union that no Soviet leader could conceivably calculate victory from such an attack. When the Soviets achieved the same capability, around 1969, a mischievous detractor of the strategy renamed it *mutual assured destruction,* reducible to the acronym MAD, which is what that analyst thought the strategy was.

The operative dynamic of assured destruction is something called the "hostage effect." In a world without defenses against strategic rockets, either the United States or the USSR can attack the other, who has no hope of blunting the attack. Deterrence derives from the recognition that doing so invites a devastating response that will also destroy the aggressor. Americans are effectively Soviet hostages, as Soviets are of Americans; both have the capacity to execute the other in the event of a nuclear transgression. Because the suicidal consequences of launching an attack are recognized, deterrence is maintained.

The strategy reflected its time. Most of its ideas were drawn from the scholarly community's golden age, and it was therefore embraced. Moreover, the strategy was both realistic and economical. Its realism consisted of aiming forces at those Soviet urban areas where the hostages were and which relatively inaccurate missiles could hit. It was economical because there are a finite number of cities worth hitting in the Soviet Union or anyplace else before one reaches the point of diminishing returns (or gets less "rubble for the ruble" because one is forced to hit smaller and smaller communities). Once a force large enough to hit the major Soviet cities is assembled (which it was in 1965), there is little need to build more.

Like massive retaliation, assured destruction had within it the seeds of its own discrediting. Soviet ICBMs made massive retaliation outmoded, and the Soviet achievement of nuclear parity with the United States affected assured destruction similarly. When the United States could assuredly destroy the Soviet Union without being similarly threatened, the strategy was believable. When the Soviets caught up to us in nuclear terms, it meant that an American-assured destruction retaliation (second strike) would invite a Soviet third strike. Carrying out the assured destruction threat became tantamount to committing suicide.

The Nixon-Ford Years (1969–1977)

Richard Nixon became president at a traumatic period in American history; Vietnam, a defense and foreign policy issue, underlay the trauma. In some ways, his election to the nation's highest office resembled his election as Dwight Eisenhower's vice-presidential candidate sixteen years earlier. Eisenhower had been elected on the pledge to end an unpopular war initiated by a Democratic president, and Nixon rode to victory in part on a similar promise regarding Southeast Asia.

The clearly dominating influence on domestic and international policy was Vietnam. The Tet offensive that began on January 30, 1968, had destroyed remaining public trust in the war effort and in Lyndon Johnson, who declined to seek renomination in 1968 because of public revulsion at a war for which he was blamed. The antiwar movement reached its peak at the star-crossed Democratic party convention that year, and no candidate in either party could seriously expect to win the presidency without a purported way to end the war.

The problem was how to end it. Three years of apparently inconclusive combat suggested that a purely military solution was not practical, and the North Vietnamese seemed uninterested in negotiating a settlement that preserved a shard of dignity for the United States. Despite those difficulties, American relations with the Soviets continued to improve: The Russians and Americans negotiated and ratified the Strategic Arms Limitation Treaty (SALT) accords—the pinnacle of detente—while Americans continued to fight and die on Vietnamese battlefields.

The process of extrication from Vietnam undercut trust in public officials and spurred a major debate about conventional defense policy. Just as the public had reacted to the outcome of the Korean conflict by demanding no repetition in the future, so the lesson of Vietnam was "no more Vietnams," the meaning of which is still being debated.

There was also a domestic debate over strategic nuclear policy. Led by detractors of assured destruction, it took two different directions. On one hand, there were those who criticized the strategy as bizarre and grotesque. The threat underlying the strategy was, after all, a promise to engage in massive genocide against the Soviet population in the event of a Soviet attack; such a threat violates all canons of civilized behavior. This position was stated in 1983 in the Catholic bishops' pastoral letter on nuclear war.

The other, ultimately more telling, criticism was that the assured destruction threat was simply not believable. In a "MAD" world, the critics maintained, carrying out the threat means committing suicide. The only believable circumstances for an assured-destruction retaliation is in direct response to a massive attack against American cities. The Soviets realize this, so it is their least likely form of attack. Thus, assured destruction emerges as an effective deterrent against the least likely aggression. At the same time, an assured-destruction response to a limited Soviet aggression—by definition, more likely—is not credible. This argument was captured in President Nixon's lament that an American president should not be faced with the options only of carrying out the assured destruction attack or doing nothing after a limited Soviet first strike.

Strategic nuclear policy was most affected by international factors. A major influence was the continuing growth of Soviet nuclear forces. Spending up to $150 billion more than the United States during the 1970s, the Soviets caught up to and surpassed the American arsenal in all categories of measuring peacetime arsenal sizes except total warheads. The question was why this buildup continued, and what it meant for U.S. strategy.

The other international influence was the SALT process. Originally scheduled to convene in 1968, the talks were postponed by the Soviet invasion of Czechoslovakia that May. The new president was personally ambivalent about SALT but knew the talks would have to be conducted because of general public support for arms control efforts. Moreover, any agreement would clearly have an impact on the nuclear balance between the superpowers and, hence, create either opportunities or limitations on nuclear strategy.

The period was one of great technological activity. On the strategic nuclear level, two mutually supportive technologies that have a continuing impact reached fruition. The first was multiple warhead technology. First developed by the United States, the multiple independently targetable reentry vehicle (MIRV) was first deployed in 1970 and entered the Soviet arsenal in 1975. The MIRV allows more than one warhead (or nuclear explosive) to be launched from a single rocket, which can thus attack multiple targets.

The second technological influence was great improvement in missile and warhead accuracy. Breakthroughs in inertial and terminal guidance systems reduced the inaccuracy of nuclear missiles from errors formerly measurable in miles to 0.1 or 0.2 miles.

These two innovations made it possible to think about targeting, and possibly attacking, one another's missile forces. With single-warhead rockets, great inaccuracies, and roughly equal numbers of missiles, such calculation had little meaning. Accurate multiwarhead rockets meant that a fraction of one's forces could be dedicated to the other's ICBMs with a good prospect of arriving at and destroying their targets.

From this milieu came the defense policy known as *realistic deterrence.* It was realistic in adapting to the situation which it confronted. At the strategic level, the reality was Soviet achievement of an irreversible nuclear parity, with which American defense policymakers would have to learn to live. At the conventional level, popular reaction to the Vietnam War meant the need to pull back and avoid Third World engagements.

Strategic nuclear policy evolved under the leadership of two Republican presidents as it had done under two Democrats. President Nixon first announced that American nuclear strategy would be organized around the principle of *strategic sufficiency*—the name originated in 1955 by the Eisenhower administration, in which then Vice President Nixon had served. Deterrence was based on the United States' maintaining four force characteristics. None represented a radical change in policy.

Four criteria restated assured-destruction force requirements. The first was the need to maintain a secure second-strike force capable of deterring an all-out attack on U.S. strategic forces. The second was that forces should be designed to give the Soviets no incentive to attack them during a crisis: they should be safe from attack so that they could retaliate. The third requirement was that the Soviets should not be able to do substantially more damage to the United States than the United States could do to them. Destructive parity was acceptable but should not be upset. Finally, American forces should be capable of repelling small or accidental attacks. This final criterion justified a light antiballistic missile (ABM) system to defend against a Chinese attack, but defenses were dropped when a Chinese nuclear threat failed to materialize.

If this initial formulation was much like assured destruction, the critics of MAD eventually gained sway in the Nixon White House. As a result, a new strategy was announced by the administration and later embraced by Nixon's successor, Gerald Ford: *limited nuclear options* (LNOs).

Limited nuclear options responded to the criticism that assured destruction was ineffectual against a measured, or limited, provocation by the Soviets. It maintained that such an attack is deterred by a series of available proportional responses, or limited nuclear options, appropriate to whatever level of attack was contemplated. Soviet knowledge that the United States could respond appropriately would better deter them from action.

Conventional policy, at the same time, had to contend with an antimilitary resurgence caused by Vietnam. That reaction included demands to end conscription and institute all-voluntary military service (Americans were last drafted in 1972), to cut back the size of the armed forces (the army was halved in active-duty strength after the war), and to further limit military spending.

The answer was the Nixon Doctrine. Harking back to the 1950s, this was an attempt to eliminate direct American military involvement with ground forces in the Third World, especially in Asia. The doctrine asserted that the United States would limit assistance to beleaguered Third World governments to the provision of supplies and war materials and the training of indigenous forces. Beyond that, countries would be expected to help themselves, aided, it was hoped, by other regional powers.

The Nixon Doctrine reemphasized American commitment to NATO. During Vietnam, American men and supplies originally intended for Europe had been transferred to Southeast Asia; Presidents Nixon and Ford reinstituted American presence at previous levels. The two Republican presidents, in essence, returned the United States to a one-war footing. In light of a public mood very antagonistic to defense and defense-related matters, very little else could be sustained.

The Carter Years (1977–1981)

When the first post–Civil War southerner elected to the presidency arrived in Washington, "Vietnam hangover" was his most prominent defense inheritance. A product in part of the antimilitary backlash himself, Jimmy Carter had campaigned on a pledge to reduce defense spending in absolute terms at a time when double-digit inflation was seriously undermining the buying power of the dollar.

A continuing public desire to ignore military matters was the primary domestic political consideration facing the new president. Although the evidence suggested that the all-volunteer concept was producing an inferior fighting force, the mere suggestion of reinstating registration for the draft (not of actually reactivating the draft itself) was greeted with strong objections. Spending proposals were also met with great skepticism and reluctance.

There was some domestic interest in strategic arms control. Negotiations for a successor to the 1972 SALT I agreement had been ongoing since the Vladivostok Accords were signed by President Ford and Premier Leonid Brezhnev in 1974. Within months of his inauguration, Carter made his own "comprehensive proposal" to reduce U.S. and Soviet arsenals by 25 percent. When Carter and Brezhnev signed SALT II in Vienna in June 1979, strategic arms control reached its high mark to that point.

International events in the late 1970s aided recovery from the Vietnam hangover but also undercut the euphoria surrounding the SALT treaty. The major event was the Soviet invasion of Afghanistan two days after Christmas in 1979. The event accelerated a gradual erosion of antimilitary feeling and served as the death knell for SALT II in the U.S. Senate.

Following shortly after the fall of the Shah of Iran to the militant, anti-American Khomeini theocracy, the Soviet invasion was doubly ominous. First, it further destabilized the Persian Gulf area, the single largest source of the world's petroleum energy. Second, it appeared a blatant case of Soviet aggression, and many in the West wondered if it was not simply a Soviet stepping-stone toward control of the gulf region. Soviet-American relations had cooled during the Carter presidency over alleged Soviet violations of the human rights of Soviet Jews and others. When the United States responded to the Soviet invasion of Afghanistan by suspending grain sales to the Soviets and boycotting the 1980 Summer Olympics in Moscow, these relations began a precipitous plunge.

The arms race, meanwhile, continued. More sophisticated weaponry was added to the U.S. arsenal to take advantage of overall American technological superiority that could compensate for Warsaw Pact superiority in men and quantities of arms. "Technological substitution" was intended to produce "force multipliers": weapons could be so qualitatively superior to the enemy's that they made up for the inferiority in numbers of soldiers. Critics countered that these highly sophisticated weapons were often so expensive that they could be bought only in small and generally inadequate numbers. Moreover, the ability of the average soldier to operate highly sophisticated equipment in wartime was questioned. Even more ominous, most agreed that the Soviets were, in any case, narrowing the technological gap, an assertion that would only be disspelled with time.

The trend toward increasingly accurate MIRVed weapons centered on the MX missile system. Although work on MX began in the early 1970s, it became a cause célèbre during the Carter administration for two reasons. Because it carried 10 highly accurate warheads, the missile was criticized as provocative, a first-strike weapon better suited for attacking the Soviet Union preemptively than for retaliatory use. At the same time, a parallel increase in Soviet missile accuracy raised the specter that all land-based missiles were becoming vulnerable, thus casting doubt on whether there was any safe way to base MX.

There was also renewed interest in ballistic missile defense (BMD). The idea of developing an active defense against missile attacks had suffered a serious blow with the signing of the Antiballistic Missile (ABM) Treaty in 1972, since the treaty severely limited ABM deployment. By the end of the decade, BMD supporters were back in the public eye, working seriously on the potential of "exotic" defenses using space-based lasers and charged-particle beams. Although President Reagan popularized this concept in his famous "Star Wars" speech of March 1983, it was actually a product of the Carter Pentagon and earlier research efforts.

Essential continuity was most evident in conventional force policy. The Vietnam hangover left little support for an aggressive policy or for the spending that would accompany such a policy. The American people simply did not want to be bothered by discussions about conventional defense and the possibility of war.

During the early Carter years, the American posture was designed around the one-war philosophy. Popularly mandated budget restraints and the greater expenses associated with all-volunteer armed forces actually eroded American capabilities, in particular the capacity to engage in anything beyond the NATO European war scenario. Carter has been criticized for allowing American conventional capabilities to deteriorate, as in candidate Ronald Reagan's reference to the Carter defense policy as one of "unilateral disarmament." Given the public mood, it is hard to imagine how Carter could have done much more.

Policy development had to wait on events, primarily on those in the Persian Gulf. The jackhammer 1979 events in Iran and Afghanistan shocked a president who, to his later embarrassment, said he learned more about Soviet behavior in the twenty-four hours surrounding the Soviets' landing in Kabul than he had in his previous three years in office. The American public was aroused by our apparent impotence in the face of these events, and the mood of strident antimilitarism that preceded those startling occurrences began to shift.

Carter made two distinctive contributions to conventional policy in reacting to the Persian Gulf events. First, he declared the security of the

Persian Gulf and its oil to be a vital U.S. interest. This announcement, part of his 1980 State of the Union address, instantly became known as the Carter Doctrine and later provided the policy justification for removing Iraq from Kuwait (the Persian Gulf War). It placed the gulf along with western Europe and Japan as places the United States would certainly defend with force. The problem was absence of an obvious U.S. military capability to project significant power into that distant region.

His second contribution was to authorize a force to defend American interests in Southwest Asia (as the gulf area is also known): the Rapid Deployment Force (RDF). The idea was to create a highly mobile strike force that could rapidly be inserted into a distant trouble spot. No new forces were added in the process; instead, existing units were given additional responsibilities with the RDF. The RDF evolved into the U.S. Central Command (USCENTCOM), which had operational responsibility for conducting the Persian Gulf War.

Strategic nuclear policy also evolved in the Carter administration. When the Georgian came to power, he recruited two individuals who had gotten their professional start as defense policymakers in the early McNamara Pentagon. His secretary of defense was Harold Brown, a physicist who helped invent the hydrogen bomb, former president of the California Institute of Technology, and secretary of the air force under Lyndon Johnson. His secretary of energy was James Schlesinger, author (as secretary of defense for President Ford) of the strategy of limited nuclear options.

Carter's strategic policy, adopted in 1978, was the *countervailing strategy*. At its heart was limited nuclear options. It accepted the logic of the critics of assured destruction, and the idea was that the United States must have appropriate and proportional responses to meet any Soviet provocation. The Soviets would be deterred by recognizing the futility of expecting to gain from any contemplated aggression. As Brown himself put it in his last annual report, "Our countervailing strategy tells the world that no potential adversary of the United States could ever conclude that the fruits of his aggression would be worth his own costs." Reflecting the ambivalence of his past in the McNamara Pentagon, Brown frequently mused that assured destruction might well be the outcome of nuclear war, despite efforts at limitation.

The countervailing strategy evoked a curious response. When it was initially announced, it brought essentially no negative reaction, which was remarkable because it directly rejected the assured-destruction strategy of which many liberal intellectuals had been enamored for a decade.

Public reaction awaited the heat of the 1980 election campaign. In August 1980, Secretary Brown announced a new directive for nuclear targeters, Presidential Directive (PD) 59, based on the dictates of the countervailing strategy. The directive emphasized selectivity in what was targeted by nuclear forces and highlighted the priority assigned to military targets. The latter emphasis explicitly rejected assured destruction, because the hostage effect required targeting population centers. The result was a furor that probably cost Carter votes and that would form part of the environment in which Ronald Reagan took office.

The Reagan Years (1981–1989)

Ronald Reagan rode into the White House on the crest of a wave of interest in defense issues. During a sometimes bitter campaign against President Carter, he had consistently portrayed himself as much more supportive of the military and had characterized his opponent as weak, especially in his dealings with the Soviets.

Several changes in the international setting and domestic political scene facilitated Reagan's harder line on defense. Internationally, there were changes. The first was an altered U.S.-Soviet relationship. The "spreading glow of detente" announced by Secretary of State Kissinger in the early 1970s had been replaced by an increasingly cool relationship, much of it created in the wake of the Soviet invasion of Afghanistan and Carter's responses to that event. The Soviet thrust into and occupation of Afghanistan stood as a continuing reminder of Soviet brutality that the new president would seek to exploit.

The failure to ratify SALT II was the single greatest symbol of the breakdown of Soviet-American detente. Reagan had campaigned vigorously against the treaty, charging that its provisions favored the Soviets and that the entire treaty was thus "fatally flawed." At that, both sides adhered to SALT II provisions through the life of the document, which lapsed formally at the end of 1985. In the wake of the 1985 Gorbachev-Reagan summit, arms control negotiations resumed in Geneva, but the road to a new comprehensive agreement was clearly long and arduous.

The second area of continuing international concern was the Middle East. In the Persian Gulf, the revolutionary government of Iran became embroiled in 1980 in a war with neighboring Iraq that raged on until 1988. The conflict between Israel and its neighbors simmered, boiling over into open warfare in Lebanon in 1982.

The new president presided over a polarization of public opinion on military issues. International events created a more anti-Soviet attitude and willingness to spend on defense; both the president's typification of the Soviet Union as the "evil empire" and his calls for record defense budgets struck responsive chords in the populace during his first term. Reagan also denounced SALT II, called for massive modernization and expansion of American strategic nuclear forces, and bitterly attacked Soviet nuclear intentions. These actions helped create a loose coalition— calling for a nuclear freeze and movement toward nuclear disarmament —that resembled antimilitarist reactions two decades earlier.

Changed public perceptions and the president's overtly anti-Soviet attitudes would suggest a good deal of conceptual change in defense policy in the new Republican administration. At the rhetorical level, there was significant change: the president called for a major expansion of American military capabilities, and rhetoric aimed at the Soviet Union was increasingly hostile. Some critics remarked sourly that American foreign policy consisted mainly of calling the Soviets nasty names during the first Reagan term.

The rhetoric was not, however, matched by any fundamental changes in policy. The Reagan administration waited until 1985 to give its policy a name, reviving "flexible response" as a title. Examined closely, its strategies primarily extended policies developed under Carter and before, although it significantly expanded several programs. The Strategic Defense Initiative was an exception to the continuity with Carter administration policy.

At the conventional level, the main thrust was on rearmament to improve the quality of America's fighting forces. The Rapid Deployment Force was upgraded to the Central Command (CENTCOM) to place greater emphasis on its importance. There was renewed interest in the Special Forces and their unconventional warfare role, and the deployment of Pershing II and ground-launched cruise missiles (GLCMs) in Europe was designed to enhance NATO capabilities. None of these measures represented a novel direction, but all were intended to increase American ability to respond to a variety of military challenges worldwide. If there was a change, it was in emphasis. The Reagan administration appeared more willing to spend on defense than its predecessor, and apparently was more favorably disposed to military solutions to problems, as in Grenada and Libya. The ability to sustain the large increases in spending initiated during Reagan's first term was challenged in 1985 by the Gramm-Rudman balanced budget bill. Reconciling budgetary limits with defense preparedness continued to be a major theme in the second Reagan term. Moreover, the apparent decline in the Soviet threat also began to raise the question about how much was needed, a prime question facing the successor Bush administration.

Incremental change also marked strategic nuclear policy. In October 1981, the president announced a major force modernization proposal that included the MX (Peacekeeper) missile, the Trident IID5 missile for the Ohio-class submarine, the B1B and Advanced Technology Bomber (ATB or Stealth), ballistic missile and civil defenses, and improvements in command/control/communications and intelligence (C^3I) endurability. The Carter administration had advocated all elements of this package except the B1B bomber, if at a slower procurement rate. The countervailing strategy remained the underlying concept, although now under the flexible response label. This continuity was first stated publicly by Secretary of Defense Weinberger in his *Fiscal Year 1984 Report to the Congress:* "The Soviet leadership, in calculating the risks of aggression, recognizes that because of our retaliatory capability, there can be no circumstance in which it would benefit by beginning a nuclear war at any level or of any duration." This construction, of course, is essentially identical to that of the countervailing strategy.

The Reagan security policies moderated somewhat during his second term in office. The harsh rhetoric that had characterized the first term gave way to a more measured tone as Mikhail S. Gorbachev consolidated power and began to instigate apparently meaningful reforms. At the same time, both sides demonstrated a renewed interest in arms control, culminating in the 1988 Intermediate Nuclear Forces (INF) Treaty, which banned all nuclear-armed missiles with ranges between 300 and 3,000 miles.

Several things coalesced to create this moderation in U.S. policy. First and foremost was the rise of Gorbachev in 1985 and the institution of his policies of *perestroika* (restructuring), *glasnost* (openness or criticism), and the "new political thinking" in foreign policy. The domestic elements of the policy were aimed at resuscitating a Soviet economy that the Russians admitted had been in decline for over a decade and had the effect of limited democratization of the Soviet state. The foreign policy initiatives, most dramatically demonstrated by the Soviet withdrawal from Afghanistan and the breakdown of communist hegemony in much of eastern Europe, were clearly aimed at reducing East-West tensions.

A second factor helped fuel policy changes. During the first Reagan term, defense spending increased at the most rapid rate in peacetime history. This spending was, of course, accompanied by a 25 percent cut in personal income taxes. The result was a trebling of the national debt, including the holding of a substantial amount of that debt by foreign nationals, notably the Japanese.

Concern over the federal deficit side of the "double deficits" (the other being the negative balance of trade between the United States and the rest of the world) triggered legislation to force deficit reduction. The Gramm-Rudman-Hollings bill, named after its Senate cosponsors, mandated a balanced federal budget by 1993, with gradual reductions annually along the way. The largest target of budget cuts was defense.

The two factors combined. Although many members of the Reagan administration were initially skeptical about the new Soviet leader's reforms, warmer Soviet-American relations could help reduce the threat component of national risk. This was particularly desirable in that budget cuts meant capability would be reduced as well.

A third factor also helped undermine support for national security: growing public disaffection with the heavy defense commitment. In some ways, this disillusion was no more than an outgrowth of traditional American attitudes discussed in Chapter 3. In the second Reagan administration, however, at least two other factors contributed to the erosion of interest and support.

The first of these was a growing belief that defense monies were not being spent well. Amid sensational accusations about $600 toilet seats, many came to feel that so-called "waste, fraud, and abuse" marked defense spending. Second, the Iran-Contra episode, in which high government officials apparently engaged in illegal acts in the name of national security, further eroded public confidence.

The Bush Years (1989–1993)

George S. Bush entered the presidency at an extremely dynamic, fluid time when traditional elements of the policy environment were undergoing rapid, possibly fundamental change. Nowhere was this change more obvious than in the international environment in which a threat is defined. At the same time, domestic priorities made demands both on the resources available to deal with national security and on the priorities of the American people.

The world climate in 1989 was especially charged. In the Eastern bloc, which had historically provided the greatest threat content, there was virtual disarray. Political democratization mixed with ethnic unrest, demands for greater ethnic autonomy, and a continuing—even deepening—economic crisis in the Soviet Union. President Mikhail Gorbachev, desperate for economic success to assure his own continuation in power, turned openly to the West for help, promising peace in return. At the same time, waves of perestroika lapped over eastern Europe as well: a noncommunist government was formed by Solidarity in Poland; Hungary removed the word *socialist* from the country's name, Republic of Hungary; and the Berlin Wall fell literally amid East German demands for democratization, triggering the rapid movement toward German reunification. By the end of 1992, there was not a single acknowledged communist state in Europe, and the Soviet Union had quietly dissolved into fifteen successor states. The changes were stunning even to a world grown accustomed to rapid change.

These changes raised the prospect of a new East-West power map in which military confrontation between NATO and the Warsaw Pact might dissolve into what Gorbachev called the "common European home." At the same time, the possibility of meaningful progress in arms control improved dramatically. At the Strategic Arms Reduction Talks (START), progress was made to cut nuclear arsenals nearly in half, and at the Conventional Forces in Europe (CFE) talks, begun in early 1989, there appeared to be an end to the impasse on reducing those forces that had characterized earlier negotiating efforts under the forum Mutual and Balanced Force Reductions (MBFR). The Warsaw Pact voted itself out of existence in mid-1991, and the demise of the former Soviet Union completed the collapse of the old threat.

The Bush administration, dominated by longtime Cold Warriors, reacted slowly to these changes, fearing their reversal. However, reduced East-West tensions accompanied by force reductions clearly had popular appeal in the United States. First, reduced forces could conceivably translate into lower defense spending. Such savings could be applied to Gramm-Rudman-Hollings guidelines or to a host of new domestic priorities that had accumulated during the Reagan years. In particular, such problems as repairing the American infrastructure (for example, bridges and roadways), revitalizing the education system, and eradicating home-lessness seemed ready candidates for released defense dollars.

Second, nontraditional sources of national security concern had arisen on the American agenda. Two of these, in particular, were the "war" on drugs and American economic and technological competitive-ness in the twenty-first century. The drug problem, rooted especially in crack cocaine but with ever more exotic drugs such as methamphetamine ("ice") looming on the horizon, was seen as critically undermining Amer-ican youth and contributing predominantly to crime in America's cities to such an extent that the entire society was placed at risk. Partly in re-sponse to the drug problem, Bush authorized the invasion of Panama in December 1989 (Operation Just Cause) to stem the flow orchestrated by Manuel Noriega and to restore political democracy usurped by the strongman. At the same time, the great growth in Japanese economic prowess, especially in production at the cutting edge of high technology, had put American economic competitiveness at risk in increasingly global world markets. What came to be seen as at stake was nothing less than American prosperity.

Faced with these problems and others, such as continuing instability and violence in Central America, the Bush administration initially pro-ceeded with some caution. The president's first act was to order a full-scale strategic review of American security policy, and he surrounded himself with conservative, pragmatic advisers. These included Secretary of State James Baker, Secretary of Defense Richard Cheney (named after Bush's original choice, former Senator John Tower of Texas, was forced to remove himself from consideration), and National Security Adviser Brent Scowcroft.

What Bush believed to have been the crowning achievement of his administration began with the invasion of tiny, oil-rich Kuwait by the Iraqi forces of Saddam Hussein on August 2, 1990. Acting with swiftness and resolution, Bush received United Nations authorization to raise an international force in opposition to the forceful annexation of Kuwait by Iraq and ultimately to drive the Iraqis from Kuwaiti soil. Operation Desert Storm was such a towering military success that Bush's approval ratings in public opinion polls rose to over 90 percent, the highest for any president since such polls have been conducted.

The essential caution of the new administration was particularly evi-dent in its approach to change in the Soviet bloc. There was, of course, widespread disagreement within the policy community about what was transpiring, how transient or permanent the changes were likely to be, and what those changes meant for American and allied security policy. The initial Bush reaction was to adopt a wait-and-see approach, but events began to transpire so rapidly in the fall of 1989 in eastern Europe that the president became a cheerleader of sorts for change, his enthusi-asm extending to his December 1989 summit with Gorbachev aboard naval vessels in the Mediterranean Sea and the June 1990 summit in Washington.

In these circumstances, basic changes in policy had to be deferred until the winds of change stabilized in direction and strength. In the strategic nuclear area, work continued on implementation of the Reagan strategic modernization program, although with some congressionally mandated limits on the Strategic Defense Initiative (SDI) and the B-2 (Stealth) bomber. At the same time, American negotiators continued to pursue nuclear arms reductions with the Soviets at the START forum. In conventional terms, sentiment for conventional arms reduction through the CFE process continued to grow both in the United States and in western Europe. At the same time, much emphasis shifted to the Third World, notably Operation "Just Cause" in Panama and "Desert Storm" in Saudi Arabia.

The Clinton Years (1993 to the Present)

Bill Clinton, the five-term governor of Arkansas, inherited the end of the Cold War and, hence, the problem of trying to adjust to the new, evolving nature of the national security problem. During the 1992 campaign against President Bush, national security was not a major issue; the Clinton-Gore campaign emphasized domestic policy, especially the American economy, and the Bush-Quayle campaign had little more to say on the subject, other than attempting to bask in the glow of the Persian Gulf War victory.

Obviously, the overarching international reality (as discussed in Chapter 1 and elaborated throughout this book) was the collapse of the communist threat and the need for the national security apparatus it had created. Arbatov had been right; the United States had been deprived of a reliable enemy. Lacking that enemy, the rationale for the strategies, missions, and forces that had provided the underpinning for defense policy had to come into question.

Domestically, the condition of the American economy was the major concern of the self-admitted "policy wonk." Firmly believing that America's future lay in reviving the economic vitality of the United States to compete in the increasingly global economy, the new president moved swiftly, if with varying success, on a number of fronts, including deficit reduction, health care reform, and "reinventing" government, to deal with these problems.

Clinton was clearly less comfortable with foreign and defense matters than his predecessor, and he sought initially to delegate those concerns to his national security team of Secretary of Defense Les Aspin (replaced in 1994 by William Perry), Secretary of State Warren Christopher, national security advisor Anthony Lake, and holdover chairman of the Joint Chiefs of Staff General Colin Powell (who was replaced by General John "Shali" Shaliakashvili upon his retirement at the end of September 1993). No member of this group was known for having strong philosophical feelings about defense issues, thus reflecting the president's lack of known ideology.

Following the 1996 election, Clinton replaced virtually the entire team. Madeleine Albright was promoted from UN Ambassador to Secretary of State, former Republican Senator William S. Cohen became Secretary of Defense, and Samuel R. (Sandy) Berger was promoted from deputy NSA to national security advisor. General Shaliakashvili is scheduled to retire in September 1997. The most interesting chemistry is likely to be between Albright, who has somewhat hawkish views on defense (she was once quoted as saying, "what is the use in having armed forces if you aren't going to use them" in reference to Bosnia), and Cohen, who has a more restrained view on the use of force.

Clinton initially stumbled, as noted in the first chapter, over the issue of gays in the military, in the process reinforcing the skepticism of many uniformed officers about his attitudes toward defense. As part of his economic stimulus package, however, the president called for reductions in defense spending beyond those projected by the outgoing Bush administration. He called for the acceleration of reductions in nuclear arms levels, although these efforts were stymied for a time by the unwillingness of Ukraine to turn over weapons stationed on their soil to Russia. Moreover, he moved to expand the reach of the Nuclear Nonproliferation Treaty (NPT), especially to frustrate the reported North Korean nuclear weapons program.

A coherent, comprehensive Clinton defense program has not yet emerged. Partly, this reflects confusion about what the new international system is like and what the role of American force should be in that world. In 1993 alone, leadership by the United Nations in solving world problems was first embraced, then backed away from by the administration. Until there is something like a consensus within the administration or the broader national security establishment, it will be difficult to fashion a national security policy with the clarity and precision of the policy of containment that organized American efforts for nearly forty-five years.

A new example of the difficulty of fashioning a coherent defense strategy has been the question, What should the U.S. role be in responding to the series of heavily violent, often atrocious wars that have broken out in recent years in places like Liberia, Rwanda, Somalia, and Bosnia? These "new internal wars" are discussed in detail in Chapter 10, but they pose a policy quandary that has defied consensual solution. On the one hand, the atrocity and human suffering attending these conflicts creates pressure for an international response in which the United States would be expected to assume a major leadership role. On the other hand, the lack of traditional U.S. interests in most of the countries in which these conflicts take place combines with a lingering public disdain for the outcome of American efforts in Somalia (a prototype of this kind of war) to inhibit activism. Coherent and consistent policy is the victim of this ambivalence.

CONCLUSIONS

This review of defense policy as it has evolved since 1945 highlights dramatically the difference between the Cold War period and the contemporary environment in which policy is being fashioned. The concerns and even the basic language are different. The Cold War period was dominated by the ever-present Soviet threat and concern about how to keep it at bay. Policy changed only gradually about what the problem was and how we should deal with it. The overall structure of the external environment changed very little until the rise of Mikhail S. Gorbachev and his reformers in the middle 1980s in the Soviet Union. The internal environment, although jolted by the Vietnam experience, remained relatively steadfast toward the major opponent.

The pillars of policy, nuclear balance, and the conventional NATO-Warsaw Pact confrontation in central Europe evolved as immutable symbols as well. They spawned a language and set of constructs from assured destruction and the hostage effect to follow-on forces attack (FOFA) that were argued and debated with great passion and conviction at the time. Even a few years after the curtain descended on the Cold War, these terms and constructs seem archaic, even surreal in the contemporary environment.

There is considerable instructive value in the review as it applies to the past and the future. A whole generation of policymakers and analysts, many of whom are still active participants in the policy- and strategy-making system, are products and shapers of this now displaced set of concerns. Moreover, the fact that very few people envisioned a defense environment devoid of the Cold War means there was relatively little anticipation of or preparation for a radically different environment. If there is a lot of confusion about the shape of future policy, much of that confusion is based in adjusting to the radical departure from the past.

Suggested Reading

Brodie, Bernard. *Strategy in the Missile Age.* Princeton, N.J.: Princeton University Press, 1959.

Fallows, James. *National Defense.* New York: Random House, 1981.

Gaddis, John. *Strategies of Containment.* Oxford: Oxford University Press, 1982.

Halperin, Morton. *Defense Strategies for the 1970s.* Boston, Mass.: Little, Brown, 1971.

Hartmann, Frederick H., and Robert L. Wendzel. *To Preserve the Republic: United States Foreign Policy.* New York: Macmillan, 1985.

Kaylor, William R. *The Twentieth-Century World: An International History.* 3rd ed. New York: Oxford University Press, 1996.

Kahan, Jerome. *Security in the Nuclear Age.* Washington, D.C.: Brookings Institution, 1975.

Mandelbaum, Michael. *The Nuclear Question: The United States and Nuclear Weapons, 1946–1976.* Cambridge, U.K.: Cambridge University Press, 1979.

Moulton, Harland. *From Superiority to Parity: The United States and the Strategic Arms Race, 1961–1971.* Westport, Conn.: Greenwood Press, 1973.

Nye, Joseph, S., Jr. *Bound to Lead: The Changing Nature of American Power.* New York: Basic Books, 1990.

Quester, George. *Nuclear Diplomacy.* New York: Dunellen, 1970.

Snow, Donald M. *Nuclear Strategy in a Dynamic World.* Tuscaloosa, Ala.: University of Alabama Press, 1981.

Chapter 5

The Decision-Making Process

The process of governmental decision-making clearly affects the character and content of decisions reached in any area of government, and the area of national security policy is no exception. Here, in fact, policy-making is particularly intense—and sometimes idiosyncratic—because of the weighty issues to be considered. Large amounts of money are involved: the defense budget has traditionally been the second largest federal expenditure (after entitlements). Although declining defense spending and increasing deficit spending have caused debt service (paying the interest on the federal debt) to surpass defense spending, the latter remains substantial. The critically high stakes involved in national security—up to and including national survival—imbue national security decision-making with a conservatism not found in other areas. Moreover, since defense spending is widespread in the United States, national security decisions have direct impacts on many individual communities.

The decision-making process is always problematical and often controversial. The process requires the interaction of people with differing personal, political, and institutional perspectives on policy issues. By design and evolution, the system promotes rivalry among and within the branches of the government as policy questions move toward resolution.

The heart of the decision-making process is the both formal and informal system of checks and balances that was the legacy of the Constitutional Convention of 1787. The founding fathers who wrote that document were profoundly suspicious of the ability of government or of any one person or group to accumulate power, especially of its potential tyrannical exercise. To prevent such an occurrence, the framers divided authority among the three branches of government (the executive, legislative, and judicial branches) so that no branch could unilaterally act on important matters; moreover, they gave the executive and legislative branches each the effective ability to veto acts of the other. The Congress, for instance, effectively controls much presidential action by possessing the power of the purse; it authorizes the president's expenditure of public monies. In turn, the president can exercise a direct veto on congressional actions of which he disapproves.

Beyond the formal checks and balances embedded in the Constitution, informal checks are built into the system as well. Within the executive branch, for instance, various executive agencies compete for scarce resources; in the process, they point out unwise proposals or practices of rival agencies. More microscopically, within the Department of Defense, the various armed services compete for their shares of the defense budget and, hence, act as a check on one another.

These informal checks work within the Congress as well. The heart of congressional operation, of course, is the committee system, where bills are considered, where information and testimony are collected, and where congressional expertise lies. The committee system, however, is really two systems: a series of *authorizing committees*, whose purpose is to approve programs and legislation, and a series of parallel *appropriating* subcommittees of the appropriations committees. The two sets provide two parallel considerations of policy matters.

Although we will not deal with them directly, an extensive set of interest groups and think tanks surround the formally prescribed institutions, covering the gamut of policy positions that seek to inform or influence the various branches of government. At the same time, the often aggressive electronic and print media monitor and publicize the process and its outcomes.

The system is complex and cumbersome, and it rarely does its job quickly or efficiently. The fact that the federal budget is only occasionally passed before the beginning of the fiscal year is testimony to federal inefficiency. When it operates correctly, however, the system is effective. The veritable maze of checks and balances in the decision-making process virtually ensures that all points of view on a policy issue will be given a thorough airing before decisions are made. One's particular position will not always prevail in the policy competition, but everyone gets to play. The system is often referred to as an "invitation to struggle," but in meticulously grinding through issues, lawmakers usually make effective decisions.

In some cases, the system gets short-circuited, generally with disastrous results. A case in point was the so-called Iran-Contra scandal of the mid-1980s, when Reagan administration officials illegally sought to sell weapons to Iran and use the proceeds to support Nicaraguan forces seeking to overthrow their government. The painstakingly long task of pushing policy through the system of checks and balances was short-circuited in the name of secrecy and national security. In that case, effectiveness was sacrificed to efficiency, and the result was disaster. It was efficient in that the goals of trying to influence Iran and supplying the Contras in Nicaragua were carried out. It was ineffective, however, because the ill-advised and, in some cases, illegal policies led to a devastating public scandal.

In that sense, the Iran-Contra example does not demonstrate the weakness of the system but, instead, shows its strength. Had the initiatives that composed Iran-Contra been exposed to the multiple formal and informal checks and balances of the national security decision-making process, it is absolutely certain that the initiative would have been vetoed by someone or some group. The lesson is not that the process failed; it is, instead, that policy fails when the system is subverted.

THE EXECUTIVE BRANCH

The heart of the national security decision process is the National Security Council system. When the Constitution was written, the clear intent was that the president would be a strong force in foreign and, hence, national security, policy. It could hardly have been any other way in dealing with foreign governments: one voice, that of the president, had to possess sovereign authority. The Congress, on the other hand, is in essence two large committees composed today of 535 people, and they rarely speak with one voice on anything.

As pointed out in Chapter 4, thinking about America's relations with the world in national security terms is largely the product of the post–World War II period. Before the war, foreign relations were a relatively small part of the national agenda and were handled almost exclusively by the State Department. After the war, a large and continuing American involvement in international affairs was clearly dictated. Because the environment was largely defined as hostile, American security became the prime issue and definition of policy content.

In that set of circumstances, the National Security Council (NSC) system came into being, and its organizational pattern was formed in a way that has defined the process ever since. The most important formative act was the National Security Act of 1947. That landmark piece of legislation made several fundamental structural changes in the process, as well as providing a format in which matters of security interest are viewed within the government. For instance, the act created the Department of Defense by placing the old Departments of the Army and Navy under its umbrella, created a Department of the Air Force as a separate service, and authorized the first peacetime civilian intelligence organization, the Central Intelligence Agency (CIA).

More fundamentally, the act created the National Security Council as the chief adviser to the president. By statute, the permanent members of the council are the president, the vice president, the secretary of state, and the secretary of defense. The president may add any other officials he likes to that group, and the NSC is advised—once again by statute—by the Director of Central Intelligence (DCI), the Chairman of the Joint Chiefs of Staff (CJCS), and others he may designate (for instance, the director of the Office of Management and Budget). Over time, the staff (directed by the Assistant to the President for National Security Affairs) that serves the NSC has expanded in size and function to become a sort of personal foreign and national security staff to the president.

Creating the NSC system as the pinnacle of decision making had enormous symbolic value in how the United States conceptualized and dealt with the world. The system, for instance, implicitly defines all foreign policy problems as having national security overtones. The inclusion of the secretary of defense as a full member, on a par with the secretary of state, adds further stature to the national security thrust of policy. It remains to be seen whether that thrust will need to be re-examined and additional (or different) actors included in the process, in light of the extraordinary events that signalled the end of the Cold War. Hence, the dominant national security concern remains to be determined.

Powers of the President

Although presidential leadership in national security decision making is well accepted in principle, in operation there are always differences, principally between the executive and legislative branches, about the extent of that role. The sources of executive advantage, however, are principally two: constitutional (as supported by court interpretations) and political.

Because it was written in a simpler time when America's interaction with the world was much more limited and when that condition was expected to continue, the Constitution says relatively little about the delegation of authority in the national security area. At heart, the document mentions three areas with which we would invest national security relevance.

The first area is the designation of the president as the commander-in-chief of the armed forces. This means that the entire military chain reports ultimately to the president, a designation originally devised to ensure civilian domination of the army. Presidents have interpreted the designation to include empowerment to commit armed forces to combat in situations short of a formal declaration of war, a precedent that goes back domestically to President Washington's calling out the militia to quell the Whiskey Rebellion and to President Jefferson's using the Marines to punish the Barbary pirates.

The president's power is neither complete nor unfettered. Although he commands the armed forces, Congress has the constitutional authority to raise the armed forces and, through the appropriations process, to set limits on how much money is spent in support of those forces and how that money is spent. Moreover, since only Congress can declare war, employment of force is constitutionally limited. That limitation has become controversial; since signatories to the United Nations Charter renounced the right to go to war (except in self-defense), wars are no longer declared. Thus, the extent of congressional prerogative has become controversial, as indicated by the ongoing controversy over the War Powers Act (see next paragraph).

The second presidential constitutional power is to negotiate treaties: only the president or his representative (plenipotentiary) can enter into formal, government-to-government negotiations with other sovereign governments. Once again, the Constitution provides a check on this power in the form of a requirement that two-thirds of the U.S. Senate must provide its positive advice and consent to a treaty before it achieves legal effect. In practice, that check is limited by the widespread use of *executive agreements,* intergovernmental agreements that do not require ratification.

The third specific area of constitutional authority is the power to appoint federal officials. At the time the Constitution was written, this power applied principally to ambassadors, but over time it has been extended to a range of executive branch agency "political appointments," which number in the thousands. The purpose of the constitutional grant was to ensure that the president could have like-minded, loyal officials serving his interests and carrying out his policies. The power to appoint also serves important patronage functions, allowing successful presidential candidates to reward loyal supporters and contributors.

This power is also circumscribed in the Constitution, which provides that the Senate must approve presidential appointees. While this power is not used often, it can be, and is, a real power. A negative vote by the Senate Armed Services Committee forced President Bush's initial nominee for secretary of defense, former Texas senator John Tower, to withdraw his name from consideration, and the prospect of a similar outcome caused Anthony Lake, Clinton's first term NSA, to withdraw his name from consideration as Director of Central Intelligence in March 1997. Within the power to appoint is also embedded the power to remove those officials the president (or his predecessor) has appointed; it is the single constitutionally mandated power of the president that does not have a congressional check.

Were the provisions contained in the Constitution the president's only basis of advantage, it would be fair to conclude that his predominance was minimal. Such a conclusion would, however, be mistaken. The president has a number of important political advantages that assist him in providing effective leadership in national security affairs.

The first political advantage is that the president is the *only national politician.* This means that the president of the United States is the only politician elected by the entire American electorate and, hence, is the only politician with a truly national mandate. All other officials are elected from more parochial bases and thus have narrower mandates. A senator can claim to speak for his or her state and a representative for his or her district within a state; only the president of the United States can say, "I speak for the American people."

The fact that the president is the only nationally elected politician provides him with a second political advantage: *superior access to the media.* Simply put, what the president does and says is news. There is, after all, an entire press corps whose sole job is to report to the people anything of news value that relates to the president. Thus, if the president wishes to influence the American public on some matter of national security significance, he has a ready-made, full-time conduit for spreading the word. If he wants his views on the record, he can stand in front of the cameras at a press conference, a form of communication especially favored by President Clinton; if he does not, he can simply wander into the Press Room, declare the session "off the record," and become "an authoritative White House source." Despite the enormous growth of the specialized electronic media, no congressman or senator has available that breadth of instant exposure. (It might, of course, be mentioned that having such close coverage has its negative side. A senator can trip getting off an airplane, as President Ford did in 1975, and not have to watch the instant replay on the evening news.)

A third advantage is that the president enjoys the *prestige of office*. In the American system, the president essentially wears two "hats." On the one hand, he is the head of government: the highest elected official in the country, but essentially the country's most successful partisan politician whose mandate is to try to implement a partisan political program. On the other hand, the president is also the head of state: the symbolic head of the country, a nonpartisan figure who symbolizes and epitomizes the American state.

Put another way, the president has two roles: president and guardian of the presidency. In some systems, such as Great Britain's, the two roles are separated. In the United Kingdom, the head of government is the prime minister, who fills a partisan political role. At the same time, the nonpartisan, noncontroversial role of head of state is occupied by the king or queen. The advantage of having both roles is that the president enjoys the additional prestige of the presidency, and it is difficult to criticize the person (head of government) without attacking the institution of the presidency (head of state). This problem was probably most dramatically illustrated during the tribulations leading to the resignation of Richard Nixon. Although many felt the president should step down for his transgressions, others feared that attacking the politician would also demean and weaken the presidency.

A fourth advantage of the president is closely related to the prestige of office. By virtue of being head of state and chief representative of the U.S. government in international affairs, the president has *recognition as a world leader*. This means the president has access to other heads of government that no other American politician has, and that access means that the president can claim a personal relationship with and an understanding of other world leaders that no other politician can claim. The result, of course, is to give greater weight to the president's authority.

A fifth advantage is that the president *"controls" the federal bureaucracy* in the sense that all members of executive branch agencies ultimately work for the president. The term "control" was set off purposely. As anyone who has ever been around a bureaucracy knows, the sensitivity of employees protected by the civil service laws to presidential direction varies considerably, and thus the responsiveness of some agencies to the direction of particular presidents varies as well.

This distinction returns the discussion to an earlier point. Although most federal employees enjoy a form of tenure through civil service protection that makes it very difficult to remove them even if they are insensitive to policy direction, there are other members of the bureaucracy. As mentioned earlier, the president has the authority to name several thousand so-called political appointees to important policy-making positions at the secretary level or below, and he has a personal staff of foreign policy advisers in the form of the National Security Council staff. All political appointees serve at the pleasure of the president for as long as the chief executive desires; they can be fired. Such individuals are clearly more sensitive to carrying out the president's will than someone not subject to that consequence.

The importance of control of the bureaucracy is that it provides superior access to the expertise of the entire federal government's store of knowledge on any given subject. If a national security event is occurring, the president has all the expertise of the State Department, the Defense Department, and the intelligence community at his beck and call. Members of Congress, on the other hand, have only the resources of their personal staffs, agencies such as the Library of Congress, or assistance from an executive agency to gain information. The information revolution—notably, outlets such as Cable News Network (CNN)—are changing somewhat the informational balance of power, because news of breaking interest is often reported by the electronic media before formal government agencies become aware of or can analyze them. The president, however, still has the clear advantage.

A final advantage is the *nature of Congress*. The president, as an individual, can speak with a reasonably consistent voice on policy matters, and he can provide a continuity that gives coherence to policy. (This does not, of course, always happen.) Congress, on the other hand, is a large committee of diverse individuals with diverse views, and it rarely, if ever, speaks with one authoritative voice on any topic. The view of the president on any issue can be known and carries with it the prestige of presidential stature; the Congress *per se* hardly ever has *a* view of anything. The contrast can appear to be one of order versus chaos. The fact that the membership of Congress changes somewhat every two years and that the Congress varies from periods of activism to periods of acquiescence to presidential leadership only adds to the presidential advantage.

The National Security Council System

The heart of presidential decision making in the national security area is the National Security Council system. The core of that system are the individuals, with their support agencies, named as members or advisers by the National Security Act of 1947. These people can be referred to as the *core actors* in the process, because they are always involved in recommending actions to the president. At the same time, when their particular areas of responsibility are affected by a given policy situation, a group of *peripheral actors* from other executive branch agencies become part of the advisory team. The result, within the executive branch, is an informal set of checks and balances that reasonably guarantees that the range of policy perspectives is considered before decisions are reached.

Each actor, core or peripheral, brings a distinct institutional perspective to the council. The council is a recommendatory, not a policymaking, group. It takes no votes; rather, its members offer their perspectives and advice to the president, who then reaches his own decisions.

The two chief advisers within the system are the secretaries of state and defense. The institutional role and perspective of the State Department is to maintain the best and most favorable diplomatic relationship between the United States and other governments. As such, the secretary of state looks at problems as political and diplomatic in nature and is predisposed toward the diplomatic instrument of power to solve problems. As noted earlier, prior to World War II the secretary was virtually the only adviser to the president in foreign policy matters.

The responsibility of the secretary of defense is to view national security matters as primarily military in nature and to assess the propriety of employing the military instrument of power to solve problems. This does not necessarily mean that the secretary of defense more often advocates the military instrument of power to solve problems, although he must provide professional advice as to the advisability of military action and the military consequences of different forms of action. In fact, during the Reagan administration, Secretary of Defense Caspar Weinberger reportedly sought to restrain the use of military force suggested by Secretary of State George Shultz, a relationship that may find a parallel in the Clinton cabinet between Secretaries Albright and Cohen, as suggested in chapter 4. It is a matter of record that the Defense Department opposed sending the U.S. Marines into Lebanon for the second time in 1983, when their presence resulted in the truck bombing that killed 241 of them.

The difference in perspectives between these two paramount agencies means there is a certain healthy rivalry, assuring that each scrutinizes the activities of the other as a check against unwise policy. This oversight is even institutionalized. Within the Department of Defense, then Secretary Aspin reorganized assistant secretary positions so that they parallel and can monitor activities within the State Department. Similarly, the State Department has its Bureau of Politico-Military Affairs, whose operation is often referred to as running the State Department's defense department.

Other core actors bring their distinct perspectives as well. The director of central intelligence brings the perspective of the intelligence community to bear on decisions. Especially since the Goldwater-Nichols Defense Reorganization Act of 1986, the chairman of the Joint Chiefs of Staff (designated by that legislation as the chief military advisor to the president) is responsible for providing military counsel.

The other interesting core position that has evolved over time is that of assistant to the president for national security affairs (national security adviser, or NSA). The National Security Act made no direct provision for such a position, although it did anticipate that the NSC would have a staff and that someone would be in charge of it. In the early years, that position was largely restricted to being a kind of super office manager. In the Kennedy administration and after, the position began to expand in power and responsibility.

Two presidents, in particular, expanded the role of the NSA. During the Johnson presidency, his NSA, McGeorge Bundy, acted as a primary assistant to the president in managing the war in Vietnam, which brought the NSA into much more intimate contact with actual decision making than had previously been the case. The NSA became especially prominent, however, with the appointment of Henry Kissinger to the job by Richard M. Nixon in 1969.

Nixon's expansion of the NSA to the role of chief foreign and national security adviser reflected his desire to dominate foreign policy and his inherent distrust of the State Department. The NSA and other members of the NSC staff are, after all, the president's personal staff. All are political appointees who serve at the pleasure of the president, they are not subject to Senate confirmation, and they cannot be subpoenaed to testify before Congress. Located as they are in the Old Executive Office Building on the White House grounds, they are also very accessible. For a president who wishes a highly responsive, politically loyal group to carry out his distinctive bidding in the national security arena, a powerful NSC apparatus is very appealing. It is especially attractive if the president does not believe that the traditional bureaucratic actors, notably the State and Defense Departments, will be highly responsive, as Nixon suspected of State.

The relative power balance between the NSA and the secretaries of state and defense (particularly, state) has become a good indicator of the degree of presidential activism in national security affairs. Richard Nixon wished to conduct policy himself, and he therefore elevated the position. Others, such as Presidents Ford and Reagan, who were less personally involved, instead delegated power to State and Defense. Presidents Carter and Bush sought a balance of advice and influence from the NSA and the secretaries, a perspective largely shared by President Clinton.

The NSA position became highly controversial during the Iran-Contra affair, because it was members of the NSC staff—notably, Marine Lt. Colonel Oliver North and, apparently, NSAs John Poindexter and Robert C. "Bud" McFarlane—who were instrumental in arranging and carrying out the various shenanigans that marked the affair. To some, the abuse of power that Iran-Contra represented was evidence of a need for greater control over the NSA and NSC staff. To others, the lesson was that the system itself was not at fault; rather, the difficulty was in the avoidance and ignoring by individuals of how the system is intended to work.

The core NSC is assisted by a series of working committees made up of officials from the various NSC-related agencies in an institutional relationship begun under President Bush and continued by President Clinton. Directly beneath the NSC is the *Principals Committee*, which is the NSC meeting without the president (either because direct presidential involvement on a particular issue is unneeded or to increase the candor of the discussion). Next is the *Deputies Committee*, composed of the chief assistants of the members (e.g., deputy secretary of state) and chaired by the NSA. Finally, there are the *Policy Coordinating Committees*, a series of functional and geographic bodies chaired by assistant secretaries of state for particular geographic regions or their equivalents. When a problem such as drugs is discussed, it is usually by a functional PCC; if an area of the world such as Latin America is the topic, a geographic committee is called. Generally speaking, the lower the level of the committee, the greater the detail of its considerations.

In addition to the core executive branch actors in the national security policy area, there are also peripheral or occasional actors, as well. At one time or another, almost any governmental agency can and does have its interests affected by issues with a mostly national security content. For instance, the grain embargo imposed on the Soviets by the Carter administration in retaliation for the invasion of Afghanistan in 1979 affected U.S. farmers and, hence, required bringing the Department of Agriculture into the decision-making process. National security has historically been used as the reason for denying the former Soviet Union access to categories of U.S. goods, such as computers, that could have military applications, thereby involving the Department of Commerce in the decision-making process.

Two points should be made about the involvement of peripheral actors. First, the involvement of institutional agencies representing all interested groups means that an important informal check and balance system exists within the executive branch. This involvement means that all points of view are likely at least to be considered in the decision-making process. The fact that there are parallel congressional committees that oversee various functions further ensures a thorough, effective (if not necessarily efficient) consideration of points of view. Second, as conceptions of what constitutes national security broaden to encompass more than national defense, many of these peripheral actors will have enhanced roles. For instance, economic competitiveness and economic security are major concerns for the 1990s, thereby virtually guaranteeing expanded roles for the secretary of commerce and other economic advisors, as exemplified by the roles of former Secretary of Labor Robert Reich and

CASE IN POINT

The Brown Mission and National Security

The mission on which Secretary of Commerce Ron Brown and a group of business executives were embarked when their plane tragically crashed on its approach to the Dubrovnik, Croatia, airport in April 1996 vividly represents the changing nature, conceptualization, and set of actors who are part of the national security equation.

The mission's major reference point was American participation in the NATO-sponsored Implementation Force (IFOR) that was monitoring the ceasefire in Bosnia. There was general agreement that IFOR was doing a commendable job of preventing the resumption of fighting. The consensus was that unless economic conditions in the war-ravaged country improved (or showed any possibility of improving), the prospect of political reconciliation and tranquillity after the scheduled withdrawal of IFOR at the end of 1996 was bleak. The failure to increase economic prosperity in the region could undermine the long-term success of the mission.

To attempt to deal with this problem, enter Ron Brown, U.S. secretary of commerce, with a group of international corporate executives in tow, into the national security arena. The purpose of the mission was to try to identify projects in which private businesses could invest, thereby creating economic opportunities for Bosnians and Croats that would contribute to their return to economic prosperity. In this manner, the late secretary sought to become a part of the positive state-building process necessary if the Bosnian peace is to have a reasonable chance to succeed.

the late Commerce Secretary Ron Brown, before his death in an airplane crash over Croatia in 1996 (see the accompanying Case in Point box "The Brown Mission and National Security"). Whether these changes in emphasis will be accompanied by a revision of the provisions of the National Security Act or will be done informally remains to be seen.

The president thus has an impressive array of resources for dealing in the national security arena. It is a system that, when operated in the manner it was intended, provides both formal and informal checks and balances that virtually ensure a thorough consideration of policy options. Because policy is ultimately a human endeavor, it does not necessarily produce wise policy or prevent the attempted abuse of the system, as Iran-Contra demonstrated. Moreover, there are practical constraints on presidential freedom in addition to institutional and constitutional bounds.

Constraints on the Executive

The Constitution, of course, provides the major constraint on executive behavior, mostly through the provision for congressional authority (discussed in the next section). At least five practical and political constraints, as well, limit the president's conduct of national security policy. The first of these is *past policies and programs*. Any president enters office within certain confines of what he can accomplish, a phenomenon sometimes called *the limits on policy possibility*. Although he may wish to change policy, even in fundamental ways, his ability to do so is limited by what his predecessors have done.

This makes sense. For example, U.S. policy toward the former Soviet Union was developed and shaped over a period of time; based on experience, it had a certain logic and wisdom that successful application over time gave it. Even a president such as Ronald Reagan, who entered office with fiery rhetoric about the "evil empire," came to realize that policy cannot be moved rapidly. At the same time, much of what one can do in the national security arena is the result of the forces one has to work with. This is especially true of the large military equipment in inventory (the "force in being") when a president assumes office. President Reagan, for instance, entered office convinced that American military might had seriously eroded since the end of the Vietnam War, and he proposed massive military spending to rectify what he termed "unilateral disarmament." Much of the building Reagan proposed is still going on, and it provided the force for Reagan's successors, Presidents Bush and Clinton, rather than for Reagan himself during his own tenure.

A second restraint comes from *bureaucratic responsiveness* or, in most cases, its absence. To reiterate, the federal bureaucracy is made up of two groups of professional employees, political and career. Political appointees, such as members of the NSC staff or Cabinet members, are appointed by the president and serve as long as he wants them to serve. Presidents, of course, appoint people who generally agree with their positions, so that political appointees usually are sympathetic to presidential ideas and, hence, want to implement the president's programs. At the same time, if they do not carry out the presidential will, they can be sacked.

Career civil servants are another matter. They are, after a probationary period, given job protection through the civil service laws that allows them to be fired only for gross malfeasance, criminal behavior, or some other extreme cause. Opposition to a particular president's policies or foot-dragging are not among the offenses for which a career civil servant can be fired. Such a person can be transferred to other positions (within limits) in which he or she can wreak less havoc to presidential policies, but the degree to which interference can be reduced is mostly related to the obscurity of the position to which the miscreant is assigned.

A third limitation, related to the second, is what might be called the *constriction of policy possibility*. Presidents enter office on the heels of successful campaigns for that office, often accompanied by reasonably grandiose policy promises and the intent radically to alter policy, whether it be in the national security area or elsewhere. Once they attain office, however, they come to realize (and are helped to realize by the bureaucracy) that the real policy options are much more narrow, or constricted, than they appeared from the outside. As a result, each president goes through a period of adjustment of his rhetoric, promises, and ideas to fit the realm of possibility.

The "war on drugs" that was a centerpiece of the 1988 Bush campaign illustrates this dilemma. When George Bush entered office, he vowed a broad, sweeping program to eradicate the crippling effects of drugs on American society, a policy emphasis supported by the vast majority of the American people. To activate the war, he appointed a "drug czar," William Bennett (the secretary of education under President Reagan), and gave him a broad mandate to come up with a battle plan.

Solving the problem, however, was not as easy as all that. Almost all the strategies that have been designed to deal with drugs—destroying coca plants at their source, interdicting drugs illicitly entering the country, or educating Americans on the evils of drug abuse—either do not work or require the infusion of resources (people and money) that are simply unavailable. This problem is examined in more detail in Chapter 8, but it illustrates the point that practical constrictions on what policies can, in fact, be implemented do serve to constrain the executive in shaping policy. Symbolically, President Clinton quietly cancelled most of the "war effort" in 1993. The popularity of attacking the drug problem, however, caused him to appoint the retiring commander of the U.S. Southern Command (which has operational responsibility for interrupting the flow of illicit drugs from Latin America), Gen. Barry R. McCaffrey, to spearhead a revived effort in 1996.

A fourth constraint is the *nature of the international environment*. National security problems, whether they deal with conventional military threats or a broader array of concerns, share the commonality that they are responses to challenges from the outside world. Presidents deal with the risks and dangers that are dealt them, not the ones they might prefer.

The seismic events swirling through eastern Europe recently illustrate this influence. In 1981 Ronald Reagan entered office intent on a massive buildup of American military strength. The international environment, notably the Soviet Union, cooperated in helping him justify the policies he believed were necessary; Soviet force expansion during the 1970s (at a time when the United States was not spending as much on defense, in reaction to Vietnam) made the military balance appear ominously unfavorable to the United States.

Contrast that circumstance with the 1990s. Were President Clinton desirous of further military capability expansion today, he would have a very difficult time making the justification. The lessened military threat of a disintegrated Warsaw Pact, whose former members clamor for full membership in NATO, and the promise of reduced force levels through venues such as the Conventional Forces in Europe (CFE) negotiations alter the threat and the realm of possible responses.

A fifth constraint is *public opinion*. In a political democracy, the only policies that ultimately can be sustained are those that have popular support—or, at least, the absence of popular opposition. Although the influence of public opinion on national security policy is more general than specific, it nonetheless is a consideration that no president can ignore.

The impact of public opinion on most national security issues is limited by the fact that most Americans are either ignorant of or uninterested in national security affairs, unless their interest is directly stimulated or they are directly and personally affected. The vast majority are part of what is known as the "uninformed public,"—those who do not follow or act to keep themselves informed of foreign and national security affairs. These people tend to become interested only if someone solicits their interest. Often the person trying to do so is the president, but it may also be members of Congress or interest groups opposing presidential policy. When a president proposes or seeks to implement any policy, he must consider whether public opinion can be rallied for his position.

Public opinion also becomes a factor if the public is directly affected by a decision. In the most extreme case in the national security arena, the decision to commit American forces to combat illustrates this condition and the need to rally public support behind policy. (As noted in Chapter 1, public opinion serves as the main constraint on the use of force by the market-based democracies of the First Tier.) In less extreme cases, however, spending on defense (as in deciding to build an airplane in one state rather than another) or savings (base closings) will catch the attention of otherwise unconcerned citizens.

THE CONGRESS

The other branch of the U.S. government with major responsibility in national security affairs is, of course, the Congress. Through most of American history, the role of Congress in what is now national security policy was limited and reactive. The sources of that limitation arose partly from constitutional constraints, partly from the nature of international relations, and to some degree from the relative isolation of the United States from the rest of the world. As the United States emerged as a global power with major and expensive national security obligations, the congressional role has expanded.

The constitutional role of the Congress in national security is, as demonstrated earlier, largely defined in terms of providing a check on presidential powers. Thus, it has the constitutional prerogative to raise and maintain those armed forces of which the president is commander-in-chief, and only the Congress can formally declare war. At the same time, the Senate must give its positive advice and consent on those treaties that the president (as sovereign representative of the state) negotiates in order for ratification to occur, and the upper house of Congress must also confirm presidential appointments to important positions.

These are largely formal powers that do not represent the heart of the system: no war has been declared since 1945 (in fact, only five of the 125 or so shooting conflicts in which the U.S. has been involved in its history has been accompanied by a formal declaration of war), and only a tiny fraction of the agreements between the United States and foreign governments are handled as treaties. The Congress gains some of its real clout from two *implied powers* in the Constitution.

The first is the *power of the purse.* According to the Constitution, all money bills (bills appropriating federal funds) must be initiated in the House of Representatives, and Congress must approve both the amount the federal government can spend and the purposes of that spending. This means that Congress must approve both revenue and spending bills. In an era where the White House is often controlled by one political party and the Congress by the other, the "battle of the budget" is the most clear annual demonstration of partisan politics; the annual battles between President Clinton and the Republican-controlled Congress in 1995 and 1996 are particularly clear evidence of this problem. Control of the budget is Congress's most important lever over the president, which is why the fight is so important.

The other implied power is *oversight and investigation.* Congress not only appropriates funds, it is responsible for making sure that monies are spent for the purposes for which they were appropriated. This gives Congress the right to investigate how those in executive agencies spend money, the so-called "watchdogging" function. Because the federal budget is so huge and because impropriety meets with great public scorn, the investigatory power gives Congress the considerable ability to embarrass an administration. Charges of waste, fraud, and abuse in defense spending and the Department of Housing and Urban Development (HUD) scandal rocked the Reagan administration, in particular. One recently retired senator, William Proxmire (D-Wisconsin) made a niche for himself by bestowing his Golden Fleece awards for alleged abuses of the public coffers.

Not only does the president have important political advantages over Congress, but Congress has several disadvantages in trying to perform detailed scrutiny of national security affairs. The first limitation is the *volume and complexity of international issues.* Clearly, a lot is happening in the world, and keeping up with events in a detailed enough manner to make responsible judgments is beyond the physical ability of most members of Congress. Relatively few members come to Washington as foreign policy experts, and they generally do not have the expert staffs to provide them with the same volume and quality of analysis and advice as is available to the president through the NSC system.

A second disadvantage is the frequent need for *speed and flexibility* in decision making. National security decisions are often made in crisis conditions, where failure to take prompt action could compromise the ability to pursue self-interest successfully. Clearly, many decisions have to be made in a more efficient manner than through complete congressional debate and scrutiny. In such cases, a balance between efficiency and effectiveness is often attempted by the executive branch through consultation with the relevant congressional leadership before decisions are made.

A third and very controversial problem is the need for *secrecy*. It is the nature of relations between adversaries that they feel the need to keep secrets from one another. Those secrets often involve both what they know about one another and how they know what the other knows. Moreover, information held secretly inevitably becomes part of the basis on which decisions are made.

Secrecy is a problem in two ways. On the one hand, it restricts access to the information base on which decisions are reached and, thus, compromises the ability to assess the wisdom of the decision. The outsider is assaulted by the decision maker with the charge, "If you knew what I knew, you would reach the same conclusion. But I can't tell you what I know, so you will have to take my word for it." On the other hand, holders of secrets tend to be very protective of them and to fear (some would argue excessively) their disclosure. The White House and the Congress, for instance, are constantly accusing each other of breaching classified information. One of the less decorous aspects of the televised congressional hearings on Iran-Contra was the confrontation between Lt. Col. North and a number of committee members about who "leaked" worse, the executive branch or the Congress. The need to keep large amounts of information secret will presumably lessen as the post–Cold War world evolves.

Finally, Congress tends to have *greater concern for domestic than for national security issues.* Each member of Congress must vote on legislation covering the gamut of domestic and foreign policies. Because members were elected to represent a state or a district within a state, they must be particularly sensitive to the interests of their constituents and vote in ways that defend their interests.

When the perspective of a member of Congress is put in this light, it is not surprising that most representatives place their primary attention on domestic policy areas. Except in limited cases, such as in a district heavily dependent on defense spending, the interests of most of a representative's constituents are most directly affected by domestic concerns. Assuming that representatives are going to represent their constituency responsibly and that they cannot possibly become experts on everything, they are quite naturally going to concentrate on issues with the broadest constituent interest. For most, that means domestic issues. Advisers to the president in the State and Defense Departments do not have an equivalent constraint.

Committees: The Heart of Congress

Faced with these inherent limits, the Congress nonetheless has the constitutional and political responsibility to oversee the executive branch's conduct of national security (as well as all other) policy. The major vehicle through which it does so is the committee system.

To do most of its work, both houses of Congress are organized into a series of committees. The particular pattern of the committee system basically parallels the organization of the executive branch. There is, in other words, a congressional committee that monitors each executive branch function; roughly speaking, for every major executive branch agency, there is a corresponding committee in each house of Congress.

The committee system operates at two levels. The committees that parallel executive functions are known as *authorizing* committees: their role is to review the activities and proposals of the agencies they oversee and to authorize various programs. The second set of committees are the *appropriating* committees. These are actually subcommittees of the Appropriations Committee in each house, and there is an appropriations subcommittee for each authorizing committee. As the name implies, these committees appropriate monies to fund authorized programs. The two sets, however, do not always agree on what should be authorized or appropriated.

The committees are the source of congressional expertise in issue areas. Generally speaking, the people who become members of particular committees do so either because they have some inherent interest in its issue area or because the interests of their constituencies militate toward their gaining such expertise. The members of the Senate Armed Services and House National Security committees and parallel appropriations subcommittees are Congress's major experts on national security affairs, although significant additional expertise on such matters as intelligence and foreign affairs is available in other committees (see below). Moreover, each committee has a staff of paid analysts who augment the committee's activities.

Of special importance to understanding Congress and how it reaches decisions is the role of committee chairs. The chair is, generally speaking, the senior member (in terms of length of service on the committee) of the committee from the party that has a majority in that house. In the Congress elected in 1992, for instance, the Democrats controlled both houses. As a result, all important committees in each house were chaired by Democrats, with a Democratic majority on each committee. Thus, the chairman of the Senate Armed Services Committee was Sen. Sam Nunn of Georgia, and his counterpart in the House Armed Services Committee was Rep. Ronald Dellums of California, who succeeded Les Aspin of Wisconsin when Aspin became Secretary of Defense. When the Republicans gained power in 1994, Strom Thurmond of South Carolina became chair of the Senate Armed Services Committee, and Floyd

D. Spence, also of South Carolina, became chair of the House National Security Committee.

Committee chairs wield enormous power in Congress. First, their seniority and accumulated expertise means that they are viewed as the resident experts of the Congress in the areas over which their committees have purview. When it comes time to vote, many members who are not experts in the particular issue area vote with the committee chair out of deference. Second, the chairs organize the agendas of their committees, and since they lead the majority on the committee, they generally can control what bills are reported favorably to the floor of either house. Third, the committees also serve as the chief investigatory arm of the Congress in overseeing their parallel executive agencies. A president or agency that incurs the ire of a powerful chair is simply asking for trouble. President Clinton learned this early in his first term when he found himself at odds with Nunn over the status of gays in the military.

What emerges from this profile is that there are in the national security area a small number of representatives who have considerable expertise and power. In their particular areas of concern, they have nearly the power and prestige of the president, and a president ignores these chairs at his own considerable peril. If one wants to know what the Congress thinks about a particular issue and whether Congress and the president are in consonance or disagreement, comparing the position of the relevant chairs with that of the president is the fastest way to make a determination.

Within the national security field, roughly five committees in each house have the most authority and power. Three are substantive and oversee specific agencies within the NSC system. The Senate Armed Services and House National Security committees oversee the Department of Defense and deal with military matters. The Senate Foreign Relations and House International Relations committees oversee the Department of State and foreign policy issues. The Senate and House Select Committees on Intelligence oversee the intelligence community and intelligence issues. At the same time, the appropriate subcommittees on the Senate and House Appropriations committees are critical in deciding who gets how much of the federal pie, and the Senate and House Finance committees are critical to the overall budget.

Congressional Militancy and Activism

While the balance between executive and congressional power and authority in the national security area has traditionally favored the president, Congress has become gradually more assertive in the decision-making process. The root of increased militancy and activism was reaction to the Vietnam War and the belief that Congress had been neither fully consulted nor completely informed of the prosecution of that conflict. In the wake of the Watergate scandal that brought down President

Richard M. Nixon, the power and advantage of the president has diminished and the role of Congress has expanded.

There are several reasons for increased congressional activism. One cause is the *increased U.S. role in international relations.* In the more laconic times that preceded World War II, the United States was largely aloof from international affairs, and events abroad had little noticeable effect on most Americans. Accordingly, foreign relations made little difference to most Americans, and the Congress reflected its constituencies' lack of interest.

That situation has, of course, changed. As the postwar world evolved, national security affairs became an everyday part of the national agenda, competing with other national priorities and resources. National security has become important to Americans, and their elected representatives are responsive to those interests.

This raises a second, related point. In the prewar period, it was said that "politics ends at the water's edge." This phrase meant that foreign relations should not be the subject of partisan political bickering between the political parties or between Congress and the president. Rather, the country should show a united, bipartisan face to the rest of the world. Such bipartisanship worked as long as there were no domestic—and hence, partisan—consequences of national security decisions. That condition no longer holds: *almost all foreign policy decisions have domestic implications.* Politics no longer ends at the water's edge, and as long as the consequences of foreign policy decisions have direct and measurable effects on individual Americans, their representatives and senators are going to demand an active voice in national security decisions. The debate over the North American Free Trade Agreement (NAFTA) revealed this phenomenon with particular clarity.

A third source of congressional activism is *presidential misdeeds and bungling,* which have decreased public confidence in the presidency and have led to congressional action to place additional checks on executive discretion. The list of such misdeeds is familiar: the cumulative decisions that entangled the United States in Vietnam, the Watergate scandal, the *Mayaguez* incident of 1975 (where the United States unsuccessfully attempted to rescue the crew of an American merchant ship, the *Mayaguez,* from Cambodian pirates), the Iran hostage crisis of 1979–1981, and the Iran-Contra affair, to name a few. The typical congressional response after such events has been an outcry of alarm and the demand for statutory or other restriction on unilateral executive action.

A fourth factor is *internal changes in Congress.* Members of Congress are generally younger than their counterparts of an earlier era, and they are better educated on national security matters. In the last twenty years or so, there has been something like a 300 percent increase in the size of congressional staffs, giving both individual members and committees considerably more human resources for investigating and raising questions. Moreover, such activism as there used to be emanated mostly from the Senate, whose members are elected only every six years and thus have the "luxury" of spending time on matters such as national security affairs that lack direct constituency impact. But as the constituency salience of national security affairs has risen, so has activism in the House of Representatives. In contrast to their greater education on national security affairs is a steady decline in the amount of military experience that members possess. Since the last Americans were drafted in 1972, very few middle- and upper-class Americans (those groups most likely to reach Congress) have volunteered for and served in the U.S. military.

A fifth and final source of congressional activism is *the impact of the media*. As noted earlier, the emergence of the electronic media, especially organizations like Cable News Network (CNN), has generally raised public awareness of international events. Moreover, the great sophistication of the electronic information industry has dramatically increased the opportunities for individual members of Congress to communicate directly with their constituents. Ten years ago, your representative could make his or her views on matters of state known only through newspaper interviews or newsletters. Today, that same member can easily be interviewed live on your local evening news, even though he or she is in Washington.

When one combines the greater public awareness of national security affairs with the increased ability of members of the legislative branch to air their views to their constituents, the basis for activism is there. Representatives do not want their constituents to believe that they are either not knowledgeable on the issues or powerless to influence them. The chemistry leads toward a more activist Congress.

Presidential-Congressional Interaction: The Budget Process

The budget process and its outcomes represent politics in its purest form. From the outside, that process and its outcomes may seem sterile and incomprehensible to the average American. Yet, if politics is the process by which scarce resources are allocated (the definition offered in Chapter 2), then the budget process is the essence of politics.

Despite its importance, the budget process is among the least-understood aspects of government activity, and this is especially true in the case of the defense budget. The sheer size and complexity of the defense budget and the extremely technical nature both of how the process works and of many of its items—such as weapons systems—makes it difficult to comprehend.

The budgeting process can, for our purposes, be broken down into two subparts. The first is the preparation and rationalization of the budget within the Department of Defense (DOD), a process known as the planning-programming-budgeting system (PPBS). The second component is the legislation of the budget through the interaction of the presidentially proposed budget and the Congress. Congressional action, of course, is dominated by the actions of the appropriations committees.

The PPBS is a product of the McNamara Pentagon of the 1960s. It is a complex process with bewildering details that go well beyond our present concerns, particularly the details of reviews and counterreviews that are important to participants in the process but probably not to the average student.

The PPBS process is an ongoing, year-round enterprise. In essence, it consists of three forms of activity, each corresponding to one of the three letters of the PPBS acronym.

The first stage is *planning*. Beginning in January of each year, this phase consists of two essential activities. First, the Joint Chiefs of Staff, with the assistance of U.S. military leaders worldwide (the Commanders-in-Chief, or CINCS, of the various commands) prepare an estimate of the global threat and the resources necessary to negate that threat. The resulting documents are tantamount to military wish lists. At this point, the process is not encumbered with restrictions about what resources will likely be available, and the result is a request in excess of what the budget will provide. (Knowing this, the services routinely request much more than they expect to get, since they know that the other services are doing the same and that each will have its request cut.)

The documents are then sent to the Office of the Secretary of Defense (OSD), which assesses the requests, incorporates likely budgetary restraints, and produces the draft of a document called the Defense Guidance (DG), which, in its final form, will be the Pentagon's chief planning and programming document. The draft is reviewed both within the services and OSD. On the basis of comments in those reviews, a final DG is produced in April or May of the *following year* (this is by far the longest phase in the process), ending the planning stage.

The second stage is *programming*, which begins with the end of the planning stage and lasts through August. In this phase, the military departments propose programs that respond to emphases in the DG. After these are prepared, they are reviewed and combined within OSD and readied for submission as part of the overall federal budget.

The third stage is *budgeting*, the preparation of a final Department of Defense budget proposal, its submission to the White House for review and incorporation into the overall budget request by the end of December. This budget is then proposed to the Congress to fund the fiscal year that begins in the following October. At the same time, work begins on assembling the budget for the following years.

This process takes almost three years, as shown in Figure 5.1. The budget proposal for fiscal year (FY) 1998 (beginning October 1, 1997), for instance, was begun in January or February of 1995, and the planning phase ended in April 1996. The programming stage extended through August 1996, and budgeting was completed in December 1996. The budget proposal was then incorporated into the overall federal budget sub-

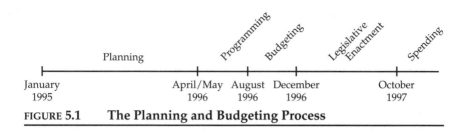

FIGURE 5.1   **The Planning and Budgeting Process**

mitted by the president as part of the 1997 State of the Union address. Spending on that budget began on October 1, 1997, assuming Congress had acted on it.

This lengthy process also means that the Department of Defense is, at any moment, working on three budgets: one it is beginning to assemble, one that has been submitted to Congress, and one from which is expending appropriated funds. Thus, on January 1, 1998, the DOD begins the planning process on the budget for FY 2000 at the same time as its proposals for FY 1999 are being reviewed and it is spending funds appropriated for FY 1998.

The formal actions of the Congress are in principle, if not necessarily in practice, more compact and straightforward, consisting of three basic steps. First, the Budget committees of the two houses of Congress receive and analyze the executive's budget proposal, both overall and by category (one of which is national defense). This review established likely budgetary ceilings overall and for each category, and these are supposed to result in passage of a *budget resolution,* the guideline for future actions.

Second is the authorization process, wherein the authorizing committees review the proposal programmatically and make recommendations about which programs should be funded and at what levels of support. Third, this action is supposed to be followed (although in fact it usually occurs more or less simultaneously) by the appropriating subcommittees' conducting their own investigations and making funding recommendations, which ideally, are close to those of the authorizing committees. The two houses of Congress, however, are rarely in agreement on the defense budget; the authorizing and appropriating committees often contradict one another, requiring considerable negotiation within and between the two houses.

The process is rarely as straightforward or as rational as it has been portrayed here. The organizational details of budgeting within the Pentagon are mind-numbing to all but the most interested, and the interactions within and between the houses of Congress are often chaotic—as well demonstrated by the Republican-controlled 104th Congress that convened in January 1995. It is, for instance, difficult to depict the steps in adopting the defense (or any other) budget for FY 1996 (which theoretically began on October 1, 1995) when, as of April 1996, no budget had yet been passed.

The process represents politics at all levels. During the preparation of the budget request within the Pentagon, the services vie for maximum shares of the overall budget (one of the first things officers working within the Pentagon do when a new budget comes out is to see if their service's percentage of the budget increased or decreased). When the budget gets to the White House, it must compete with the requests from other agencies in an environment wherein there are not enough resources to fund all requests. In addition to fighting within the Congress itself, a great deal of political maneuvering goes on during the period between presidential submission of a budget and Congressional enactment. For example, during the period when Bill Clinton's presidency coincided with Republican control of both houses of Congress, the Congress constantly tried to pass larger defense budgets than the president requested.

Aside from its sheer size, the defense budget and, hence, the process by which it is reached is a matter of great interest within the government. Defense spending affects large numbers of people and locales—in short, Congressional constituencies—through base locations, national guard armories, defense industry contracts, and the like.

At the same time, the defense budget contains the largest number of "controllable" elements in the federal budget. An item in the budget is said to be controllable if it must be specifically appropriated on an annual basis. (So-called uncontrollable elements such as entitlements are appropriated automatically unless legislation rescinds or reduces an entitlement—a major issue between President Clinton and the 105th Congress.) Almost 70 percent of the defense budget is controllable, and that amount is two-thirds of the entire controllable federal budget. Controllable funds are particularly vulnerable to the budget cutter's axe. Although the Republican majority in the 104th Congress was able to protect the defense budget, it is not clear what will happen in the future, particularly in the 105th Congress (that was seated in January 1997) with its strong rhetorical commitment to a balanced budget.

CONCLUSIONS

The era of congressional activism has brought a closer balance of power between the two principal branches of government in the national security area. The increased influence of Congress has clearly come at the expense of presidential autonomy and discretion. Whether one applauds or decries that shift in the balance of power generally depends on what one thinks of individual presidents and Congress.

One thing that is fairly certain is that the Congress is unlikely to restrict its own role voluntarily. For the reasons already stated, Congress feels a real need to involve itself in national security affairs, and that need is likely to continue. Three ongoing forces illustrate that continuing involvement.

The first is the great turmoil in the contemporary world. Changes in eastern Europe, the former Soviet Union, and elsewhere are rapidly transforming the power map in ways that only a fool would try to predict with any precision. Who, for instance, would have had the temerity to predict at the beginning of 1989 that by year's end communist governance in most of the Warsaw Pact would be crumbling?

The changes are, however, producing major national security repercussions. At one level, the old system of threats and risks around which American defense policy, strategy, and forces were built has disappeared as surely as the Berlin Wall. Certainly, the confrontation between NATO and the Warsaw Pact that has dominated thinking and planning and that has devoured as much as 60 percent of defense budgets has disappeared, replaced with a concern over how best to welcome former enemies to NATO.

The decrease in traditional defense problems has led to a second level of change, a debate about those additional concerns that compose national security. In addition to blunting military threats, what constitutes the conditions under which Americans feel and are secure? Viewed in this way, national security and security policy encompasses a broad range of considerations, from terrorism to economic competitiveness, to the environment. The debate over these and other issues will be spirited and highly visible in the electronic age. Congress will demand its share in the debate.

A second factor has to do with congressional success in eroding presidential discretion. Congress has had what it feels to be success in harnessing a reluctant executive branch and even in reforming the defense sector. Along the way, a number of members have developed expertise and power that they are unlikely to relinquish willingly.

The Goldwater-Nichols Department of Defense Reorganization Act of 1986 well illustrates this phenomenon. Named after the retired Arizona senator and the late Alabama member of the House, the bill sought to reform the Defense Department. Starting from the premise that organizational problems underlay much of the defense problem—especially the waste, fraud, and abuse problem—the bill forced a reluctant Pentagon (which opposed it) to reorganize. Greater authority was given to the Joint Chiefs of Staff, a "procurement czar" was created to oversee all purchases of military equipment, and an assistant secretary's position for low-intensity conflict (LIC) was recommended by the act (and subsequently created a month later by the Cohen-Nunn Act), to name a few of its provisions.

The overall effects of Goldwater-Nichols are still unfolding in areas such as "jointness" (the requirement for greater interservice cooperation and interaction). Secretary Weinberger actively opposed many of the provisions that reorganized and strictured the operation of his own office, and the resultant foot-dragging irritated members of Congress and contributed to their continuing belief in the need for the bill. The point is that

Goldwater-Nichols is an example of Congress's seizing the initiative on a national security issue and winning. The taste of victory is always sweet, and there is little reason to believe that Congress as an institution will conclude anything from the experience other than the wisdom of their continued militancy.

Third, and finally, is the legacy of Iran-Contra. One of the predictable consequences of major executive branch malfeasance such as the Iran-Contra affair has been a major effort to restrict the executive branch through legislation. As first the Tower Commission and then the Joint Congressional Committee conducted their investigations, one thing many observers expected was a similar spate of legislating. Because the National Security Adviser's position figured prominently in the scandal, speculation about requiring senatorial confirmation of the NSA was particularly strong.

But it never happened. After all the deliberations were completed, there was no formal demand for reform. The consensus was that there was nothing wrong with the National Security Council system as such; rather, it was those who sought to subvert its strictures and undermine its principles that caused the problem.

In the midst of momentous change, the system continues to grind along. It is seldom very efficient, but it remains relatively effective. The system of formal and informal checks and balances both within and between the executive and legislative branches ensures that the "invitation to struggle" will continue to dominate the national security decision-making process.

Suggested Reading

Crabb, Cecil V., Jr., and Pat Holt. *Invitation to Struggle: Congress, the President and Foreign Policy*, 2nd ed. Washington, D.C.: Congressional Quarterly Press, 1984.

Edwards, George C., III. *At the Margins: Presidential Leadership of Congress*. New Haven, Conn.: Yale University Press, 1989.

Franck, Thomas M., and Edward Weisband. *Foreign Policy by Congress*. New York: Oxford University Press, 1979.

Hilsman, Roger. *The Politics of Policy Making in Defense and Foreign Affairs: Conceptual Models and Bureaucratic Politics*, 3rd ed. Englewood Cliffs, N.J.: Prentice-Hall, 1993.

Inderfurth, Karl F., and Loch K. Johnson. *Decisions of the Highest Order: Perspectives on the National Security Council*. Belmont, Calif.: Brooks-Cole, 1988.

Lowi, Theodore. *The Personal Presidency: Power Invested, Promise Unfulfilled*. Ithaca, N.Y.: Cornell University Press, 1985.

Rosati, Jerel A. *The Politics of United States Foreign Policy*. New York: Harcourt Brace Jovanovich, 1993.

Rose, Richard. *The Postmodern President: The White House Meets the World.* Chatham, N.J.: Chatham House, 1988.

Rourke, John. *Congress and the Presidency in U.S. Foreign Policymaking.* Boulder, Colo.: Westview Press, 1983.

Snow, Donald M., and Eugene Brown. *Beyond the Waters's Edge: An Introduction to U.S. Foreign Policy.* New York: St. Martin's Press, 1997.

Spanier, John, and Eric Uslaner. *How American Foreign Policy Is Made,* 2nd ed. Holt, Rinehart and Winston, 1978.

Stubbing, Richard. *The Defense Game.* New York: Harper and Row, 1986.

Chapter 6

The Nature and End of the Cold War

For most adult Americans, the Cold War is the major foreign and defense policy reality of the period since World War II. For nearly forty-five years, the politico-military rivalry between the United States with its allies and the Soviet Union with its allies was the single most important feature of international relations—an overarching phenomenon in terms of which all other matters gained their meaning.

The contemporary debate about defense policy can be fully understood only in the context of the Cold War. Those in charge of making policy were reared and educated with the Cold War as their point of reference. Strategy, tactics, and weapons systems were developed to deal with the threat posed by a heavily armed Soviet Union and its Warsaw Treaty Organization compatriots. The rationale for the entire existing defense structure and effort was predicated upon the problem posed by the split between communism and anticommunism.

As already noted, the crashing end of the Cold War was unanticipated even by communism's most vocal critics. As the second half of the 1980s unfolded, it was clear that the leadership of Mikhail S. Gorbachev was somehow different from that of the grim, gray men who had preceded him, but hardly anyone at the time guessed—or could guess—at the profound change over which Gorbachev would preside. It is almost certain that Gorbachev himself had no inkling that he was undoing the Bolshevik Revolution of 1917.

The entire international system has been transformed as well. The old rules of the game were built around Soviet-American rivalry and competition. Managing that competition in its numerous facets was the major international concern, especially keeping the Cold War from becoming a hot nuclear third world war.

These concerns have, of course, faded, replaced by a more nebulous, less focused set of international concerns. The Cold War, for all its perils, was a comfortable intellectual construct: everyone knew who the enemy was and what was to be done about him. The new environment lacks such clarity.

In this chapter, we examine the Cold War as the framework from which the new order is evolving. We begin by looking at the essence of the Cold War relationship as a distinct international system. We then focus on the military confrontation that invigorated the competition. That relationship eventually became deadlocked by the sheer weight of the military confrontation, leading to the dynamics that caused the Cold War to end. Some residue remains, however, that affects both European security and security in the former Soviet Union. Finally, we will make some assessment of what the end of the Cold War means for American national security policy.

THE ESSENCE OF THE COLD WAR SYSTEM

The backdrop from which the Cold War evolved was the end of World War II, which had effectively destroyed the European-dominated system of the previous 300 years. (The modern international system is normally dated back to the Peace of Westphalia, which concluded the Thirty Years War in 1648.) During the war, the United States and the Soviet Union had stood as the bulwarks of the alliance that defeated the fascist coalition led by Germany, Italy, and Japan. The war ended with the physical defeat of the fascists and the exhaustion of most of the victorious allies. Only the United States and the Soviet Union came out of the war with the energy, resources, and power to reshape the system.

How the postwar world would evolve was largely a question about whether the Americans and the Soviets would continue their wartime collaboration. The two powers were firmly united in their opposition to Hitlerian Germany, although Soviet strongman Joseph Stalin harbored a deep and not altogether mistaken suspicion that the Western allies—principally the United States and the United Kingdom—had dragged their feet in opening the Western front, content to let the Nazi and Red armies exhaust one another.

Those who planned the postwar system in Washington were hopeful, but not optimistic, that collaboration could continue. The centerpiece of the new system was to be the United Nations, and its charter provided for both cooperation and competition between the major parties. If the Americans and the Soviets could agree on a common status quo, the provisions of Chapter VII created the framework for an effective collective security system that could enforce an agreed peace. If they could not continue to collaborate, the veto in the Security Council disabled the UN from taking actions obnoxious to one or the other. Article 51 made provision for "individual and collective self-defense," thereby providing the legal cover for the alliance systems both evolved.

Events described in Chapter 4 quickly laid to rest any romantic notions about continuing friendship. Instead, the ideological divisions between two contradictory evangelical systems overrode the wartime cooperation. The Soviet Union installed communist puppet states in the eastern and central European countries it occupied, thereby providing a *cordon sanitaire* (buffer zone) between itself and the West that the West felt violated the wartime agreements on the postwar world. Virulent anticommunism—punctuated by the hysterical witch hunts of Senator Joseph "Tail Gunner Joe" McCarthy—gripped the United States. By the time North Korea invaded South Korea on June 25, 1950, the competition was comprehensively joined.

How can we describe the Cold War system? At the risk of some oversimplification, we can organize an understanding around six related observations.

First, the Cold War was the *central reality of the international system.* Particularly during the early period after World War II, the Soviets with their large army of occupation and the Americans with their nuclear weapons and large stash of dollars to finance recovery were the only countries capable of wielding power in the world. Their grip gradually diminished as the countries of the First Tier became reinvigorated and as the Second Tier emerged from colonial bondage. Still, at that, the nuclear arms race and the possibility that the superpowers could go to war that might extinguish human civilization meant that the Soviet-American relationship remained the crucial reality of international politics even after it ceased being the only reality in the system.

Second, the Cold War rivalry was a *pervasive political and military competition.* Both sides viewed—or came to view—their rivalry as an all-encompassing affair. As the Cold War began to evolve in the latter 1940s and early 1950s, a broadly held belief was that there were no points of commonality between the two; their political values were so completely opposite that there was no room for agreement or cooperation on any items; the world was a zero-sum game in which one side could gain only at the expense of the other.

The diametrical opposition at the political level extended to the military as well. The Soviet Union never demobilized the huge conventional armed forces that it had raised to fight the Germans (contemporary observation suggests one reason may have been their inability to absorb military personnel back into the civilian population), and the Red Army of occupation in eastern and central Europe both facilitated the communization of those countries and served as a vivid symbol to the West of hostile Soviet intent. Why, many in the West asked, would the Soviets maintain such large forces unless they had an aggressive intention toward western Europe? In 1949 the United States, Canada, and the major western European countries countered with the formation of NATO; on May 14, 1955 the communist countries reacted to West German rearmament by forming the Warsaw Treaty Organization. The two alliances eyed one another across the barbed wire fences that composed the "iron curtain" until the structure of division began to unravel in 1989.

Nothing more completely symbolized the military aspect of the competition than the competition in nuclear arms. The United States first possessed the atomic (or fission) bomb, successfully testing a prototype at the Trinity Site in New Mexico on July 16, 1945, and employing two atomic devices against the Japanese cities of Hiroshima and Nagasaki on August 6 and 9, 1945, in an effort to convince the Japanese leadership of the futility of continuing the war effort. The Soviets exploded their first atomic device in 1949. In 1952 the United States exploded the first hydrogen (thermonuclear) device; the Soviets followed suit in 1953. The nuclear arms race was off and running.

Once joined, the nuclear arms race developed a momentum of its own that virtually defies conventional logic. The deadliness of the competition (described more fully in the next section) spiralled to proportions where it became impossible to relate the use of even a small part of the arsenals in anger to any rational political end. The purpose of building and development became *deterrence*, possessing such awesome retaliatory capability as to dissuade the other side from launching an attack. A fatalistic popular culture developed in the 1950s that asked not if nuclear annihilation would occur, but *when*.

Third, the conflict was viewed as *protracted*, a long-term competition for which only great patience would suffice. The policy of containment was extended—to the dismay of its original champion, George F. Kennan—around the Sino-Soviet periphery to form a kind of line in the dirt beyond which the communists were not to cross. The West flirted with the idea of "rollback," pushing back the outward frontiers of the communist world, but concluded that doing so would probably result in a war all would lose.

Nothing better symbolized this longstanding, unchanging situation than the conventional balance in Europe, where huge peacetime allied armed forces faced one another across the iron curtain. Elaborate war plans were developed and practiced, and enormous resources (an estimated 60 percent of the American defense budget was devoted to NATO by one means of accounting) were expended simply to form a barrier to invasion one way or the other. For most of the Cold War period, these expenditures and efforts were beyond criticism except among the political left in some western European countries.

Fourth, the perception of a protracted conflict meant there was *little consideration of how the Cold War might conclude;* that is to say, there was no planning for an endgame. The idea of a political settlement of the divide between East and West was considered by most "serious" thinkers to be so unlikely as to be utopian. The vibrancy of the West might not be matched physically in the communist world, but the solidity of the Soviet bloc was not seriously questioned. The Soviet bloc countries were ruled by force and coercion, but the idea that the situation would be reversed was hardly mentioned.

Part of the reason for the absence of a vision of how the Cold War might end is the result of the implicit assumption that the only way it could end was by general war that might destroy both. This conviction provided a powerful incentive to maintain the status quo, even if the status quo was not the way one would like things to be. Cold war, however, was infinitely preferable to a hot nuclear war. If one's operating assumption was that the only alternatives were cold or hot war (which most believed), then cold war was the best we could do.

This conceptual limitation helps explain why the process of change that unravelled the Cold War was so poorly anticipated and why most were so stunned by it when it occurred. In retrospect, the decline of the Soviet Union and the increasing hollowness of the military competition (which caused the Soviet leadership to end the Cold War) seem, if not obvious, at least not impossible to have been observed. The problem was that our own concepts of the nature of the Cold War prevented us from being receptive to the possibility of fundamental change.

Fifth, the Cold War competition *extended globally*, encompassing every region of the world to some degree. The competition began, of course, in Europe in the aftermath of World War II. A major consequence of the war's exhaustion was that the major colonial powers who controlled most of Africa and Asia had neither the resources nor the will to reimpose their authority. Demands for political independence spawned by the war began to emerge in the 1940s on the Asian subcontinent and in Southeast Asia, and by the 1950s the phenomenon extended to Africa as well.

The result was the emergence of a large number of new, independent, and mostly underdeveloped states in the Second Tier. They uniformly lacked political experience and wealth, and their demand was for assistance in development. As such, they became a competition ground for the superpowers, as each tried to gain influence or at least sought to deny influence to the other.

The global extension of the Cold War took two distinct forms. On one hand, it was reflected in a series of bilateral and multilateral alliance commitments between the two superpowers and their client states. The United States system was the most extensive, ringing the Sino-Soviet periphery wherever local governments would join in assistance arrangements.

The cornerstone, of course, was in Europe, where NATO faced the Warsaw Pact. Other regional arrangements included the Central Treaty Organization (the Baghdad Pact or CENTO) in the Middle East (in which the United States played a role but was not a member), the Southeast Asia Treaty Organization (SEATO), and a number of bilateral treaties with countries such as Japan, South Korea, and Taiwan. The United States was tied for security and other concerns to the rest of the Western Hemisphere through the Organization of American States (OAS). At its height, the

United States was bound through bilateral and multilateral agreements to over forty states around the world, most of which pacts have lapsed in the wake of the Cold War's end. The principal Soviet alliance, of course, was the Warsaw Pact, and the Soviets had bilateral agreements spotted around the world in places such as North Vietnam and Cuba. The Soviets' comparative disadvantage was that often it had to compete with China when forming relationships with other communist countries.

The other form was the more limited competition for influence in those parts of the Second Tier unwilling to be tied formally to one superpower or the other through treaty obligations. Many Second Tier countries reasoned, not entirely without cause, that their interest in extracting as much developmental and military assistance as possible from the superpowers was best served by allowing the two to compete for favor, thus hopefully raising the stakes. Neutrality, it went, could increase the size of the pie, and the superpowers, as interested in denying influence to the other as in gaining influence for themselves, were often willing to oblige.

This competition was frustrated by Third World conditions. First, it often bought little influence, as cynical Third World leaders simply manipulated the superpowers. Second, the existing instability meant that there was little real advantage in currying favor, because regimes were weak. Third, involvement could mean a long-term commitment from which little was to be gained. American and Soviet backing of rival factions in places such as Mozambique and Angola are cases in point. Ultimately, as we shall see, the futility of the competition weighed more heavily on the fragile economy of the Soviet Union and played some part in the decision to call off the overall competition.

Sixth, the Cold War competition *changed over time.* It was most intense during the early postwar period, from the latter 1940s, when it was forming, through the 1950s. The political competition was especially poisonous, with both sides convinced that they shared no mutual interests and that the competition would be perpetual unless settled by a massive bloodletting that many Americans believed was necessary. The military side of the competition was equally spirited, especially in the area of nuclear weapons development. The explosives became more lethal, the means of delivery more sophisticated and less capable of defensing, and the sheer numbers grew. At the same time, the opposing alliances faced one another grimly across the barbed wire dividing Europe, each side wondering where and by whom the first move would be made.

The Cold War reached its apex at or around the time of the Cuban missile crisis of 1962. Poised as closely at the brink of thermonuclear holocaust as at any time in the competition, the experience gave the leaders on both sides a chance to peer over the brink and confront the prospects of what they were coming close to creating; they looked into the abyss and, in Kafkaesque manner, the abyss looked back.

Although it would take another twenty-seven years to evolve, one can look at the Cuban experience as the intellectual beginning of the end of the Cold War. Relationships between the two sides gradually improved, principally through signing a series of nuclear arms control agreements whose purpose was to lower the likelihood of tripping inadvertently into nuclear war that each increasingly sought to avoid. These included the Limited Test Ban Treaty (banning testing in the atmosphere), the Outer Space Treaty, and the Nonproliferation Treaty discussed in Chapter 8. This mutually recognized interest in avoiding thermonuclear annihilation was the common thread that changed the tenor of the relationship from absolute opposition to limited dialogue and cooperation for much of the 1960s into the early 1980s. The recognition that nuclear war had to be avoided at all costs helped contribute to undermining the intellectual rationale for the Cold War, as well.

One way to measure the difference made by the Cuban experience is to use it as a dividing standard for measuring instances of Soviet-American confrontation, especially in situations with some escalatory potential. Before 1962, these were fairly frequent: the Berlin Blockade, the building of the Berlin Wall, the Sino-American standoff over the Taiwanese islands of Quemoy and Matsu, the Korean War. After 1962, these kinds of confrontations simply ceased; the possible exception occurred when the Soviets threatened to send reinforcements to aid the Egyptians trapped on the Sinai Peninsula in 1973. Even that episode, however, can be used to demonstrate the point of confrontation avoidance; both sides worked feverishly to defuse the crisis and succeeded within twenty-four hours. The lesson of Cuba was that the brink must be avoided.

The contribution of Cuba can, however, be overstated, and it is easy to do so in retrospect. The competition with the Soviets continued and, in some ways, even intensified after the missile crisis. One of the immediate lessons for the Soviets was that they had to back down because they lacked both the naval strength to push the issue around the Cuban island and also because of their inferiority in nuclear arms. (The United States had about a 5 to 1 advantage in deliverable warheads at the time.) As a result, they engaged in a feverish developmental program of nuclear weapons development which, when matched by the United States, increased the deadliness of weapons inventories manyfold.

At the same time, conventional expenditures multiplied, leading former Carter Secretary of Defense Harold Brown to describe the arms race thusly: "We build, they build. We stop building, they build." In the 1980s the Reagan defense buildup was in partial response to that dynamic. As we will note, the competition became ruinously expensive for the Soviets, adding to their determination that the competition could not be sustained.

FORMS OF MILITARY COMPETITION

Part of the residue of unravelling the Cold War involves determining what of the military edifice should be retained and what can safely be dismantled without compromising national security. It is not an easy task. While admitting that the driving force behind almost all the military decisions made during the Cold War was the Soviet military and ideological threat, it does not necessarily follow that its disappearance means that the whole defense structure can disappear, as well. What it does mean is that the most significant military problem is solved; the question is what are the new military problems and their solutions.

It is a recurrent theme that the new problems are much more nebulous than those of the past, a fact that makes planning and preparation more conceptually difficult. A war in Europe, although horrible to contemplate, provided clear planning parameters in terms of the number of airplanes, tanks, artillery pieces, and soldiers its defense required. Everyone understands—at least viscerally—that the numbers and kinds of needs now are diminished. The Persian Gulf War may have been the world's last European-style mechanized conflict. But what will follow?

The forces that are being transformed are those of the Cold War. If we are to understand what is to be cut and why, we must begin by examining what exists and why. We will do this by looking sequentially at two related levels that are the direct artifacts of the Cold War: conventional and strategic nuclear arms, which are conceptually related because a conventional war in Europe always had the potential to escalate to nuclear war.

Conventional Forces

The centerpiece of Cold War military science was deterrence of, and yet preparation for, a general war centered in Europe—World War III. The focal point of that conflict, for which preparations were necessary, was a massive air and ground war in the center of Europe, notably Germany, known in NATO parlance as the "central front." The general intent was to keep such a war at the conventional (non-nuclear) level, although the possession of large stocks of nuclear weapons designed for battlefield or theater use, combined with the likelihood that the United States and its allies might lose a conventional war (because of the vast numerical advantage of the Soviet bloc in manpower and equipment), always made that outcome problematical. The Reagan administration expanded the geographic extent of that conflict with its concept of global war.

The World War III scenario, expanded to include some surrogate Third World situations, largely drove conventional force planning in all its aspects. The Army was designed as a "heavy" force, emphasizing large numbers of heavy tanks, long-range artillery, armored personnel carriers, and the like that would be used in highly mobile yet set-piece battles with the massive amount of armor and manpower that the Soviets were expected to thrust into what they hoped were weak places in NATO defenses. Light, highly mobile Special Forces and Rangers were designed to foment uprisings behind the lines in eastern and central Europe and to engage in so-called Fifth Column exercises such as blowing

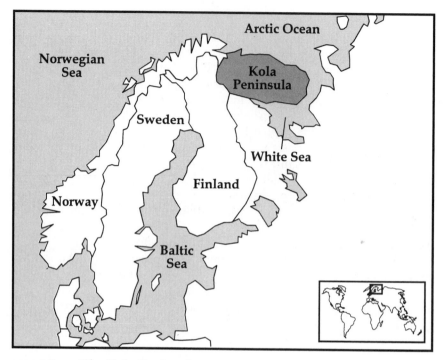

MAP 6.1   The Kola Peninsula

up bridges and disrupting power and communications systems. These forces are similar to former Soviet/Warsaw Pact *speznatz* forces.

The Navy's contribution to the European front was peripheral, but still important. The most arduous task was to secure the sea lanes between North America and Europe to insure the flow of men and supplies across the Atlantic Ocean. This objective translated into assuring that Soviet submarines could not escape their home ports, notably the Kola Peninsula, and sneak into the Atlantic to wreak havoc on the convoys making the transit (see Map 6.1).

In order to make this comparatively passive task more palatable to a Navy that preferred combat to running a "ferry boat" service, the Navy announced the Forward Maritime Strategy (FMS) in the mid-1980s. The thrust of the FMS was an aggressive maritime campaign north into the Norwegian Sea when war seemed imminent, the purpose being to sink as many Soviet attack submarines as possible and to bottle the rest of the fleet at Kola, thereby allowing the Navy to redirect Naval aviation to the air war on the continent. When President Reagan announced his intention to plan for a global war in the event of hostilities in which the United States could seize the initiative and relieve pressure in Europe, the Navy— as the most globally mobile service—saw this as an opportunity to widen its scope. The Marines' major responsibility in this regard was to land on the northern tip of Norway and deny its control to the Soviets.

TABLE 6.1   U.S.-U.S.S.R. Force Comparisons, 1980 and 1985

	1980		1985	
Element	U.S.	U.S.S.R.	U.S.	U.S.S.R
ARMY				
Manpower	774,000	1,825,000	781,000	1,995,000
Tanks	10,900	50,000	13,400	52,600
Armored vehicles	22,000	62,000	21,650	70,000
Helicopters	8,050	3,200	8,600	2,650
NAVY				
Surface (combat)	173	290	200	290
Submarines	81	240	100	270
Carriers	14	2	14	6
Aircraft (tactical)	1,200	775	1,350	875
Marines	190,000	12,000	199,000	16,000
Tactical air	415	N/A	600	N/A
AIR FORCE				
Aircraft (combat)	3,700	5,000	4,000	6,000
Transports	315	135	340	328

The Air Force had dual roles in Europe. Much of its role in the so-called *Air-Land Battle*, the joint Army-Air Force campaign on the ground, was in close air support of Army operations. Army corps commanders were given considerable leeway about where to fight (including into eastern Europe) in the highly mobile style of war demonstrated so vividly in the Persian Gulf War, where Air Force jets were used to soften up enemy forces. As part of *Follow-On Forces Attacks* (disrupting and destroying the ability of the Warsaw Pact to reinforce and replace the first echelons of attack—that is, the follow-on forces), the Air Force was to engage in interdiction campaigns in Eastern Europe (and possibly the Soviet Union itself) to break up subsequent waves of attack.

This war plan called for large, sophisticated forces on both sides. Using the International Institute of Strategic Studies' figures from *The Military Balance* as a guide, one can see the extent and asymmetry of the forces of the two sides (Table 6.1). The years 1980 and 1985 are chosen because they reflect the Reagan buildup.

Not all these figures are exactly equivalent. The Soviet Army figures, for instance, do not include the roughly 400,000 to 600,000 KGB border guards who performed semi-military duties, and the Soviet "marines" were actually Soviet Naval Infantry with lesser capability than American Marines.

The comparisons also do not reflect qualitative differences in the two forces. Because of its more advanced industrial and technological base, the United States preferred technologically superior forces (so-called force multipliers) to the mountainous numbers employed by the Soviets. Thus, the apparently great Soviet advantages in tanks and attack aircraft were diminished to some degree by the probability of lesser performance if the "balloon went up." Evaluation of the performance of the Red Army in Afghanistan during the 1980s and of the Russian Army in Chechnya during the middle 1990s suggests that the morale and fighting ability of that force, composed as it was largely of first-term conscripts who rarely reenlisted, would have been suspect, as well. (This comparison was not widely appreciated during the Cold War period itself.)

The force comparison reflects strongly the different military problem for the two sides. Because it occupied (and Russia still occupies) a significant portion of the Eurasian landmass, the Soviet Union was naturally a continental power. Its lack of significant warm-water ports (ports not blocked by ice during the winter) further influenced the Soviet calculation. As a result, the Soviets emphasized ground capability and coastal patrol for their Navy (most of their surface combatant ships were for this purpose). A heavy emphasis on the army, and air support of that army, made a great deal of sense, and it was reflected in force structure.

The United States, by contrast, is an island country for national security purposes. Large oceans protect it from foreign invasion from east and west, and it faces no military threat from its neighbors to the north and south—a situation reinforced by the implementation of the North American Free Trade Agreement (NAFTA). This happy situation has made the United States effectively invulnerable (except from a Soviet nuclear missile attack) since the War of 1812; it also influences American strategic calculus.

Since the only ways to attack the United States are by sea (an invading armada) or by nuclear missile attack, Cold War planning naturally emphasized naval forces and those elements involved in nuclear deterrence. Moreover, the chief requirement of using American forces is getting them overseas to some foreign theater of operations, notably Europe in the NATO scenario. This need places great emphasis on naval supremacy and control of the high seas during periods of conflict. These requisites give the American Navy an importance and prestige enormously greater than that enjoyed by their former Soviet counterparts.

The Persian Gulf War (Operation Desert Storm) offered the United States its one unambiguous opportunity to employ the weapons and strategies designed for Europe. The Iraqis had been armed and trained by the Soviets, thus providing a similar foe attempting to do what the Soviets might have tried to in war. In one sense, the highly mobile style of warfare was easier to implement than it would have been in Europe, where roadways and obstacles such as forests and towns would have slowed the pace. The real problem in the desert is knowing where you are (since there are no landmarks), but this problem was overcome by advanced satellite-based sensors that could tell ground forces their exact locations. (The Iraqis lacked this capability.) Arguably, the Iraqis were

TABLE **6.2**   American Force Levels in 1980, 1985, and 1990

(numbers in thousands)

Active Component	FY 1980	FY 1985	FY 1990
Army	777	781	772
Navy	517	571	598
Marines	188	198	197
Air Force	558	602	571
Total Active	2,040	2,152	2,138
Other:			
All reserves	869	1,088	1,178
Direct-hire civilians	916	1,043	1,019

inept in exercising Soviet plans with Soviet equipment, but many Russians privately express their dismay at the mismatch and wonder how much better they might have fared.

These priorities are also reflected in the numbers of people under arms. Using Secretary of Defense Frank Carlucci's *Fiscal Year 1990 Annual Report to the Congress* (the last such document issued before the sequence of events leading to the end of the Cold War began) as the source, one can see that American forces had remained basically static in size at high levels for a decade (Table 6.2).

These figures reveal a very large force: active duty forces at over 2 million for each period, and reserve forces and civilian support personnel at totals approximating 2 million; total direct-hire employees, military and civilian, for 1990 totalled 4.335 million to support the defense effort. Among the active duty personnel in 1988 (using the same annual report as data), 541,000 (about a quarter of the total) were stationed overseas. Of these, 323,000 were assigned to European (NATO) duty, and another 33,000 were categorized as "Europe, Afloat" (naval assets with NATO assignments). All of these requirements, needless to say, contributed to the very high cost of defending Europe.

The question that we must raise (with the answers deferred to Chapter 11) is how much of this structure is justified in the post–Cold War environment. The edifice for which it was erected no longer exists: the Warsaw Pact is gone, and the former Soviet military has disintegrated into lesser forces of the successor states. Russia remains the most potent of these forces, but by capability and doctrine, it is unlikely to be able or prone to conduct military actions outside the boundaries of the old Soviet Union. (The most likely use is to rescue suppressed Russian minorities in former Soviet republics or to put down internal rebellions such as that by the Chechens.)

Similarly, it is hard to imagine a replay of Desert Storm, other than possibly in the short term in Korea. A few countries, such as India and

Pakistan, possess large, European-style armed forces, but it is difficult to imagine circumstances under which the United States would become involved in a land war on the Asian subcontinent. Recognizing the element of uncertainty, it is similarly hard to envisage a war fought on the scenario of World War III elsewhere in the Second Tier. The Cold War conventional force was a First Tier force designed to fight in the First Tier. With general peace in that region, its continuing viability is certainly open to question.

Strategic Nuclear Forces

Even more than the structure of conventional forces, strategic nuclear weapons—those nuclear devices and delivery systems aimed at each other's homelands by the superpowers—are an artifact of the Cold War and its underlying mentality. Conventional armed forces share some characteristics, regardless of the situation: all armies have their "kings" (artillery) and "queens" (infantry) of battle, for instance.

The nuclear forces that evolved through the Cold War were different, for at least two reasons. First, they were unique weapons, qualitatively different in destructive capacity from any weapons they succeeded. Second, their development was a part—some would argue, the central aspect—of the Cold War competition, the situation that made it what it was.

Seminal Events

The uniqueness of nuclear forces can be seen by looking at a series of seminal events that defined the growing lethality of the nuclear balance. These include the development of the atomic (fission) bomb, the hydrogen (fission-fusion) bomb, the intercontinental ballistic missile (ICBM), the multiple independently targetable reentry vehicle (MIRV), and, at least in prospect, ballistic missile defenses (BMD). Each event contributed toward transforming and making ever more deadly the nuclear equation. Cumulatively, they defined the physical situation that existed at the time of the Cold War's end, to which the post–Cold War world is still trying to adjust.

The first event of the nuclear age was the development and detonation of the first *atomic bomb*, an occurrence without which there could have been no nuclear age. Its development, the fruit of over seventy years of international nuclear physical research, was the product of World War II: American and other allied scientists were motivated by the fear that Nazi Germany, which was engaged in atomic research when the war began, would fabricate and use such a device. (The Nazis actually abandoned their effort early in the war.) The first nuclear chain reaction occurred as part of the Manhattan project in 1942; the first bombs were dropped on Japan in August 1945.

The fission bomb is the most primitive form of nuclear explosive. As its name implies, its basic process is to break apart atoms of heavy, unstable elements, thereby releasing energy. In turn, the process yields four effects: great heat and light that create fires, great atmospheric overpressure that collapses structures, initial or prompt radiation of gamma and beta rays that cause injury or death, and residual radiation (or fallout) that returns to earth and pollutes wherever it lands.

The atomic bomb was the most powerful explosive ever devised to that point in time. Destruction that had once required literally hundreds of sorties (individual missions) by conventionally armed aircraft could now be accomplished with a single explosive. The ethics of atomic weaponry worried the physicists who developed it and others; the military effects caused military strategists and planners to seek to understand whether or how these weapons could be incorporated into war. This latter debate produced two groundbreaking works in 1946: Bernard Brodie's edited volume, *The Absolute Weapon*, concluded that deterrence of atomic attack was the only meaningful purpose of nuclear weapons; William Liscum Borden's *There Will Be No Time* reached the opposite conclusion that as weapons, they would be used, but that they were too hideous to be used against civilians.

The atomic bomb thus spawned debate over the utility of nuclear weaponry. In the early years, it was not a lively debate, however, for other events surrounding the onset of the Cold War overshadowed the nuclear debate. Until the Soviets exploded their first device in 1949, the United States had a nuclear monopoly. Moreover, the effects were relatively contained; the blast effects were measured in kilotons (KT), the equivalent of thousands of tons of TNT. A war in which a limited number of atomic bombs were used would be awful, but it would be survivable.

The second nuclear event, the *hydrogen* or *thermonuclear bomb*, changed the latter calculation by upping the lethality of the weapons. The thermonuclear, or fission-fusion, bomb is based upon a two-step process: a fission device is exploded as a trigger to create enough heat and energy to create a fusion reaction of heavy hydrogen molecules. This latter reaction, which duplicates the energy production process of the sun, creates an enormous release of energy that is measured in megatons (MT), the equivalent of millions of tons of TNT.

A thermonuclear device was first successfully tested by the United States in 1952; to the surprise of the Americans, the Soviets replicated the feat in 1953. It changed thinking about nuclear weapons use. A single hydrogen bomb could destroy a very large metropolitan area; it became less possible to calculate the survival of a society subject to even a moderate-size nuclear attack.

In the process of creating the thermonuclear explosive, parallel work was occurring that would make bombs more compact and lighter. The original bomb used against Hiroshima had weighed literally five tons itself, and simply taking off with it aboard taxed greatly the ability of the B-29 Superfortress (the *Enola Gay*) that carried it. At that, it produced "only" an explosion of 12–15 KT (no one knows for sure). As long as bombs remained so large, they could only be delivered by relatively slow-moving aircraft, against which air defenses were at least theoretically possible. Making them simultaneously lighter and more powerful opened another dimension.

The third, and possibly most crucial, event of the nuclear age was the successful development of the *nuclear-armed intercontinental ballistic missile* (ICBM). This event required both the development of workable rockets capable of flight over intercontinental ranges and the compacting of nuclear explosives into packages small and light enough to be hoisted into space and returned to earth by means of missile propulsion. The Soviets did this first in 1957, testing a successful ICBM months before the more highly publicized launch of *Sputnik*. The Americans followed suit the next year.

The ICBM changed the nuclear calculus dramatically. First, it placed the United States under direct threat of nuclear attack, a condition not formerly the case because the Soviets had no real long-range bomber aircraft. Soviet ICBMs could now attack American targets. Second, there were no known means of defending against missile attacks. John Kennedy set the tone, somewhat misleadingly, by equating the problem of ballistic missile defense as "shooting a bullet at another bullet." If there was any illusion about surviving a nuclear attack previously, the ICBM laid those dreams to rest.

With ICBMs in the inventories, the only way to avoid being destroyed by nuclear weapons was to prevent nuclear war. Deterrence thus became a cardinal principle, and the period after the testing of the ICBM stimulated a mountainous amount of thinking and writing about the problem of nuclear deterrence, all aimed at devising the best conditions to persuade the Soviet Union not to employ nuclear weapons against the United States.

A fourth event, the *multiple independently targetable reentry vehicle*, reinforced the need for deterrence. First tested by the United States in 1968 and entered into the inventory in 1970, MIRV refers to the capability to place more than one nuclear device on the tip (reentry vehicle) of a rocket and to deliver those bombs against several different targets.

MIRV allowed great expansion of weapons inventories. Previously, the number of nuclear warheads deliverable by missiles equaled the number of missiles available. MIRV obviously increases that number by the carrying capacity of the MIRVed reentry vehicle. This feature was particularly alarming when the Soviets began fielding MIRVs in 1975, because Soviet rockets were much larger than their American counterparts, allowing them to stuff more warheads into the tip of a given rocket.

The result was a spiral in warhead inventories during the 1970s and early 1980s, at the very time that arms control processes were attempting to limit weapons stocks. Previously, each superpower had a few thousand nuclear devices apiece aimed at one another's territory; those numbers escalated to around 12,000 each before the Strategic Arms Reduction Talks (START) started to reverse the number.

A parallel phenomenon made MIRV more ominous and potentially destabilizing. Simultaneous to the MIRV process, breakthroughs in delivery accuracy were greatly increasing the theoretical ability to hit strategic targets with great accuracy over intercontinental range. With these increases, a warhead hurled several thousand miles could be calculated to land within a hundred or so feet of its target (the accuracy ascribed to the American MX or Peacekeeper missile). No target, regardless of the attempts to reduce its vulnerability, was safe; the proliferation of warheads placed many more targets at risk.

The last event was interrupted by the end of the Cold War, the development of *effective defenses against ballistic missiles*. The idea of building defenses capable of intercepting and disrupting or destroying offensive ballistic missiles is as old as rocketry itself, and the theoretical aspects of defense had been worked out before the first missile was fired. The problem has been executing the BMD mission: locating, tracking, calculating the trajectory and extrapolating future locations and times, and getting a defensive weapon in place and in time for interception. Given the velocity with which ballistic missiles fly, this is a very exacting and difficult task, the demands of which were just being overcome as the Cold War ended and made the effort less pressing.

Ballistic missile defenses are an alternative to deterrence. If a BMD system can be made essentially leakproof (nothing, or essentially nothing, can penetrate it), then the failure of deterrence does not necessarily entail societal Armageddon. Protecting populations from nuclear decimation is an intuitively attractive idea that has been plagued by two controversies, one practical and one theoretical.

The practical problem is demonstrating that such a system works up to acceptable standards. The requirements for comprehensive BMD are enormous: with strategic arsenals at 12,000 warheads (their levels at the height of the Cold War), for instance, a *1 percent* error means 120 thermonuclear warheads penetrate it. The practical problem extends to demonstration: it is impossible to conduct a truly comprehensive test to see in advance if there are any "bugs" in the system that would cause malfunction or degraded performance. There is little margin for error and little way to know what the margin is.

The theoretical problem with defenses is that they may cause those who have them to be more willing to engage in nuclear war than they would in their absence. Without defenses, everyone knows the consequences of nuclear war. With defenses, it is possible to calculate (or miscalculate) personal and societal survival and thus have one's inhibitions reduced. The irony is in making the calculation, then finding out that the system is faulty and that the result is destruction, not survival.

Although a limited anti-ballistic missile (ABM) system was erected and abandoned in 1975, the major effort in BMD was President Reagan's *Strategic Defense Initiative* (SDI), first announced in 1983. It proposed what was called an "astrodome" effect that would render offensive missiles "impotent and obsolete." The plan called for a complicated layered defense consisting of ABMs and laser weapons in space coordinated through satellites and computer ground links. To many, it seemed a Rube Goldberg project that could never work; the computer program to coordinate the various elements was estimated at *30 million lines* alone.

The other problem of SDI was cost. Since it was never built, we will never know what a fully deployed system would have cost, but reliable estimates went all the way from $500 billion to $2 trillion over a ten-year deployment period. With the Soviet threat extinct, such an expense could not be justified. The Clinton administration quietly announced the formal disbanding of the Strategic Defense Initiative Office (SDIO) in 1993, although some resources remain committed to a more modest program aimed at defending against small attacks, the so-called Global Protection Against Limited Strikes (GPALS) and other small projects within the various services.

Nuclear Weapons and the Cold War

Nuclear competition was the marquee item of the Cold War military and geopolitical competition. The prospect of nuclear war represented the system at its most deadly, and it is one of the salient differences between the Cold War order and the world of tiers. Military clashes during the Cold War threatened the central actors of the system and, thus, the international system as a whole. Peace among First Tier members removes that threat and leaves the system without a central system-threatening problem.

But nuclear weapons meant more than that. The defining characteristics of superpower status were largely military in content and, especially, were tied to nuclear weapons possession at the levels attained by only the United States and the Soviet Union. Nuclear weapons technology and technological competitiveness were, for a long time, thought of as synonymous, and the nuclear arms race provided a macabre fascination for experts and laypersons alike.

The problem of deterrence induced by the ICBM riveted the attention of the defense intellectual community. It produced a whole genre of so-called nuclear strategists who analyzed and passionately argued the most effective ways to insure the continuance of deterrence. In the United States, two schools of thought dominated.

The first, which owes its origins to Brodie, argued that deterrence was the only utility of nuclear weapons and that, as a result, strategy should be fashioned to maximize the deterrent effect. These analysts embraced the *mutual societal vulnerability* created by the ICBM; the Americans and Soviets could destroy one another at any time. What prevented them from doing so was a structure of nuclear arsenals such that enough would survive such an attack to retaliate and destroy the attacking society. This strategy, known as *assured destruction*, emphasized sufficient offensive retaliatory ability that no potential attacker could delude himself into believing that *he* would survive a war he initiated. A nuclear war, if it came, would likely be an all-out affair that neither side would survive. It would be a war based on *countervalue targeting* of nuclear weapons, aiming them at the things people most valued—namely, their lives and the conditions that make life commodious.

Not everyone agreed. The horrible consequences of an all-out nuclear war made it the least likely form such a war might take; hence, the problem of deterrence was to dissuade the enemy from making smaller and, by definition, more likely attacks. For limited attacks, an all-out response of the kind envisaged in assured destruction would be inappropriate because it would likely trigger a similar response. Thus, the problem became how to fashion threats and responses relevant to the actual provocations the Soviets might undertake. The answer was a strategy of *limited nuclear options*, emphasizing limited and proportional responses to measured provocations and featuring *counterforce targeting* (aiming weapons at military and military support objects), an indirect response to the legacy of Borden that the weapons were so horrible they would only be used against military targets.

All this theorizing occurred in an atmosphere of great uncertainty and empirical deficiency. No one knew when a heretofore conventional war would become nuclear (the so-called nuclear threshold), because it had never happened. The ability to limit nuclear hostilities (which is key to the advocacy of assured destruction or limited options) is similarly factually opaque because of the absence of observation. Moreover, deterrence strategies assumed that the Soviets needed deterring—that in the absence of action by us, war would occur.

In nuclear terms, the Cold War ended happily. We had the perfect number of nuclear wars: none. Whether the outcome was the result of great thinking or diligence or the simple avoidance of what would have been the stupidest (and probably final) decision in human history remains moot. In the current climate, large stocks of weapons remain in the hands of both the Americans and Russians (as discussed in Chapter 11), but it is difficult, if not impossible, to imagine circumstances in which one country would use them against the other.

During the Cold War, nuclear weapons were highly controversial, largely because of the awful consequences of their use and the belief held by many that the longer they existed, the more likely was their use. It was hard to think of nuclear weapons as having a positive, stabilizing influence that could contribute to peace rather than to war. In retrospect, nuclear weapons had a positive influence on ending the Cold War, a subject to which we now turn.

DEADLOCK OF THE COMPETITION

Although it was difficult to see at the time, the beginning of the end of the Cold War can be dated back to the latter part of the 1970s. At that time, the sclerosis of the Soviet economy set in, stifling growth and beginning the atrophy that would result in the collapse of Ronald Reagan's "evil empire." The Soviet Union was doomed; it just took a little while for that to become apparent.

Two phenomena related to the systemic rot in the Soviet Union contributed to its determination to terminate the competition and ultimately to the demise of the Soviet Empire. The first of these was a deadlocked military competition with the United States that could not be won in any meaningful sense and the pursuit of which became increasingly burdensome (especially after Reagan's aggressive force buildup raised the ante). The other was the growing economic and technological gap between East and West that required jettisoning of a Stalinist economic and political system that simply did not function and, therefore, could not compete.

The two problems fed upon one another. Spending large amounts on the defense establishment and broader geopolitical competition robbed the system of resources that might have been used to stimulate economic growth. The military competition became an albatross. At the same time, a faltering economy and technological base weakened the military's ability to be competitive with a highly technologically advanced West. Economic and military failure went hand-in-hand.

The Military Deadlock

During the 1970s, a furor arose in the United States over the extensive military buildup underway in the Soviet Union and the military advantages that expansion could provide for the Soviets. At the time, estimates of the Soviet defense effort approached as much as one-quarter of Soviet gross national product (although estimates of Soviet spending were always suspect, because they were based upon Western costing methods). Lost in the discussions was the possibility that the expenditures were economically ruinous to the Soviet state.

By the end of the 1970s, and certainly by the time Mikhail S. Gorbachev rose to power, it was—or should have been—clear to all that the military competition between the two countries was also in a state of deadlock. Simply stated, the superpowers had armed themselves to such an enormously deadly degree that any conflict between them threatened both their existences and could scarcely be related positively to any meaningful political objective.

At the center of the deadlock, of course, were the nuclear arsenals each country possessed. Both countries had heeded the nuclear strategists, at least to the point of devising arsenals that could survive an initial attack from the other and thus be capable of a devastating retaliation. The result of a nuclear strike and counterstrike could destroy both as functioning societies and possibly produce ecological effects that could endanger the rest of the world as well—so-called "nuclear winter."

The result was a "necessary peace" between the two: a peace born not of good will but of the simple realization that war between them was impermissible. American presidents as far back as Dwight D. Eisenhower and Soviet leaders as far back as Nikita S. Khrushchev had expressed clearly and unambiguously the belief that nuclear war simply could not be allowed to occur. Their entreaties were generally taken as rhetoric; they were, instead, stating the obvious. Nuclear weapons served the useful purpose of "clarifying the mind" to the reality of the consequences of World War III.

What was less obvious was the extension of nuclear-necessary peace to any violent conflict between the two countries. The escalatory possibility—that a non-nuclear conflict could somehow expand into a nuclear conflict through dynamics unknown and with equally unknowable consequences—had been a part of nuclear theorizing for some time. What was missing was the next step in the argument: necessary peace extended to *any* East-West conflict. Because any war between the superpowers was a potential nuclear war, all wars between them had to be avoided.

The military competition, in other words, had become hollow and ritualistic. Plans were devised and practiced—wreaking havoc on valuable German farmland—to fight a war that was to be avoided at all costs. Yet, neither side could afford to act any differently as long as the adversary continued the game: if one side considerably cut back on its military effort, the other might calculate gain and try to take advantage of it.

The problem, especially from a Soviet but also from an American vantage point, was that the competition was ruinously expensive. In the West, it had always been assumed that the authoritarian nature of the Soviet Union meant it could and would spend as much as it wanted on military power. A generation of Soviet intellectuals coming of age in the 1970s saw things differently; when Gorbachev succeeded to power in 1985, they had a champion who believed that the competition could not be sustained without ruining the Soviet system.

The Reagan defense buildup of the early 1980s fed this growing concern among Soviet intellectuals. Reagan sought to reverse what he saw as a deficiency in American defense spending—what he called "unilateral disarmament" in the 1980 presidential campaign—by engaging in the largest military spending program in peacetime American history. Many of those who supported Reagan hoped this effort would convince the Soviets of the futility of trying to compete. The evidence, taken largely from conversations between Americans and former Soviets since the end of the Cold War, suggest that the buildup did contribute to the ultimate Soviet determination to conclude the Cold War.

What particularly concerned the Soviet military was the amount of American effort devoted to technological innovation. This concern was particularly symbolized by the Strategic Defense Initiative: although most Soviets never seriously believed that it would yield the defense system that Reagan proposed, they did apparently fear it would produce other capabilities that would endanger them.

The military competition had become a millstone for the Soviets by the time Gorbachev came to power. It was vastly costly in direct terms and had led the Soviets to provide large amounts of resources in support of basket case Communist states such as Cuba and much of Eastern Europe and in support of farflung Third World conflicts in places such as Angola and Mozambique. With an economic crisis looming in the Soviet Union itself, the competition simply became unaffordable.

The Economic Dimension

The economic crisis that began to develop in the Soviet Union during the 1970s also eluded Western observation. What Soviet reformers labelled the "era of stagnation" was a phenomenon where growth in the economy simply ceased during the second half of that decade; by some measures, the only growth industry was the production of vodka for a notoriously unproductive Soviet work force. This trend continued into the 1980s, a time of enormous growth in the economies of the First Tier. The gap was large and growing between the socialist and capitalist worlds.

The crisis was recognized by Soviet economists, but they were powerless to act until Gorbachev, whose favor they had curried, came to power. The connection between Gorbachev and what became the reformers occurred largely through Gorbachev's wife, Raisa, who was a faculty member at Moscow State University and a colleague of many of the would-be reformers.

The details of reform do not concern us here. They began with comparatively mild criticism of the ongoing system directed at the cronies of deceased leader Leonid Brezhnev—the *nomenklatura*—who presided over the stagnating economy. The early goal was simply to make socialism work better, not to undo it and replace with a market economy. The early reforms did not accomplish this purpose, and the openness (*glasnost*) that accompanied them increasingly was voiced as open criticism of the Communist Party and its leaders. The Soviet Union was beginning to democratize, almost by accident.

A leading cause of Soviet comparative economic stagnation was lack of progress in science and technology. Fueling the economic growth among the First Tier was the high-technology revolution of which they were all an integral and interdependent part. Explosive growth in knowledge generation (the product of computing) and knowledge dissemination (telecommunications) was resulting in an economic and technical advantage that was rapidly creating a chasm between East and West.

The Soviets and their allies sat outside the general prosperity. To some extent, it had been a conscious part of Soviet policy to remain aloof from the global economy, due to the artificial structure created by such factors as the subsidies and price supports that underlay the Soviet economy. At the same time, the Soviets were not allowed to participate in the technology revolution, because of the *dual-use* nature of most technologies—that is, having both civilian and military applications.

The Soviets were well aware that as long as they remained outside the global technological and economic system, they would fall further and further behind, ultimately to the status of a "Third World country with nuclear weapons." In order to be allowed to join in the global economic activity, they would have to join the world. The Cold War had to go.

Convergence

The first real hint that the Soviet leadership might be considering fundamental change came with the publication of Gorbachev's *Perestroika: New Thinking for Our Country and the World.* The book contains two distinct parts: a detailed discussion of the internal reform plan in both its economic and political dimensions, and a new view of the way the Soviet Union proposed to participate in the international system. Central to this vision was Gorbachev's avowed intention to transform the Soviet Union into a "normal" state by virtue of such changes as avowed noninterference in the affairs of other states and renunciation of the so-called Brezhnev Doctrine that had been used as the justification for forceful intervention in eastern Europe and Afghanistan. Initial reactions in the West ranged from skeptical to mildly hopeful. Most considered the pronouncements largely propaganda or disinformation.

But actions followed words. In 1988 the Soviets completed their withdrawal from Afghanistan, a traumatic and largely unsuccessful military adventure that had proved very unpopular in the Soviet Union. Fundamental change, however, occurred in the summer of 1989. Gorbachev and Foreign Minister Eduard Shevardnadze travelled to the capitals of Eastern Europe with an apparent message to the communist leaderships: come to terms with your people. If you do not, there will be no Soviet tanks to save you this time.

The Poles were the first to test the new Soviet policies. In the September 1989 elections, the communist party was defeated handily and a government made up of supporters of the Solidarity Union took over. When the Soviets did not respond by crushing the new leadership, it was seen as a signal. Communist governments rapidly fell throughout the region and, eventually, in the Soviet Union itself. When the Soviet Union formally dissolved itself with the first tick of the clock in January 1992, the Cold War was over.

Why did Gorbachev act to end the Cold War? The short answer was that he had no choice. The old system was broken; it could not be revived without considerable outside assistance economically and technologically, and Gorbachev and those around him understood that the *sine qua non* for assistance was to end the Cold War and remove its most obviously annoying symbols: the Iron Curtain, the Berlin Wall, and, most importantly, the structure of military confrontation.

The military and economic dimensions converged and reinforced the decision. The Soviet Union could not sustain the levels of military spending it had endured and remain an economically viable system. The professional military itself recognized the nature of the societal problem, and although they were reluctant to vacate their privileged position within society, they realized that an ailing economy and technological base could not produce the advanced, sophisticated weaponry with which to compete with NATO. The wretched performance of the Iraqis in the Persian Gulf War using Soviet weapons and employing Soviet strategies and tactics only reinforced the wisdom of ending the competition.

An end to military confrontation both removed part of the burden on the economy and opened the way for the Soviets and their successor states to turn to the West for help and to try to join the First Tier. There were, of course, no guarantees of success, but there was the certainty of failure in the absence of taking the chance.

Framed in this manner (and with the considerable luxury of hindsight), the decision to end the Cold War makes perfect sense. As the 1980s wore down, Gorbachev was left with a devil's choice: he could resist fundamental change and watch Soviet power dwindle, or he could embrace change and hope for the best. Neither alternative was easy.

Observers—especially former Soviets—now concede that what has happened to the former Soviet Union was inevitable: marxist socialism was simply a failure, a flawed idea. Kennan was proven correct. In a sense, the Americans—notably, the Reagan administration—probably accelerated the process of self-realization by throwing down the military gauntlet in the early 1980s. Without that stimulus, the Reaganites contended, the collapse of the Soviet Union might have taken a few more years, but it would have happened nonetheless.

THE END OF THE COLD WAR: WHO WON?

The period beginning with reform in the former Soviet Union and extending to the present has been one of the most remarkable in modern history. In a period of less than three years, the entire security structure of the post–World War II period crumbled. Peaceful decommunization, an idea formerly thought of as ludicrous and impossible, swept through Eastern Europe and engulfed the Soviet Union itself. As late as 1988, it was a standard rhetorical device to ask how many countries had removed communist governments and to answer the question, "None!" as evidence of the power of communist rule and protracted conflict. But the answer changed quickly.

In the process, both the basis and the structures of confrontation disappeared. At heart, the Cold War was an ahistorical confrontation between rival political and economic systems. At that level, the West clearly "won" the competition. Given the opportunity, the people of eastern Europe and most of the successor states of the former Soviet Union abandoned communism in a heartbeat. The embrace of market economics has been tortured in most places because there is no blueprint for the transformation of command to market economy. Freedom from communist rule has not meant the triumph of western-style democracy everywhere among peoples with no experience at it; in many places freedom has meant the most exclusionary forms of national self-determination. Indeed, exclusionary nationalism has become a major problem for the international system.

The pace of change has been overwhelming, to the point that we have become jaded. The truly dramatic has become commonplace when it should not be. The *peaceful,* voluntary dissolution of the former Soviet Union—the dissolution of an empire—is a virtually unprecedented act. States and empires have dissolved before, but normally only as part of the outcome of major wars. The Soviet Union simply ceased to exist. Coming hard on the heels of the formal dissolution of the Warsaw Treaty Organization by vote of its members, the Cold War's institutional base disappeared as well. Had someone suggested even as late as 1989 that the pact would disappear and that its members would apply for membership in NATO through something like the PfP, we would have thought that person insane.

The dissolution is remarkable for several other reasons. First and foremost is the peaceful nature of the change. Americans and Soviets were mortal enemies one moment and friends the next (which may say something about the depth of the animosities, but also, about the current friendship). Second, the end of the Cold War left the world for a time without a great ideological divide. Fundamentalist Islam offers something of a challenge to Western political notions, but its appeal is narrow. The Cold War has not meant the end of dictatorship or thuggery, but no one is publicly espousing these forms of governance. Third, the end of Cold War has helped create the possibility of change elsewhere. The beginning of a peace process in August 1993 that could end the Arab-Israeli conflict is an example of something that likely could not have occurred within the Cold War framework.

Who won? At the most obvious level, the United States and the other industrial democracies of the First Tier triumphed: our systems endured, while authoritarian communism largely failed. Communism as an official ideology continues to exist in isolated pockets such as Cuba, North Korea, Vietnam, and the People's Republic of China. In the latter case, the Communist Party retains control (although one can reasonably wonder how long that will continue), but its leaders privately counsel visitors not to follow Marxist precepts; it is Leninist authoritarianism that is the remaining precept. Vietnam has joined the capitalist-based Association of Southeast Asian Nations (ASEAN) and openly recruits Western investment. Francis Fukuyama's controversial "end of history" is upon us for a time: there are no viable ideological alternatives to market democracy other than negative, reactionary creeds such as sectarian, fundamentalist Islam.

In a broader sense, the system as a whole is the major beneficiary. The Cold War was very serious business, a matter of life and death not only for Americans and Russians but potentially for everybody else as well. Future historians may well question whether the fervor and passion with which the Cold War was waged had an adequately firm basis to warrant the effort; Americans and Russians have not, historically, had much if any animosity toward one another. Nonetheless, a great deal of energy and a lot of resources went into elaborating the rivalry.

And now it is gone. Will we miss it? At one level, the answer is clearly that we will not. The national security problem that the Cold War created was taxing and dangerous in ways that are not revisited in the current situation. It sounded slightly corny to many listeners in the 1992 Presidential campaign when George Bush said of the new order that at least now children did not have to go to bed worrying about the prospect of waking to a nuclear war. But to a generation who grew up with nuclear war drills as part of the classroom experience and who debated solemnly not whether but when nuclear war would come between the United States and the Soviet Union, that statement carries a different meaning.

The new system's problems are real, but smaller. National security challenges are not so clearcut, not wrapped in threats to the national existence or basic geopolitical vital interests. There is little, if anything, that threatens the physical well-being of Americans in the way that a hostile Soviet Union did. Whether that improved condition is transitory or of long-term duration remains to be seen.

What we currently miss about the Cold War, ironically enough, is its order. The Cold War had become a comfortable intellectual construct around which to base and understand the national security problem. The Soviet military threat was tangible; the ways to counter it were likewise concrete. We might argue about a specific Soviet intention or an appropriate response to a particular perceived provocation, but the basic framework remained to channel how we thought.

Moreover, the transformation is hardly complete and may even be partially reversible. The resurgence of the Russian communist party in the 1995 and 1996 elections was not so much a matter of nostalgia as it was a response to the failures of change: a destroyed "social net" of guaranteed standards of living, lawlessness and chaos in the streets, and the loss of international status, to name three complaints. There was even open talk among Russian hard-liners and former communists of trying to revive the Soviet Union itself (Vladimir Zhirinovsky served as a lightning rod for this argument).

The emerging order lacks the focus of the Cold War period. The remaining challenges are indirect and diffuse; there is no consensus either about the extent to which they affect American security or the extent—if any—to which we should respond to them. An intellectual framework to replace the Cold War organization of thinking has yet to emerge.

COLD WAR RESIDUES

Even if the Cold War has ended, there still remain some remnants of the great confrontation that dominated the Eurasian land mass for over forty years. Most of this residue has to do with the way that security will be accomplished within the part of the region most centrally affected by the Cold War itself. What will replace the old structures to ensure a sense of security for changed circumstances?

There are two principal concerns here. The first has to do with the formation of a successor framework to replace the NATO-Warsaw Pact structure, a need made all the more pressing by the institutional inability of Europe to deal effectively with the Bosnian crisis for nearly three years. The second, and partly overlapping, problem is in the evolution of the successor states, as they lurch uncertainly through the process of political and economic change within a climate of instability and uncertainty.

The European "Architecture" Problem

The division of Europe into two opposing military alliances imposed a certain order and predictability to security concerns. Problems within NATO countries, while infrequent, were NATO's problem, and the same was true for the Warsaw Pact. Each side had well-established bureaucratic organizations that facilitated chain of command, division of labor, and setting of priorities and responsibilities.

That situation has, of course, changed markedly. At the most obvious level, the Warsaw Pact physically voted itself out of existence in 1991, meaning that there is no real security-oriented organization among the former communist states. On paper, the former Soviet Union has the Commonwealth of Independent States (CIS) as a mechanism to coordinate defense matters, but it exists on paper only. NATO remains intact—if with lower troop commitments—but a military alliance that lacks an opponent looks increasingly forlorn; military alliances without a common mission to unite and give them common purpose tend to diffuse or wither.

What, then, should Europe do to reorganize its security "architecture" (the awkward term most frequently used in discussions of the subject)? Should Europe move to a more exclusive arrangement that includes only European members? Or should it become even more inclusive, embracing parts or all of its former adversaries in an enormous framework through Partnership for Peace (PfP) or something similar?

The answers to these questions must begin with an assessment of the current security situation in Europe. Among the prosperous First Tier states, there are no real security problems. Where there are problems, however, are in parts of the former Second World, including the former Soviet Union. Some of these are problems of political and economic development as states formerly in bondage struggle to adopt and learn how to operate democratic political forms and market economies; this is no small task, and it remains at various levels of incompleteness in different countries.

Bosnia has been and may again be Europe's current nightmare, and a European security mechanism that serves European purposes must be capable of preventing future Bosnias or, failing in that, to handle and contain such situations at far lower levels of violence than have occurred in that small, incendiary part of the Balkans. There is a pressing need to erase European shame at its impotence in the face of communal bloodshed. At the level of European security, there are other potential conflicts, not unlike what has happened in former Yugoslavia, in the former communist states of eastern Europe and in and among the successor states of the former Soviet Union.

Three European-based alternatives are generally put forward as proposals for European security. Each has advantages and disadvantages, depending on one's perspective and preferences. The first and most frequently mentioned is an *expanded* NATO that gradually is enlarged to include some or all of the states of the Warsaw Pact and at least the European-oriented successor states (Ukraine, Belarus, Russia, Moldavia, and possibly the Baltic states and the states of the Caucasus). The loosely defined Partnership for Peace is the current apparent mechanism for association—at less than full membership.

The great advantage of NATO is that it already exists (see Map 6.2), with a well-established organization and bureaucracy and forty years of organizational and operational experience. Moreover, NATO continuation guarantees an ongoing American commitment to European security (a disadvantage in the eyes of those who would like to see a more exclusively European organization). NATO's disadvantages include the fact that it was organized for a far different purpose and might not survive the institutional trauma of embracing its former enemies without being fundamentally altered. Whereas it was formed as a military entity to confront a concrete foe, the new architecture will have to operate in a much more fluid environment when yesterday's enemies are today's allies.

The Partnership is the interim solution, although it does not truly satisfy any of the states who are part of its associational status, and it also reflects the real difficulty of devising a permanent security system. In early 1996 there were twenty-two members of PfP in addition to NATO's sixteen full members. The PfP members fall into three general categories: *successor states to the Soviet Union* (Azerbaijan, Estonia, Georgia,

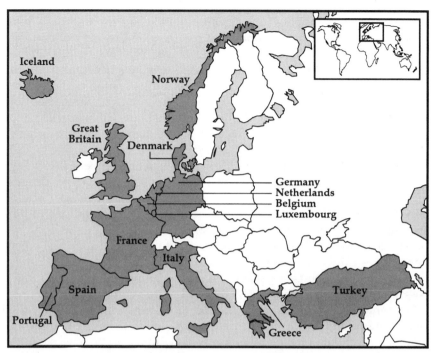

MAP 6.2   NATO Membership (not including Partnership
           for Peace affiliates)

Iceland	Luxembourg
Great Britain	Italy
Norway	Spain
Denmark	Portugal
Germany	Greece
France	Turkey
Netherlands	Canada (not shown)
Belgium	United States (not shown)

Kazakhstan, Krygyzstan, Latvia, Lithuania, Moldova, Russia, Turk-
menistan, Ukraine, and Uzbekistan); *former members of the Warsaw Pact*
(Bulgaria, Czech Republic, Hungary, Poland, Romania, Slovakia); and
Cold War neutrals (Albania, Finland, Slovenia, and Sweden). A number of
these states have applied for full NATO membership, and the number of
such applicants is expected to increase over time.

PfP status puts the states who are members in limbo. It is not clear,
for instance, what NATO protection they would have in the event of an
attack against any of them; there is clearly no firm guarantee. Since most
of them fear a resurgent Russia more than anything else, the rise of Russian expansionist rhetoric, should it continue to grow, can only increase
demands for full NATO membership. These were all great issues when
NATO met in July 1997 to consider which—if any—PfP members would
be granted full membership.

Granting such applications has been held at bay for essentially two reasons. The first is Russian opposition; within the Russian political debate is the widespread feeling than an expanded NATO would be an encircling, potentially hostile threat to Russia, a perception that feeds on Russian humiliation at the loss of empire and thus reinforces the expansionists. One solution is to admit Russia as a full member (Russia has not applied and currently favors an associate status) but with a special position akin to that of the United States (a status many Europeans believe the Russians do not deserve). The second reason for foot-dragging on full membership is that it is not at all clear that current members, especially the United States, are interested in committing themselves to defend many of the new applicants. How many Americans, for instance, would be willing to see U.S. troops dispatched to defend Bulgaria (one of the states that has applied for full membership)?

Because the NATO/PfP option appears to be the solution, the other possibilities can be dealt with more succinctly. The second candidate is the *Western European Union* (WEU), a smaller body of nine of the members of the European Union (EU). The WEU is the darling of those Europeans who would like to make Europe more independent of both the United States and the former Soviet Union. Before the Cold War's end, there was even talk of expanding the WEU within Europe to make it an independent counterweight to both superpowers. To supporters of WEU, NATO will forever be a Trojan horse by means of which U.S. influence subverts their plans for a truly united Europe, organized, for instance, around EU. The EU and WEU are further linked through the Maastricht Treaty (Title V) that increases European economic unity.

The WEU option has relatively few champions. First, most Europeans prefer an American presence in Europe, at least for purposes of security. Since all members of WEU are also members of EU, the precedent has been set that one must qualify for EU membership before becoming eligible for WEU. The informal criteria for EU membership require that a member be a working, stable democracy and have a prosperous market economy—criteria that the formerly communist states will not be able to meet in the foreseeable future.

Politics and economics intermix with security concerns in the WEU option. If the evolving European economic and political association aspires to a more independent stance from the United States—possibly challenging American leadership of the First Tier—then an autonomous arrangement may prove attractive. On the other hand, if the GATT agreement signed in December 1993 lowering overall trade barriers results in greater economic interdependence within the First Tier, then such independence may prove unnecessary or even counterproductive.

The third option is the *expansion of the functions of the Organization* (formerly *Conference*) *on Security and Cooperation in Europe* (OSCE). This organization, an outgrowth of the Helsinki Accords of 1975, is the most inclusive of all. It contains all the members of NATO and the old Warsaw

Pact, as well as the neutral states of Europe. Before the unification of Germany, its members included 35 states. With the inclusion of the successor states of the former Soviet Union, former Yugoslavia, and the bifurcated Czechoslovakia, its membership stands at 53 states.

The current problems of OSCE are twofold. The first comes from its old name: OSCE has been more a *series of conferences* than it is a real organization. It created a small secretariat (bureaucracy) for itself in Prague in late 1992, but it is clearly neither large nor robust enough to handle difficult security issues, especially when members are at odds—which they would often be. Moreover, OSCE's rules call for unanimity in decision making, which would probably be paralytic in times of crisis.

The need to have an effective mechanism to respond to future Yugoslavias before they get out of hand creates a consensual agreement that something must be done to establish a new security organization or to modify an existing one. Although the options are not forestalled at this point, the most likely—or least unlikely—scenario involves a gradual expansion of NATO to the point that, somewhere in the future, its membership would approximate that of OSCE, so that they would meld into a single, encompassing architecture.

Security in the Former Soviet Union

The peaceful dissolution of the former Soviet state has been accompanied by a process of fundamental change, both within individual successor states and between those states that pose concrete difficulties within the physical territories of the former communist giant and, possibly, beyond those boundaries. These problems include achievement of economic and political stabilization; elimination of internal, ethnic violence within the successor states and dealing with the problem of minorities, especially Russians living outside Russia; control of nuclear weapons; and the possibility of a resurgent, aggressive Russia.

That political and economic change has been difficult should come as a surprise to no one. In Russia, the largest and most populous successor state (half the population and three-quarters of the land mass of the former Soviet Union), the process has been chaotic. When, for instance, Russian President Boris Yeltsin dissolved the Congress of People's Deputies (a holdover from the Soviet state and the refuge of "former" communists), and the Congress responded by impeaching Yeltsin in September 1993, there was initial dismay and fear of civil war or worse.

The crisis passed, and Russia bumps along, with its leaders trying to figure out how to run—or develop—a democratic political system for which Russian history leaves them nearly totally unprepared. The coup attempt of 1991 and the confrontation of 1993 share a common characteristic: the amateurism of the parties in the game of state-building. The process reveals what we already knew; in terms of political and economic development, Russia and the other successor states are indeed "Third

World states with nuclear weapons." The most heartening sign in this chaos has been the highly restrained, professional bearing of the Russian military. At the same time, the revival of the Communist party indicates that all vestiges of change have not been positive and that there is residual support for the old regime.

There is also the problem of communal, ethnic violence and civil war within a number of the successors. The most notable conflicts have been, unsurprisingly, in those areas along the border between the old Soviet Union and the Islamic Middle East where religions and ethnicities collide to form a volatile mix. Civil war raged in 1993 in Tajikistan and Georgia; in Armenia and Azerbaijan, a bloody five-year war has raged over the Christian Armenian enclave Nagorno-Karabakh in Muslim Azerbaijan and the Azeri enclave of Nakichevan in Armenia. Within Russia itself, the brutal application of military force has not succeeded in killing Chechen separatist sentiment.

The prospects for peaceful settlement remain slender in any of these conflicts. The Russians have threatened to intervene, to the universal dismay of those in the successor states, many of whom believe the dissolution of the Soviet Union, in fact, freed them from the *Russian* empire. If these conflicts fester or worsen (both possibilities) or, for instance, if Middle Eastern countries such as Iran decide to come to the aid of coreligionists (also a possibility), the First Tier could conceivably be drawn in against its will and best interests. Whether this prospect extends to China is discussed in the Amplification box "Is China a National Security Problem?"

The prospect of Russian military involvement outside of Russia—but within the old Soviet Union—is particularly great in areas where significant Russian minorities reside. It was a conscious policy of Joseph Stalin to encourage emigration of Russians to the outlying republics, and the best estimates suggest that around 25 million Russians live outside Russian jurisdiction, generally in a minority status.

These Russians are often resented because they brought with them programs of russification that independent states seek to expunge. Nowhere is this sentiment more strongly held than in the Baltic states, which were annexed to the Soviet Union in 1940. Sizable Russian minorities now live in those states and are—certainly in the case of Lithuania—subject to political discrimination. There have not been more than a few, isolated instances of physical abuse of Russian expatriates, although that was threatened in 1992 in Moldova. The physical suppression of Russian minorities would almost certainly evoke a Russian military response in the offending successor state. The systemic response to such actions would be problematical.

There is also the question of former Soviet—now Russian—nuclear weapons and, especially, unaccounted-for fissile materials. The process by which strategic weapons stationed in Ukraine, Belarus, and Kazakhstan came under Russian control has received extensive publicity. What is somewhat less certain is the physical location and security of stocks of intermediate and battlefield nuclear weapons scattered throughout the

CASE IN POINT

Is China a National Security Problem?

The Soviet Union was not the only communist state viewed as a national security problem during the Cold War. For a time, as noted in Chapter 4, the United States followed a two-and-a-half-war strategy that included the prospect of a war with China as well. The generally growing economic relations between the United States and China, centering around the Chinese adoption of capitalist economics in the Special Economic Zones (SEZs), sublimated the national security aspect of the relationship; Chinese rocket tests near Taiwan that were intended to influence the 1996 Taiwanese presidential election reminded Americans of the military dimension.

The China "problem" combines economic, political, and military concerns. Economically, China is the world's second largest economy in terms of consumptive ability and is projected to have the world's largest economy by the year 2020. Thus, there is a powerful incentive to court Chinese goodwill that comes into conflict with political and military concerns. Politically, continued authoritarian rule and human rights abuses cause concerns that sometimes turn into advocacy of economic sanctions to force changes in the nature of rule. The problem is the lack of support for sanctions by other states, notably Japan, which uses U.S. sanctions as an opportunity to expand its own economic presence in China.

Military concerns are also ambivalent. When China sought to intimidate Taiwan, the United States moved the Sixth Fleet to the vicinity to thwart any contemplated invasion, thus temporarily straining relations. Most of the time, however, the military dimension is latent or nonexistent. China has the world's largest armed force, with an active-duty strength of 2.93 million and reserves of 1.2 million, but the People's Liberation Army (PLA) is generally considered not very potent and is useful mainly for defending Chinese territory. At the same time, China poses no direct physical threat to the United States: China possesses nuclear weapons and ballistic missiles, but they are not of sufficient range to target the continental United States.

successor states, to say nothing of stored chemical weapons. More ominously, Soviet procedures for safeguarding weapons-grade fuel used in power plants and experimental reactors were notoriously lax, and the problem is getting worse. Apparently orchestrated by Russian mafiosi, stolen quantities of weapons-grade plutonium have been seized in the more-or-less open market, a problem Russia has not yet overcome.

These weapons raise two horror scenarios. One involves the introduction of nuclear battlefield explosives into the conflicts—say, in Georgia or in the war between Armenia and Azerbaijan. A Russian invasion of a successor state to protect Russian minorities could also engender such use. The other scenario has Muslim successor states imbued with Islamic fundamentalism furnishing nuclear explosives to terrorist states such as Iran.

The final possibility, already mentioned, is that a newly resurgent Russia will seek to reverse some of the humiliation caused by its descent from major power status. Certainly that was the theme of Russian ultranationalists in the 1996 presidential election. The terribly inept performance of the Russian military during the Chechen campaign, however, raises serious questions about the physical capability of Russia to reannex its neighbors.

CONCLUSIONS

Basic change in global power configurations that alter national security problems occur only occasionally. Normally, they occur at the end of major wars that consume the major actors and that end with winners and losers who demand alterations in the old relationships. The world wars of the twentieth century, the Napoleonic Wars, and the Thirty Years War all produced such changes.

One of the most fundamental concerns of those who form new orders is that of war and peace. What was it about the old system that led to central war? What can be done to minimize the likelihood that the new arrangements will lead to a new central conflict?

It takes time to answer these kinds of questions. The aftermath of central war makes the answers more compelling: dealing with the massive dislocation and human suffering that accompanies central war provides an immediacy to the effort that we currently lack.

We are in the midst of a major transition distinguished by the fact that it did not come about as the result of a systemic war. It is, nonetheless, analogous to system change that accompanies the end of war. An analogy to the world immediately after World War II may be instructive.

There were two major variables that would form the parameters of the post–World War II system. The first was whether the wartime collaboration between the United States and the Soviet Union could be sustained. As we have noted, there was not great optimism that cooperation would prevail, but it took a matter of years for the shape and extent of animosity to congeal. Had comity between the superpowers been the norm, one kind of system—probably based in United Nations collective security that may be a basis of the new order—would have evolved. Since comity was not possible, we had the Cold War.

The other great national security question was about the difference made by nuclear weapons. They were the unique military technology to emerge from the war. How would they be treated? As just another form of explosive in the evolutionary path of lethality? As something unique that changed the way the world thought about armed conflict?

In 1945 the answer was not clear (if it is now). Brodie and Borden, the earliest apostles of the nuclear age, reached diametrically opposed conclusions, and thinking and writing about nuclear weapons throughout the Cold War diverged both on the likelihood and consequences of nuclear conflict and on how best to avoid nuclear confrontation. All we know for sure is that nuclear war was avoided; we cannot say with absolute certainty why.

We are at a point of similar uncertainty today. The power distribution in the world has changed, not because one side lost a shooting war, but because the geopolitical struggle ended with the implosion of one of the contestants. Resuscitating the remnants of the fallen former Soviet Union is a concern, but not one with the urgency of restoring warravaged Europe and Japan at the end of World War II.

What is emerging, instead, is an international system with two distinct tiers, as argued in the introductory chapter. Each tier has its own distinct rules and set of problems. Within the First Tier, military problems are virtually absent; political democracies, especially with the interlocked economies possessed by the First Tier states, simply do not go to war with one another. It is hard to imagine circumstances that would change that situation in the near term. The problems the First Tier countries face among themselves are, by and large, economic, dealing both with their interactions and with coming to grips with the regulation of what is becoming a truly global economy that defies regulation by states.

The world's current chaos exists in the Second Tier nations that comprise the vast majority of humankind. Violence and instability are staple items in much of the Second Tier. There is nothing new in this; a pattern of instability accompanied the physical granting of independence throughout the Second Tier. But there are two differences. First, the absence of Cold War competition refocuses our attention; we are more aware of the Second Tier's problems because we have fewer of our own. The relentless, omnipresent eye of global television reinforces our awareness of that which we previously sought, usually successfully, to ignore.

Second, the wave of exclusionary nationalism that manifests itself in ethnic and communal violence behind the mask of self-determination has intensified in the wake of the Cold War. In the old socialist world, the end of authoritarian rule has allowed the primordial expression of ancient hatreds long suppressed in parts of the former Soviet Union (notably the Caucasus, but potentially elsewhere), in the Balkans, and into parts of Africa. The potential for this phenomenon to spread to its own territory, ironically, forms part of the rationale for continued Chinese authoritarian rule. In the old Third World, the withdrawal of superpower presence appears to have reduced constraints on the expression of similar hatreds in places ordinary citizens are only slowly beginning to recognize.

The national security problem for the United States resides at the intersection of the Tiers. The United States *is* the only remaining superpower in that we are the only state with both significant economic *and* military power. Our economic strength makes us a major player within the First Tier; our economic and military power make us the only true candidate to provide leadership in how the First Tier relates to the Second Tier. Moreover, the nearly universal desire to emulate the political democracy and market economy of which the United States is the prototype endows the country with a great deal of soft power (the appeal of American ideals).

How this intersection should be dealt with lacks the consensus of the Cold War both in the United States and in the First Tier generally. One major strand of argumentation maintains that American national interest is served only in a condition of global stability. If that is the case, this liberal interventionist school of thought argues for a highly active, aggressive American posture toward the violence and instability of the Second Tier and maintains that the United States is obliged to form a First Tier consensus on that ground.

The other major school of thought, which its advocates prefer to label as realist, counter that the guiding light for American activity should be American geopolitical vital interests. Their first question about how to approach any conflict is: how will any outcome affect the United States and American citizens? Their answer for most of the Second Tier is cautionary: except where access to petroleum is involved, there generally are not important American interests put at risk. The United States should not play "globo-cop" where we are not directly at risk.

This is not a new debate. During the Cold War and before (for instance, the 1919 debate between President Woodrow Wilson and the Senate over the Versailles Peace Treaty ending World War I), these same schools of thought conflicted over the extent to which the United States personally should enforce the sanctity of the containment line. The liberal interventionists argued for a more proactive position; they "won" the day in Vietnam. The realists argued that while the containment line was important, the United States should only become *personally* involved at key places where our vital interests were clearly on the line. Such reasoning, they argue, would have prevented the Vietnam debacle.

Neither of these arguments was overwhelming during the Cold War, and there is little reason to expect one or the other to be decisively triumphant in the new order. Rather, sometimes the interests in a global order will prevail, while at other times reserve and caution will rule the day. It may be that the liberal-realist paradigm is itself the problem, forcing us to think in terms that are inappropriate to the structure of policy challenges in the environment.

Suggested Reading

Asmus, Ronald D., Richard L. Kugler, and F. Stephen Larrabee. "Building a New NATO," *Foreign Affairs* 72, 4 (September/October 1993):28–40.

Bialer, Seweyrn, and Michael Mandelbaum (eds.). *Gorbachev's Russia and American Foreign Policy.* Boulder, Colo.: Westview Press, 1988.

Brzezinski, Zbigniew. "The Cold War and Its Aftermath," *Foreign Affairs* 71, 4 (Fall 1992):31–49.

Fukuyama, Francis. "The End of History?" *National Interest* 16 (Summer 1989):3–18.

Gaddis, John Lewis. *How Relevant Was American Strategy in Winning the Cold War?* Carlisle Barracks, Pa.: Strategic Studies Institute, 1992.

Heisbourg, Francois. "The Future of the Atlantic Alliance," *Washington Quarterly* 15, 2 (Spring 1992):127–140.

Mearsheimer, John J. "Why We Shall Soon Miss the Cold War," *Atlantic Monthly* 266, 2 (August 1990):35–50.

Roberts, Brad. "Arms Control and the End of the Cold War." *Washington Quarterly* 15, 4 (August 1992):39–56.

Simes, Dimitri. "America and the Post-Soviet Republics," *Foreign Affairs* 71, 3 (Summer 1992):73–89.

———. "The Return of Russian History," *Foreign Affairs* 73, 1 (January/February 1994):67–82.

Snow, Donald M. *The Necessary Peace: Nuclear Weapons and Superpower Relations.* Lexington, Mass.: Lexington Books, 1987.

Chapter 7

National Security
in a Tiered System

The 1990s security environment scarcely resembles the 1980s or any of the decades since World War II. The sharp geopolitical hues of vivid reds and blues that denoted the communist and noncommunist world on maps have given way to a gray pastel. Now it is often difficult to distinguish friend from foe, to calibrate degrees of threat and risk, and to decide when basic interests are engaged or not.

This is a systemic problem: the international system is undergoing a fundamental transformation from the Cold War bipolarity to a world of tiers wherein power and political relationships will be different than before. The question is how they will differ.

Although the problem transcends the United States, Americans have a special place in the new order. The United States is, at least for the time being, *the* remaining superpower—the only country with the full array of instruments of power available to it. Given its special status, the world increasingly looks to the United States to provide leadership in shaping the new order.

It is not merely chauvinistic to say this. The evidence of the short period of post–Cold War history provides testimony to the proposition. When the world learned of the genocide by starvation in Somalia, it turned to the United States to relieve the problem. When Israel and the Palestinian Liberation Organization (PLO) and then Israel and Jordan reached accord on recognition and the beginning of a peace process, they went to the White House lawn to sign accords negotiated quietly and secretly in Oslo, which may prove a significant precedent for the future. The symbolism was clear: only an American imprimatur (with the Russian foreign minister as an important secondary presence) could sanctify and guarantee the accord. When the world dithered over Bosnia, international eyes turned to the United States.

The debate about America's leadership role in the new order is both necessary and consequential. Wistful sentiment notwithstanding, the

United States has no real option to withdraw from providing leadership in forming the new order. Our involvement within the First Tier is inextricable; only the United States has the global reach to influence events worldwide. What we decide will have a good deal to do with the nature of the international order—or disorder. One can overstate the role—many things will happen regardless of where and how the United States stands—but one cannot reject it.

The world has changed, but have American interests changed as well? As noted in Chapter 2, one normally thinks of interests in enduring terms: secure national boundaries, access to important markets and sources of natural resources, and freedom to pursue economic well-being do not change over time. What *do* change are the circumstances that facilitate or impede the pursuit of those interests—that is to say, the structure of threats to interests and the consequent risks one entails in realizing one's interests.

The structure of threats has changed greatly. In the old system, it was a hostile Soviet Union and its allies and fellow-traveller communist states that posed the major threats, with phenomena such as militant Islam a distant second. The dissolution of that central threat structure is what most affects the national debate about security in the future.

In traditional terms of interest, we face an *interest-threat mismatch*. During the Cold War, interests and threats had a neat symmetry: our primary interests (for example, a free and accessible Europe and Japan) were threatened by a concrete opponent; the process of matching threats and interests and devoting resources to reducing the consequent risk was straightforward, even deductive.

Today the situation is one of mismatch: *where America's most vital interests exist, there are essentially no threats (with the possible exception to Persian Gulf petroleum). Conversely, where there are threats (most of the Second Tier), hardly any important interests are at stake.* Threats and interests not only do not coincide, they hardly overlap at all. Put another way, American national security as traditionally conceived is hardly in jeopardy anywhere on the globe.

How do we respond to this situation? In the short run, complacency is an option, although that might well simply make the threats worse (if not necessarily threatening interests in the process). Inaction in Bosnia for three years certainly qualified in this regard. We can also redefine interests, extending the importance of situations in nontraditional ways. We have also done this by condoning—at least selectively—the idea of "humanitarian vital interests" put forward by UN Secretary General Boutros Boutros-Ghali: that certain crimes against humanity are so atrocious as to demand international rectification. The initial, fuzzy rationale for American involvement in Somalia sprang from such intellectual roots.

The mismatch suggests that some redefinition of interests, especially vital interests, is required for the United States to be involved militarily in much of the Second Tier. As noted earlier, one of the definitions of

vital interest is that a situation is worth going to war over; in a traditional geopolitical sense, very little of the Second Tier's woes meet that
definition.

The American response to this changed circumstance to date has
been ambivalent, revealing a lack of consensually agreed-upon principles
about what will and will not activate the United States into various forms
of action. Much anticipation and hoopla was expended when the United
States forged the Desert Shield/Storm response to Saddam Hussein's
conquest and annexation of Kuwait in July 1990. The expansive hyperbole of a "new world order" was raised as heady wine, only to fade into
oblivion when the Iraqi dictator, defeated but unbowed, remained in
power and unleashed his fury against those who had, with what they
mistook as American blessing, risen to overthrow Saddam Hussein following George Bush's call to revolt. When the United States created de
facto statehood for Kurdistan (Operation Provide Comfort) and an in-
country sanctuary for Shiite rebels (Operation Southern Watch) within
Iraq, talk about new orders and new principles promptly ceased. The incursion by Iraqi forces into Kurdistan in 1996 in support of one Kurdish
faction (the Kurdish Democratic Party) and their subsequent withdrawal
accompanied by U.S. protests merely reemphasized the U.S. predicament
of how the United States might possibly be able to withdraw in the future
without leaving the Kurds in jeopardy.

Similarly, what are the principles to be learned from Somalia and
Bosnia by others (such as the Sudanese, currently) who would starve
and exterminate ethnic groups within their boundaries? Is it that the
system operates when the task seems easy, as it initially appeared in
Somalia, but not where the job is difficult, as everyone assessed it to be
in Bosnia? Do we follow the slightly tongue-in-cheek canard that "the
Army does deserts (Kuwait, Somalia); it doesn't do mountains (Bosnia)"?
It is not clear.

Also, as suggested earlier, it may be that the terms of reference of the
Cold War framework do not match evolving reality. Basing U.S. action
solely on traditional vital interests could paralyze the United States in situations where American leadership might help. Our Clausewitzian
framework, with its implicit Napoleonic tendency to act only for large
purposes and in decisive ways could similarly keep the United States
from smaller and less decisive actions designed to assist but not necessarily to solve problems that may be unsolvable.

It is within this framework of uncertainty and questions that the
present discussion will proceed. We will begin, in the next section, to
look at the general dimensions of the national security debate as it is
emerging in the United States. From there, the discussion will move to a
more detailed examination of interests and their translation into action
through the instruments of power. We will then attempt to link these
ideas together, concluding with an impression of the new "menu" of opportunities for American national security involvements.

THINKING ABOUT SECURITY

As was pointed out in Chapter 2, security is both a physical and a psychological phenomenon: safety and a sense of safety. For Americans throughout most of our history, the physical sense has been relatively unimportant because no state or group of states could convincingly threaten the integrity of American soil. The threats were limited (the exposure of the Hawaiian Islands to the Pearl Harbor raid) or historical (the British invasion during the War of 1812). Now, although Russia technically could still destroy American society with its remaining nuclear weapons, its obvious lack of motivation for doing so leaves that a matter of only slight concern.

Americans have always been ambivalent about the psychological dimension: what threats external to the United States and not directly menacing the United States make us uneasy enough to contemplate the use of force? George Washington's farewell address and Thomas Jefferson's first inaugural speech set the cautionary tone that guided American opinion through most of its history before World War II. Elements of the American military tradition, such as the myth of the citizen-soldier and the mobilization-demobilization tradition, reflect the general historical correlation of security and aloofness.

Retreat from the world stage no longer remains an option. The debate over what actions the United States should be prepared to undertake and what actions should be avoided in the name of American security proceeds within bounds that begin with not *whether* the United States has a role in global security but, instead, about the *nature and extent* of that involvement.

The debate has multiple facets. For present purposes, six will be identified and introduced: (1) the focus of security on the national or international level; (2) the extent or amount of activism of American action; (3) the question of whether the United States is overextended, given its capabilities; (4) the balance between domestic and international priorities; (5) the efficacy of American involvement; and (6) the nature of the interests that come into play.

Security Focus

The question of whether American security policy should emphasize the national level of security or the security of some other units is a rather recent phenomenon. *National security*, of course, takes the security of the American state as its primary value and is the traditional way in which the state system has defined security affairs. What, then, are the alternatives?

Two other levels were mentioned briefly in Chapter 2. *Individual security* takes the individual person as its focus; this position is not a particular part of the debate, except to point out that actions, such as sending people to war, taken in the name of national security may come at the expense of the individual security of those asked to serve.

The real alternative notion in the current debate is so-called *international security*, which begins with a concern for the sanctity of the system as a whole rather than that of its constituent members. Those who advocate a central emphasis on the overall system generally make one or both of two arguments. On one hand, they argue that states, acting on their own narrow concerns, often take actions that endanger the security of other members or the system as a whole. One state arming against another may, for instance, lower the sense of security of the second state. This is an important part of the essence of the security dilemma. At the same time, a decision by the superpowers during the Cold War to employ nuclear weapons could have endangered the entire system.

The second argument, which is likely to be increasingly heard in the debate, is that the security of the individual states is best served by a primary concern for the stability and security of all states. The proposition is, of course, debatable. Its currency takes on added momentum in an international milieu of tiers.

The idea of international security is particularly appealing to the states of the First Tier. Certainly, the relations *among* First Tier states reflect this "all for one, and one for all" orientation toward the central questions of peace and stability. In addition, the spread of stability within the Second Tier is clearly desirable for the First Tier, as a means of providing a more dependable economic climate and of avoiding even the prospect of First Tier members being sucked into Second Tier conflicts.

One possible focus for international security sentiment is the United Nations and the implementation of its *collective security* provisions. If First Tier states are in reasonable agreement that systemic peace and stability are desirable and an important systemic (or, for that matter, individual state) interest, they should also agree that the burden should be shared. That means both gaining a consensus and sharing the physical burden of contributing forces. The mechanism for achieving these ends is often likely to be the Security Council of the UN, where the important players (the permanent members) who will be expected to enforce collective security have a veto. This will be especially true when (or if) permanent membership is extended to Japan and Germany. For some special cases, the G-7, or especially NATO, may be the authorizing agent for collective actions in the name of international security—the precedent for the Bosnian IFOR operation.

Ironically, the most resistance to embracing this kind of concept is likely to come from some Second Tier states, which are likely to cling tightly to national security as the base concept. For one thing, most of the collective security actions one can conjure will be taken against Second Tier states, and in some cases, the states or governments acted against will not want those actions. The system, in other words, will impose settlements where not everyone involved wants them; they may be good for the overall system, but not necessarily for all (or any) of the individual parties to the dispute. It will be ironic when the authorizing agent is the United Nations, long the stronghold of the Second Tier for voicing its grievances with the First Tier (largely through the General Assembly).

A second reason for a Second Tier preference for definitions of national security is that collective actions taken for systemic reasons will often violate the sovereignty of the states against which actions are taken. An emphasis on national security, of course, flows from the idea of national sovereignty as the first principle of the international order. Often, it is the mask for the rogue state, which can use sovereignty as a screen behind which to suppress its own people or subvert others. The actions in the aftermath of the Persian Gulf War to protect the Kurds and Shiites from the Iraqi government represent one example. In Somalia, U.S. forces entering the country under UN auspices were not there at the invitation of any government, since there was no government (which, of course, was the heart of the problem). Somali genocide was a problem the international system could not abide; Somali sovereignty was of a lesser importance.

There is one other dimension to thinking about security in international rather than national terms. As a practical matter, an orientation around traditional national security is likely to lead to substantially fewer involvements for First Tier states in Second Tier conflicts. The reason is simple: a national security orientation leads one to think of actions taken on the grounds of *national* interest, which triggers the interest-threat mismatch. Thinking in terms of international security, on the other hand, is a way to move the definition of interest more closely to the structure of threats in the world.

It should also be noted, however, that there is no consensus within or between states on the principle of international security, nor is there agreement on what situations should trigger a systemic response. The system intervened in Somalia and eventually in Bosnia; it has done nothing (other than to pass toothless condemnations) effectively to end the religiously based insurgency in Sudan.

Extent of Involvement

The willingness to consider broadened definitions of security is related to general orientations toward American activism or passivity with regard to security in the world. In the current debate, the poles of that debate are internationalism and neoisolationism.

As already noted, the isolationist strand is as old as the country itself. Many of the first Americans who immigrated did so first to escape the tyrannies of European lands and later to flee the authoritarian systems of Asia and Latin America. The notion that America is a special place—what, most recently, former President Reagan referred to as the "shining house on the hill"—runs deep in the American tradition. So does the notion that most of the rest of the world is somehow tainted.

The tradition of aloofness began to break down in the first half of the twentieth century, as the United States vacillated between lesser and greater involvements in world affairs. In World War I, the United States embarked on a moral crusade to "make the world safe for democracy," although some Americans grumbled that we were pulling European "chestnuts out of the fire" to indicate our inherent superiority. The aftermath of the experience caused the United States to retreat into "splendid isolationism," only to be drawn inexorably into World War II. As one of the two remaining poles at war's end, total retreat ceased to be an option.

The end of the Cold War allows the debate to reopen, although within somewhat constrained parameters. Neoisolationism cannot be as absolute as was interwar isolationism because of global interconnectedness; internationalism is constrained by restraints on American resources and by an American public that does not show consistent support for an aggressive, intrusive role in the world.

The neoisolationist position, probably best associated with conservative columnist and Republican presidential aspirant Patrick Buchanan, suggests that the United States should and must scale back its internationalist activity now that the Cold War is over. He and others cite several reasons for this. The declining threat to American interests means that Americans no longer need to bear such a large portion of the global burden, most of which does not affect the United States in important ways. The end of the Cold War creates the opportunity to redirect American resources formerly directed toward the Cold War competition to domestic priorities. The United States may be the only global power, but the United States' position is not so far above others as it once was. The United States cannot, and should not, retreat altogether, but others, such as Japan and the countries of the European Union (EU) should increasingly share the load.

The internationalists take exception to this limited, even gloomy, prospect. This strand argues that retreat is both irresponsible and impossible as a practical matter. It is irresponsible because the United States is the only country with the physical resources, international political standing, and prestige to provide global leadership. If the United States does not lead, no one else can or will. Neoisolationism is impractical because the world has become so interdependent—economically and politically—that a retreat cannot be sustained. Moreover, American interests are so globally extensive that the chaos that would accompany any retreat would disserve the United States. The United States must lead because it has no practical alternative.

Much of the internationalist-neoisolationist debate centers on the use of American military force in the new order. Where the United States should employ force is a matter of resource allocation (overseas deployments are expensive) as well as a question about where Americans should have their lives put at risk. The contemporary debate has tended to focus on the role of the United Nations and the extent and nature of U.S. participation in UN-sponsored military actions, although within policy constraints dictated by wavering support for the UN. At the same time, there is the increasing prospect that the United States might act unilaterally, in conjunction with NATO or some other organization, or that it might use a UN mandate as a cover for one of the other options. As one might expect, the internationalists are more enthused about consigning American forces to any of these kinds of actions than are the neoisolationists.

Much of this debate reflects an assessment of America's relative standing in the world. How much does the world need the United States? And how much does the United States need the world? If the United States is the only pole in the new system, how relatively big a pole is it? And is the pole growing in relative stature or contracting?

America's Standing in the World

This side of the debate was stimulated by the 1987 publication of a controversial book by Yale University history professor, Paul Kennedy. The thesis of his book, entitled *The Rise and Fall of the Great Powers*, has become known as *declinism*. According to this notion, great powers have traditionally expanded to the point of overextension, usually through excessive commitments to military spending and power. In the process, they overreach their natural capacities, and once this occurs, they go into decline. Much of his historical analysis dealt with the building and decline of the British Empire in the nineteenth and twentieth centuries; his contemporary examples are the Soviet Union and the United States. One can argue his thesis proved decisively true for the former Soviet Union; the question is whether it is equally applicable to the United States.

Kennedy put his thesis forward at a time when American predominance was being questioned on a number of fronts. American scientific, technological, and, especially, manufacturing prowess was being seriously challenged by the Japanese and members of the EU, and the question of American competitiveness heading toward the twenty-first century was being widely raised. In many measures of productivity and advanced status, the United States was not competing very well in relation to market share in a broad variety of products (especially those at the high end of the technological spectrum), standardized scores on international science and mathematics tests, and the like. The overextension of American military commitments was at least partly the villain in this decline.

The result was a picture of the United States as a state in decline on the world stage. The declinists argued that the United States was becoming just another member of the international community rather than the preeminent state and that Americans should learn to accept this lessened status and its consequences. According to them, the United States can no longer afford the luxury of projecting worldwide power or providing comprehensive global leadership.

The existence, inevitability, and permanence of the declinist phenomenon have been widely attacked. Those who oppose the declinists— as Harvard political scientist Joseph S. Nye, Jr., does in his book, *Bound to Lead*—maintain that the data on which American decline is premised is misleading and that Kennedy and his supporters effectively "cook the books." The declinists start with data on the American economy immediately after World War II, when the American share of global gross national product (GNP) was at an artificially inflated level of about 40 percent. As the world's economies recovered, the American share quite naturally declined to around 20 percent, still quite high given that the American population is only about 6 percent of the world total. Moreover, the percentage has stabilized or even increased slightly since the early 1970s. The evidence for decline is thus less than overwhelming.

Moreover, opponents argue, the declinist thesis is both self-fulfilling and self-defeating. If the United States comes to think of itself as in decline and pulls back on its global military and other commitments, then its influence will, in fact, decline, regardless of whether the American condition requires that retreat from global involvement. Moreover, if the United States sees itself in the positive terms that the antideclinist contingent feels is more realistic, then continued American vitality will ensure that the twenty-first, like the twentieth, will be an American century.

The neoisolationist and declinist positions are obviously quite closely related, as are the position of the internationalists and those who oppose declinism. Much of their difference hinges on optimism or pessimism about the American future: in one analogy, it is a matter of looking at the American condition and viewing it as a glass half full (optimistic) or a glass half empty (pessimistic). The debate clearly hinges on what the United States can and cannot afford in the future. As the United States girds for the future, where do our priorities lie?

American Priorities

Much of the 1992 election campaign was framed in terms of the balance between domestic and foreign priorities. Buchanan challenged incumbent President Bush in the Republican primaries, touting the neoisolationist line and accusing the president of continuing the liberal internationalist tradition of the Cold War period. In the general election campaign, Bill Clinton argued for greater domestic activism—suggesting less international involvement—whereas Bush preferred to dwell more on foreign policy accomplishments resulting from American leadership in instances such as the Persian Gulf War.

The early performance of the Clinton administration belied the ability to make as sharp a distinction between domestic and foreign priorities as the campaign had implied. The new president clearly entered office with domestic issues on his mind: deficit reduction (actually reduction in the rate of deficit accumulation), health care, and the "reinvention" of government clearly most engaged the self-styled "policy wonk." But the world, and the American place in it, would not leave the new administration alone. The situation in Bosnia and Herzegovina would not go away, nor would the deteriorating situation in Somalia. More positively, the Israelis and the PLO found the White House lawn a symbolically appropriate place to begin their peace process, effectively locking an American guarantee to that process by so doing. Moreover, the longer he remained in office, the more comfortable he became in dealing with foreign and defense matters, jetting to capitals around the world at a dizzying pace and authorizing major military deployments in Somalia, Haiti, and Bosnia.

The question is one of the relative allocation of scarce resources to foreign and defense priorities as opposed to more traditionally domestic ones. Should the United States attempt to lead the new international system's attempt to maintain order and stability? Doing so would deflect resources that could be devoted to the multitude of domestic needs: rebuilding infrastructure components such as highway bridges and railbeds, increasing allocations to education, rebuilding the inner cities, combatting alarming increases in street crime, battling the deficit, or generally investing in the American industrial and technological base.

Positions form along predictable lines. Those who support the neoisolationist-declinist school of thought de-emphasize the foreign priority, although they differ on how the resources saved should be used. If a reversal of decline is the goal, then investment is the priority; others see the opportunity to "get government off the people's back" (Reagan's phrase) by reducing taxes and the like. Internationalists counter that there are adequate resources for both efforts in an American system that is much more vital than the declinists will admit, and that the United States has a moral obligation to lead in a system where no one else can.

The Clinton position falls between the extremes. His often-stated interest in domestic priorities and his sense of government activism suggest that he leans toward a greater emphasis on domestic priorities. At the same time, he apparently believes that the United States must provide global leadership in such areas as support for American participation in UN peacekeeping and other military matters. His second-term plan to combine a foreign policy emphasis on promoting global free trade with a domestic emphasis on education to make the United States competitive in a free-trading world illustrates his current synthesis of foreign and domestic priorities—the essence of the national security strategy of "engagement and enlargement" of the number of market-based democracies.

How much the United States should involve itself in the world system and its security affairs is also a matter of the extent to which the situations are amenable to solution by the application of force, including American force. No matter what the moral imperative of a given situation, the question of "can do" or its obverse must be an important consideration.

The Efficacy of U.S. Involvement

The utility of employing American military forces in the kinds of Second Tier conflicts for which they may become eligible is also a matter of considerable disagreement. These problems are discussed in detail in the chapters that follow and will only be introduced here. They do, however, follow from the two basic views of America's general inclination toward the post–Cold War environment.

For the "realists" and neoisolationists and their supporters, the opposition is both philosophical and practical. At the philosophical level is the question of interests: most Second Tier conflicts do not entail the traditional American vital interests that would trigger an American military response. Unlike the so-called "central battle" between NATO and the Warsaw Pact, it is often difficult to see how Americans would be better or worse off, regardless of the outcomes of many of these conflicts. The exception, of course, is where vital resources, notably petroleum reserves in the Persian Gulf, are involved.

At the practical level is the question of efficacy. Most of the conflicts that have erupted since the end of the Cold War are internal in nature: civil wars between ethnic and other groups either to cleave states or to gain control of them. For outsiders to become involved effectively in such conflicts requires both a clear understanding of the dynamics of these conflicts and, hence, their solutions (which are always political), as well as a military capability that can effectively produce the political climate necessary for political solutions to be reached.

The military problem in most of these situations is akin to the problem of counterinsurgency. The history of successful counterinsurgent operations by outsiders (especially racially distinct outsiders, as would have been the case when First Tier states intervened in Second Tier conflicts) during the Cold War was sufficiently bleak to suggest that efficacy is difficult—even impossible—to achieve. The American involvement in Vietnam and the Soviet intervention in Afghanistan stand as Cold War monuments to this difficulty. The failure to pacify Somalia gives pause about the new system, as well.

The current efforts to use American forces in Second Tier conflicts centers around the United Nations and the world organization's attempts to define its own role in the new order. The UN itself, of course, lacks the resources, the expertise, and the military capability to intervene in these conflicts. Only the First Tier states have the military muscle. It is unclear, however, whether they have either the political or military doctrines and strategies to do much more than recolonize chaotic states such as Somalia.

The enormous suffering and atrocities that accompany many of these kinds of conflicts make them difficult to ignore—particularly when they are televised. While there is little evidence in the policy community—especially its nonmilitary sector—of an appreciation of the inherent difficulties of such operations, there is considerable pressure to "do something" when one sees massive carnage and human suffering. The internationalist instinct is that we have to become involved, reflecting the implied belief discussed earlier that there can be no security for the United States in a situation of international chaos.

Part of the difficulty of knowing what, if anything, to do is a matter of sorting out interests and priorities. If traditional definitions of interest yield negative evaluations of where and when involvement should occur, should interests be redefined to make them compatible with international activism?

The Nature of Interests

When does a situation warrant the use of military force by the United States (or anyone else)? When the interest is vital. When is an interest vital? When it is important enough to go to war over. The circularity of this distinction divides the policy community. Among those who would increase American assertiveness in the new system, the tendency is to begin with the situations the system presents and to alter their notions of interest to accommodate those deemed important. From the standpoint of those who would restrict American involvement (prominently including large sectors of the military), the question should begin with the act of war such contemplation implies. The serious nature of committing acts of war—especially when success cannot be assumed—mandates caution in choosing any action.

A major question facing the evolving international order is whether the traditional, interest-driven paradigm is in tune with the contemporary system. It is arguable, at least, that the new system is, indeed, more driven by a sense of international security that renders obsolete more parochial definitions of when force should be used. Are we entering an era of *international* vital interests where the system's interests override national interests?

Moreover, something called *humanitarian interests* or even humanitarian *vital* interests have emerged. These are defined loosely as interests of the totality of humankind and the globe itself by the promotion and protection of human rights against atrocity by governments. Former UN Secretary Boutros-Ghali was a vocal advocate of this asserted interest, especially in light of very public violations throughout the Second Tier of states.

How interests are defined will have a visible effect on the extent of American military activism in the new order, as well as framing the size, extent, purposes, and content of military and nonmilitary actions. Embrace of an expanded, internationalist definition of interest will create a very large number of situations for which First Tier (including U.S.) force might be eligible. A more traditional, restricted definition would reduce the candidate situations markedly.

TABLE 7.1   Aspects of Security

Facets of Debate	Narrow	Broad
Focus	National	International
Involvement	Neoisolationism	Internationalism
Standing	Declinism	Antideclinism
Priorities	Domestic	Foreign/system
Efficacy of force	Narrow	Necessary
Interests	Traditional	Expanded

We can summarize the foregoing discussion of security by looking at a summary of the various dimensions we have analyzed (Table 7.1).

There is really nothing new about the poles of this debate. The portrayal is of two broad schools of thought and how they respond on a series of facets of the current debate. A sizable part of the American public and its leadership has always believed that U.S. security is best served by restricting American involvement in foreign affairs, another segment of the populace has always called for greater American involvement in the world. But three aspects of this topic are somewhat different now than they were in the past. First, the parameters of discussion have shifted. It is no longer possible to start from the position of near-total isolationism as one extreme in the debate: such a position is not sustainable in an interdependent world from which the United States simply cannot withdraw. Rather, the boundaries of debate are the extent or degree of American activism. Second, the end of the Cold War relaxes a number of American security concerns. The basic physical security of the United States is not the pressing concern it was when a plausible case of Soviet animosity made the nuclear threat lively. The debate now occurs at the margins of physical security in the realm of security's psychological dimension.

Third, the interest-threat mismatch has created a vacuum for thinking about and planning for the country's security. If one begins from the narrow interpretation of national security requirements and obligations, then the military component of American society has a much more limited role than was previously the case. Such an interpretation is clearly implied in the administration's stated intention to reduce American standing military strength by one-third of its Cold War level, apparently expecting that responses to the new challenges can be accomplished by smaller, even less-expensive, commitments.

The question of interests is pivotal in deciding what constitutes national security in the future. How does one realign interests and threats? Answering that question requires us to look in some detail at the whole question of interests and the range of instruments of national power by which they are enforced.

THINKING ABOUT INTERESTS

Although it is bandied about lightly and used to justify broadly varying conditions and positions, the concepts of *interest* and, more specifically, *national interest* are both hazy and controversial. The dictionary provides a wide variety of meanings for the word *interest*, ranging from something that stimulates intellectual curiosity ("that's interesting") to money paid for the use of money (interest payments).

In a political sense, interest combines two definitional elements. The first is the idea of common purpose, goal, or principle held by a number of individuals—the idea associated with interest groups. The second is the notion of advantage or benefit—the best interests of some unit. From this, political interests can be thought of as *the shared goals, deriving from some common political principles, that provide entities with a perceived political advantage.*

Although any entity (including a single individual) can have interests, the ones that count are those of groups. Due to the principle of sovereignty, states have traditionally been endowed with the most important interests. Indeed the survival and prosperity of individual states is the highest value of the Westphalian system. Thus, *national interests*, defined by *The American Political Dictionary* as "the concept of the security and well-being of the state, used in making foreign policy," have underlain the criteria for making national security policy. The most common principle of the state system is national security.

The haziness of the term *interest* comes from two sources. The first is the diverse uses to which it is subjected. The problem is akin to the term *strategy;* although its only clear meaning is in reference to military strategy, the term has been diluted to the point that almost every kind of group and even individuals have strategies to cover the gamut of activity. In a similar vein, everyone seems to have interests, and national interest is used to enshrine all forms and focuses of activity.

Of more consequence is the second source of haziness: because interests are perceived conditions, they are matters on which individuals and groups can—and do—reasonably disagree. Like the psychological dimension of security, what is in the national interest is largely what people *think* serves that interest. Notions of security and interest are thus very closely intertwined.

The notion of national interest is controversial because it is so clearly associated with the "realist" school of thought about foreign and defense policy. The concept derived over time from the idea of *raison d'etat* (reason of state) developed by Niccolo Machiavelli in the sixteenth century to justify national security and advantage as the primary determinants of state behavior. As a guide to state action, foreign policy rooted in national interest takes national advantage as its first premise; whenever other, conflicting values such as moral principles compete, national interest prevails. It is in this sense that a national-interest-driven policy is often referred to as Machiavellian.

The controversy about the term is that it is too restrictive and conservative for the contemporary world situation. Although there is nothing inherent in national interest to suggest an incompatibility between pursuit of national interests and international human rights (a world where human rights are enforced could arguably be a more tranquil and secure place), traditional usages have implied a hierarchy of values that internationalists feel unduly restricts American activity in the world. Moreover, in a world of increasing interdependence, the extent to which such a framework adequately encompasses reality is also a contemporary concern.

Confusion and controversy notwithstanding, the concept of national interest remains the bedrock on which national foreign policy decisions are grounded. National security policy comes into play when the debate comes to focus on whether interests are vital or not.

Determining National Interests

In Chapter 2, the idea of vital interest was first introduced to help explain the need for military force in an anarchic world and the inevitability of an anarchic world as long as vital national interests exist. In this section, we will look at the concept in more detail, including differentiating between the conditions being sought and the importance or intensity of the interests in question.

In this analysis, we will lean heavily on the work of Donald Nuechterlein, who has created a very useful matrix for organizing the discussion of national interest in a series of books, most recently in his 1991 book, *America Recommitted: United States National Interests in a Restructured World* (see the end-of-chapter suggested reading section for complete citation). His basic vehicle is the "National Interest Matrix," reproduced as Table 7.2.

The table classifies interest in two dimensions: the basic interests or conditions to be promoted, and the intensity or importance of each interest in providing the perceived political advantage included in the definition of interest. In each case, the categories are arranged in descending order of vitality. (For example, the defense of homeland is more important than promoting American values, and vital interests are more important than peripheral interests.)

The definitions, paraphrased from Nuechterlein, are straightforward. *Defense of homeland* refers to the ability to protect the country from invasion, conquest, or destruction by an enemy. For the United States, this has seldom been a particular problem, given the accident of geography. A signal exception was (and is) the physical ability of the Soviet Union (Russia) to decimate the American homeland with nuclear weapons.

Economic well-being refers to the promotion and protection of an environment conducive to economic success and prosperity. For the United States, this means, for instance, free and unfettered access to markets, trading routes (sea lanes and air space), and access to natural resources (such as

TABLE 7.2   **National Interest Matrix**

Basic Interest	Intensity of Interest			
	Survival	Vital	Major	Peripheral
Homeland defense				
Economic well-being				
Favorable world order				
Value promotion				

petroleum) necessary for American prosperity. *Favorable world order* refers to a peaceful systemic environment conducive to a state's success. An optimal world order for the United States would include stability spreading from the First Tier to the Second. Finally, *value promotion* refers to a situation in which states have similar political and economic philosophies. The extension of market democracy to parts of the world that do not currently embrace the system would be an obvious example for the United States.

Which of these conditions have national security, including military, implications? A traditional, "realist" analysis would suggest that the two most important categories, defense of homeland and economic well-being, have such implications, but probably the lower two do not. Clearly, the United States (or just about any other country) would fight to maintain the integrity of its borders; a state that cannot guarantee its own existence is not of great utility to its citizens. As noted, however, this is much more of a problem for most other countries of the world than it is for the United States. The virtual absence of homeland-threatening conditions is one of the unique attributes of the American strategic culture, as noted in Chapter 3.

Economic well-being is slightly more complex. Certainly, the United States has been willing to use force in defense of its economic interests. The need to enter the world wars in Europe can be justified in economic terms: a German-dominated continent (and conceivably a German-dominated North Atlantic Ocean) would almost certainly have excluded American products. Although it was touted as a favorable world order motivation (the "new world order"), American participation in the Persian Gulf War was largely the result of the economic consequences of losing access to petroleum from the region. When initially questioned about why we were organizing the coalition to reverse the Kuwaiti annexation, Secretary of State James Baker replied, "jobs," in apparent reference to the number of American jobs that would be lost if the annexation stood.

Generally speaking, the promotion of world order and values occupies a lower order of priority, below the level at which military force will be contemplated. There are, however, exceptions in the immediate American past. Operation Just Cause, the invasion of Panama to install a democratically elected government and staunch the flow of narcotics from South America to the United States through its Panamanian funnel, can be viewed only as a world order condition. The invasion of Grenada in 1983, Operations Provide Comfort (1991) and Southern Watch (1992), and Operation Restore Hope in Somalia (1992) provide other examples where the American homeland was not threatened and no particular economic interests were involved. The same is true of the mission to Bosnia, which President Clinton justified rhetorically as "the right thing to do," and of U.S. intervention in Haiti.

It is not coincidental that the most recent uses of force have been in situations where force has not traditionally been thought of as justified. It is the essence of the interest-threat mismatch that traditional values are not threatened (defense of homeland, economic well-being) and that the threats are to lesser priorities (world order and value promotion). The implications are explored in the Amplification box "Expanding Definitions of Interest" shown on page 181.

The discussion gains added focus when we include the categories indicating the intensity of interest involved. *Survival* (or what Nuechterlein also terms *critical*) interests, as the name implies, concern imminent threats to the national existence. Kuwait, for instance, faced a threat to its survival when Iraq invaded. *Vital* (or *dangerous*) interests involve situations that are not willingly tolerated and, as such, represent conditions over which states are normally willing to commit military force. *Major* (or *serious*) *intensity* refers to conditions where interests are affected adversely, but not so fundamentally as to be intolerable. These are conditions that may be remedied by some form of action but probably not by the use of military force. Finally, *peripheral* (or *bothersome*) *conditions* reflect adverse conditions that are troublesome to some portion of the population but that are otherwise not intolerable; these are annoying circumstances but not situations one would do much to change. With these definitions in mind, we can reconstruct and add to the matrix, as shown in Table 7.3.

Two additional notions are included in the combination and elaboration of the table. The first is a depiction of the difference between the

TABLE 7.3   National Interest Matrix Elaborated

Basic Interest	Intensity of Interest			
	Survival	**Vital**	**Major**	**Peripheral**
Defense of Homeland Economic Well-being	(Physical)			(Psychological)
Favorable world order Value promotion				

physical and psychological dimensions of security. The boxed upper left-hand cell (homeland defense, survival) is the single national security interest that clearly represents a physical threat to security. All the other cells (combinations) affect the commodiousness of national life to one degree or another but not to a life-threatening extent. As a result, both are included in the psychological dimension of security, where there is room for disagreement and debate.

The second addition is represented by a vertical solid line surrounded by dashed lines between vital and major intensities of interest, and counterpart (horizontal) markings between economic well-being and favorable world order. The solid lines denote the traditional boundaries for determining the employment of military force. The dashed lines bordering the solid lines are meant to suggest that there are no consensual boundaries but rather a confidence interval. Within the confidence interval are the disagreements about when force should and should not be used that form the parameters of ralistic debate over security policy.

Look at the distinctions. The vertical line (or confidence interval) divides vital and less than vital interests; the definitional boundary line delineates when force will and will not be contemplated. But where does any real situation fall in that regard? Take the 1980s conflict in Nicaragua between the American-backed Contras and the Marxist Sandinista government. Was the overthrow of the Sandinistas vital to the United States? The Reagan administration seemed to think so, taking the lead in creating and supporting the opposition Contras (and providing dubiously legal support in the so-called Iran-Contra affair). Others, including a majority in Congress, disagreed with this assessment and forbade certain kinds of support for the Contras, notably American government funding under the various Bolland amendments.

The example points to the boundary as a confidence interval where the location of the line is a point of contention. The same question, engendering the same disagreement, could be applied to any number of concrete situations in terms of their impact on the United States. Indeed, much of the security debate can be conceptualized in terms of whether to push the line to the right, making traditionally major interests candidates for military force (a position congruent with the activist, internationalist strand in the debate) or pushing the line to the left, making the criteria for using force more restrictive (a position congruent with the traditional realist strand).

The same kind of application can be made to the line/interval between economic well-being and favorable world order. A traditional analysis suggests that the line should be maintained or even pushed upward further to restrain when force can be employed. By contrast, the internationalist strain, particularly when it begins to advocate humanitarian vital interests, for example, is, in effect, advocating an extension of the line downward to encompass world order values among those things for which force might be employed.

Two other points can be made about the matrix. The first has to do with the interest-threat mismatch. The portion of the matrix in the upper left quadrant defined by the solid lines (wherever they are placed within the confidence intervals) clearly mark the country's most important interests: those over which the country will consider the use of force. If one were, in a traditional geopolitical sense, to place specific parts of the world inside those boundaries, the most obvious areas would be Europe, Japan, and the oil-rich portions of the Middle East (in addition to the United States itself). These are the areas that were most threatened during the Cold War, thereby aligning interests and threats.

In the new system, these areas of vital interest are hardly threatened at all, except in the Middle East. Outside this quadrant is most of the Second Tier, which is the source of virtually all the instability and violence that produce threats to the peace. It is also, however, the part of the world where interests are lesser: major and peripheral intensity, world order or value promotion content. This image helps clarify the mismatch in terms of the nature of interests. If the mismatch is to be resolved, then either the definition of vital interest will have to be adjusted to incorporate world order concerns, which the current administration has suggested in selective situations, or heretofore major interests will have to be upgraded in importance.

The second point has to do with the instruments of power that are incorporated to pursue various levels of interest. Of the three general categories identified in Chapter 2 (economic, military, and political/diplomatic), the only ones where military power would be contemplated are in the upper left quadrant, especially in the upper left cell. Diplomatic power is the only form that most likely would be used in circumstances falling in the lower right corner of the matrix (peripheral and value promotion interests), whereas one might contemplate the additional use of economic power in situations where world order and major interests are involved.

The orchestration of instruments of power was suggested in the brief case study dealing with the Iran hostage crisis in Chapter 2. Within each category, however, there are several wide, varied, and graded kinds of action that can be undertaken in pursuit of policy goals. Our interest here is particularly focused on the military instrument, although that instrument is often associated with other instruments as well.

APPLYING INSTRUMENTS OF POWER

The contemplation of applying power to alter a situation in which the state's interests are in some danger is, as noted earlier, situation-specific, making generalization about what instrument of power will apply to any category difficult in the abstract. Moreover, the invocation

AMPLIFICATION

Expanding Definitions of Interest

The Cold War came to epitomize the Clausewitzian view of the use of force as the servant of the political purposes of the state. This was especially true in the United States in the wake of Vietnam, for two reasons. One was that the Vietnam war was conducted against an opponent whose views were based in the philosophy and strategy of Mao Zedung, which were heavily Clausewitzian (Mao had read and admired Clausewitz). The other was that the military itself was disillusioned by what it viewed as the failure of support from the American people. Feeling it had been abandoned, it could and did adopt the Clausewitzian trinity that stresses the need for interactive support between the army (military), the people, and the government.

Embedded in the Clausewitzian scheme is an implicit Napoleonic tendency to elevate the purposes for which force is used. Since Clausewitz's *On War* was based on his observations of the Napoleonic wars, this is not surprising. What it does, however, is to suggest that force is properly attached to large causes with decisive outcome, such as the spread of the democratic principles of the French Revolution. In the process, it implicitly downgrades more limited applications of force for less than decisive purposes. The mission to Bosnia has such a limited purpose: it does not seek to solve the problem of the Bosnian polity but only to provide a breathing space for the actors to try to establish peace. As such, there are no truly vital U.S. interests at stake, and the outcomes will likely be modest.

The question is whether definitions of interest should be expanded to normalize this more limited use of U.S. force in the service of more modest purposes. The troublesome situations in the world more closely resemble the Bosnias and Haitis of the world than they do the Cold War confrontation in Europe where vital interests were clearly at stake.

The 1996 edition of *A National Security Strategy of Engagement and Enlargement*, the U.S. government's official statement, answers this question by delineating three categories of situations where the application of American forces might be contemplated. The first involves U.S. "vital interests," which is the standard condition. In addition, however, two other categories are added: cases where "important, but not vital" interests are involved; and "primarily humanitarian interests." Figure 7.1 shows how this expands the Neuchterlein outline to encompass the potential use of force into almost any cell of his matrix.

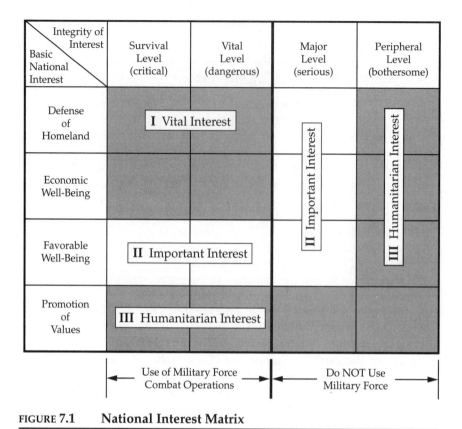

FIGURE 7.1   **National Interest Matrix**

of a particular instrument implies the capability to carry out the promise—whether in the form of negative threat or positive benefit—and the likelihood that the particular action will, indeed, result in the desired behavior to bring the situation into conformity with the national interest.

The status of states, especially in the post–Cold War world, can largely be measured by the variety of the instruments available to them. In the Cold War, superpower status was bestowed for military and, more specifically, thermonuclear, power; it was the possession of great nuclear arsenals that defined the superpower "club" of the United States and the Soviet Union.

Military power alone, however, is an inadequate measure of the ability to exercise power in the new, tiered system. Supreme military power is not relevant to the relations *among* First Tier states; threatening to employ military instruments of power to force, for instance, the EU to change agriculture policy (a longtime thorn in the side of EU-American relations) would be totally hollow. The general utility of military instruments is, rather, relevant only within the Second Tier and, on some occasions, in the relations between the First and Second Tiers. Within the First

Tier, diplomatic and political instruments have relevance, and some of those instruments are also salient in relations between the tiers.

The assertion that the United States is *the* remaining superpower now rests on the fact that it is the only country that possesses the full array of instruments of power. Because different forms of power are relevant in different situations in different parts of the world, this means that the United States is the only country capable of influencing events globally. This does not imply that the United States has the ability to control the outcomes of all situations or that it is overwhelmingly more powerful on any particular measure; it does mean that the U.S. arsenal of instruments of power is greater than that of anybody else. The rest of the world knows this and, thus, expects an American leadership that cannot be avoided.

Choosing instruments of power can be thought of as a three-part process. The first part is an assessment of the threat posed in a specific situation; it involves the question of interests. The second part involves looking at the array of instruments available; it is a process of inventorying possible means to achieve ends. The third part involves assessing the effectiveness of any particular instrument or instruments.

Threat Assessment

The solution begins with the problem. An event or situation poses a threat to some interest, and the question is what, if anything, will be done about it. Inaction is a form of response, as are the variety of actions one might take.

The assessment can be conceptualized in terms of five questions, using the Iraqi invasion of Kuwait as an example. The first and most basic is, *"What has happened that affects American interests?"* In this case, the invasion—especially coupled with Iraqi intent to annex Kuwait as the "19th province" of Iraq, was the precipitating event.

The second question is, *"What are your interests in the situation? How are you potentially affected?"* The answer here was at least threefold. Iraqi success would give them control of Kuwaiti oil reserves and, hence, a greater capability to interrupt the flow of Persian Gulf oil to the West (an economic well-being interest). Iraq could also use Kuwait as a staging ground either to menace or to invade that part of Saudi Arabia where the oil fields are located, thereby gaining even further control of oil reserves. In addition, there was the matter of precedent: Iraqi success flew in the face of norms found in the UN Charter (of which Iraq is a signatory) that forbid military aggression (a favorable world order interest).

The third question is, *"What threatens your interest? What happens, or may happen, if you do nothing?"* The minimal answer to that question was that Iraqi aggression would be rewarded with the prize of Kuwait. At worst, Iraq could gain control of most of the Persian Gulf's oil reserves. This assessment leads to the fourth question, *"How important are the interests?"* Given Western, including American, addiction to Persian Gulf oil, the answer was relatively easy: an interruption of petroleum from the Persian Gulf for any extended period of time would threaten the productive capacities of the First Tier. From this point flows the fifth and final question, *"How tolerable is failure to achieve your interests?"* Put in terms we have already introduced, would that failure be merely bothersome, serious, dangerous, or critical?

The reply to the fifth question was that failure to reverse the results of the invasion would be dangerous, a matter of vital interest that would affect the economic well-being of the First Tier and, thus, would be intolerable to the United States and its fellow developed states. Within this context, the array of instruments of national power, including military force, was available to deal with the concrete problem. Despite Bush administration denials in its aftermath, the response was precedential, sending a message that the First Tier would not tolerate instability and violence that interfered with the general prosperity of the First Tier. The occupation of Kuwait would have to be reversed.

The Inventory of Instruments

When the interests involved and the tolerability of various outcomes have been established, the next question is what can be done about the problem? In this case, what would cause Saddam Hussein to leave Kuwait?

The United States had available to it a range of options in terms of instruments of national power. A representative, but by no means exhaustive list, grouped by traditional categories, is presented in Table 7.4.

Several points should be made about this list. First, it is not inclusive of all possible acts that the United States or some other state might consider in any given situation. There are, for instance, a number of nuances within the economic list, and the list does not include highly unorthodox acts, such as Saddam Hussein's "environmental warfare" when he ignited fires in the Kuwaiti oil fields during the Persian Gulf War. Second, the list appears to be skewed toward military options because this is a book about national security. Were the subject matter diplomacy or international economy, those instruments would be more extensively elaborated.

Third, the arrangement of the list is in a kind of ascending order of activism and effort. It takes relatively less effort for the president of the United States to make a public show of concern at a news conference than it takes to mount a successful special operation (for instance, sending in a Delta Force or Ranger team to kidnap an opposition leader, as was disastrously attempted against Somali strongman General Mohammed Aidid) or to mobilize or employ military forces.

Fourth, this list also suggests—at least roughly—which instruments will be employed for what kinds of goals. The mildest actions will normally be the extent to which the country will act on peripheral, value questions such as, say, rigged elections somewhere in the Second Tier. As situations approach major interest proportions, then more vigorous ac-

TABLE 7.4   **Instruments of Power**

Diplomatic/Political
Publicity
Public show of concern
Behind-the-scenes diplomacy
Offer to mediate or reconcile
Building international consensus
Presentation of UN Security Council resolution
Rallying allies, coalition-building
Break in diplomatic relations

Economic
Offer of humanitarian or technical assistance
Change in economic or trade policy
Offer or withdrawal of economic assistance
Limited economic sanctions
Economic embargo

Politico/Military
Covert action
Military assistance
Military embargo
Special operations

Military
Show of force
Increased surveillance
Mobilization or alert status of forces
Evacuation of American nationals from scene
Movement of forces
Threats to use force
Formation of military coalition/alliance
Limited attacks
Injection of forces into scene
Invasion

tions, such as the various forms of economic sanctions or even covert actions such as placing propaganda stories in a country's press, might be employed. Even the more symbolic uses of military power, such as anchoring a carrier battle group off the coast (show of force) or increasing the number of overflights (surveillance) can attach to major interest threats. The more vigorous military actions are reserved, by definition, for matters of vital interest.

Fifth, progress through the options is normally sequential: one begins with the most modest, least strenuous applications, then gradually moves to more strenuous applications as the severity of the situation dictates. Along the way, some instruments may be bypassed or discarded as inappropriate, but policymakers will almost always be guided by the principle of least strenuous—and least traumatic—action.

Sixth, the instruments of power represent the operational effects of force reductions in the current American debate. When one cuts back on, for instance, military capability by reducing the defense budget, the bottom line is a decreased capability to do some things. When aircraft carrier battle groups (CVBGs) are reduced from fifteen to twelve (the Clinton plan), fewer will be available for shows of force; in a particular instance, the reduction might mean that a CVBG cannot be steamed somewhere in a timely manner, thereby eliminating use of that particular instrument. Given the array of possible situations and uses of military force, a prudent approach to reductions considers the effects on the instruments of national power.

The Persian Gulf War example shows the process in operation. Once the invasion became known, it was widely publicized, and the president condemned it and demanded that the Iraqis retreat. Behind-the-scenes diplomacy attempted to find ways to mediate the crisis, and the United States moved quickly to introduce United Nations resolutions that initially imposed economic sanctions and were gradually escalated to include the authorization to use force. A coalition of states was assembled along the Saudi-Kuwaiti border.

When nonmilitary instruments failed to dislodge the Iraqis, the American-led coalition gradually shifted to escalating military action. Carrier battle groups were dispatched to the Persian Gulf area along with a naval armada to enforce economic sanctions. The American embassy in Kuwait City was evacuated as American reserve forces were mobilized. An international arms embargo was put into effect, and the coalition forces moved into place for direct action. When these acts failed to cause Iraq to quit Kuwait before the January 15, 1991, deadline, the coalition air forces attacked in strength, accompanied by psychological operations ("psyops," a form of special operations), such as leaflets aimed at undermining the morale of Iraqi troops. Finally, the across-border invasion of Kuwait had to be undertaken.

The Persian Gulf War represented a particularly and unusually strenuous test of the instruments of national power. The reason, of course, was the intransigence of Saddam Hussein, manifested in the inability to bring him to heel with less than the application of all available instruments of power. Most situations are not so difficult. As one assesses the range of threats in the system and the number and capability of instruments necessary to deal with them, few situations will likely present themselves with the same vigor as the situation in Iraq, which was a kind of "worst case scenario" for the new order. As capabilities are diminished through cutbacks, however, some of the flexibility of action available to the United States in the form of multiple instruments of power will undoubtedly be diluted as well.

Assessing Instruments of Power

Situations in which power must be asserted are inherently difficult because they involve contests of will and ability wherein one or all of the contending parties are forced to accept solutions to problems they do not want. These situations are also difficult because, by definition, they occur in adversarial circumstances that contain at least some uncertainty on the part of the parties about motivations and more or less acceptable outcomes.

As a result of these considerations, the selection of appropriate instruments of national power in given situations will always be an inexact science and will routinely require trying multiple instruments until an effective one can be found that produces the desired outcome—if that is possible at all.

We can, however, suggest four criteria that help direct the selection of appropriate tools. The first is *controllability*, which refers to the ability to bring the instrument of power to bear on the situation. In the case of responses to the Bosnian tragedy, this was a particularly poignant criterion for the Clinton administration. Its preferred method to end Serbian and Croatian assaults on Bosnian Muslim enclaves was punitive air strikes coordinated through NATO, an action it periodically threatened and finally carried out on April 11, 1994. The Serbs, in particular, were unimpressed, recognizing the unwillingness of European NATO allies to become entangled in the Bosnian affair, especially those (such as Britain and France) with peacekeepers on the ground who might be victims of reprisal should such attacks occur.

The second problem is *relevance*, which refers to the applicability of the instrument to the problem at hand. Somalia comes to mind as an example. When American forces were first sent into Somalia, their mission—and accompanying capability—was to relieve starvation, which they did. But the problem, and the reason for most of the famine, ran deeper: the existence of virtual anarchy that had clan-based maurauding bands using food as a weapon to subdue their enemies. The solution was to create a legitimate government, a task for which the United States Marines and Army are not ideally suited.

The third criterion is *effectiveness:* will the instrument work? In the early 1970s, as discussed earlier, the United States government became upset by the rule of Ugandan leader Idi Amin Dada, who was engaging in a campaign of virtual genocide against members of rival tribes. The tool chosen to pressure Amin was economic sanctions, forbidding the import of Ugandan coffee into the United States. Unfortunately, Uganda was not heavily reliant on the coffee trade with the United States. Amin was subsequently forced from power by a more relevant instrument of power, an internal insurgency supported by the Tanzanian armed forces.

The fourth criterion is *credibility*, the perceived believability of the threat to employ the instruments of power. For the United States, the problem is largely the question of public support. Citing the Bosnian example again, much of the reason the Serbs ignored American entreaties and threats to "do something" to lift their sieges of Muslim cities was that they viewed the threats as hollow expressions that the United States was unwilling to back with actions. Their calculations, of course, proved correct for a long period of time.

CONCLUSIONS

The problems confronting American security policy are simultaneously less demanding and more problematical in the evolving international system. There are no security threats that resemble in severity and potential danger a clash between the American-led NATO and the Soviet-dominated Warsaw Pact over the heart of Europe. The problems are now more diffuse and their relevance more arguable.

The Cold War structured the security debate around highly tangible concerns that are now lacking. When the poles were peace or extermination, debates about how much involvement the United States should undertake in the world were academic; we were talking about nothing less than the physical survival of the country.

A world of tiers has changed all that. There is an ongoing security debate that can honestly and forthrightly question fundamental premises long held dear. Containment, the backbone of foreign and security policy for over forty years, is no longer relevant; the promise of containment has been realized, just as George Kennan suggested that it could be in his famous article, "The Sources of Soviet Conduct," in *Foreign Affairs* in 1947.

The new security agenda emphasizes choice, a theme that the Clinton administration began to advertise in late 1993. A speech in September 1993 by national security advisor Anthony Lake set out the agenda of choice in terms of four priorities of apparently descending importance. The first was strengthening the already tight bonds between the "core of major market democracies." The second imperative was to promote enlargement of the circle of market democracies in the former Second (socialist) World, "where we have the strongest security concerns and where we can make the greatest difference"—that is, the former Soviet Union and eastern Europe. The third priority was aimed at promoting stability elsewhere in the world by "minimizing the ability of states outside the circle of democracy and markets to threaten it." Finally, he added a concern with so-called "humanitarian interventions" in areas of great tragedy which, he admits, "increasingly may be driven by televised images." These basic themes remain as pillars in Clinton's second term policy of engagement and enlargement.

This list need not be taken as sacrosanct, nor its details as binding. Nonetheless, it does provide some definition to the debate and how it will drive the continuum that defines security, interests, and instruments of power in a world of tiers that it implicitly embraces.

Four priorities speak to concerns we have raised throughout this chapter and in the introductory chapter. The first admits the existence of the First Tier and says that we should strengthen the bonds between First Tier states. The effect of doing so is to reduce even further threats to the most important interests of the United States. The instruments of power necessary to do so are principally diplomatic/political and economic, and they entail American leadership. To the extent that military instruments are involved, it concerns the important question of where and how First Tier states will be employed in Second Tier conflicts.

The second priority concerns the old source of security concerns, the formerly communist world. The Soviet Union and its former allies have ceased to be an active threat, and it is in the interest of America—and other Western nations—to reinforce the process of "normalizing" those societies—that is, making them like us. One can debate the extent to which the United States and its fellow First Tier states can promote market democracy in countries that lack either tradition. The implications for security policy are clear: American security is best served by fostering the embrace of our system by our former enemies. Aiding the transformation is a matter of vital interest, and the instruments of power applicable to the task are primarily political and economic. If one needs precedent or rationale for the endeavor, the transformation of Germany and Japan at the end of World War II can be cited.

The third and fourth priorities relate directly to First Tier and, hence, American relationships with the Second Tier states in traditional national security terms. The third priority relates to "rogue" states in the order: Second Tier states whose behavior threatens their regions or, in a few cases, where nuclear, biological, or chemical (NBC) weapons and ballistic missiles are present, offer greater systemic problems. The fourth priority concerns the development of a coherent strategy to guide First Tier involvement in normally internal conflicts—often, ethno-religious in origin in so-called "failed states"—in the Second Tier.

These latter priorities go a long way toward defining the military dimension of contemporary American national security policy. They implicitly recognize the interest-threat mismatch and the need to resolve it. Maximum tranquillity in the areas outside the acknowledged First Tier of nations is clearly identified as a prime, and occasionally vital, interest for which military force will sometimes be necessary.

With security and interests in the process of definition, the policy process must now move to the identification of instruments of national power that can meet the criteria of applicability in dealing with the problems identified. Where existing instruments are inapplicable and cannot be linked to ongoing national security challenges, they will become candidates for the budgeter's axe. Where priorities are established but clearly effective instruments are unavailable, appropriate instruments will have to be fashioned.

The process of readjustment triggered by the post–Cold War debate over national security and America's place in the new order will not be easy. A security establishment developed and rationalized for one set of concerns will be asked to redefine itself in terms of new definitions of interest that have quite unfamiliar parameters and implications. Moreover, the new problems bear little operational or conceptual resemblance to Cold War constructs. Preparing for war in Europe, in a word, does little to prepare for intervening in Somalia. Defining these new problems will be the task of Chapters 8 and 9.

Suggested Reading

Brodie, Bernard. *War and Politics*. New York: Macmillan 1973.

Burton, Daniel F., Victor Gotbaum, and Felix Rohatyn (eds.). *Vision for the 1990s: U.S. Strategy and the Global Economy*. Cambridge, Mass.: Ballinger, 1989.

Harris, Owen. "The Collapse of 'the West,'" *Foreign Affairs* 72, 4 (September/October 1993):41–53.

Luck, Edward C. "Making Peace," *Foreign Policy* 89 (Winter 1992/93):137–155.

Luttwak, Edward N. *Strategy: The Logic of War and Peace*. Cambridge, Mass.: Belknap, 1987.

A National Security Strategy of Engagement and Enlargement. Washington, DC: The White House, February 1996.

Nuechterlein, Donald E. *America Recommitted: United States National Interests in a Restructured World*. Lexington, Ky.: University of Kentucky Press, 1991.

Pfaff, William. "Invitation to War," *Foreign Affairs* 72, 3 (Summer 1993):97–109.

Rogov, Sergei. "International Security and the Collapse of the Soviet Union," *Washington Quarterly* 15, 2 (Spring 1992):16–28.

Smith, W. Y. "U.S. National Security after the Cold War," *Washington Quarterly* 15, 4 (Autumn 1992):21–34.

Ziemke, Caroline F. "Rethinking the 'Mistakes' of the Past: History's Message to the Clinton Defense Department," *Washington Quarterly* 16, 2 (Spring 1993):47–60.

Chapter 8

Ongoing Challenges in the Second Tier

In his September 27, 1993, address to the United Nations, President Bill Clinton laid out his vision of foreign and security policy for the future. He sounded two broad themes about what most interested the United States. The first had to do with "widening the circle" and strengthening the bonds between the market democracies of the First Tier. Making reference to the general tranquillity among First Tier states, he offered a welcoming hand to states in regions such as Latin America and the successor states of the Soviet Union to join the greater prosperity—the basis for the national security strategy of engagement and enlargement.

The second theme addressed the violence and instability of the Second Tier. Noting that the end of the Cold War had lifted the veil from a large cauldron of ancient, yet suppressed, animosities, Clinton argued that it was in the best security interests of the United States and the international system at large to see an end to this cycle of violence and a gradual integration of the Second Tier into the First.

The problems Clinton discussed in that speech have become familiar themes of national security analysis in the new international order, and they are topics we will address in this chapter. We begin with the most stunning and unsettling phenomenon of the post–Cold War world, the widespread outbreak of internal violence that threatens groups and states from Africa to the Caucasus region of the former Soviet Union, and beyond (a phenomenon that will be described as new internal war). The most prominent early examples of these conflicts were in Bosnia, Somalia, Rwanda, and Liberia, where systemic reaction has been mixed, at best. At least some of the reason for this problem has to do with the removal of old constraints imposed during the Cold War and the failure to date to replace those constraints with new and enforceable rules of behavior.

The discussion will then move to so-called regional conflicts, wars and potential conflicts between longtime enemies whose behavior is no longer influenced as it once was by superpower rivalry and assistance. Although the historical rivalry between Israel and its neighbors—for a long time, the most prominent regional conflict—appears to be on the bumpy road to resolution, other conflicts remain in south and southeast Asia, the Persian Gulf, and Africa. These situations have been exacerbated by the proliferation of deadly weapons, notably nuclear, biological, and chemical (NBC) munitions and ballistic missiles—all capabilities that President Clinton has publicly sought to halt and outlaw.

It is worth repeating that most of these problems are not new to the places where they occur. Animosities between groups within states have long existed, and it has only been the removal of authoritarian constraints within states and the removal of superpower restraints on former clients that has accompanied the end of the Cold War that has allowed their reassertion. Indeed, it is one of the ironies of the new order that freedom and hatred have so often coincided, and they threaten to continue to do so. Regional conflicts, although generally without missiles and NBC weapons, have also been with us for some time. The Cold War competition may have dampened these conflicts because the superpowers sought to avoid any escalation that might have drawn *them* into direct confrontation, but the underlying animosities were present to fuel the superpower competition. They are now simply freer to express them.

It should also be noted at the outset that these problems were largely overshadowed by the Cold War. The result was that little energy was exerted to understanding and solving them. Yugoslavia's disintegration, for instance, was widely predicted for a decade or more before it happened; creating a peaceful solution was simply not high enough on the international agenda to command compelling attention. Maybe a solution was not possible. In any case, the upshot is that the system, including the major players such as the United States, has more questions than answers about who, how, and what can be done in the volatile Second Tier.

THE SYSTEMIC TRAGEDY OF NEW INTERNAL WAR

Possibly the least-well-anticipated change, in an international system where change has been rapid and poorly predicted generally, is in the spate of internal violence within states of the old Second and Third Worlds. During the Cold War, internal violence in the form of civil wars was generally ideological, with at least nominally communist and anticommunist factions competing as insurgents/government. These contests for political power normally had a Cold War aspect, with the United States generally supporting a beleaguered government and the Soviet Union, the insurgents. (Ronald Reagan, of course, reversed that association by supporting revolutionary groups in Afghanistan and Nicaragua under a policy known as the Reagan Doctrine.)

These "traditional" Cold War-related forms of internal violence have, to a large extent, disappeared for the time being. The end of East-West rivalry means there is not much monetary or military backing for traditional insurgencies, and an ongoing insurgency such as the *Sendero Luminoso* (Shining Path) in Peru, which originally was a classic communist movement, has devolved into little more than a criminal insurgency with the sole purpose of protecting the drug traffickers from Peruvian authorities. About the only outside source of support for internal conflicts anywhere may come from Islamic fundamentalists in Asia and Africa on behalf of Islamic movements (a particular problem in former Soviet central Asian republics and northern Africa). Only in a few isolated places, such as Angola, are there ongoing insurgencies of the traditional variety, and a peaceful solution to that tragic conflict seems inevitable. Laurent Kabila's revolution in Zaire is the closest internal war to the old mold of insurgency.

The end of communist rule in eastern Europe and the Soviet Union and the disintegration of the Soviet Union itself were initially greeted with great optimism and hope for a new wave of democratization and self-determination throughout the international system. That optimism was short-lived, as the cause of self-determination quickly showed an uglier side in the form of ethnic violence that threatens to tear apart fragile, "failed" states.

This phenomenon is widespread and growing. Political freedom in parts of eastern Europe and many of the successor states of the Soviet Union has not translated into political democracy. In many places, the old communist leaders have simply disavowed their communist roots, but remain in power. More to the point, freedom of expression has often revealed the darker side of self-determination: an exclusionary, primordial, and narrow sense of nationalism that bares deep hatreds and animosities that most had presumed had disappeared years—even generations—ago. Self-determination allows the creation of fractured political entities where former suppressed minorities take on the role of suppressing majorities.

Ethnic violence and its companion, ethnic "cleansing," are such a different phenomenon in contemporary times (although certainly not in history) that we have trouble describing their dynamics. To this point, it has been confined to places such as the former Soviet Union, Bosnia, and Rwanda, where a formerly authoritarian rule has collapsed and not been replaced by a new and stable political system. Shorn of points of political reference, peoples have reverted to old means of identification, especially ethnicity (presumed or real) and religion. Where elements of the population are divided by one or both of these factors, animosities once thought extinguished can experience spontaneous combustion and explode. It is hard to recall, for instance, that Sarajevo prided itself as a model of intercommunal tolerance and progress only a few years ago.

Ethnic conflict is only part of the new pattern. In a number of states, principally in Africa, the phenomenon of new internal war has taken on a newer and uglier face. Manifested most publicly in Rwanda, it is war fought for no discernible political purpose but with a special level of viciousness. The sight of marauding bands of teenagers terrorizing the population in Somalia gave us a glimpse of this cruel, non-Clausewitzian violence. Liberia, Sierre Leone, and other states in Africa have given us a foretaste of this kind of war, fought not for lofty political ideals but for criminal gain or for no reason at all; the so-called narco-insurgencies of South America are variants on the theme.

Unfortunately, this combination of ingredients can be found in large parts of the Second Tier. In Africa, ethnicity is usually defined tribally, and tribes are often divided between Christianity, Islam, and more native animistic forms of religion. In the swath from central Asia extending west to the Balkans, ethnicity blends with religious differences in those places where Islam and Christianity collide.

The world's two most populous states are not immune from this potential. India hosts multiple religious groups (Christians, Muslims, Buddhists, and Hindus) and a broad array of ethnic nationalities. Fragile democracy may or may not be capable of keeping India intact or of containing violent change to India itself. To India's north, the rulers of China do not confront major ethnic differences but justify continuing authoritarian rule on the ground that if it granted freedom to everyone, the country could be torn apart worse than the former Soviet Union. Authoritarianism thus can become the bulwark of national integrity.

When this primordial nationalism or worse is invoked, the results become very difficult to contain. Like most internal wars, they become especially brutal, as amateur, largely undisciplined civilians take up arms to defend themselves against equally untrained and undisciplined neighbors. These wars become very personal, and they generate further passions that make peaceful resolution and reconciliation even more difficult.

Moreover, it is also not at all clear how to deter these wars from occurring or how to end them, including how to use outside force to stop the fighting and start the process of rebuilding. The traditional literature (see, for instance, my *Distant Thunder*) suggests that threats from outsiders rarely deter internal groups; the existence of a standing United Nations force, as some have suggested, would be of dubious deterrent value. Ending the fighting is usually made difficult by the fact the side that is succeeding does not want a cease-fire until it has achieved all of its goals. Likewise, the side that is losing may wish to continue fighting in the hope of reversing its fortunes. Moreover, the history of outside intervention to create or impose a solution—an exercise in counterinsurgency—has a sufficiently dismal record as not to encourage future endeavors. At the bottom line, these are political problems that can be solved only by the parties themselves.

The new internal wars where there are no political objectives add to the difficulty of knowing what to do. Most of our understanding of counterinsurgent and outside intervention is based on confronting traditional insurgencies: a government besieged by an insurgent force whose overt purpose is to seize power and rule. In a place like Liberia, there was neither a real government nor any intent on the part of the insurgents to gain or exercise power. It is questionable whether approaches designed for dealing with traditional insurgencies are relevant in these cases.

Why do we as Americans worry about these wars that rage in distant places where traditional American national interests are hardly involved? More specifically, where and why would the United States consider injecting American armed forces into harm's way in these kinds of contests? This latter concern is especially poignant for a country that remembers its experience in Vietnam and whose professional military suspect (not without justification) that most of these potential involvements have distinctly Vietnam-like characteristics.

There is no current consensus on these questions, either in a generalized way or in specific instances. President Clinton, in his UN speech, did suggest at least some of the parameters of the policy area that includes some of the criteria necessary to frame answers.

A first concern is the sheer *volume* of potential ethnic violence. In his talk to the United Nations, the president cited the existence of seventeen ongoing United Nations peacekeeping missions involving 80,000 troops on four continents, in comparison with thirteen missions (some ongoing) for the entire Cold War period. And that total does not include forces that might be sent to quell ethnic cleansing anywhere in the former Soviet Union or in Sudan or elsewhere in Africa, where ethnic hatreds express themselves in blood. Secretary-General Boutros-Ghali predicted that by the end of the century, the current 188 members of the United Nations could rise to 400, as states dissolve. While that prediction is certainly hyperbolic, it remains likely that most of the increases will not occur as peacefully as the bifurcation of Czechoslovakia into Slovakia and the Czech Republic. Between thirty-five and forty of these wars are ongoing at any point in contemporary time, mostly in the poorest and, in American eyes, most obscure places in the world.

A second concern, and one of particular concern to President Clinton, is that *atomization runs counter to trends in the international economy.* The economy is becoming global, with activity leapfrogging national boundaries and creating demands for larger economic areas such as that found in the European Union, the North American Free Trade Area (the basis for the proposed Free Trade Area of the Americas), and the Asia-Pacific Economic Cooperation. Aggregating existing political units creates parallel phenomena in the economic and political realms, whereas atomization reverses this trend, making it more difficult for Second Tier states to participate in the global economy and move toward membership in the "circle of market democracies" that the President extols. To become players on the economic stage, Second Tier states have to make themselves attractive both as markets and producers. What private firm would, in the foreseeable future, consider developing markets or setting up manufacturing enterprises in the remains of states such as Liberia and Somalia?

In a number of places, anarchy is atomization's handmaid, with the same effect. It is striking how much of the ethnic and nonpolitical violence is occurring outside the general emerging prosperity of the EU, NAFTA/FTAA, and APEC (arguably the basis of the globalizing economy). The spate of uncontrolled, self-destructive violence in the poorest parts of the world simply reinforces their unattractiveness as candidates for the greater prosperity that might contribute to their stabilization.

A third aspect of the problem is that it represents an *assault on the sovereignty that underlies the system's operation*. The Westphalian principle of state sovereignty collides with the Wilsonian conception of self-determination. The Westphalian standard proclaims the state's right to existence as the central systemic tenet—an idea in place for almost 350 years. Wilsonian self-determination suggests a contrary "right" of groups of people to redraw political maps so that they may live in states of their choosing.

This dispute has both philosophical and practical aspects. At the philosophical level, the two concepts confront one another on the issue of the right to secede. Traditional international law, grounded in Westphalian principles based on the legal philosophy of positivism, does not recognize the right of secession implicit in the right to self-determination. If the right to secede (based in natural law philosophy) is accepted in law, then under what circumstances can states resist and in which cases must they accept the breaking away of parts of national territory? This controversy affects international legal, national security, and human rights debates.

The practical side of the secession issue is the imperfection of the world's map along ethno-religious, national lines. The extreme outcome of self-determination would be a system in which all ethnic groups live in states that include all members of the nation and in which no nationals from other states reside, thereby perfectly aligning nation and state. There are no such states in the world today. Creating such a map, if possible, would atomize the world into literally thousands of political entities, in which it is hard to imagine historical animosities among national groups being lessened by noncontact. Such a system might reduce internal violence and war; it would almost certainly increase wars between states.

Moreover, many believe that the alignment of nation and state would be undesirable on other grounds. Such an alignment might be heavily antidemocratic, if one accepts the proposition that democracy breeds best in an atmosphere of understanding and tolerance of those different from you. Economically, such a system would be chaotic and would run counter to the internationalization of economic activity wherein firms are becoming much more multinational on all grounds (management, work force, and ownership).

A fourth problem of dealing with the new internal violence has to do with *citizen—even elite—understanding*. Most of the spate of violence is occurring in isolated parts of the Second Tier about which most Americans, including their leaders, have little knowledge. Area expertise within the government generally, but especially within the military, which may be asked to intervene, is scanty and diffuse. Moreover, where there are pockets of expertise (as among the desk officers in the State Department), it is often not shared with other agencies. When events flare and there appears to be a need to cooperate and pool information to make recommendations, the system is often unwieldy.

The area in the southern successor republics of the former Soviet Union offers a particularly vivid example of the absence of information among elites and the general public. In late 1993, fighting was occurring actively in three republics. In Georgia, the government of former Soviet Foreign Minister Eduard Shevardnadze was under siege by Abkhazian separatists seeking to secede and form a separate state of Abkhazia. In Azerbaijan and Armenia, fighting raged over Nagorno-Karabakh and Nakhichevan. More recently, the Republic of Tajikistan has been beset by Islamic fundamentalist violence of a quality, if not level of publicity, similar to the violence in Algeria. All three continue to flare from time to time. How many Americans had heard of Chechnya before its attempted secession hit the airwaves?

To most Americans, these were strange-sounding places that might as well be on the moon. In large part, the lack of general understanding was the result of concentrating over the years on the part of the Soviet Union that caused the greatest threat: the part centered in Moscow. Even among former Soviet experts, it is difficult to find many Tajikistan experts. Moreover, there are very few Americans who trace their heritage to these areas, with the exception of Armenia, and who, thus, have an interest in raising the consciousness of the American public.

Lack of general knowledge contributes to the fifth and sixth problems. Fifth is the *difficulty of selling the American public on the importance of these conflicts.* Whether Abkhazia remains a part of Georgia or achieves independence obviously has great importance to the contestants, may have important precedential value in the region, and, if fracturing occurs, may compromise the economic transition in that small part of the world. In turn, the outcomes may make the international relations of the region more or less difficult in the future, thereby creating at least an abstract reason for the United States to involve itself.

But all that means little—if anything—to average Americans who might be asked to support whatever actions seem appropriate in a systemic view. Why should the United States participate in or underwrite a UN peacekeeping mission to Georgia or Azerbaijan? What American interests are served if we do? Why not let the people directly involved (including the Russians) solve their own problems? (See the Case in Point box "Azerbaijan, Chechnya, and U.S. Security.")

The inability to rally public support is complicated by a sixth factor: *the inability to propose affordable solutions to these kinds of problems.* Internal

---

CASE IN POINT
_____

Azerbaijan, Chechnya, and U.S. Security

Are the outcomes of the war between Azerbaijan and Armenia and the war within Chechnya of consequence to the United States or the American citizenry? Although most Americans are unaware of it, the answer in both cases is a clear and compelling "Yes."

The reason is oil. The world's second largest oil reserves are found under the Caspian Sea in territories controlled by Azerbaijan, and negotiations on exploration and exploitation rights are currently being conducted between the Azeri government and the major oil companies. Once oil and natural gas begin flowing from these fields, U.S. and other First Tier reliance on Persian Gulf oil may be greatly diminished (depending on the actual size of the fields and the accessibility of the energy), conceivably to the point of being able to avoid involvement in a future Persian Gulf war. Less dependence on the Persian Gulf definitely represents a U.S. interest.

The connection to the wars comes from the potential location of the pipelines to carry the oil and gas to market. There are two viable options (a third, piping it southward through Iran to the Persian Gulf, would obviously subvert the purpose of lowering Persian Gulf dependency). One is to build pipelines from Azerbaijan across Turkey to the Mediterranean Sea; the other is to traverse Russia to the Baltic Sea. Both Turkey and Russia are highly interested in the transit fees that would be involved.

Wars affect both routes. As long as the ongoing violence—or its plausible recurrence—between Azerbaijan and Armenia continues, both routes are vulnerable to Armenian subversion (as the one across Turkey could be threatened by Turkish Kurdish separatists). The Russian route, which is the more likely choice on geopolitical grounds (it would provide a great boost to the Russian economy), goes directly across Chechnya.

---

war is difficult enough to solve through the intermediation of outsiders, whose presence will be resented by some or all of the contestants (certainly those whose success is likely to be compromised). Moreover, these are generally total wars, in the sense that their goal is to gain total control of government; one side wins and the other side loses.

These situations are rarely settled by negotiation and intermediation unless one or both of two conditions occur: the physical exhaustion of one or both, or the loss of sustaining assistance to one or both. Those conditions occurred in El Salvador in 1992, but only after ten years of grueling, brutal fighting, replete with atrocities on both sides, and the withdrawal of assistance by Cuba (which had lost assistance from the crumbling Soviet Union). In the absence of such conditions, it is difficult—often impossible—to force the contestants to stop fighting.

The inability to provide solutions may have a deeper base: there may simply be no peaceful outcomes that are acceptable to all parties. It is hard to find, for instance, a solution to Nagorno-Karabakh that simultaneously preserves Azerbaijani sovereignty over the enclave and provides an adequate amount of perceived security for the Armenians who live there. Armenia has acted to annex the territory separating Armenia proper and Nagorno-Karabakh, thereby guaranteeing transit and defense as well as complicating the oil problem. The loss of formerly Azeri territory has created a flood of Muslim refugees fleeing the Armenian army. Where is the basis for compromise?

Ethnic hatreds further poison and corrode these disputes, hardening positions that might otherwise be negotiable. Moreover, the logic of ethnic hatred is separation and partition, but that is also fraught with difficulties. As noted, partition simply aggravates the tendency toward politically atomizing a system that is fusing economically. In addition, habitation patterns seldom conform to easy partition. Due to planned or unplanned migrations, ethnic groups have intermixed, and existing boundaries are often arbitrary. (Both phenomena were conscious Stalinist policies.) The result is inability to separate groups in a way that both secures their futures and satisfies their material and psychological needs. Forced population migration does not facilitate peace and the healing of wounds.

The problem of expense is made worse when these wars take place in extremely poor places that require the massive infusion of outside public or private capital, which is generally unavailable. The ill-fated Brown mission to encourage private investment in Bosnia represented an attempt to address this problem in a war-torn country that is, compared to other countries where new internal wars tend to occur, fairly affluent. What are the prospects of attracting direct foreign investment in post-war Liberia?

The seventh factor is the *frustration of having to view ethnic violence without being able to solve it.* Thanks to the technology of global television, we are made intimately aware of death, suffering, and atrocity wherever the cameras of CNN, the British-based Independent Television Network (ITN), and others record man's inhumanity to his fellow man. ITN pictures of so-called detention camps hastened our awareness of suffering in Bosnia; CNN pictures of starving Somalis made us aware of that country's tragic fate.

These television images impel us to action that might not take place in their absence. The problem is that television images are fleeting (the average televised news story is only a minute or two long) and may be misleading. They may impel us to do something without first gaining an in-depth understanding of the entire situation that might encourage different, more cautious approaches.

It may be that we are becoming conditioned to worldwide violence by the sheer repetitiveness of worldwide situations. Images of starving Kurds in the Turkish mountains activated American action, but the siege of Sarajevo and other Muslim towns in Bosnia and Herzegovina created cries for help that were mostly unanswered. The image of suffering overwhelmed the policy process in one case but not in the other.

The impulse to help has faded. The fighting in Georgia and Armenia have been given wide publicity on global television, but there are no cries for American assistance there. Why not? Is it because misery and suffering in marginal places has become so commonplace that we are conditioned by it and accept it? Are we effectively desensitized to the appearance of remote suffering? We ignored the carnage in Rwanda and Chechnya. What will happen if the widespread atrocities in Sudan and Angola catch the camera's eye? Will the sheer extent of suffering leave us jaded? These are interesting questions that will have a good deal to do with likely American responses in the future, but the answers are not readily available now.

American—and, indeed, global—policy is in limbo with regard to this growing phenomenon. The virtual euphoria over using the United Nations as the institution of choice has given way to much more caution. In his September 1993 UN speech, Clinton noted the need to be selective in choosing where to become involved and where not. He paraphrased Anthony Lake's four rules for intervention: "Is there a real threat to international peace? Does the proposed mission have clear objectives? Can an exit point be identified for those who are asked to participate? How much will the mission cost?"

Part of the problem with involvement has been conceptual. Whether American or United Nations involvement can be successful depends on the degree to which the parties desire an end to hostilities. Where they do, traditional United Nations *peacekeeping* missions may be appropriate and effective. Where the situation is ongoing war, where one or all sides prefer its continuation to peace, then the much more difficult—and possibly futile—mission of *peace enforcement* or *peace imposition* (discussed in detail in Chapter 10) may have to be invoked if action is undertaken at all.

The other part of the problem is experiential. Since the end of the Cold War, the system has witnessed and become involved in two great internal conflicts with ethnic implications, in Bosnia and Somalia. Each presented a different challenge, and each was handled differently. They share the common thread of being misperceived, of being handled poorly because of that misperception, and of sending a strong cautionary message for further involvement by the international community. The direct lesson for the United States arose primarily in Somalia, where direct American intervention occurred; our intrusion into Bosnia was decidedly more cautious until the peace process produced a ceasefire that could be enforced.

BOSNIA AND SOMALIA: WHAT'S A WORLD TO DO?

On the surface, the crises in Bosnia and Herzegovina (hereafter referred to as Bosnia for shorthand purposes) and in Somalia would appear very distinct. The countries in which they occurred are separated by continent, by historical experience, by culture, and in a host of other ways. Structurally, their problems were distinct: the breakup of the Yugoslav state and starvation-produced anarchy in Somalia. Moreover, the initial responses were very different: dithering that contributed visibly to the conflict in Bosnia, in contrast to apparently swift and decisive action to stem the starving in Somalia. Ethnicity was a major factor in Bosnia but not in Somalia, where inter-clan violence pretensively aimed at seizing power provided the rationale.

Despite these differences, there is much in common between the events and the way the international system, including the United States, reacted to them that both help define the problem of internal conflict and the likely pattern of responses. The general points of similarity include the evolution of each crisis, the fact that each operated at two levels of complexity, the inappropriateness of outside reaction, the eventual ingratitude of those we attempted to assist, their contribution at first to euphoria and then to skepticism about the UN, and the American response to each.

In terms of *evolution*, each crisis followed a similar course. Each crisis was predictable but was ignored until it reached fever proportions. The initial efforts of outsiders to deal with each problem were botched and probably contributed to the lingering problem. In each case, attention was paid at the wrong time.

The breakup of Yugoslavia had been predicted since the 1970s, when Yugoslav President Josip Broz Tito's mortality was recognized. When he died in 1980 and a committee arrangement whereby the Yugoslav presidency would rotate among the republics came into full force, anarchy was predicted. When the fragile state began to disintegrate in 1991 and fractured irreparably in 1992, the pundits seemed almost relieved.

That the crisis should focus on Bosnia was also entirely predictable, since it was the most integrated (by design) of the republics in terms of Serb, Croat, and Muslim proportions of the population. Yet, when Croatian independence—on the heels of a similar declaration by Slovenia and both rapidly recognized by Germany—was followed by a declaration of a sovereign Bosnia by its Muslim plurality, everyone seemed surprised at the fury. The UN reacted inappropriately at this point in time, dispatching a lightly armed, defensive peacekeeping force, UN-PROFOR (UN Protection Force) to patrol a fragile truce between Croatia and Serbia when peace was not going to hold.

Somalia was similar. Somali history is a patchwork of chaos when there is no single authoritarian ruler who can unite enough of the fifteen clans to maintain order. In 1991 Siad Barre, the Somali leader, was forced to flee after his soldiers opened fire on the crowd at a soccer match in Mogadishu, where some people booed the President's name. That chaos would ensue as the clans maneuvered for position was likewise predictable. When efforts at mediation broke down in confusion during the summer of 1992, the warlords began to use scarce food supplies to subdue their rivals. Against a backdrop of years of drought, the result was devastating.

The response in Somalia, led by the United States, demonstrated a resolution sadly missing in Bosnia. American troops stormed ashore (including some sheepish American SEALs who landed at night on the beaches to be greeted by reporters with spotlights), restored a semblance of order, and began to make sure that food got through. The Americans apparently failed to recognize that their actions worked to the political detriment of Somali factions. When the latter—most notably, Mohammed Aidid—failed to gain American backing, they came out in opposition to the Americans and their mission.

This leads to the second point of similarity: *both crises were two-level problems, where responding to the first level failed to address the second level.* One can think of each crisis as displaying this characteristic: at one level was a public display of suffering and anguish that gripped the world outside and appeared to demand redress. The problem in each case was that what we saw—Somalis starving, gaunt detainees in Bosnia—was a symptom of a deeper underlying cause. Global reaction was to "do something" about the symptom: feed Somalia, condemn Serb atrocity.

The difficulty is that there were underlying, much more difficult problems that the actions invoked by the "do something syndrome" did not and could not solve. Starvation was the symptom in Somalia; the underlying cause was the anarchy of Somali clan politics. It was only in late September 1993 that the American government acknowledged the real problem as state-building (which the Marines sent to feed starving Somalis were poorly equipped to undertake). In Bosnia, the underlying problem was how to find a basis for partition that was minimally acceptable to all parties. As suggested in the preceding section, the nature of habitation patterns and the like make such a solution difficult and could reignite the conflict in the future.

The third problem was *inappropriate physical responses* to the situation. In the case of Somalia, the handiest American forces were sent into the country to protect supply lines and to distribute food. The Marines initially appeared to be doing a fine job, but the seeds of problems were sown. On the one hand, the rules of engagement (ROEs) under which the forces labored suggested that this was a peacekeeping situation, when it was not. There was a lull in the fighting while the internal factions sized up the Americans; that is not the same thing as a peace to be kept. Marines are elite assault troops, not military police, but the functions assigned them were quasi-policing functions. When the Marines were not replaced by military police—or something similar—soon after landing, the first deadly incidents between the Americans and the Somalis became inevitable.

The situation was even worse in Bosnia. As noted, a UN peacekeeping force was inserted into a war zone during a temporary lull in the fighting. When UNPROFOR wandered into Sarajevo in search of a pleasant headquarters and found themselves in the midst of a military siege, the mismatch between the peacekeepers and their situation was nearly complete. By contrast, the Implementation Force (IFOR) dispatched in December 1995 to help implement the Dayton accords arrived configured as a heavy war-fighting force in what was pretensively a peace zone.

These inappropriate responses led to a fourth common thread: *the eventual ingratitude of the beleaguered toward those dispatched to assist them.* Why is this the case? In Bosnia, no one was particularly happy with the role played by the UNPROFOR peacekeepers. Bosnian Muslims (who now refer to themselves as Bosniacs) have been dismayed at the lack of any real protection from their Croatian and Serbian attackers and by the apparent willingness of the UN forces to acquiesce to Serb demands, especially in such matters as blocking the shipment of food and medicine to besieged towns. The Serbs and Croatians, for their part, treated UNPROFOR as little more than an annoyance—a "speed bump" in their campaigns to gobble up Bosnian territory. A more robust IFOR has not been subject to these kinds of criticisms; the more common concern has been about the potential resumption of the fighting after their departure.

Successful peacekeeping operations have several characteristics that are discussed more thoroughly in Chapter 10, but two stand out. One is neutrality: the peacekeeper is respected as long, and only as long, as he remains neutral. UNPROFOR attempted to be neutral; the structure of the situation did not allow them to remain so. The second characteristic that permits neutrality is the existence of a peace that both or all sides desire and that they view the peacekeepers as helping to maintain.

Such was clearly not the case in Bosnia. Bosnia was a war zone; if the UN had a role, it was to *create* peace. Peace*keepers*, in other words, were sent into a peace*making* (what the U.S. government calls, euphemistically, *peace enforcement*) situation. They could have had the purest motives in the world, but the simple fact remained that any efforts they made to create peace had to come at the expense of those who were winning and preferred to continue the war. UNPROFOR's *effect*, despite its *intentions*, could not be neutral. On the one hand, the Muslims were resentful that the UN did not protect them, even though to do so would have been partisan in Serb and Croat eyes. On the other hand, to the extent that UN action relieved Muslim suffering in the besieged towns, they were considered by Serbs to be pro-Muslim. The overwhelming force that IFOR presented made resistance impossible. That does not mean that those disadvantaged by the agreement they enforced (the Serb former residents of Sarajevo suburbs turned over to Bosnian control, for instance) were not resentful.

As a parallel in Somalia, there is no doubt in the public record that the United States launched Operation Restore Hope (renamed Maintain Hope after the initial American withdrawal in the Spring of 1993) for purely humanitarian, nonpartisan reasons: we went in to save lives, and nothing more. Our motives were pure, but the effects of our actions were not. Since food and starvation were weapons in the internal power struggle in the country, the impact of getting food indirectly aided some clans at the expense of others. There is little evidence those in charge of the relief effort realized that effect, but it was there.

In the early months of Operation Restore Hope, the various clan leaders, notably Mohammed Farah Aidid, courted American favor in the hopes of furthering their own political prospects. When the Americans hewed assiduously to a neutral position and consciously avoided actions disadvantaging any side, the clan leaders—especially Aidid—came to see the American presence as an opportunity. When they returned as part of the UNISOM (United Nations in Somalia) II mission and began disarming his militia members, he came to see the United States as an intrusion blocking his successful rise to power. At that point, Aidid and the others wanted the Americans—and the UN—out. The booby traps and gunfire began; when American forces fired back in self-defense, with inevitable civilian casualties, larger portions of the population turned on the Americans. The fighting culminated in the ambush of American Rangers attempting to capture Aidid, in which eighteen U.S. personnel perished.

Americans were shocked and mortified at this show of ingratitude in a way reminiscent of the reactions of soldiers returning from Vietnam. We had, after all, saved their country from starvation, and this was the thanks we got for our efforts.

Unfortunately, the reaction in Somalia was *absolutely predictable in advance*. Somalia was Vietnam in the sense that outside intrusion interfered with local politics and, eventually, was resented by the "ingrates." Anyone conversant with the dynamics of counterinsurgency understands this problem; external forces cannot solve internal political problems. The more they get in the way, the more they are resented. When that resentment turns violent and is reciprocated, the noble instincts that impelled initial action begin to melt into disillusionment. Both cases mirror a similar lesson: neutrality of intention is not the same thing as neutrality in effect on the situation.

This process leads to the fifth phenomenon surrounding these two cases: *an initial euphoria, largely inspired by the UN, that degenerates into skepticism*. This is more obvious in the Somali than the Bosnian case. In Bosnia, the dispatch of UNPROFOR was so clearly inappropriate and inadequate to the actual situation that hardly any period of positive impact resulted from the presence of the peacekeepers. In the debate leading up to their authorization, of course, the idea of UNPROFOR was extolled as yet another bit of evidence of the expanding role of the world organization in shaping the peace in the new order. Conditioned by the UNPRO-

FOR failure and perceptions of the intractability of the situation, most Americans initially opposed the IFOR deployment.

A much clearer euphoria surrounded the arrival of the Americans, deputized to do the UN's initial work, in Mogadishu and elsewhere in Somalia. The American forces, life-sustaining food in hand, were initially greeted as liberating heroes. Television screens were filled with acts of friendship and altruism as the Marines handed out candy bars and taught Christmas carols to obviously grateful Somali children—most of whom, of course, were Muslims.

Then the operations went sour. In Bosnia, the mismatch between UN mission and the means to implement it meant that the UN's effort never had a chance from the beginning; only war exhaustion or victory could solve the problem. In Somalia, the first withdrawal of the Americans and their replacement with other UN peacekeepers started the resentment. Partly, the contending Somali factions preferred dealing with the Americans rather than the UN. Many were suspicious of Boutros-Ghali from their dealings with him when he was Egyptian foreign minister; others did not trust the Italians, Pakistanis, and others who replaced the Americans.

If 1992 was the year of the United Nations, 1993 became the year of disillusionment with its expanding role, when the President of the United States told the world body it had to learn how to say no to involving itself in some Second Tier conflicts before the United States would say yes in support. The years 1994 and 1995 and beyond have seen further attempts at a dialectical process to reconcile euphoria and skepticism into realism.

These common characteristics of the two situations are important in their own right, but they are also predictive of likely characteristics of proposed interventions in Second Tier conflicts in the future. Bosnia and Somalia are not the last cases of poorly anticipated and misunderstood situations where initial reactions make matters worse. The temptation to react to horrifying atrocities that are symptoms of deeper, more intractable political dilemmas will recur, and it does not defy the imagination to see inappropriate, inadequate responses. It is important to understand that purity of motives will not prevent resentment from growing among those we go to help; the structure of the situations virtually ensures that outcome. Restraint on euphoria may soften disillusion later on.

The sixth and final concern is *American policy response* and what it portends for the future. In both cases, the urge to become involved, to "do something," has recurred. In Bosnia, that reaction was initially limited. The Bush administration resisted pleas to become militarily involved, taking heed of the cautionary advice from the military, especially Chairman of the Joint Chiefs of Staff, Colin Powell. As probably befits a more generally activist president, President Clinton sought to act, airdropping (ineffectually) food supplies to besieged villages during the coldest days of winter 1992–1993, later reactivating proposals to bomb Serbian positions, backing away when allies (who had forces on the

ground they feared would be the objects of reprisal) protested, and finally carrying out limited strikes. He later took the primary leadership
role in brokering the peace process. The lynchpin of that success, and a
harbinger for future situations, was the promise of direct American military participation.

Policy in Somalia vacillated as the on-ground situation changed. The
initial intervention was certainly successful in alleviating the symptom,
and the American presence was so apparently overwhelming that there
was no real resistance. The only disagreement was between Boutros-
Ghali, who insisted that the Americans should systematically disarm the
roving bands of armed teenagers who called themselves "technicals,"
openly brandishing heavy machine guns mounted on the beds of Toyota
4 X 4s, and the Americans, who insisted that doing so would exceed their
mandate. In retrospect, Boutros-Ghali's insistence, on the grounds that
disarmament of the factions was a necessary preface to a durable peace,
looks better than it did at the time; today, only an uneasy peace exists
and the formation of a real government remains elusive.

The situation deteriorated after the Americans left, punctuated by an
attack on Pakistani peacekeepers that killed twenty-three and that helped
prompt the Americans to return in the form of Rangers and Delta Force
teams, which attempted to capture Aidid. Reaction to the general deterioration of the situation and fears of an open-ended commitment prompted
demands for the withdrawal of all American forces, which was completed in March 1994.

The Clinton administration has drifted from an activist to a more restrained stance regarding either unilateral or multilateral involvement in
future ethnic conflicts. The President's criteria for involvement (a real
threat to peace, clear mission objectives, an exit point, realistic cost estimate) are clearly conservative, since in any concrete case it will be difficult
to find positive responses to all of them. At the same time, the apparent success of the "intervasion" (part intervention, part invasion) of Haiti in 1994
and the early success of IFOR may have whetted his appetite. Neither "success," however, guarantees the stability of either country after the interveners leave, as is happening in Haiti and is scheduled in Bosnia in 1998.

REGIONAL CONFLICTS: WHO CARES?

The other form that violence in the Second Tier occasionally takes
arises from rivalry between states within various regions. Many of these
regional conflicts are extremely old, stretching back for centuries, or even
milennia—for instance, the rivalry on the Asian subcontinent between
India and China. Many such conflicts were repressed during the period
of colonial rule and have resurfaced as that rule receded first in Asia,
then in Africa. The most prominent example at the end of the Cold War
involves the Persian Gulf War: is it a harbinger of problems to come?

Regional Conflict and the Cold War

The Cold War system helped both to shape and to manage most regional conflicts as part of the general competition between the opposing sides. The motives underlying East-West involvement were scarcely pristine. Both sides curried favor and influence (or sought to deny influence to the other) in regions, and participation in regional rivalries provided an opportunity to curry influence. By definition, regional conflicts had a military aspect, hence a nearly insatiable appetite for arms that could be supplied by the superpower rivals.

In most cases, the superpowers sought to counterbalance one another, with the Soviets providing the majority of assistance to one side, and the Americans to the other. Thus, in the Arab-Israeli conflict, the United States was the primary sponsor and armorer of Israel, the Soviet Union of Syria, Iraq, and, until 1975, Egypt. This relationship extended to the Persian Gulf, where, until the Iranian Revolution of 1979, the United States armed Iran, and the Soviets Iraq. India got most of its help from the Soviets, and the Pakistanis from the Americans. South Vietnam was supported by the United States, North Vietnam by China and the Soviets. And so on. This rivalry and counterbalancing was not unlike the pattern of support for contending sides in internal wars.

The rivalry also produced constraints on the levels of violence that would be tolerated by the sponsors. With assistance also came commitments—sometimes vague in content—to assist "clients" should they come under siege. The United States, for instance, always provided an unspoken guarantee for the existence of Israel against its numerous enemies, many sponsored by the Soviets. As part of their commitment to the area, the Soviets threatened in 1973 to air drop commandos into Egyptian lines to save them from Israeli decimation when they were pinned with their backs against the Suez Canal during the Yom Kippur War.

Sponsorship begat constraint in that a basic underlying rule of superpower rivalry in Third World regions was not to allow conflicts to escalate to the point that the superpowers were somehow inadvertently drawn into a shooting war that might somehow spin out of control and eventuate in general war between them. The calculation was hardheaded: the interests that both sides had in any regional conflict were well below vital and thus should not be allowed to escalate. The potential dangers of a failure to restrain one's client adequately were demonstrated in the Yom Kippur War, when the Soviet threat to intervene caused the United States to go to a high global alert status (Defcon three) and cause a furtive twenty-four hours of shuttle diplomacy that resulted in the Israelis backing away and thus defusing the situation.

There was, of course, a certain level of cynicism in all this; the outcomes of regional conflicts would be determined in large measure not on the basis of regional interests but, instead, in ways suitable to superpower interests. At the same time, the result was constraint. The most obvious example was the eight-year-long war between Iran and Iraq. Although not precisely a conflict pitting a Soviet client against an American client (since both had broken, partially or in total, from their old sponsors), it was a war carefully choreographed by those supplying arms to ensure that neither state either won or lost the contest decisively. The war ended in an Iraqi victory of sorts, but not enough of a triumph to give Iraq clear hegemony in the region.

The end of the Cold War removes this overlay from regional conflicts. As discussed previously, the overwhelming economic burden of conducting the competition was one of the reasons the Soviets wanted to end the overall competition. In addition, the Soviets came to realize that the expenses involved were hardly ever matched by beneficial advantages.

The early post–Cold War experience of removing Cold War constraints has been ambivalent. On the positive side, the lack of a superpower to prop up their positions almost certainly contributed to progress in the peace process between Israel and her old rivals, so dramatically and symbolically accentuated by the PLO's Yasir Arafat shaking hands with Israeli Prime Minister Yitzak Rabin as President Clinton beamed his approval, followed by the successful completion of peace negotiations between Israel and Jordan and the opening of talks between Israel and Syria. Such an event would have been unthinkable in a Cold War context.

The success in defusing regional conflicts has extended beyond the Arab-Israeli context. The Indo-Pakistani dispute has been dormant since 1990, when it threatened to heat up again over Kashmir. Despite some saber-rattling and the destabilizing influence of serious food shortages in the north, the Koreas remain at peace, and there has been positive progress in Northern Ireland.

The Clinton administration has become the common denominator and prime mover in this process. Acting from its position as the remaining superpower, the administration has become the central force for regional stabilization. Whether the parties are responding positively to American initiatives because there is no alternative force to turn to if they disagree is uncertain. That they have felt the need to take heed is undeniable.

But the prospects are not entirely positive. In a period in which the old constraints were missing but no new set of rules was in place, Saddam Hussein calculated that the system would not respond to his invasion and annexation of Kuwait. Many analysts look at alternative ways to bolster regional stability—a concern most pointed when one or both rivals are armed with NBC weapons and/or ballistic missile capability.

The Desert Storm "Precedent"?

The Iraqi annexation of Kuwait and its reversal by the American-led, United Nations–sponsored coalition was one of the most dramatic events of the 1990s. Coming when it did, it has been both extolled as the first defining moment of a "new world order" and dismissed as the last dying gasp of the old system. It marked the activation of a UN system formerly paralyzed by the veto powers of the Cold War superpowers, who stood together on the issue.

What is the precedent of Desert Storm for the new international system and, especially, for the problem of regional conflict? Was it an aberration or a portent of the future? What lessons can be learned from it, particularly in the context of First Tier dealings with Second Tier conflicts?

Assessing the precedential quality of the Persian Gulf War requires two separate but related judgments. The first has to do with the nature of the situation itself, including prominently Saddam Hussein himself and the actions he took. Are there more Iraqs and Saddam Husseins out there to be dealt with, and what may they have learned from the Gulf War experience? The second judgment has to do with the coalition response and asks, with particular reference to the United Nations, whether the collective security response sets a precedent for future Second Tier conflicts.

Saddam Hussein's Iraq represented a new and potentially dangerous phenomenon. Through a program of systematic investment in weaponry (including the so-called Iraqgate scandal, in which American farm subsidies to Iraq were diverted to buy American arms), Iraq had emerged as a state with military power disproportional to its status otherwise. It had become what the political columnist Charles Krauthammer termed a "weapon state," an otherwise unimportant regional actor that gained status because of its large store of weapons. Included in this inventory were some primitive ballistic missiles that were used in the Gulf War (the Scud B), a nuclear weapons program reported nearing fruition, and an active chemical and biological weapons capability. (Iraq used chemical weapons against both Iran and its Kurdish minority in 1987.) Disarming the NBC capability would become a postwar point of contention between Iraq and the UN.

The purpose of much of this armament was to promote Saddam Hussein as the leader of the Arab world—and possibly beyond. Just as Iraq had become the prototype of the weapon state, Saddam Hussein had become the symbol of a potentially dangerous *regional hegemon* intent on self-promotion. Grabbing Kuwait and its oil riches could only add to the capability for Saddam to enhance his power, inspiring a particular fear in the neighboring Saudis. The handling of this regional hegemon, it was argued, would send a message to other aspiring hegemons.

The other question of precedent has to do with the response that was mounted to reverse the effects of the invasion. Its precedential quality, in turn, requires looking at three facets of the situation and asking whether the situation demanded a special, or what will become a standard, response.

The first facet was the nature of what Saddam Hussein did when he conquered and annexed Kuwait. In essence, he violated two basic norms, one of the general international community and one internal to the Arab world. At the general level, the action represented the first time in the history of the organization that one United Nations member, in strict violation of its duties and obligations under the Charter, invaded and conquered another member. A United Nations (especially one freed of an automatic Cold War–based veto) that could not respond to such a challenge was of dubious value, at best. At the same time, Saddam Hussein violated an unwritten code of the Arab world that forbade altering the 1919 boundaries of the Arab world by force.

In this light, UN sponsorship and the shape of the coalition mounted in the desert are less amazing than they seemed when the operation was forming. Who needed a United Nations that could not act when its basic principles were subverted? At the same time, the participation of a number of Arab states (Saudi Arabia, Egypt, and Syria, for instance) alongside Western states against a fellow Arab makes sense. The precedential question is whether a similar coalition could be mounted in the absence of such egregious violations.

The second facet of the response was where it happened. When Secretary Baker replied after Operation Desert Shield (the name of the effort before combat began, whereby allied forces shielded Saudi Arabia from invasion) was announced that its purpose was to save the jobs that would have been lost had Iraq been allowed to control as much of the world's oil supplies as it would have had the conquest stood, only slightly cynical analysts questioned the fervor of response had there been no oil in Kuwait.

The third facet of the response was the nature and precedential quality of invoking the United Nations' collective security as the vehicle for organizing the coalition effort. Operation Desert Storm was the first time since Korea that the organization was the vehicle for turning back a major invasion, and the Korean action happened only because the Soviet Union was boycotting the Security Council (over seating the new People's Republic of China rather than Nationalist China), making it something of an aberration. In the case of Desert Storm, there was no veto.

Two points should be made about UN participation. One is that the collective security action authorized was not the kind envisioned in the Charter. The Charter calls for a standing armed force composed primarily of the permanent members of the Security Council to carry out actions, a scenario that forms the basis for a few current advocacies, such as that of former Senator David Boren of Oklahoma, of a standing UN armed force. In approving the action for freeing Kuwait, the Security Council authorized force and called for volunteers for enforcement. This was the collective security model for the League of Nations during the period between the world wars, and it proved spectacularly ineffective in preventing the violent rise of the Axis powers.

The other point is that, for many purposes, the UN imprimatur was little more than window dressing for an action the United States would have undertaken unilaterally (or in concert with close allies like Great Britain) had there been no UN authorization. Given the enormity of the effort and the overwhelming role of the American armed forces in its success, one can only wonder what kind of a UN action could be mounted *in the absence* of American participation. Put another way, does the United States have an effective veto on large UN actions even if it chooses not to exercise its formal veto? This informal veto could be important if a proposed UN action should require using U.S. airlift and sealift assets to get to the scene, which it would if a sizable deployment were anticipated.

An intangible factor in all the crisis was the role of Saddam Hussein, especially his often haughty intransigence in the face of global rebuke (which he displayed regularly for global television). Saddam Hussein came across as a caricature of villainy, a leader whom the world could love to hate and against whom it was easy to unite. One wonders how a less villainous leader doing the same thing would have been treated.

Does Saddam Hussein's action and the systemic counteraction represent a portent of future situations and responses? The first part of the question asks whether there are other regional hegemons leading weapon states and what they may have learned from the outcome. The second part asks whether the system will act similarly in the future.

Most observers question the current existence of other Saddam Husseins, suggesting that his actions were *sui generis* and, as such, unlikely to recur. General Powell raised this perspective on the eve of the one-hundred-hour ground campaign that dislodged the Iraqis from Kuwait, arguing that he could not think of any leader who would spend (or have the ability to spend) the estimated $50 to $60 billion Saddam Hussein had invested in making his country a weapon state. Moreover, a system becoming sensitive to Saddam-like characters and especially attuned to avoiding proliferation of deadly capabilities (see the following section) might be unlikely to *allow* another Iraq to arise.

Saying there are no current Saddams on the horizon should not create undue relief or optimism. There are dangerous states, such as North Korea while the processes of reunification unfolds, and volatile situations exist that could explode either inadvertently or purposely, as between India and Pakistan. A nuclear-armed North Korea in conflict with the more prosperous South Korea is a prospect that certainly has Japan's attention, as well as the attention of the United States by extension. How and whether the major powers would react to a major war—especially one employing NBC weapons and ballistic missiles—is problematical. Also, change is inevitable. A new and unpredicted threat could emerge, just as Iraq did.

Will the systemic response in Kuwait chasten aspirant regional hegemons against similar actions? The answer probably depends on two critical matters. The first is an assessment of whether the United States would become directly and personally involved. Here the Desert Storm precedent must be contrasted to the situation in Bosnia before 1995. What happened there qualifies on grounds of outrage and atrocity with the Iraqi action in Kuwait, but the Serbs, in particular, calculated that threats to intervene were hollow, and they proved correct for a long time. Does the United States act only when traditional vital interests such as oil are involved (as in Kuwait) or when the situation appears easy to handle on the surface (as in Somalia)? We Americans appear not to know the answers to those questions. How is a foreign despot to know?

The other question is how the United Nations will respond. Structurally, the formation of a permanent armed force as envisaged in the Charter would have far greater deterrent power than the uncertain prospects of calling for volunteers and having none arise. Mounting such a force in sufficient strength for large operations requires American participation, and that is unlikely on political and constitutional grounds. Politically, it is inconceivable that Congress would mandate placing American young people under other than American commanders, a position shared by President Clinton. Constitutionally, giving over command and employment of American forces to the UN may violate Congress' authority to declare war. Without American participation, such a force would be far less formidable and deterring. In its support, the United States has often been financially fickle, sometimes paying its UN budget and peacekeeping assessments and sometimes not, depending on whether it has agreed with UN missions.

The final concern about Desert Storm is what can be learned from the experience that may be relevant to the future. Lists of "lessons learned" vary considerably, depending on the purpose of the exercise. The perspective here is the lesson for American defense policy and the United States military. Two overarching lessons stand out as key elements in the national security debate.

The first lesson revealed by Desert Storm is the enormous military gap between countries of the First Tier and those of the Second. The gap between Western (American, British, and French) and Iraqi capabilities was startling. The Western states, especially the United States, had superior technology, superior strategies for employing that technology, and superior personnel who were capable of employing their capabilities to maximum effect.

This superiority encompassed the range of military categories. American satellites and associated electronic equipment surveilled the Iraqis in great detail; after the first day of the air war, Iraqi surveillance was literally reduced to what its forward-most personnel could see with the naked eye. The air belonged to the Allies, who could use that superiority further to disrupt the Iraqi effort and to demoralize Iraqi forces on the ground. Superior range and accuracy of tanks and artillery meant that the coalition was usually operating out of range of counterpart enemy capabilities. All these advantages are the result of the ongoing Revolution in Military Affairs (RMA) that is rewriting the standards of military capability.

The early reportage of the war overplayed this superiority, however, and subsequent, more objective assessment has reduced estimates of, for instance, bomb damage and accuracy. Nonetheless, there is a lesson to be learned: *if the First Tier, including the United States, chooses to employ its most advanced capabilities against a Second Tier state, militarily that state does not stand a chance.* Iraq, after all, possessed the world's fourth largest army, much of it was battle-tested against Iran, and it also had advanced capabilities. Yet, the war itself was a walkover. Unless, through arms transfers or failure to maintain the technology gap, the First Tier abnegates its advantage, it can retain it for the foreseeable future.

The second lesson is more cautionary and complex. Because all the major First Tier countries are political democracies responsible to their publics, *involvements in major regional conflicts will have to be infrequent and selective.* This is especially true for the United States, for two reasons. First, the structure of the American armed forces in 1990—a condition magnified by force reductions—required the activation of significant numbers of reserves (a matter of conscious policy to assure the commitment of the public to a major endeavor), and any future involvement would require a mobilization as well. There are real limits on how often the American public will support the activation of its "friends and neighbors." The only other large-scale mobilization was in Korea, forty years earlier. Whether there would be support where no obvious American interests were jeopardized is especially questionable. This question of reserve mobilization will also apply to smaller involvements, because some missions, such as civil affairs, are entirely reserve functions.

Second, the technological gap is based on highly sophisticated but very expensive weapons systems. In the Gulf War, much of the expense was absorbed by contributions from countries such as Germany, Japan, and Saudi Arabia that, in effect, subsidized the American effort financially. Such subsidies may not be available in future situations. If foreign subsidies are necessary to permit American participation, that in itself may say something important about the extent of American leadership. Moreover, the United States depleted large portions of its stocks of many munitions—such as "smart" bombs—that are time-consuming and expensive to replace.

In sum, we are saying that where the First Tier—and, especially, the United States—decides to involve itself in Second Tier conflicts, it will likely prevail, whether the operation has United Nations sanction or not. At the same time, such involvement will have to be selective, probably decided on a case-by-case basis. From the vantage point of Second Tier regional rivals, the secret will be in guessing where the First Tier will and will not decide to act.

DEADLY QUARRELS: NBC AND MISSILE PROLIFERATION

Part of the calculation of involvement in Second Tier regional conflicts revolves around how dangerous the conflicts are to the regions and, potentially, to the system. A major criterion for assessing these dangers is the degree to which regional rivalries have been enlivened by the individual or mutual possession of particularly lethal nuclear, biological, and chemical (NBC) weapons and the means to deliver them (ballistic missiles). President Clinton has made the control of proliferation and elimination of these capabilities a major priority of his foreign and national security policy.

Although each capability presents certain unique challenges and problems, they share at least five notable characteristics that help enliven concern about them. These include their currency in regional conflicts, the difficulty they pose in controlling proliferation, their increasing sophistication, their ability to expand the number of states at risk, and their escalatory potential.

Characteristics of the Lethal Capabilities

The first characteristic is that *these capabilities currently exist and have been employed with effect in war.* Table 8.1 shows the states that currently have, or are believed to have, one or another capability. As the table reveals, one or another of these weapons capabilities, often in combination, are held by a number of Second Tier states, including a kind of who's who of potentially unstable, troublesome nations such as North Korea, Iran, and Iraq. Moreover, a number of regional rivals who have previously fought have one or both capabilities that could be employed in a future conflict. India and Pakistan stand out with particularly chilling prominence.

These weapons have been employed in war, notably by the quintessential weapon state, Iraq. The Hussein regime used chemical weapons against Iran during the latter stages (1987) of their war, and there is evidence to suggest that the attacks helped push an already war-weary Iran over the edge to sue for peace. That same year, the Iraqi government also gassed Kurdish villages within its own borders to bring about an end to opposition from the Kurds. Reports in late 1993 suggested that Iraq attacked Shiites in the southern exclusion zone with air-delivered chemicals.

Iraq also employed Russian-built Scud B missiles in terrorist attacks against both Israel (to provoke an Israeli retaliation that might have splintered the coalition) and Saudi Arabia. One Scud attack resulted in the largest single instance of American deaths in the war, when an errant missile slammed into a dormitory in Dharan, killing twenty-seven Pennsylvania reservists.

The second common characteristic is the *difficulty of preventing proliferation of NBC and missiles capabilities.* The control and/or elimination of both sets of capabilities is a major national security priority of the Clinton White House, but it is beset by at least two difficulties. The first is the ability to produce many NBC weapons in relative secrecy. The elements of chemical weapons, for instance, are commonly available and legally obtainable substances that can be purchased almost anywhere in the

TABLE 8.1   Missile Possessors

Country	Nuclear	Biological	Chemical	Missiles
Algeria	T			P
Ethiopia			P	
Libya		P	P	P
South Africa	P		P	
Egypt		P	P	P
Iran	T	P	P	P
Iraq	T	P	P	P
Israel	P	P	P	P
Saudi Arabia			P	P
Sudan			?	
Syria		P	P	P
Afghanistan			?	
China	P	P	P	P
India	P	P	P	P
North Korea	P	P	P	P
South Korea			P	P
Myanmar			P	
Pakistan	P		P	P
Taiwan		P	P	P
Thailand			P	
Vietnam		P	P	
Argentina	*		P	P
Brazil	*		?	P
Chile			?	
Cuba		P	P	

T=Trying to Develop   P=Possessing NBC and Missiles
?=Sources express doubt   *=Mutually agreed not to develop but possess capability

SOURCES: *Countering the Chemical and Biological Weapons Threat in the Post-Soviet World.* Committee on Armed Services, House of Representatives, 103rd Congress (2nd Session), February 23, 1993; *Proliferation of Weapons of Mass Destruction: Assessing the Risks.* U.S. Congress: Office of Technology Assessment, 1993.

world. The ease with which the materials were bought and the chemical explosive built that destroyed the Murrah Federal Building in Oklahoma City in 1995 is testimony to the problem. While the intention of large purchases of the component parts is obvious, buying small amounts of each substance from different merchants in different places can produce enormous monitoring difficulties. Moreover, a plant devoted to producing chemical fertilizers—or the notorious baby formula plant in Baghdad during the Persian Gulf War—can be quickly converted to chemical weapons production that can be detected only by human intelligence agents (humint) on the ground. The Iraqis demonstrated their ability to produce weapons-grade plutonium for nuclear weapons clandestinely by using centrifuge technologies long since discarded by the West as inefficient; because the Western states did not use the technology, they failed to look for signs of its employment.

The other proliferation problem is the fact that a number of Second Tier states, including some rogue states, produce these weapons for resale. North Korea, for instance, will build either a chemical weapons or missile plant for anyone with the requisite cash in hand. And, despite pressures from the Clinton administration (such as threats to retract most favored nation status), China continues to be an exporter of missiles, especially to Pakistan. A major thrust of administration policy is to widen the number of Second Tier states who are parties to various conventions prohibiting the production and sale of these capabilities.

A third problem is the *increasing sophistication of the weapons being produced, especially missiles.* In the past, most of the missiles produced have been relatively unsophisticated copies of primitive major power weapons. The Scud B is an example; it was primitive enough that it could be successfully intercepted using a defensive missile (the Patriot), which was designed as an antiaircraft, not an antimissile, system.

This scenario is increasingly unlikely in the future. Thanks largely to the overseas training of Second Tier scientists who have returned to their native lands, Second Tier states are now able to conduct research and development programs that allow them to produce their own sophisticated designs. India, for instance, has flight-tested a satellite-launching rocket which, if converted to a ground-to-ground missile, would be capable of flights over a 2,500-mile range.

The fourth common characteristic is that *these capabilities expand both the quality and quantity of states at risk.* NBC capabilities are primarily terrorist weapons effective against defenseless civilian—especially urban—populations, although nuclear weapons may have some battlefield applications. As such, they raise qualitatively the horror and terror of warfare, a condition especially onerous in the flashpoint Middle East, where most states have only a few urban centers at risk. The terrorist use of one of these kinds of weapons against a First Tier state remains a horrifyingly vivid prospect.

Quantitatively, missiles, in particular, extend the "reach" of their possessors to the extent of the range of the missiles they have. Almost any missile-possessing state in the Middle East, for instance, can attack the capitals of any enemy with missiles (possibly tipped with NBC munitions), and major portions of the former Soviet Union are within range of Second Tier possessors. Although no Second Tier state (other than Russia) can currently target the entire United States or a significant part of it, it is only a matter of time until the range is achieved.

The fifth and final shared characteristic is the prospect that possession by one state in a regional rivalry will trigger *an escalatory cycle of measures and countermeasures.* These can take one of two forms. One would simply be for a state faced with the offensive threat of NBC munitions or missiles to match the rival's capability. The motive of this offensive countermeasure would be to pose a deterrent threat: if you use gas (or agents of biological origin or nuclear weapons) against me, I will retaliate in kind. The dangers of this situation are twofold: such a balance could up the likelihood of war starting in a crisis if it produces a "finger on a hair trigger"; likewise, it could produce an escalating cycle of arms racing in other dangerous and deadly weapons.

The other form of escalation would be an offense-defense escalatory cycle, a prospect most obviously attaching to missiles, regardless of their payloads. In the Persian Gulf War, the answer to Iraqi offensive Scud missiles were Patriot defensive missiles. The Patriots, however, were effective only against relatively primitive rockets like the Scud. As more sophisticated offensive weapons enter inventories, it will be necessary to develop more sophisticated antiballistic missile (ABM) systems to create the counterweight. The Global Protection against Accidental Launch (GPALS) and similar systems that are the remaining component of the cancelled Strategic Defense Initiative (SDI) program of the Reagan years is a prime candidate for this role—a potentially lucrative American export.

NBC Weapons Problems

Each capability, as noted, adds certain special problems to regional conflicts. In the case of NBC munitions, there are four such concerns: the increased regional status possession brings; the effects of use in war; the added uncertainty produced by possession; and the difficulty of controlling the substances.

The first problem is the perception that *possession of NBC weapons enhances the prestige of regional actors.* In the Cold War competition, nuclear weapons were often viewed as the "membership card" for major power status, and some residue of that perception lingers in parts of the Second Tier. For those unable to obtain nuclear weapons or unwilling to violate the Nonproliferation Treaty (NPT) governing nuclear weapons possession, the alternative may be to acquire "poor man's" substitutes in the form of chemical or biological weapons. For better or worse, a country that acquires one or the other is afforded a military status quite unlikely to accrue without them. This fact significantly raises the prospects of an action-reaction phenomenon of armament and counterarmament with these weapons among rival parties.

This result raises the second problem, which is the *acquisition of deadly capabilities for planned use in war.* If this purpose is publicly known, it can only heighten the terror that already attaches to the prospects of war, particularly against civilian populations. Chemical and biological weapons are often especially hideous in terms of their effects on humans, raising great anxieties about their possible employment. One only has to remember the tremendous anxiety that the prospect caused among Israelis during Saddam Hussein's Scud attacks during the Persian Gulf War. The danger is that such plans will only add to the desperation of contending sides in conflicts that are already highly emotional, where that emotion may cloud more sober calculations.

The problem of planned usage of NBC weapons contributes to the third difficulty, the *added uncertainty that NBC weapons bring to regional conflicts*. Traditional regional conflicts were bloody and unpredictable enough when conducted with traditional military means and directed more or less exclusively at combatants. The evidence from the one regional conflict in which chemical weapons was used, the Iran-Iraq War, provides evidence that such weapons are efficacious in a limited way. That evidence is of limited instruction, however, both because the use was limited in nature and duration and because only one side employed the capabilities.

An all-out regional conflict in which both sides possessed one or more of the lethal capacities would be another matter. The weapons, if used at all, would almost certainly be used against civilian populations, since NBC weapons are most effective against unprotected civilians. They would clearly jack up the lethality index and incite passions and anxieties missing or suppressed in their absence. The urge to vindictiveness and vengeance would be particularly great among the survivors of an NBC attack, making peaceful resolution more difficult. A conflict with these weapons is simply more difficult to contemplate than one without them.

Fourth, and finally, is the *difficulty of stopping chemical and ABO capabilities*. This problem has two aspects, one already raised and the other not. The familiar part is the difficulty of detecting and monitoring the possession and production of either capability if those possessing or developing the capability actively seek to conceal it. It is part of the problem that the kinds of states likely to engage in clandestine development/deployment are going to be closed, hostile states where the intelligence-gathering capabilities of the major powers is very limited. Pre–Persian Gulf War Iraq was a case in point; years of isolation had reduced the on-the-spot intelligence operations of the major powers to virtual impotence.

The other aspect of difficulty is in dealing with these capacities if they are actually used. Both chemical and biological weapons are extremely difficult to apply in a controlled manner. A chemical attack's effectiveness is subject to the whims of something as simple and uncontrollable as changes in the direction of the wind. The same is largely true of many of the viruses (such as anthrax) employed in biological weapons; even if their original application is limited and controlled, spread into the ecosystem is hard to predict or control.

Although the majority of the strategic community agrees that NBC proliferation is undesirable, a minority wonders if this is always the case. In assessing the 1990 Indo-Pakistani dispute and why it did not escalate, one possibility was that "opaque proliferation" provided a brake. This means that both sides were widely believed—including by the other—to have nuclear capability but neither side would admit possession (proliferation was not clear and open but, rather, opaque). In that circumstance, both sides may have been dissuaded by the possibility that the other might have and use its nuclear weapons.

Ballistic Missile Problems

The introduction of ballistic missiles to one or both parties in a regional conflict also creates its own unique difficulties. Five stand out: added lethality; the vulnerability and crudeness of the capability; additional parties placed at risk; visceral fears of terrorist attacks by irresponsible leaders; and difficulties in controlling missile proliferation.

The *increased lethality* that missiles bring to warfare comes from two characteristics: the increased range for delivering weapons and the inability of almost all states to defend against them. These combine. Aircraft, after all, are capable of delivering various kinds of munitions over long ranges (in some cases ranges longer than those of available missiles), but airplanes are interceptible by other airplanes or missiles. Launched missiles are invulnerable to attack unless they can be attacked before launch, and they thus can be used against targets that could not be otherwise attacked either because of range or defensive protection.

As noted, however, the missile capabilities of many Second Tier countries are *primitive and vulnerable* before launch. Most must be launched either from stationary or mobile platforms out in the open and above ground. In such a configuration, they are vulnerable to destruction by like systems before they are launched. This creates a problem known in the business as "use 'em or lose 'em." What that means is that in a crisis situation, one or both sides may conclude that they must fire first, thereby initiating hostilities, for fear of a preemptive attack that would destroy their capability. Such a perception can only add to the desperation, and even panic, that associate with the presumed slide toward war and result in war where it might otherwise have been avoided.

An associated third problem is that of *the visceral fear of terrorist attacks*. Missiles are especially frightening weapons; not only are there few reliable defenses against sophisticated missiles, but they land without warning or sight. A missile launched in Iraq can attack a target in Israel (as during the Persian Gulf War) *in six minutes*. Even with advance warning, there is hardly enough time to take cover. Moreover, you cannot see the attack coming; the first physical warning may be the sound of the missile just before landing. There is no greater nightmare in war than being unable to see or hear your attacker and, hence, to be able to counteract. When that attacker is someone of unpredictable character—a Saddam Hussein, for instance—the prospects are especially frightening.

Finally, *missile proliferation is proving difficult, although not necessarily impossible, to control.* The regime currently attempting to stop missile spread is the Missile Technology Control Regime (MTCR), whose growing effectiveness is a major part of the Clinton strategy to prevent proliferation. It is not a formal treaty but an informal agreement that began within the Group of Seven (G7) economic giants and had been acceded to by a total of well over 20 states as of late 1995. The problem is that some of the Second Tier states who produce and distribute missiles are either nonparticipants in MTCR (such as North Korea) or are reluctant participants with questionable track records of compliance (such as the People's Republic of China). Chinese compliance with the MTCR is a major ongoing bone of contention between the Chinese government and the administration in Washington.

CONCLUSIONS

The old structure of violence and instability has become restructured in the international system of tiers. A peaceful set of relations has replaced the communist-anticommunist confrontation of the Cold War. There are no systemic threats to the existence of the system, and the prospect of war between First Tier states is farfetched. Part of the tapestry of world violence has simply vanished.

The tranquility of the First Tier accentuates its opposite in the Second Tier. The disintegration of the old Second World, especially the atomization of the former Soviet Union, has cast areas of the old communist sphere into the maelstrom of violence and instability that already plagued much of the Second Tier. The spate of ethnic violence and internal instability played out so gorily in Bosnia and Somalia has already spread to the southern regions of the old Soviet Union (Armenia, Azerbaijan, Georgia, and Tajikistan); that pattern may well spread to other parts of the old Soviet empire and beyond. The prospects of ethnic purification in the Asian subcontinent and parts of Africa are particularly chilling. The growth of new internal wars, mainly but not exclusively in Africa, is alarming.

Of the two forms of violence, internal war and regional conflicts, the former will be quantitatively the greater problem; there will be more wars fought among factions within states than there will be wars between states. To counterbalance that quantitative balance, such regional conflicts as do occur are likely to be more qualitatively difficult, thanks in large measure to the introduction of deadly new capabilities to Second Tier arsenals.

What's a world to do about all this? That policy question is at the bottom line of the policy debate about America's role in the new international system that was highlighted in the previous chapter. The problems associated with various solutions are discussed in the final part of this book, following a discussion of new and unique nontraditional national security problems in Chapter 9.

Suggested Reading

Bandow, Doug. "Avoiding War," *Foreign Policy* 89 (Winter 1992/93): 156–174.
Bell-Fialkoff, Andrew. "A Brief History of Ethnic Cleansing," *Foreign Affairs* 72, 3 (Summer 1993): 110–121.

Bundy, McGeorge, William J. Crowe, Jr., and Sidney Drell. "Reducing Nuclear Danger," *Foreign Affairs* 72, 2 (Spring 1993): 140–155.

Deutch, John M. "The New Nuclear Threat," *Foreign Affairs* 71, 4 (Fall 1992): 120–134.

Doder, Dasko. "Yugoslavia: New War, Old Hatreds," *Foreign Policy* 91 (Summer 1993): 3–23.

Etzioni, Amatai. "The Evils of Self-Determination," *Foreign Policy* 89 (Winter 1992/93): 21–35.

Krauthammer, Charles. "The Unipolar Moment," *Foreign Affairs* 70, 1 (Winter 1990/91): 23–33.

Metz, Steven. *The Future of Insurgency.* Carlisle Barracks, Pa.: Strategic Studies Institute, 1993.

Neuman, Stephanie G. "Controlling the Arms Trade: Idealistic Dream or Realpolitik?" *Washington Quarterly* 16, 3 (Summer 1993): 53–73.

Radu, Michael (ed.). *The New Insurgencies: Anticommunist Guerrillas in the Third World.* New Brunswick, N.J.: Transaction Books, 1990.

Snow, Donald M. *Distant Thunder: Third World Conflict and the New International Order.* New York: St. Martin's Press, 1993.

Spector, Leonard S. *Deterring Regional Threats from Nuclear Proliferation.* Carlisle Barracks, Pa.: Strategic Studies Institute, 1992.

Chapter 9

Nontraditional Problems

In a world where our physical sense of security is hardly threatened at all, there are two ways to think about the question of U.S. national security and the role of national security policy within the framework of national policy generally. One approach is to consider a reduced role and mission for the various parts of the national security community, notably the military. The current reduction in the physical size both of the standing force and its supporting budget reflects this perspective.

The second way is to expand the definition of what composes the country's security. Given the general military tranquillity of the First Tier and the consequent lack of direct physical assaults, any expansion would have to come from the psychological realm of security: that is, what would make us *feel* safer?

The national security community, especially the professional military, is struggling with this problem and has yet to resolve it satisfactorily. With the anti-Soviet mission completed (with the lingering exception of former Soviet nuclear weapons) and an amorphous set of concerns not clearly relevant to the vital interests of the United States, the search is ongoing for sustaining missions that can justify the retention of a potent standing force.

Another way of looking at the problem is in terms of a paradigm change, a perspective raised earlier. The traditional realist paradigm based in vital interests suggests a considerable lessening of the security problem when threats to the vital interests of the United States are virtually nonexistent. This is not to suggest that the world is trouble-free, only that most of the problems, from economic underdevelopment in the Second Tier to environmental degradation, fall outside the realist framework of highly actionable concerns. That framework, highly Clausewitzian and Napoleonic in tone, suggests two general levels of response: large, even all-out actions when vital interests are engaged, inaction when they are not.

Many contemporary problems are not captured well in this framework. These are the so-called nontraditional problems that were ignored conceptually during the Cold War and its primary concern with competition. That framework may be inappropriate for the post–Cold War world; an alternate paradigm may be needed.

The search for a sustaining military role reveals at least two problems from the vantage point of the military itself. First, many of the proposals for an expanded notion of security have little, if any, military role or component. Environmental security is a case in point; more dramatically, economic security suggests—if anything—a narrower military role as resources formerly devoted to defense become candidates for diversion to economic priorities.

Second, those expanded roles that do have a military component are often "nontraditional" in terms of their military implications and the kinds of military forces applicable. Counterterrorism, discussed at length in the next section, is of this nature: the military component requires a few specially trained forces, not large formations of mechanized infantry. Moreover, these missions are generally in areas where the military has little experience or training and in which it consequently may not perform well; in the case of terrorism, the military is prevented by law from participating in dealing with the domestic variety (*posse comitatus*) in which citizens are most interested.

The result is a kind of flailing for missions that will sustain the force. As one listens to discussions within the military community itself, one senses something bordering on desperation for sustaining roles that will keep the force strong and ready enough to be effective in the event of some unpredictable conflict. Who, for instance, would have predicted a large war with Iraq even a few weeks before the Iraqi invasion of Kuwait?

This searching has come to resemble a reaching for straws that has been occasionally embarrassing to a proud professional military establishment. Nowhere has this been more apparent than in the so-called *war on drugs*, declared with great fanfare by the Bush administration and revived by the Clinton administration for the 1996 presidential campaign. Because it represents both the kinds of nontraditional problems the country faces and the difficulties inherent in translating them into what the U.S. Army, in its most recent edition of *Field Manual 100-5*, calls operations other than war— or OOTW (and what more recently has been dubbed military operations other than war, or MOOTW), it is worth detailing.

The motivation for a concerted effort against drug use in the United States neatly fits an expanded role of what constitutes the psychological sense of security. The streets of many cities have become unsafe because of the drug-related crime that has eroded inner city families and neighborhoods and that had, by the middle 1980s, spread to the suburbs and beyond. Security against the ravages of drugs became a central issue in the broader emphasis on reviving family values. Attacking the problems arising from narcotics was and is a problem on which there can be little dissent.

The difficulty—one of those so-called devils in the details—has been how to solve the drug problem. In the Reagan administration First Lady Nancy Reagan's exhortation to "just say no to drugs" focused public attention on the problem. When he was elected president in 1988, George Bush elevated the priority to a "war on drugs"; like all good wars, it was a priority in which the military would play a prominent role. President Clinton reinforced this military emphasis by appointing retiring Gen. Barry McCaffrey, outgoing commander of U.S. Southern Command (which has responsibility for Latin America, where most of the drug effort is concentrated), as his chief assistant on drugs.

Particularly as the mission was dawning and forming, the professional military had very ambivalent feelings about enlistment in this war. On the one hand, there were many who felt that drug trafficking was not a problem on which military force could successfully be brought to bear; involvement in the drug war might well mean frustration, at best, and tarnish for the military, at worst. On the other hand, as the war on drugs was being declared, the traditional military mission was evaporating. In that context, enlistment offered the hope of a new mission that might justify budget and force level requests in otherwise rocky times.

A combination of executive-level insistence and the need for a new mission won out, and the national security establishment gradually reoriented itself toward fighting the war on drugs. Enthusiasm was never great, and the results have consistently justified the suspicions.

The "war on drugs" always suffered difficulties because of the analogy it suggested. In the case of Lyndon Johnson's "war on poverty" in the 1960s, the analogy was never taken literally, but in the case of the drug war, it was. One problem this created was the danger of hyperbole— an overstatement both of the problem and the means of its solution. For instance, the actual campaign focused almost exclusively on one substance, cocaine from South America, and ignored other sources and drugs such as Asian heroin and locally produced methamphetamine. Thus, the war on drugs arguably became the "skirmish on cocaine."

The more important problem was how to "fight" the war. From the beginning, there were two basic and conflicting approaches, so-called *supply-side* and *demand-side*. Supply-side efforts consisted of three forms of activity with the common purpose of making drugs less available: source eradication, interdiction, and strict enforcement of narcotics laws in the United States. Demand-side advocates sought to reduce the market for drugs, emphasizing drug treatment programs and education to reduce demand. A minority even advocated legalization (or decriminalization) of drugs.

Supply-side efforts clearly had more potential military relevance than did demand-side approaches (although the military itself had remarkable success in eliminating drug use within the ranks through a combined program of education and testing). As a result, the "war" would be fought by the United States military principally in the two areas of supply where it could legally operate, eradication and interdiction. (The laws that bar the military from participating in antiterrorism within the territorial United States also apply in this case.)

Eradication of cocaine at the source meant a campaign in the three South American countries where the coca leaves that form the basis of cocaine are grown and processed. The coca plants grow in the high mountain valleys of Peru (notably the Upper Huallaga) and Bolivia. Raw coca leaves produced in those countries are bought by Colombian drug traffickers (the *narcotraficantes*), who take the coca to Colombia for chemical processing into cocaine in jungle laboratories. From there it begins its journey to the United States.

Source eradication created several problems, especially in Peru, where the effort was most concerted. First, it required an alliance with a highly unstable Peruvian government faced with a violent insurgency led by the *Sendero Luminoso* (SL, or Shining Path) that was itself allied with the peasant growers of coca leaves (which have been cultivated for centuries). Involvement with the Americans was problematical, since they were mostly worried about coca, while the government necessarily was primarily concerned with the insurgent SL.

Moreover, attempts to eradicate by spraying chemical defoliants or slash-and-burn techniques further alienated the peasant growers from the government and drove them reluctantly into the arms of the Shining Path. What was supposed to be good for the United States was not necessarily good for Peru. The same was true for Colombia, where the United States pushed the government toward a more aggressive campaign to locate and destroy laboratories, thereby putting the government effectively at war with the highly armed and wealthy drug cartels. The effect on the Andean countries was simply destabilizing.

The second supply-side effort was interdiction of cocaine coming into the United States. Because the drug traffickers employed all three avenues (air, land, and sea) to transport their merchandise, it was an effort in which all major services had a part. Air Force planes could be employed in surveillance of suspicious aircraft headed toward the country (and even possibly force planes down, although the risk of shooting down an innocent flyer has always been a nightmare scenario). The Navy and, especially, the Coast Guard were each given tasks for interrupting the supply headed for the United States by sea. Although it never came to particular fruition, an Army role in patrolling the Mexican border, across which most of the cocaine was smuggled, was also suggested. (The major Army role has been confined to eradication at the source.)

The problem with supply-side solutions was that they did not work, at least as measured by any visible interruption of the amount of cocaine available in the American market. Attempts at source eradication simply drove the growers further into the jungle, contributing to the destruction of more of the jungle rain forest, pollution of ground water through the use of the defoliants, and even diversion of farmers from growing coca to culturing the less visible and more profitable poppy for heroin.

Interdiction suffered similar problems. Sea and air attempts were crippled by the highly sophisticated equipment available to the smugglers and the nature of the areas into which smuggling took place. Very fast speedboats, for instance, could dart from behind the protective covering of Cuba and make a fast dash to one of the thousands of inlets on the Florida peninsula before the Coast Guard could detect and attempt to intercept them. The use of Panama as a funnel for the transshipment of drugs (apparently orchestrated by strongman Manuel Noriega) was one prominent reason for the American invasion of that country under the banner of Operation Just Cause in December 1989.

The bottom line of several years of supply-side efforts is that there is no clear evidence of success. The supply of drugs available on the streets has not lessened, especially in the inner cities where the problem and its manifestation in terms of crime are most acute. To those who argue that the effort is inherently flawed—a misapplication of expensive resources—the answer is to redirect efforts from the supply to the demand side of the drug equation.

During the 1992 presidential campaign, candidate Clinton attached himself to a demand-side approach featuring greater public education and treatment of hard-core offenders. Although his first budget—like all first presidential budgets, little more than a fine-tuning of a budget prepared by the preceding administration—did not represent a major shifting of resources (nearly 70 percent of available funds still went to supply-side efforts), he announced in 1996 a revitalization of the entire effort as part of his family values campaign. He proposed substantial increases in antidrug efforts, with most of the additional funds targeted at antidrug education.

The reason for this lengthy discursion is that the war on drugs may represent a parable of sorts for future efforts to redefine the national security mission. The enthusiasm and subsequent disenchantment with participation in United Nations–sponsored peacekeeping missions (see Chapter 10 for details) represents a similar kind of evolution, although one condensed in time largely because of the number of casualties inflicted on American troops.

Anthony Lake's four rules were applicable to the war on drugs, and had they been invoked, the result might have been different. Was the use of force in South America and along the air, sea, and land routes in America's interests? Maybe. Could that force actually do any good? Not demonstrably. Was the cost acceptable? A lot of money was spent, but the results were pretty slender. Finally, was there a way out? The answer was, a very quiet reorientation toward a demand-side strategy.

We will use the experience of the drug war as a caution in dealing with the other nontraditional roles discussed in this chapter. The first two roles have some clear military content, so-called *low-intensity conflict* and *terrorism*, although we will raise questions about the propriety and prospects for success in both cases. The other two, so-called *transstate issues* and *economic security*, have less direct national security content in the traditional sense of that term.

LOW-INTENSITY CONFLICT

The curious term "low-intensity conflict" (LIC) is largely an artifact of the Cold War, in two distinct regards. The first is contextual and arises from the way the American military classified the different military problems they faced. The second attempts to be descriptive of a distinct style and form of warfare.

The terminology in which LIC is included came into general usage in the early 1980s, when the Cold War was still in full form. It was part of a taxonomy that sought to describe, in rank order of importance, the various military tasks facing the armed forces. At the upper end was *high-intensity conflict* (HIC), referring to a general, probably nuclear, war between the United States and the Soviet Union. Then came *middle-intensity conflict* (MIC), conventional war fought by the United States against a somewhat lesser foe than the Soviets; Desert Storm would be an example of a fairly large MIC. At the lower end of the scale was *low-intensity conflict* (LIC), with reference to unconventional wars fought in the Third World (Second Tier) that were smaller in terms of military scale.

The ordinal ranking served three purposes. First, it ranked potential conflicts in terms of their importance and consequences, with a thermonuclear HIC at the top of the consequence heap and a Third World LIC at the bottom. Second, the classification served to show the inverse relationship between likelihood and importance; there were, and continue to be, many LICs and no HICS in the world. Third, the categories served to define military missions and requirements; preparation for HIC (which one sought to deter) required robust thermonuclear forces and a large, heavily armored conventional force, while LIC does not.

The term also sought to be descriptive of a category of wars in the Second Tier. The low-intensity part of the definition refers primarily to the way the wars are fought. This means that most are insurgency-style wars fought with relatively light equipment (mostly hand-carried) and relatively small military formations (company size or below) in which there are very few large, pitched battles. Thus, LICs look smaller (of lower intensity) than the combat one would have expected between NATO and the Warsaw Pact in Germany.

These kinds of wars often had a distinctly Cold War overlay to them. In most cases, LICs pitted a government usually supported by the United States against an insurgent group sponsored or assisted by the Soviets. The major exceptions were the Contras fighting the Sandinistas in Nicaragua and the Afghan rebels fighting the Afghan communist government, in which cases the Americans supported the insurgents under the Reagan Doctrine. For the Americans, the problem was normally one of counterinsurgency—how to help a beleaguered government maintain itself in power. The operational question was the proper extent of direct American involvement in someone else's internal affair.

In the post-Vietnam period, the American military developed a reasonable level of expertise in this area, a direct reaction to a Vietnam experience that began as a LIC (although the term was not used at the time). The question is the degree to which that experience is relevant in the contemporary milieu.

The Cold War overlay has clearly disappeared; the United States, in observing a LIC, no longer has to question whether there is Soviet activity underlying the conflict or how a communist victory would destabilize a country or region. At the same time, internal violence, often in the form of ethnically based conflict, has become an even more prominent part of the landscape of violence. Dealing with it is a nontraditional problem for which our understanding of LIC is directly relevant in some cases but not necessarily in others.

This fact suggests the direction of our discussion. We will begin by defining LIC largely in terms of insurgency and its characteristics, relying heavily on analyses prepared by the U.S. armed forces themselves. This will be followed by a discussion of counterinsurgency, especially the difficulties of outside intervention in internal war. The overarching model is that of the classic Maoist mobile-guerrilla style and strategy of war, which was a traditional form of warfare that fit neatly into the Clausewitzian framework, since its principal author, Mao Zedung, was a student of Clausewitz's *On War*. Its applicability to the non-Clausewitzian new internal wars and to operations like peacekeeping will also be examined.

LIC Defined as Insurgency

One of the most difficult problems of gaining a command of LIC is that so many different terms are used to describe it. LICs have variously been described as guerrilla wars, small wars, insurgent wars, and partisan wars. The term LIC itself is objectionable to many because it suggests a lack of urgency—even importance—that is terribly misleading.

A clear way to think of this style of warfare is as *insurgency*. A working definition is provided in a 1986 publication of the U.S. Army Intelligence Center and School at Ft. Huachuca, Arizona: insurgency is "a protracted political-military activity directed toward completely or partially controlling the resources of a country through the use of irregular military forces and illegal political organizations." To accomplish their goals, insurgents engage in a variety of actions, "including guerrilla warfare, terrorism, and political mobilization . . . designed to weaken government control and legitimacy, while increasing insurgent control and legitimacy."

These definitions point to the unique character of what can be called traditional insurgent warfare (in contrast to new internal war), the intimate and reciprocal relationship between the political and military aspects of insurgency. While war is always fought at the military level to achieve political objectives, in insurgency there is a blending and inter-twining of the two not evident in more conventional warfare. The objec-tive of traditional insurgency—to gain control of government—is both a political and a military phenomenon. Politically, it is a contest of political organization for loyalty and, hence, legitimacy—what Lyndon Johnson first called the "battle for the hearts and minds of men." Militarily, it is a contest to topple one side or the other in which the political impact of in-dividual military actions also weighs heavily.

The political element of insurgency cannot be overstated. As *Field Manual* (FM) *100-20* (1989 edition), the U.S. Army's primary doctrinal statement on the subject, puts it, "Insurgency is focused and directed po-litical violence" where "each side seeks to demonstrate that it can govern better." The seed bed of insurgency is governmental malfeasance, a situa-tion where "the government is unwilling or unable to redress the de-mands of important social groups." As such, the sheer existence of an insurgent movement should give caution to any outsider thinking of sup-porting the government in power. The antidote to insurgency is good government; where good government does not exist, insurgency may.

This notion of insurgency reflects its Maoist roots. In essence, Mao brought three influences to insurgency. First, Mao was a Clausewitzian who believed deeply in the subjugation of military action to the politi-cal purposes for which war is fought. Second, he was a Marxist, which adds the ideological element and makes insurgency a battle of ideas. Third, he was also a student of the ancient Chinese military theorist Sun Tzu, who added military caution and limitations on the carnage of war to the overall mix.

The physical conduct of insurgency requires considerable patience. Especially during the Cold War period, governments were typically heavily armed as the result of Cold War competition for influence, mean-ing that insurgencies usually began in a position of considerable military disadvantage. To deal with that circumstance, many insurgent move-ments adopted the *mobile-guerrilla-warfare strategy* perfected by Mao Tse-tung during the Chinese Civil War.

The mobile-guerrilla strategy is depicted in Table 9.1, borrowed from the Army Intelligence Center and School. The table puts forward a four-step plan of activity, beginning with the preinsurgency, when per-ceived misdeeds lead to the formation of a movement.

Once a leadership has emerged, insurgencies enter the organizational phase. At this point, the insurgency is quite fragile and vulnerable to de-struction by the capture and suppression of its leadership and cadre. As a result, the purpose of the insurgents is to maintain a low profile, avoiding capture while they engage in a campaign of political conversion, normally in the countryside where alienation from the government is greatest and where the government is least effective. In the process, domestic support is built, which results in the creation of a sanctuary where the citizenry will

TABLE 9.1   States of Insurgency

Stage	Insurgent Action	Government Response
Preinsurgency	Leadership emerges in response to domestic grievances or outside influences.	Minimal.
Organizational	Infrastructure built, guerrillas recruited and trained, supplies acquired, and domestic and international support sought.	Counterinsurgency organization created.
Guerrilla warfare	Hit-and-run tactics used to attack government. Extensive insurgent political activity—both domestic and international—may also occur simultaneously during this stage.	Low-level military action initiated. Political, social, and economic reforms; civic action programs; psychological operations; and amnesty programs may also be initiated to counteract the insurgents' political activities.
Mobile conventional warfare	Larger units used in conventional warfare mode. Many insurgencies never reach this stage.	Conventional military operations implemented.

protect the insurgents, as well as provide them with a source of sustenance and recruits for the armed force that is being put together.

The insurgency becomes active when it gains enough strength selectively to confront government forces in guerrilla warfare situations. Using tactics first articulated by Sun Tzu (*The Art of War*) over 3,000 years ago, the emphasis is on small-unit engagement, with platoon-size forces selectively finding isolated small government units in vulnerable situations where tactics like ambushes are effective. Whenever the tactical situation is disadvantageous, the guerrillas simply quit the field, melting back into the population.

This style requires considerable patience, but it is highly purposive. Fighting only when certain of victory saps the morale of government forces, while simultaneously building insurgent spirit. Frustrated government forces begin to desert—some joining the insurgency—thereby contributing to a gradual shift in the balance of power between the government and the insurgency. In the process, the insurgency appears progressively to look like a winner, thereby increasing its political appeal.

An insurgency that has reached the guerrilla warfare stage is extremely difficult to defeat unless its leadership acts in such a manner as to alienate the population. Insurgencies do engage in selective acts of terror and atrocity, normally directed against the government and often to provoke governmental overreaction that further alienates the population. Such acts tend to be spotlighted by the insurgency's opponents to prompt images of the insurgents as atrocious, even monstrous figures. That image distorts the central purpose, which is the transfer of political loyalty away from the government. As *Field Manual 100-20* clearly states, "Each side seeks to demonstrate that it can govern better." An active guerrilla movement normally has effected much of that transfer.

When the balance of power has been decisively shifted, the insurgency enters its final stage, employing conventional warfare to crush the government's forces and to establish itself in power. The large, conventional forces necessary for this decisive action have been developed throughout the campaign but withheld until they are clearly superior to what is left of the government's forces.

Traditional insurgency is "poor man's war." It typically begins in situations of underdevelopment where governments, through ineptitude, corruption, venality, or insensitivity, have been ineffective in meeting the demands of a population but where an opposition must confront weakness that reflects societal conditions. The strategy attempts to turn warfare on its head, emphasizing the political elements as a way to overcome military disadvantage. In some regards, the military element is less important than the political process of persuasion, although military action is necessary both to demonstrate appeal and to protect those engaged in the political process. As a problem for American national security policy, the difficulty is that the underlying conditions in which insurgency arises are widespread in the Second Tier.

The Problem of Counterinsurgency

Countering an insurgency that has become established (reached the point of actively attacking the government) is especially difficult work. At one level, the existence of an insurgency suggests that part of the population is alienated from the government by policies and practices from which the government's supporters presumably profit in one way or another. At the same time, insurgencies are most vulnerable when they are weakest; ironically, at the point of vulnerability, they are least likely to be recognized as enough of a problem to be dealt with. Only when insurgencies reach the point that they are difficult to extinguish is counterinsurgency likely to be seen as important.

The object of both insurgents and counterinsurgents is the same: to win the loyalty of the population. This is the crucial "center of gravity" of both sides. The problem is that the mere existence of an insurgency demonstrates that part of the population rejects the government, demanding changes in governmental policy to better reflect their interests. Insurgents demand reform of existing conditions, but reform more than likely comes at the expense of those in power, who are likely to resist change.

This dynamic sets up the two alternative emphases that can be employed in dealing with insurgents. One way is to think of insurgency as a primarily—but not exclusively—political problem, the solution to which is political reform. The alternative is to define the problem as primarily military—the physical crushing of the rebellion. The difficulty, of course, is that insurgency is both a political and a military phenomenon that can be successfully dealt with only by a combined strategy of political reform and military suppression. The key, however, is the battle for people's loyalties.

The difficulty of counterinsurgency is that governments are likely to resist reform and lean toward a military approach that not only fails to respond to the political demands of those supporting the insurgency but exacerbates the problem. The result is a campaign where the symptoms, not the underlying problems, are attacked. As A. J. Bacevich and his colleagues put it, "The short-range fix is to go up the hill and kill the guerrilla; but that's addressing the effect, not the cause."

El Salvador's long civil war is an example. The insurgency's demand in that country was land reform; a handful of very wealthy land owners controlled the government and virtually all the productive land, which is in short supply. Political reform meant giving up both power and property, which they opposed. As a result, they viewed the problem as a military matter of destroying the insurgents. Only virtual exhaustion on both sides and the withdrawal of assistance coincident to the end of the Cold War produced a political compromise ending the war (which had begun in 1981) in 1992.

From the vantage point of American national security policy, the question is whether problems of insurgency and counterinsurgency remain an active concern. During the Cold War, the United States became involved in numerous insurgencies at one level or another. In places like El Salvador, we materially aided government forces; in Vietnam, we engaged in a massive, bloody campaign that tore asunder the country. In Afghanistan, Nicaragua, and, to a lesser extent, Angola, we backed the insurgents.

The common thread in all our Cold War involvements was the physical countering of movements that were avowedly or nominally Marxist and whose success presumably meant enlargement of communist dominion in the world. Clearly, that motivation is no longer present, nor is the superpower structure of support for beleaguered governments or insurgent bands. Does that mean that insurgency will disappear or that there will be little concern about it?

Five possible futures present themselves. The first is that traditional insurgencies, employing something like the mobile-guerrilla strategy, will remain the dominant form. The second is that these kinds of insurgencies will decline because of changed conditions in the world, notably the absence of outside forces willing to "sponsor" one side or another. A third prospect is that a number of movements will continue, but as long-term, low-level, yet persistent and protracted movements (for example, the Shining Path in Peru) with little prospect of either defeat or success. A fourth possibility is that the future will hold a number of pro-democratic movements that will see a shift in American support away from the government and toward the insurgents.

The fifth and most likely prospect is that internal movements will resemble the struggles in places like Bosnia and Somalia—desperate struggles sometimes for political power but often unstructured outbreaks of violence lacking any discernible political aims. These wars are very unlike traditional insurgencies in the sense that contending parties are not actively engaged in attempts at political conversion that serve to moderate the violence. Often, there is no interest in creating an alternate government at all; instead, the ostensible purpose is to create maximum disorder that facilitates the lawless terrorizing and exploitation of the population by the insurgents themselves. Although these new internal wars do not resemble traditional insurgencies in other ways, the dynamics of outside interference in them is structurally quite similar to intervention in conventional insurgencies.

The Problem of Intervention

If counterinsurgency is difficult work for a besieged government, its prospects are even dimmer for an outsider contemplating intervention. This is true for at least five reasons: the asymmetry of objectives between contending parties and the intervenor; a likely misunderstanding of the situation by the intervenor; the difficulty of properly timing intervention; the inevitable lack of appreciation shown by the host population; and the unenviable track record of outside intervention in domestic disputes. All are relevant to the so-called peacekeeping efforts of the United Nations and the United States in new internal wars in the post–Cold War world.

With regard to *asymmetry of objectives* between the contending parties and the outsider, internal wars are typically desperate affairs where one side triumphs at the physical expense of the other and where the stakes are control of government and even physical survival. Although the means of conduct may be relatively low-level (low-intensity), the purposes are total. The intervenor, on the other hand, has more limited objectives, such as the restoration of order or the ending of atrocity.

This situation creates problems for the intervenor. His objectives are less important to him than are the objectives of the parties to the dispute (hence the characterization of asymmetry). If intervention is by a First Tier country, its presence is governed by public opinion, which can recognize a comparative lack of deep interests. Thus, *Field Manual 100-20* concludes that "the U.S. must conclude such operations quickly." An objective of the parties adversely affected by intervention will be to protract an already protracted conflict or to take physical actions, such as attack-

ing the intervenors, that will turn public opinion in the intervening country against the action.

A second problem is outsider *misunderstanding of the situation.* Internal wars are typically complicated affairs in both a political and a military sense, and they often occur in places where American (or other)
knowledge of the situation is minimal—often because there are few U.S.
interests to trigger more in-depth understanding. It is, for instance, now
clear that the United States lacked a clear understanding of the situation
in Somalia when it first entered the country. It acted to alleviate a human
tragedy, but the real situation was a war zone where the weapons of war
were not guns and bullets but the withholding of food to starve portions
of the population into capitulation or death as surely as would have been
the case if the factions were shooting and killing people. American humanitarian efforts inevitably changed the military balance in ways favorable to some factions and unfavorable to others without fully appreciat-
ing the impact of its actions.

The third problem is the *difficulty of properly timing intervention.* The
dynamic here is what State Department official Todd Greentree calls the
"democratic contradiction." By this he means that outsiders are unlikely
to become adequately sensitive to internal problems until they reach a
critical stage at which they are highly visible and especially troublesome
to deal with. In classic insurgency terms, this is often late in the guerrilla
phase or early in the decisive phase, when effective action is very difficult. In more contemporary instances, this phase may be the point at
which gross atrocity becomes most evident—largely due to television
coverage—as the forces in contention are reaching a decisive stage.

This condition leads to the fourth problem: *lack of appreciation in segments of the target population for outside efforts.* When an outsider inter-
venes in an internal war, it is like intervening in a domestic dispute; it
may be in the name of the greater good, but the participants are unlikely
to see it that way. Also, there is no accepted right in international law to
intervene in an internal dispute, whether invited by one party or not. In
the Cold War, intervention was explicitly to aid one side (usually the
government), and the other side naturally opposed and resented intervention. Even in those circumstances, the longer the intervenor stays and
converts the war to his own affair, the greater the portions of the population that will be alienated. That was the large phenomenon of the American adventure in Vietnam.

In current circumstances, the dynamic is similar, but with subtle differences. In places like Somalia, the intention of outsiders is to be neutral
and evenhanded as a way to resume order. The problem is that some or
all parties to internal wars prefer the continuation of war to peace, usually because they are winning. When one interrupts the fighting, one implicitly becomes a partisan and, hence, alienates the portion of the population that does not benefit from the intervention. Even the limited
outside military intervention (bombing) in Bosnia, for instance, placed

the intervenors in effective alliance with the Muslim forces (the losing side) whether intended or not. Opposition to outside interference in Somalia, to the surprise of many, was absolutely predictable, a point reiterated in Chapter 10.

Finally, the *track record of involvement* highlights the simple matter of fact that outside intervention rarely results in the outcome desired by the intervenor. Internal wars can be successfully terminated only by the contending parties, whose interests are most intimately at stake. If one or all sides to a conflict oppose the interposition of peace, it is unlikely to work. The recent settlement in Cambodia seems a partial exception, but the final acceptance of the accord by all factions of the Khmer Rouge has yet to take place.

These rejoinders suggest a series of questions (borrowed from *Distant Thunder*) that a potential outside intervenor (considering either unilateral or multilateral intervention) might ask. The first is, "What is wrong here? What is the nature of the situation that tempts my involvement?" Second, "How do I come down on the side of the angels?" Internal wars are rarely simple matters of good versus bad; black and white fade into almost indistinguishable shades of gray. Picking good guys and bad guys is not as easy as it may seem; siding with a government requires an understanding of *what it did* to provoke war in the first place.

Third, "Does your side—or do you—have a reasonable prospect of success?" This is another way of asking Lake's question about whether intervention can do any good in a given situation, and whether the outsider's definition of doing good corresponds to that of the parties. Fourth, "Do you recognize the limits of your ability to influence the outcome?" Ultimately, internal wars are decided by the participants themselves. It is a corollary of the democratic contradiction that the effectiveness of outside influence is inversely related to the extent of involvement.

Fifth, "Do you have a viable politico-military strategy?" The heat of the moment may cause you to invoke the "do-something syndrome," as occurred in Somalia, where there was no clear strategic vision that could direct action. That is clearly a situation to be avoided in the future. Sixth and finally, "Will the American people support—and sustain support— for intervention?" In political democracies where the chief limit on applying military force is public opinion, this is clearly the bottom line consideration, to be challenged only with the greatest of care.

Insurgency and New Internal Wars

The pattern of post–Cold War violence differs from traditional insurgency. If one surveys the contemporary pattern, there is some residual occurrence of traditional insurgencies in such places as Angola (although the Clinton administration has been working to mediate that conflict, which has been going on since 1960) and Zaire. In addition, secessionary movements in such places as Georgia and Chechnya have the traditional political purpose of overthrowing and replacing a government, although they have been fought with particular ferocity and atrocity.

The new wars are different. The major subtypes are *criminal insurgencies*, campaigns of violence the major purpose of which is to promote the criminal activities of the putative insurgents (Liberia, Sierre Leone); *narcoinsurgencies*, wars the purpose of which is to protect the narcotics producers from the reaches of government authority (Peru, Bolivia, Colombia); and *Islamic fundamentalist movements*, the purpose of which is to destabilize secular government and to force governance in conformance to strict religious precepts (Algeria, Tajikistan).

The shared characteristics of these new internal wars are virtually the opposite of Maoist wars. First, the insurgents demonstrate no interest in governing the country (i.e., they are non-Clausewitzian). Sierre Leone's Revolutionary United Front (RUF), for instance, has been operating since 1992 and has never produced a political manifesto of any kind. The same is basically true of the various movements operating in Colombia.

Second, there is the absence of any political ideology underlying the movement that directs the violence and attempts to appeal to the population (i.e., they are non-Marxist). Peru's Shining Path, for instance, used to espouse an extreme Maoist ideology; since the capture and imprisonment of its founder, Abimael Guzman, such appeals have disappeared. Third, there is usually an absolute absence of military discipline or purpose (i.e., they are not followers of Sun Tzu). The image of teenage (and younger) street fighters in Monrovia, Liberia, is a particularly vivid example.

These characteristics have some decidedly non-Clausewitzian consequences. First, there are *no political objectives to limit the military actions undertaken*. Many of these wars are little more than random attacks on elements of the civilian population with no purpose save terrorizing the population. Second, the absence of political objectives leaves *no basis for postwar governance*. The very short ceasefire in Liberia that was negotiated in December 1995 and broke down completely in April 1996 is a case in point.

Third, there is *no positive appeal to a common center of gravity*. In traditional insurgencies, there is the battle for the hearts and minds of people to effect the exchange of loyalties. Finding such an appeal in Peru's Upper Huallaga Valley (where Shining Path operates) or in the slaughter of Rwanda is impossible. Fourth, the lack of political objectives translates into the *absence of military objectives and strategies*. It is not clear what the various militias and the like in the several central African internal wars seek to accomplish other than to further destabilize the country. This results in a fifth characteristic, the *very unmilitary way in which these wars are conducted*. To call those people soldiers who engage in the massive acts of atrocity against civilians (notably women and children) is to defame the military art and science. From Bosnia to central Africa, one can not help but be struck, and appalled, at how infrequently military units confront one another. Rather, the slaughter of the innocents prevails.

Sixth and finally, the *fashioning of a cease-fire to solve the problem is very difficult*. The extent and level of atrocity makes reconciliation extraordinarily difficult in places like Bosnia, Rwanda, and Burundi, where residents must wonder if their neighbors engaged in acts of atrocity against members of their families. This has clearly been a problem in Bosnia and Rwanda, which have revived the prosecution of war crimes as a way to sort out the responsibility. It also means that truces and cease-fires will be made all the more fragile because of the suspicions raised by the conduct of the hostilities.

These characteristics suggest that one cannot entirely understand these wars within the Clausewitzian framework of mobile-guerrilla warfare. Possibly we simply need a new framework to apply to these especially hideous conflicts. (See the Amplification box "Intervening in New Internal Wars.")

TERRORISM

Until the 1993 terrorist incidents in New York, the bombing of the Murrah Federal Building in Oklahoma City in 1995, and the arrest of the man accused of being the Unabomber in 1996, the problem of terrorism had only an abstract meaning for those Americans who did not routinely place themselves in the path of potential terrorist actions by travelling to parts of the world like Beirut or Northern Ireland, where such acts have become routine. The bombing of the Twin Trade Towers and the revelation of a plot to blow up the United Nations and other buildings in Manhattan, as well as to disrupt tunnels leading onto and off Manhattan Island, brought terrorism home to roost. Terrorism no longer simply happened somewhere else; it could happen here.

Americans are generally confused about terrorism and how to deal with it, for several reasons. One is the extremely evocative, emotional patina that surrounds terrorism. Acts of terror are intended to frighten populations (the Latin root from which the word derives means "frighten"), and part of the induced fright comes from the apparent randomness, even purposelessness of the actions. Randomness is usually purposive (to maximize fear of the unknown), but purposelessness often results because of fuzziness among the perpetrators of terrorist acts. When the Irish Republican Army (IRA) blows up a London subway station, its purpose (a unified Republic of Ireland in which Catholics would be a majority) is clear. When the Murrah Building Center was attacked, there was no apparent reason, probably because the bombers had no coherent purpose.

A second source of confusion arises from the meaning of terror. Terrorism is both a strategy and a tactic used by groups that do not consider themselves primarily as terrorists. Some organizations—the Iranian-backed Hezbollah, for example—are primarily terrorist in orientation and

AMPLIFICATION

Intervening in New Internal Wars

Ironically, one way in which new internal wars are similar to traditional insurgencies is in the area of the prospects of intervention. In these cases, the asymmetry of objectives will manifest itself in the desires of the intervenors to pull apart the the antagonists and stop the slaughter, while the combatants may have a greater interest in settling scores. Because these wars generally occur in remote places (at least from the U.S. perspective), the intervenors will never fully understand the situation. These wars often break out as acts of political instantaneous combustion (as did the April 1996 outbreak in Liberia) that cannot be anticipated in advance. Moreover, those disadvantaged by the imposition of peace may simply wait until intervention ends before settling scores. Finally, the record of such interventions is not especially great if successful ending of animosities is the criterion.

Systemic responses will depend on whether we can reconceptualize what we seek to accomplish by becoming involved in these conflicts. If we demand sweeping, permanent solutions, we will very likely be disappointed. Was it enough to prevent the starvation of 100,000 people in Somalia (a limited objective), or was it necessary to leave a stable peace behind (a grand, Clausewitzian objective)? By the former criterion, the United States succeeded; by the latter, it failed. The situation is similar in Bosnia. Clearly the fighting and dying was suspended by IFOR; whether that translates into a long-term peace is uncertain. Which criterion is necessary for satisfaction? and for whose satisfaction?

purpose. At the same time, most insurgent groups will, at one time or another, engage in terrorist acts for tactical purposes—for example, assassinating a recalcitrant village leader—while their broader purpose remains insurgent. This combination of usages adds to the confusion about whether to deal with terrorism as a military or a paramilitary-police problem.

Finally, the American political culture makes it difficult, if not impossible, for most Americans to gain anything like an empathetic understanding of terrorists. By and large, terrorist acts are absolutely repulsive to people from a culture that highly values individual rights, especially those of innocent citizens. We had a brief experience with home-grown terrorists of sorts during opposition to the Vietnam War (the Black Panthers and Weathermen, for instance), but we could not understand their actions except as pathology. The morbid fascination and publicity surrounding the surrender and sentencing (in the fall of 1993) of Katherine Powers, an anti-Vietnam activist who dropped out of college and participated in a bank robbery (ostensibly to raise money for the cause) in which a police officer was slain, is testimony. Our great interest in the lives and pathologies of terrorist suspects Timothy McVeigh and Theodore Kaczyinski reflect our disbelief that there are homegrown terrorists among us.

Experts in terrorism such as Neil Livingstone used to argue that an American was more likely to be the victim of a bolt of lightning than a terrorist act, but we are no longer so sure. The bombings in 1993 and 1995 brought terrorism home as a problem. Let us, therefore, look at the characteristics of terrorism and the general problems of dealing with it, distinguish between antiterrorism and counterterrorism as approaches to ameliorating the problem, and discuss how the government may seek to organize its efforts in this area of national security concern.

Characteristics of Terrorism

Understanding the motivation of individuals and groups to become terrorists requires some understanding of the nature and character of terror. What are its motives and dynamics? What causes it to succeed or fail? Who organizes and sustains terrorists? We can begin to unravel those dynamics by identifying six characteristics that apply to the phenomenon. These characteristics apply most clearly to terrorist organizations that have engaged in acts of terror for some time; they do not so clearly apply to the individual terrorists who have perpetrated acts within the United States in recent years. These seem to resemble more closely anarchistic acts, which have a long, if sporadic, history in this country.

The first is the nature of terrorist acts: *criminal acts to achieve political goals*. Terrorists engage in a wide variety of actions, all of which share the commonality of being illegal under any legal system. James J. Gallagher compiled the following list in 1992: bombing, arson, highjacking, ambush, kidnapping, hostage taking, assassination, raids, seizure of property, sabotage, and hoaxes (such as false bomb threats to dull the readiness of security employees).

If committed by an individual for personal reasons, any of these acts would doubtless be considered criminal and be prosecuted accordingly. The terrorist, however, maintains that criminality is set aside by the political purposes for which he or she acts. The capture and imprisonment of the terrorist results in martyrdom—especially if the terrorist is killed in the process. Among terrorists' peers, these criminal acts bring praise because of their political purpose.

It is from this dichotomy that the statement, "One man's terrorist is another man's freedom fighter," arises. Does the political nature of acts cancel out their criminal nature? Opponents of terror argue that criminal behavior is criminal behavior despite its motives. Proponents argue the opposite. Whether terrorism should be treated as common criminality or a political act akin to war is a major point of contention in dealing with terrorism.

What is troubling about the internal acts of terror is that they seem purposeless. Although Kaczyinski was allegedly motivated by an eccentric version of nativism as captured in his manifesto, for instance, none of the convicts or suspects in the other bombings has offered any explanation, no matter how lunatic, for their actions.

A second characteristic of terrorism is the *indiscriminate nature of terrorist acts.* As Gallagher points out, terrorist acts generally are motivated by one of several goals: to gain recognition for the movement; to coerce a population or a segment of it to engage in behavior the terrorist prefers; to intimidate a group into not doing something the terrorist opposes; to provoke an overreaction by the government that will gain sympathy for the terrorists; or, as already noted, to assist insurgents.

Terrorism coerces, intimidates, or provokes when it engenders such fear in the population that acquiescence to the terrorist's demands is deemed preferable to living in fear of attack. To try to induce this fear, the terrorist attempts to make terrorist acts so random and unpredictable that the target group lives in perpetual fear of an incident. (This unpredictability also makes terrorist acts harder to prevent.)

Third, the *goals of terrorists are generally to influence policy, not to gain control of government.* Terrorist organizations are typically small and highly compartmentalized, and the terrorist appeal is generally narrow within societies in which it breeds. Nothing approximating majoritarian appeal exists behind the terrorist's demands or program (when such exists). If it did, then the terrorist could use more traditional political tools to accomplish ends.

The goals may be more or less extensive and more or less coherent. The IRA goal to force Britain out of Northern Island as preface to its annexation to the Republic of Ireland is both ambitious and articulate, if lacking in measurable success. Organizations like Hezbollah often kidnap personnel to cause the release of "political prisoners" (generally, captured comrades convicted of criminal acts)—a clear but limited objective. The Trade Center bombers or the Libyans who reportedly placed a bomb on Pan American Flight 103, among others, never state a coherent rationale or purpose for their actions. The same seems to be true for the radical antigovernment fringe that appears to be the seedbed of American terrorism (to the extent any pattern of coherence can be ascertained).

Fourth, and related to the third characteristic, terrorism is *a tactic of the weak.* The causes in whose names terrorist actions are justified tend to be at the fringes of political reality, at least as seen from a Western vantage point. As such, their appeal is limited to those on the political fringes who are, by definition, a minority in the political spectrum. It is difficult, for instance, to imagine a meaningful terrorist appeal among Americans. White supremacists such as the Aryan Nation may be a partial exception, but they have little in the way of a coherent political program.

Fifth, despite their recent appearance in the United States, acts of terrorism worldwide are *on a steady decline.* According to U.S. State Department statistics, acts of terror peaked during the period between 1985 and 1988, averaging between 700 and 800 per year. Since then, they have declined to between 400 and 500 per year, as shown in Figure 9.1.

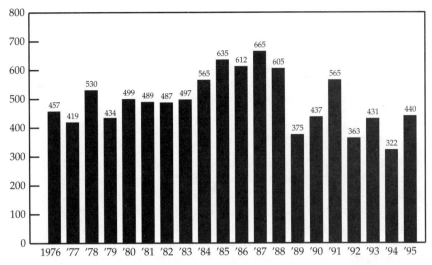

FIGURE **9.1**   **International Terrorist Incidents over Time, 1976–1995**

In past years, serious violence by Palestinians against other Palestinians in the occupied territories was included in the database of worldwide international terrorist incidents because Palestinians are considered stateless people. This resulted in such incidents being treated differently from intraethnic violence in other parts of the world. In 1989, as a result of further review of the nature of intra-Palestinian violence, such violence stopped being included in the U.S. Government's statistical data base on international terrorism. The figures shown above for the years 1984 through 1988 have been revised to exclude intra-Palestinian violence, thus making the data base consistent.

Investigations into terrorist incidents sometimes yield evidence that necessitates a change in the information previously held true (such as whether the incident fits the definition of international terrorism, which group or state sponsor was responsible, or the number of victims killed or injured). As a result of these adjustments, the statistics given in this report may vary slightly from numbers cited in pervious reports.

SOURCE: *Trends in International Terrorism.* Washington, D.C.: U.S. Department of State, 1996.

Two probable factors stand out as potential explanations. The first is the large-scale failure of terrorists to accomplish their political goals. Although individual acts continue, the list of organizations that have successfully forced target groups or governments to accede to their demands is essentially nonexistent. The second is the decline in sponsorship: the Soviet Union and several Eastern European communist countries were generally regarded as training grounds for terrorists. With the fall of communist rule, these sources have dried up.

The final characteristic deals with *sponsorship*. Sponsors come in two general varieties. The first, and least numerous, are *non-state-supported organizations*—groups privately organized and sponsored. These groups, including such organizations as the Italian Red Army (*Brigate Rosse*), tend to support themselves by criminal behavior such as robbing banks and kidnapping people for ransom. The other category, *state-sponsored organizations*, can be broken down into two groups. State-*supported* groups re-

ceive assistance from governments but operate independently of any direct orders from the sponsor. Hezbollah and the Popular Front for the
Liberation of Palestine are generally cited examples. State-*directed* groups
receive both support and operational direction from their sponsoring
governments. So-called Libyan "hit teams," such as the one that allegedly
blew up Pan Am 103 over Lockerbie, Scotland, are of this variety.

Dealing with Terrorism

If terrorists have not been spectacularly successful in achieving their
political ends, neither have forces opposed to terrorism been very successful in eliminating terrorist organizations, preventing terrorist acts, or
bringing terrorists to justice (except where the terrorists have proven in-
competent, as in New York). The reasons are multifaceted and include
general problems posed by terrorists, the balance between antiterrorist
and counterterrorist approaches to the problem, and disagreement about
whether to treat terrorists under rules of law or rules of war.

There are several bedeviling general problems. First, the clandestine,
highly fragmented nature of terrorist groups makes them difficult to penetrate. These groups are generally segmented into cells with minimal
knowledge of one another in order to limit damage if an individual is
captured. Moreover, successful groups, particularly in the Middle East,
routinely change names to thwart efforts to identify them. Several of the
more prominent Lebanese-based, Iranian-sponsored groups are, apparently, basically the same organization. The problem is even more difficult
when the terrorist is a single individual acting independently, as in the
case of the Unabomber.

Second, it is difficult to gain the initiative against terrorists, who are
able to choose the time and place of the acts to which government authorities must react. In the case of some inept groups, penetration of the
membership by government agents may allow prediction, but that is the
exception; Americans cannot always assume that future terrorists will
prove as hapless as the group that planned to attack targets in New York
or as foolish as McVeigh, who was apprehended only because he took
the license plate off his car *to avoid detection.*

Third, the terrorist acts listed earlier are highly idiosyncratic. Learning how to solve one problem does not necessarily provide much guidance for dealing with others. Kidnapping and hostage taking may have
enough in common so that lessons learned from dealing with one have
some transfer to the other, but such knowledge does not help much in
dealing with bombings or arson.

Fourth, governments often hide and protect terrorist groups effectively enough that they are outside the effective reach of those who would
penetrate and suppress them. The Bekaa Valley of Lebanon has long been
a safe haven for terrorist organizations, where they are protected by the oc-
cupying Syrian armed forces. Western intelligence services know they are

there; they just cannot get to them to do anything about them. The centers of gravity of the organizations, their top leadership and major operatives, are effectively shielded by governmental sponsors.

Finally, some of the methods for dealing with terrorists are culturally offensive to Americans. If it is often impossible physically to apprehend terrorists and, hence, to suppress their activities, then the alternative may be to convince the terrorists to cease and desist by *terrorizing the terrorists*. Such an effort may entail engaging in the same kinds of acts against the terrorists that they employ against society. Under American law, agents of the government (military or otherwise) are prohibited from engaging in illegal acts such as assassination, and many Americans object to the idea that we would stoop to the same kinds of acts that we find so repulsive when conducted against us.

The problem of dealing with terrorism in a culturally acceptable manner is reflected in the two alternative means for blunting terrorism. The first is *antiterrorism*, defensive measures taken to decrease the vulnerability of society or individuals to terrorist attacks. The effectiveness of such actions varies considerably, depending on the unit being protected. Individuals prone to terrorist attacks, such as prominent business leaders or politicians in some countries, can engage in a large array of antiterrorist actions, including varying routines to make them less predictable (one of the reasons President Clinton's penchant for jogging on the streets of Washington drove the Secret Service to distraction) and taking physically protective actions such as installing solid rubber tires on vehicles, hiring bodyguards, or wearing a bullet-proof vest.

As units get larger, antiterrorist actions become more difficult— even problematical. Installing metal detectors at airports reduces the likelihood that weapons can be smuggled onto airplanes, but it has not been totally successful in preventing airline bombings or skyjackings. Security guards at the Trade Towers did not detect the van in which explosives were located, and passive restraints (admittedly inadequate) did not prevent the lethal attack on the Marine barracks in Beirut in 1983.

The imperfection of antiterrorist approaches creates some enthusiasm for a second approach, *counterterrorism*, which is offensive action taken to suppress terrorist activities by destroying their ability to act; it includes violent acts against individuals and organizations. Counterterror involves terrorizing the terrorists. It also involves a spectrum of actions, from placing informants in terrorist cells to bring about their apprehension before they engage in terrorist acts (as in the New York case) to attacking and assassinating key personnel. Although the mission failed and could not be legally justified as such, the 1986 air raid against Libya was clearly for the purpose of terrorizing—even killing—Libyan strongman Muammar Qaddafi.

There are practical limitations on counterterrorism as described in the general problems of dealing with terrorists—the clandestine nature of organizations and protection of them by state sponsors, for instance. In foreign environments, acts against individuals and groups are much more operationally difficult than popular images would suggest.

Counterterrorism is also affected by the perception of terrorism as a legal or a politico-military problem, a distinction with both jurisdictional and operational consequences. Jurisdictionally, the conceptualization determines which elements of government will respond to terrorist threats or acts. Within the territorial United States, the distinction is clear; only law enforcement agencies have the legal right to operate in a policing capacity. The jurisdictional issue is not so clear on foreign soil, especially if terrorist actions are occurring in a war or quasi-war zone.

Jurisdictional and legal problems are especially difficult when dealing with efforts against domestic terror. Efforts to identify and suppress terrorists before they act require intrusive methods (such as wiretapping) that may violate civil rights. Legal delays, such as occurred in the Oklahoma City trial, further frustrate counterterror efforts by delaying justice. The Antiterrorism Act of 1996 which, symbolically, was opposed by the odd coalition of the American Civil Liberties Union and the National Rifle Association, reflects these difficulties.

The operational consequences affect how counterterror can be carried out. If terrorism is considered a political problem, it is, in essence, an act of war and subject to the rules of engagement (ROEs) of war and the somewhat more relaxed standards of evidence, apprehension, and confinement that attach to the rules of war. In that case, counterterrorism becomes largely a military or, at least, paramilitary activity for which special forces are clearly applicable. If, on the other hand, terrorist acts are considered as simply criminal, then such matters as rules of evidence, arrest, confinement, and trial are subject to the criminal justice system. Dealing with terrorism then becomes largely a police function.

Terrorists would like to have it both ways. They prefer to portray their acts as political, acts of war against injustice. At the same time, they believe that their actions should fall under the jurisdiction of the criminal justice system, the requirements of which greatly restrict the ability to apprehend and interrupt terrorist activities. From the vantage point of the counterterrorism community, notably specialized units such as the Army's Delta Force, treating terrorism as a criminal activity unduly restricts efforts at suppression, leaving great advantage to the terrorists.

Terrorism and National Security

Until recently, terrorism has been an abstract problem that did not command great attention within the federal government. The reason, simply enough, was that neither American territory nor U.S. citizens were subject to enough dislocation and danger to warrant concerted action on the part of the government.

This environment is changing. The cases in New York and Oklahoma City indicate that terrorism is finding its way to American shores, taking away some of the abstraction. At the same time, a likely source of abrasion between countries of the First and Second Tiers will be in Second Tier sponsorship of terrorist organizations, some of which may become active against First Tier countries, including the United States. Countries with little prospect of harming or influencing the United States in more traditional ways may find government-directed terrorism a convenient way to get the Americans into or out of their affairs.

Currently, the American government is not optimally organized to deal with terrorism, reflecting both the piecemeal organization of the effort and its low priority among national security concerns. The broad form of organization is shown in Figure 9.2, which reveals a layered approach in which many agencies have some operational responsibility and in which coordination of the activities of diverse agencies occurs through something called the "lead agency" principle.

Numerous unlikely federal agencies have some responsibility for terrorist activities. For example, the Postal Service has responsibility for investigating mail bombs, the Federal Aviation Administration (FAA) for investigating airline bombings and threats (as well as security), and the Immigration and Naturalization Service for monitoring suspected terrorists entering the country.

All diverse efforts are coordinated through the lead agency concept. For terrorist acts in the United States, the Department of Justice (through its designated agent, the Federal Bureau of Investigation) takes the lead, as was the case in the successful infiltration and arrest of the New York

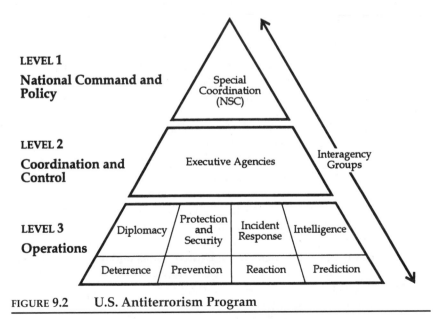

FIGURE 9.2   U.S. Antiterrorism Program

SOURCE: U.S. Department of Defense, Washington, D.C., 1991. FMFM 7–14, 2–3.

plotters. If an aircraft in flight is the subject, the FAA is the designated lead agency, and terrorist acts against Americans overseas are coordinated by the State Department. And DOD has its own interservice task force on terrorism.

If terrorism is to become a higher priority in the future, this system will have to be better rationalized in order to husband and concentrate the relatively scarce resources devoted to the enterprise. Whether this will be the case is, in a sense, up to the terrorists and how much—if at all— they step up terrorist activities in the United States or against American interests. As noted earlier, one problem of terrorism is deciding who has the initiative.

TRANSSTATE AND RELATED PROBLEMS

Both insurgency and terrorism share the commonality of being traditional national security concerns. Both are military or paramilitary in content, and each is a Second Tier problem that has some impact on the countries of the First Tier. In the past decade or so, another category of nontraditional problems has been added to the international—and even the national—security agenda. This category encompasses a series of difficulties that transcend national boundaries and are probably solvable only by multinational means.

These *transstate issues*, as they are commonly and loosely called, encompass a fairly broad range of concerns, from the environment to international migration. In one sense, they are unlike more traditional national security concerns: their military content—the way national security problems have historically been defined—is limited or indirect. They share with traditional concerns the psychological sense of security in that failure to rectify them can result in a decreased sense of safety. Moreover, they are mostly problems having their roots in the Second Tier, and the responses to them by the First Tier will help define the international relations of the tiers in the new order.

Two groups of issues are involved. The truly transstate issues are problems that transcend state in ways over which states have little control and that cannot be solved by individual states acting alone. The key defining characteristic is the *inability* of individual states to act effectively. Population migration is currently such an issue. The other related issues share the basic characteristics of transstate issues but are problems that states *could solve* if they chose to do so. Population growth is such a problem.

For present purposes, three transstate and related issues will be examined, because each touches on the United States and, by the extended definition, its security. The first of these is food, the availability and distribution of which has become an important factor in a number of Second Tier conflicts. On a macro level (global adequacy and distribution), it is a transstate issue; the use of food as a weapon in internal wars such as

Somalia is not. The second is population growth and distribution, especially the migration of populations from the Second Tier to the First. The third, which has both First and Second Tier roots and implications, is the trafficking in arms.

Food

The quantitative and qualitative adequacy of diet is a major problem throughout many regions of the Second Tier. The source of the problem is not so much that not enough food is produced globally to feed the rapidly growing population, for the "green revolution" of the 1960s created the scientific basis for growing adequate supplies for the nearly six billion people who currently inhabit the earth. Also, advances in biogenetics are projected to increase potential productivity to swell the globe's "carrying capacity" to nourish population increases into the second or third decades of the twenty-first century, when population is projected to level off.

As a purely physical matter, the problem of food is distributional and economic. While enough food is produced to feed everyone, not enough is grown at all places for adequate nourishment, and where food is in short supply, there is often no adequate means to get it to those in need. The most glaring example is the Horn of Africa (notably Ethiopia, Eritrea, Somalia, and the Sudan), where years of drought brought on massive undernourishment, exacerbated by war, and resulted in large-scale starvation. In Russia, large portions of crops routinely rot in the fields for lack of adequate means to get them to consumers. Moreover, those most in need are also generally the poorest countries, meaning that they lack the economic resources to import adequate foodstuffs and must, instead, rely on the largesse of other governments and relief organizations.

The most troubling food problem, and the one with the most direct national security consequences, is the increased use of food as a politico-military weapon. The attempt to starve populations into submission is, of course, nothing new; depriving a besieged population of sustenance is a part of the package of techniques that underlie siege warfare, one of the oldest means of bringing urban populations to their knees. The technique has been honed to particularly devastating and public effect in the post–Cold War world and has contributed to the public policy debate about appropriate involvement in Second Tier conflicts. Television's global reach has ensured that the food weapon is publicly available for inspection by global publics.

The use of food as a weapon has infected major conflicts in the new order. Saddam Hussein used the withholding of food supplies to weaken the Kurdish population, and it was CNN images of starving and diseased Kurds on a Turkish mountainside that inspired American intervention and the establishment of the Kurdish "exclusion zone" in northeastern Iraq. (The Iraqi government is "excluded" from exercising jurisdiction over its own sovereign territory within the zone.) Under the name Operation Provide Comfort, this operation continues today. In the Bosnian winters of 1992 to 1995, a primary tactic of Serbian and Croatian besiegers of Muslim cities and towns was the interruption of relief supplies of food and medicine.

Somalia, of course, represents the epitome of employing the "food bullet." There is precedent in the Horn of Africa, which only in 1993 saw its decade-long drought begin to end. The Ethiopian government long employed the withholding of food in its bitter and ultimately unsuccessful attempt to prevent Eritrean secession, and the Muslim government of Sudan has been widely accused by human rights groups of doing the same to its Christian and animist tribal minorities in the south of that country.

The interclan use of starvation for political gain reached its apex in Somalia. When negotiations to reach a political accord among the clan warlords broke down in the summer of 1992, the clans turned to scarce food supplies as the weapons of choice to impose their will on opposing clans. What Americans saw as a humanitarian problem was, in fact, a war zone where the "bullets" were bags of grain. When the United States intervened to alleviate the undeniable suffering, the effect was to remove the politico-military advantage from those clans employing the weapon, thereby affecting the balance of power. That such an interruption would eventually not be universally appreciated should have been anticipated.

Will the use of food as a weapon continue? The answer is obvious; in those parts of the Second Tier that are impoverished, where food supplies are marginal in the best of times, and where deep intergroup hatreds result in violence, clearly the problem will recur. The results will, as in Somalia, be hideous—the distended stomachs of starving children and the emaciated corpses of innocent victims. The question is what, if anything, the international community—especially the powerful countries of the First Tier—will do about the continuation of this horrible practice.

Population

Burgeoning population growth throughout much of the Second Tier interacts with other factors to inhibit development and progression toward First Tier status. Growing population strains food supplies, absorbs economic resources that could be used for economic development, places demands for social services that weaken the stability of already marginally legitimate governments, and produces a climate of misery that is the breeding ground for continued despair and the potential for violence.

The problem is easy to describe, if difficult to solve. The population growth rate (PGR) is the result of a simple formula where PGR equals the difference between birth rate and death rate, plus or minus migration. In most Second Tier countries, birth rates are steady or even declining, but, thanks to the introduction of modern sanitary and medical procedures, death rates are also declining (meaning that people live longer). Particularly, decreases in infant and child mortality have produced a younger population (compared with aging populations in First Tier states); in many Second Tier countries, a majority of the population are teenagers or younger.

Internally, the result is economic and political destabilization. Young people migrate to the urban areas, where there are neither jobs nor living facilities to absorb them. Unemployed or underemployed, they become discontented and, in some cases, violent. The teenaged Somali "technicals" marauding the streets of Mogadishu in December 1992 with their Jeep-mounted machine guns come to mind, as do the child-soldiers of Liberia.

As a First Tier–Second Tier problem with national security overtones, the real problem is *migration* from Second Tier to First Tier countries. In some cases, the reason is the hope of economic opportunity (as among many Central Americans coming to the United States); in others, it is the fear of political repression (as among Bosnian and Albanian refugees throughout Europe). In places like Haiti, both economic and political motivations combine to send populations into flight.

In the most extreme cases, refugees flee the ravages of war. Bosnia, as noted, has produced a flood of refugees to any European country that will take them; the war between Armenia and Azerbaijan has produced an estimated 1.5 million refugees (mostly Azeri). Worldwide, there were an estimated 23 million international refugees (people who had fled their countries) in the middle of 1995; the number is almost certainly larger today.

These flows create great problems in both the First and the Second Tiers. Kenya, for instance, has little vested interest in the outcome of hostilities in Somalia; at the point where Somali refugees threaten to overwhelm Kenya's ability to absorb them, however, an interest is created. Central American illegal immigrants tax U.S. southwestern states, and Caribbean immigrants create similar problems in Florida.

Europe is increasingly feeling the same pinch. France, overwhelmed by immigration from its former colonies, contemplates draconian laws to limit the flow. The refugee problem has spurred neo-Nazi violence in Germany and a constitutional amendment on immigration. The Baltic states have passed legislation making it extremely difficult for ethnic Russians to qualify for full citizenship, supplying an inducement for them to return to Russia.

The problem has definite national security overtones. Caribbean emigres have been used as the rationale for a continuing strong U.S. Navy. The mission to buttress the return of President Jean-Bertrand Aristide to power in Haiti was largely justified as a palliative to the flood of Haitian boat people attempting to enter the United States. Means of better controlling the porous U.S.-Mexican border engage the attention of many concerned with the future of the U.S. Army.

Ultimately, the population problem requires a transstate solution. As long as reduced death rates are not matched by correspondingly lower birth rates, Second Tier populations will burgeon, while First Tier states approach stasis. Only Second Tier governments can encourage those reductions, although possibly with economic help from the First Tier. Similarly, the best antidote to the urge to migrate is reduction of the misery that motivates people to move.

As a direct national security concern, the problem of refugees is the most difficult. The images of weary, starving refugees fleeing war zones with little more than the clothes on their backs is a stark artifact of the ethnic violence that is such a large part of the fabric of post–Cold War violence. Until—or unless—that trend abates, the tragic fates of the refugees will be with us. A part of the refugee problem that has received scant attention is its medical dimension. The large refugee camps so common in Africa, for instance (which had 19 million refugees in 1995), are breeding grounds for all sorts of exotic diseases. The ecola scares in Zaire are examples. It is probably just a matter of time until First Tier relief workers or peacekeeping forces are infected by some disease and carry it back to their own countries.

Arms Flow

The transfer of conventional arms to the countries of the Second Tier was a common part of the Cold War competition. As Second Tier countries emerged from colonial domination, one of the first institutions they sought to develop was the military. Motivations varied from the existence of real or imagined external enemies to the prestige of having a modern military force to suppress internal dissidents.

The superpowers, anxious to curry favor or to deny influence to one another, were more than willing to assist in the arming process. At best, real influence might be the reward from grateful recipients. By providing them with American or Soviet weapons, countries could also be made dependent for spare parts or ammunition in the future. Also, selling weapons to wealthy states, such as those in the Middle East, helped amortize research and development costs on large-ticket items such as airplanes, thereby reducing unit costs to the superpowers themselves.

The result was a flood of weaponry into the Second Tier, principally supplied by the United States and the Soviet Union. Almost everyone knew that the result of these transfers, particularly to the highly volatile Middle East, was unfortunate in terms of Second Tier stability. With the end of the Cold War, there have been great hopes that the lack of competition might allow multilateral agreements among historic suppliers to staunch the flow. To this point, however, such hopes have largely been frustrated, for at least three reasons.

The first, ironically enough, is the end of the Cold War itself. A major effect of reducing the military confrontation has been a reduction in the size of armed forces of the former adversaries. In the process, inventories of unused and now unnecessary weapons have accumulated, and some have found their way into the arms trade. The second reason is that demand remains brisk for weapons transfers, resulting in continuing supplies. For Russia, desperate for hard currency to underwrite economic transformation, the temptation has been overwhelming, and other governments as well have found the profits irresistible. Third, other Second Tier states are also actively in the business of selling arms for the same economic reasons that First Tier states become involved. Having said that, we must acknowledge that the United States is overwhelmingly the world's armorer. In 1993, for instance, 73 percent of the arms transfers from First Tier states to Second Tier countries was American.

Controlling arms transfers is a value upon which almost everyone agrees but which no state can effect unilaterally. What is needed is the equivalent of a cartel of weapons-producing states that agree to stem the flow. Unfortunately, the dynamics of cartels also include the temptation to break ranks for profit. As long as there are buyers in the market, there will be sellers, and the result will be high levels of carnage.

ECONOMIC SECURITY

As the Cold War has retreated, Americans' economic well-being—often simply referred to as economic security—has become a more prominent part of the agenda. The election of Bill Clinton in 1992 accelerated and intensified this emphasis; Clinton's greater emphasis on the domestic agenda and his particular interest in economic matters contribute to this focus. His designation of a National Economic Council parallel to the National Security Council adds symbolically to the designation.

Questions of economic security intrude on the national security debate in several ways. First, economic competition is the major source of dissent and disagreement *among* member states of the First Tier. First Tier economies do compete on a variety of levels, and national successes affect the economic well-being and prosperity of citizenries. The enormous interpenetration and interdependence of First Tier economies, brought about by international firm ownership and investment, further complicates the issue. The aggravations that economic competition create are more annoying than they are fundamental; it is very difficult to imagine any real likelihood of war within the First Tier resulting from an economic issue.

Second, questions of how to enhance economic performance and competitiveness call upon scarce resources and bring economic incentives and initiatives in direct competition for federal funds with more traditional national security claims on the budget. The Cold War prejudiced funding decisions in favor of traditional defense priorities; the eclipse of the threat leaves the national security community vulnerable to force and budget reductions ("downsizing," in the vernacular). This trend emerged in the Bush administration and has been accelerated by the Clinton administration to the point that, by 1996, interest payments on the federal deficit replaced defense expenditures as the second largest claimant on the budget. (Entitlement programs remain first.)

Third, the Clinton administration has declared its intention to move much federal research and development traditionally housed in the Defense Department to civilian priorities. As a symbol, the old Defense Advanced Research Program Agency (DARPA), the conduit for much defense-funded research, has had the "D" dropped from its title. The rationale for the change is both the reduced need for explicit weapons research and the belief that funding for civilian-oriented research is more likely to result in economically beneficial outcomes than the spinoffs from weapons research. As such, research and development has become a key element of the drive for the greater American economic competitiveness that is at the core of the Clinton industrial policy emphasis.

Economic security shares with a number of the other nontraditional security areas the dual characteristics of being non-life-threatening (the physical aspect of security) and, hence, within the psychological realm of security. It is a fact that, in an economic sense, Americans have developed over the last decade or so a decreased belief in their economic domination in the world, and many have the sense that their standards of living will likely decline in the future.

Economic security can be discussed from a number of vantage points that will frame our discussion. We will begin by looking at the question of so-called high technology, which produces the motor of economic and scientific change. We will then move to the matter of economic competitiveness itself, followed by discussion of the international implications of economic change and national security outgrowths.

The High Technology Revolution

The phenomenon of high technology—also known as the third industrial revolution—has combined with the decline in First Tier military competition and the end of the Cold War to help redefine world power and rank. President Clinton's "ring of market democracies" is defined not only as those states with free enterprise economic and democratic political systems, but also as members of the First Tier tied heavily into being part of the high-technology–based, highly internationalized global economy that both defines and is made possible by high technology. Participation or its absence in the high technology process is a major contributor to the economic instrument of power.

High technology can be defined as very rapid knowledge development and generation (largely the product of computer and computer-related technologies that allow the processing of enormous amounts of information in very little time), information processing and dissemination (the product of the parallel telecommunications revolution), and a highly diverse set of derivative technologies stimulated by the explosion in knowledge generation and dissemination.

The definition suggests that three elements form high technology. The first is spectacular leaps in the capabilities of computers and associated technologies such as microelectronics and semiconductors and software breakthroughs such as digitization. The cutting edge of computing, so-called *supercomputers* (defined as the most capable computer at any point in time), allows the analysis of information and consequent generation of knowledge at dizzying speeds inconceivable a decade ago. Moreover, the chief technology for developing future generations of computers is the capability of current computers. Because the development of new generations increasingly compresses in time, getting behind has exponentially debilitating effects.

The second element is telecommunications (also sometimes called the "informatics" revolution). The advent of satellite technology, fiber optics, and the like has increased enormously the amount of information that can be transmitted, the speed of transmission, and the global reach of dissemination. Increased capability allows, for instance, the transmission of large bodies of computer-derived data instantaneously across national boundaries. As a result, large-scale, real-time collaboration between members of the international scientific community is possible via modems linking personal computers; for the general population, outlets such as the Internet and World Wide Web promote global communications. At the same time, international commercial transactions have been automated to an extent that allows around-the-clock operations of the world's stock and commodity markets. Global telecommunications has also spawned global television networks such as the Cable News Network (CNN) and the Independent Television Network (ITN), which disseminate instantly news occurring all over the world.

The third element is derivative technologies, in which advances in computing and telecommunications stimulate other areas. A representative, but by no means exhaustive, list includes specialty materials, artificial intelligence, robotics, airframes and avionics, smart weapons, computer-aided design/computer-aided manufacturing (CAD/CAM), biotechnology, and catalysis and other chemical processes.

This impressive list underscores product development in an ever-expanding number of areas that define the cutting edge of design and manufacturing. Moreover, the pace of change in each area is accelerated by their interaction. Computer advances contribute to the design of more advanced telecommunications systems, telecommunications links facilitate greater collaboration and advances in knowledge generation, and advances in derivative technologies such as fiber optics both derive from high technology and materially contribute to advances in telecommunications. It should not be surprising that state-of-the-art projects such as the "electronic superhighway" come from the union of large corporations that combine computing and telecommunications expertise.

Economic Competitiveness

High technology provides the keystone with which economic competitiveness is built. Scientific and technological preeminence that can be translated into more advanced and desirable products represents the leading edge of applied technology. The ability to transform knowledge into commercial applications represents the forefront of production. The country that has and exploits that advantage will produce the goods and services that most people desire and thus will have the ability to provide those goods and services both to its own population and to the rest of the world.

Increasingly, technological outcomes represent advances in processes and products, especially processes with value in the international market. For instance, the placement of a CAD/CAM-designed textile plant, with robotics applied to production, can add greatly to the prosperity of a Second Tier state. The ability to choose among states that will receive those benefits can add measurably to international reputation and stature.

Most of the competition remains within the First Tier, focusing on the triangular relationship between North America (as NAFTA provisions take effect), the European Union (EU), and Japan. As the competition moves through the formation of trade blocs like EU and NAFTA (possibly expanded hemispherically as the Free Trade Area of the Americas), and around the Pacific Rim through the Asia-Pacific Economic Cooperation, there may be increased friction among the blocs unless processes through the old General Agreement on Tariffs and Trade (GATT) process now formalized as the World Trade Organization (WTO) produce generally lower trade barriers among all states.

From the United States standpoint, the 1980s and early 1990s produced a particularly sharp friction between it and Japan. Although the United States continues to have the world's strongest scientific community (as measured by graduates, Nobel laureates, and the like), the Japanese have excelled in commercializing scientific breakthrough in important commercial areas such as electronics and automobiles, leading to a great trade imbalance in favor of Japan. U.S. leadership in digital television (high definition television or HDTV) will reduce this deficit; at the same time, however, the U.S. trade deficit with China now exceeds the imbalance with Japan.

This kind of conflict has enlivened calls for greater attention to American competitiveness. Reform of education systems in the United States to produce better skilled and better educated citizens represents one aspect of this drive, as does the Clinton-Gore emphasis on industrial policy (providing governmental emphasis to selected industrial development) and the sharing of governmental research with private enterprises to stimulate advanced products and processes in areas such as environmental cleanup (a particular emphasis of Vice President Gore).

These conflicts are important, but not dangerous, in the sense of their potential to lead to war. The fact that all the First Tier countries share political form and economic systems tends to modify their conflicts. Also, one of the most salient aspects of the increasingly global economy is the extent to which economies are linked to one another via private enterpises that cut across, and often ignore, national boundaries.

International Implications

Technological change is affecting the basic structure of the world's economic system in fundamental ways that would have been impossible to imagine no more than a decade or so ago. The changes are extremely dynamic and, in many instances, unpredictable enough that any comprehensive attempt to capture the essence of change will fail. Three examples of change, however, may convey some of the import.

The first is the *internationalization of economic activity*. In the past, it was possible to talk meaningfully about reasonably autonomous and, from a national government's viewpoint, controllable national economies. The wave of privatization and deregulation of economic activity and the facilitating effects of the high technology revolution have changed that dramatically. It is now almost impossible to talk about national economies—at least, within the First Tier. Instead, a global economy linking the membership of First Tier states has emerged. It is manifested in such ways as multinational control of large enterprises. The multinational corporation (MNC) of the 1960s, a company doing business in several countries but mostly owned by nationals of one country and attached to that country, is giving way to *stateless corporations*, companies so international in ownership, management, labor force, and product mix that they cannot be meaningfully attached to any single country. Levels of investment across borders generally reinforce this phenomenon.

A second impact is the *de facto assault on national sovereignty* that the new economic system implies. National boundaries are largely irrelevant to most large commercial enterprises, which do business quite independently of any territorial imperative connected to state control or supervision. States may, for instance, want to place proprietary controls on research outcomes to enhance national advantage, but two scientists with modems living across national boundaries can simply ignore such attempts to regulate. The Chinese government's attempts to close down access to information during the Tiananmen incident in 1989 were similarly compromised by facsimile (fax) machine transmission of *samizdat* newsletters from the United States to Chinese colleges and universities.

Third, the technology revolution has *widened the economic gap between the First and Second Tiers*. Differential levels of wealth and productivity have been increased between those who do and do not participate in high technological activity. One of the apparent motives of Mikhail Gorbachev, as noted in Chapter 6, was to break down barriers to Soviet participation; that effort has not succeeded, and the successor states appear headed for the Second Tier. (Indeed, one of the interesting questions about the emerging system is which of the old Second World of communist states will end up in the First or Second Tiers.) Moreover, this widening gap, reflected in standards of living, prosperity, and stability, represents an increasingly cleaving difference between the tiers.

National Security Implications

The high technology phenomenon also has implications for national security that are affecting, and will continue to affect, how the United States deals with the new international order. Once again, it is impossible to provide a comprehensive list in a dynamic environment. Instead, two impacts will be highlighted that have already played a role in reshaping America's security.

The first impact is the *enormous gap in military capability between the states of the First and Second Tiers.* The high technological revolution has increased greatly the lethal capacity of those countries, notably the United States, that possess the most advanced weaponry, while simultaneously providing the ability for those who possess those weapons to limit greatly their own casualties in combat against technologically inferior foes. Military quality now more than makes up for quantity, evidence of the underlying dynamic of the Revolution in Military Affairs.

The gap became evident in the Persian Gulf War, which saw the first successful application of technological improvements that were occurring over a period of time. Essentially, three things came together. First, highly sophisticated weapons—precision-guided munitions, advanced satellite reconnaisance, and stealth aircraft—had been improved to the point of much greater reliability than previously attained. Second, the operators of this equipment demonstrated for the first time the ability to use the equipment to full effect. Third, doctrine, strategy, and tactics had been adapted to incorporate the new capabilities to full effect.

The result, of course, was a rout. Within hours, Iraqi intelligence had been reduced to line of sight by people on the ground and their ability to communicate to troops in the field had been disrupted by allied aircraft, which owned the skies. Air forces relentlessly attacked Iraqi forces, which had no effective means of protecting themselves. When ground combat began, the allies could generally fire upon Iraqi units outside of the range of Iraqi weaponry.

The military lesson of the Gulf War is plain: no Second Tier state can compete with the military might of the First Tier *if the First Tier decides on a vigorous application of force.* The mismatch is so great that the only way a Second Tier state can avoid defeat by the First Tier is to avoid war with the First Tier altogether or to convince the First Tier state's population not to become involved. First Tier states, as already noted, are limited in their application of force principally by public opinion, which combines an aversion to both casualties and the high cost of modern war. That, however, is their only limitation.

The second impact is an artifact of telecommunications: *conflict has become extremely public due to television coverage.* War and violence anywhere in the world are available on television virtually as they happen. We now witness the carnage and atrocity of war at a level of intimacy previously unknown.

We have already seen some of the consequences. Television coverage of the Kurds suffering when they fled the wrath of Saddam Hussein after the Gulf War led directly to Operation Provide Comfort, which created for them an American-enforced sanctuary in northeast Iraq (the so-called exclusion zone). Pictures of Somalis starving contributed visibly to the creation of Operation Restore Hope, while Bosnian suffering activated public outcry but no sustained action.

The impact of telecommunications is ambivalent at this time. The initial actions in Iraq and Somalia suggested that public policy, swayed by television images, would create a "do-something syndrome" impelling the U.S. government to take action to alleviate suffering everywhere. As the hastily conceived mission in Somalia produced negative results, however, a backlash took place; the scene of a dead American serviceman's body being dragged through the streets of Mogadishu created an equally loud cry to abandon the mission. The slaughter in Rwanda evoked hardly any international outcry at all. It is also not clear whether desensitization will occur as the public becomes inured to Second Tier suffering, and whether the "do-something syndrome" will be reduced to the "let's-appear-to-do-something-syndrome."

These two phenomena are related. Technology has produced the physical capability for the United States to intervene with great *military* effect in a broad range of situations that the same technology makes us much more aware of than in the past. Capability and awareness must, however, be combined with strategy and policy that discerns in which conflicts the United States will and will not involve itself—a challenge for policymakers largely created by technology.

CONCLUSIONS

The post–Cold War pattern of national security concerns is broader, if less deep, than it was before. We no longer have to be concerned with a problem where the survival of the United States and the whole international system is in the balance. Recognizing that things could change and that new threats as ominous as those of the past could return, we at least have an interlude during which we have the "luxury" of considering matters broader and less demanding than the problems of the past.

The new list is, of course, not really new. Insurgency and terrorism were part of the pattern of problems during the Cold War, as were the bases of the transstate issues and the technological revolution. What is new, however, is that these issues no longer are obscured by the vivid, overarching hues of the Cold War. With that threat faded, we are simply able more clearly to see these nontraditional problems.

Suggested Reading

Bacevich, A. J., James D. Hallums, Richard H. White, and Thomas F. Young. *American Military Policy in Small Wars: The Case of El Salvador*. Cambridge, Mass.: Institute of Foreign Policy Analysis, 1989.

Bell, Daniel. "The World and the United States in 2013," *Daedalus* 116, 3 (Summer 1987): 1–31.

Burton, Daniel F., Jr. "High-Tech Competitiveness," *Foreign Policy* 92 (Fall 1993): 117–132.

Davis, Vincent (ed.). *Civil-Military Relations and the Not-Quite Wars of the Present and Future*. Carlisle Barracks, Pa.: Strategic Studies Institute, 1996.

Forester, Tom. *High-Tech Society: The Story of the Information Technology Revolution*. Oxford, U.K.: Basil Blackwell, 1987.

Gallagher, James J. *Low-Intensity Conflict: A Guide for Tactics, Techniques, and Procedures*. Harrisburg, Pa.: Stackpole Books, 1992.

Greentree, Todd R. *The United States and the Politics of Conflict in the Developing World*. Washington, D.C.: U.S. Department of State Center for the Study of Foreign Affairs, 1990.

Hilsman, Roger. *American Guerrilla: My War Behind Japanese Lines*. Washington, D.C.: Brassey's, 1990.

Ohmae, Kenneth. "The Rise of the Region State," *Foreign Affairs* 72, 2 (Spring 1993): 78–87.

O'Neill, Bard E. *Insurgency and Terrorism: Inside Modern Revolutionary Warfare*. Washington, D.C.: Brassey's, 1990.

Paschall, Rod. *LIC 2010: Special Operations and Unconventional Warfare in the Next Century*. Washington, D.C.: Brassey's, 1990.

Shafer, Michael D. *Deadly Paradigms: The Failure of U.S. Counterinsurgency Policy*. Princeton, N.J.: Princeton University Press, 1988.

Snow, Donald M. *Distant Thunder: Third World Conflict and the New International Order*. New York: St. Martin's Press, 1993.

———. *UnCivil Wars: International Security and the New Internal Conflicts*. Boulder, Colo.: Lynne Rienner Publishers, 1997.

U.S. Army. *Guide to the Study of Insurgency*. Ft. Huachuca, Ariz., 1989.

Chapter 10

Systemic Responses
to Internal War

In the immediate wake of the Cold War, there was a mixture of euphoria and apprehension in the defense community. The euphoria came from the tearing down of such visible symbols of the Cold War as the Berlin Wall; there was a sense of victory and accomplishment. We had won.

But there was also apprehension, centering on where we were going next, what new roles and missions would replace the Cold War responsibilities. Saddam Hussein's invasion of Kuwait and the international response to it diverted our attention. The Iraqi armed force that had to be dislodged from the Kuwaiti desert resembled the former Soviet adversary in equipment, training, and tactics. Here was an opportunity actually to employ the strategies and tactics designed for the European plain but without the obstacles posed by German towns, forests, and the like.

Iraq appeared on paper to be a worthy foe. At about 400,000 strong, its army was the world's fourth largest. It had been battle-tested in the eight-year-long war with Iran, and it would have the further advantage of fighting on the defensive, with interior lines of supply and communication. The problem appeared formidable; during Senate debates as the operation mounted, there were wildly varying predictions of casualties, with Senator Ted Kennedy of Massachusetts suggesting the numbers could end in the tens of thousands, a prediction echoed by prominent private citizens such as H. Ross Perot.

The assessments of Iraqi prowess, of course, turned out to be illusions. The Iraqi army was, indeed, large, but most of the troops in Kuwait were Kurdish and Shiite conscripts who lacked the motivation to fight. The Iraqi Air Force never got off the ground except to fly some planes to Iran to avoid their destruction on the ground in Iraq. The experience of fighting another Second Tier state was meaningless against highly professional First Tier armed forces. Interior lines of communication and supply meant nothing once those lines had been severed by coalition domination of the skies.

The Gulf War was also the first time since the Korean War that the United Nations was used as the instrument for organizing and justifying an action. The reason was that the veto was not employed as a Cold War instrument; as a result, the Security Council could now act through a series of resolutions, first invoking sanctions against Iraq and ultimately authorizing the use of force. The coalition of over twenty-five First and Second Tier states under American leadership included First Tier European, Second Tier Arab, and others. It seemed a marvel of international cooperation, portending what President George Bush extolled at the time as the harbinger of a "new world order."

The rhapsody continued throughout the war's conduct. The air war that began at the end of the network evening news in the United States on January 16, 1991, was an unremitting string of successes. The marvel of precision munitions being guided down an air duct in a Baghdad building or a cruise missile literally chasing an Iraqi through the door of a bunker was the stuff of global television reporting. The lightning 100-hour ground campaign that drove the Iraqis out of Kuwait while incurring fewer than 150 American casualties was also a smashing reaffirmation of American military prowess.

It was a heady experience that seemed to portend a bright future for the international system. International collaboration in the face of aggression and brutality appeared the wave of the future. The United Nations was especially awash in the glory of the moment; the future would be one, Secretary-General Boutros-Ghali intoned, where the world organization would be "empowered" (his term) as the agent of choice to organize and maintain the peace.

In retrospect, the picture was too rosy. Disagreement broke out almost as fast as the last shots were fired regarding whether we had done enough or whether we had stopped too soon. Saddam Hussein remained defiantly in power, with his best forces (the Revolutionary Guards) still intact; as the smoke cleared, he turned his forces loose with a vengeance against the Kurdish and Shiite rebels who had risen to the bait offered by Bush on February 15, 1991, to "force Saddam, the dictator, to step aside." His brutal campaign forced the Kurds into the Turkish mountains and resulted in Operation Provide Comfort; the campaign against the Shiites forced them into the marshland of southern Iraq, where they are now protected from aerial assault by Operation Southern Watch; this situation is jeopardized by Iraqi plans to drain the marshes, thereby making ground assaults against the Shiites practical. More ominously, Iraq's NBC weapons capability apparently escaped the war as well.

No institution benefitted more from the glow of Desert Storm than did the United Nations and its Secretary-General. It is not unfair to call 1992 the year of the UN, as the body assumed major new obligations and prestige. Unfortunately, the organization also overextended its very limited human and financial resources, thereby causing a retrenchment in 1993. The argument over operational control of the United Nations peacekeeping force in Somalia, composed of contingents from twenty-nine countries in October 1993, highlighted both the limits of UN power and even disillusionment with the world body. When it came time to enforce the peace in Bosnia, it was NATO, acting as an executive arm of the UN under UN authorization, rather than the UN itself, that got the call.

It is within this framework of events that U.S. policy is evolving. The crises in Iraq, Somalia, and Bosnia were accompanied by a debate over whether conventional notions of national interest could encompass the new challenges from the Second Tier, or whether alternate, enhanced definitions of interest are now needed. Because of its prior experience, the United Nations has preferred to conceptualize these new situations within the confines of peacekeeping, a role nowhere found in the UN Charter but, nonetheless, a form of activity with which it is identified. Unfortunately, it is not at all clear that the peacekeeping framework is appropriate to places such as Somalia and Bosnia.

These experiences have also raised questions about the propriety of outside interference in what are generally internal affairs, both in terms of the likelihood of success and the precedential impact of such interventions. Finally, the question of the role of the United Nations in future conflicts has come to center on how much authority the organization should exercise in defining and controlling those situations in which the global community will become involved. Within a narrower American context, the debate centered for a time on whether to subordinate American forces to UN command, a possibility that President Clinton firmly ruled out when the official American position, contained in Presidential Decision Directive (PDD) 25, was announced in May 1994.

THE PRECEDENTS: IRAQ, BOSNIA, SOMALIA, AND BEYOND

The end of the Cold War left the West, including the United States, with no clear paradigm to guide it regarding where and when force should be employed, especially in the Second Tier where the only previous standard had been the East-West relevance of any particular conflict. The system did not, however, allow the luxury of reflection. The crisis in Iraq was followed quickly by the breakup of Yugoslavia, focusing on Bosnia and Herzegovina, the horror of Somalia, and ongoing tragedies in such places as Liberia, Rwanda, and Sudan.

Lacking a set of first principles to guide action, the United States was forced to react in piecemeal fashion, deciding discretely whether and how to react in each instance. In the circumstances, it could do little else. The problem with the approach is that it runs one of two risks. It may become such an inconsistent policy that neither the United States itself nor those against whom it might intervene can gauge properly the likely American responses. At the same time, the precedents of Iraq, Bosnia, and Somalia may form, by means of induction, a pattern of behavior that might not have been adopted if one had started from first strategic principles.

The specific issues and dynamics underlying these instances of international reactions to communal violence are substantially distinct, but they do have similarities that can feed into precedents for the future. All three involved large-scale violence and atrocity by one group within a country against one or more other groups, and that violence was made dramatically public by CNN (the Kurdish refugee camps in Turkey), ITN (the Bosnian detention camps), and the universal coverage of Somali suffering. That publicity made it impossible for the world to avoid the bloodshed, which it probably would have done prior to global television. At the same time, all three crises appeared at the extremities of the area stretching east from the Balkans across Asia Minor into central Asia, where Islam and Christendom (as well as sects of both) collided, leaving simmering hatreds that can produce similar conflicts in the future. What is principally different about the three is the international reaction in each case: swift and effective relief for the Kurds, much handwringing and very little succor for the Bosnians until 1995, and a massive intervention in Somalia that began as a humanitarian effort and gradually devolved into a UN involvement in the underlying Somali chaos that created the need for aid.

Operation Provide Comfort initially seemed little more than a footnote to the Persian Gulf War, a loose end in the implementation of UN Security Council Resolution 687 specifying cease-fire conditions. As noted, the problem had its root in the reaction to Bush's call for the Iraqis to rise and overthrow Saddam Hussein.

The administration's motives in this regard were almost certainly mixed. The entreaty was almost certainly aimed at "moderate" Sunni Iraqis in the military and elsewhere, although there were questions at the time whether any so-called moderates had survived Saddam's periodic purges. At any rate, the administration actively opposed successful rebellions by either the Kurdish or Shiite populations on the grounds that the result could be three successor states to Iraq (Kurdistan in the north, a Shiite state in the south, and what was left of Iraq in the middle), none of which could serve as an adequate counterweight to Iran after the war. At a purely tactical level, the admonition probably hoped that any rebellious activity that could be stirred up in Baghdad would undercut the effectiveness of Iraqi forces in the anticipated ground war that was only a little over a week away, thereby protecting American lives.

The Bush administration, of course, got the rebellion it did not want. When the Iraqi army was freed from the Allied onslaught, it turned its remaining (and quite formidable) fury against the rebels. Iraqi helicopter gunships were unleashed with particular effect against Kurdish villages in the Zagros mountains, leading to widespread panic and rumors of genocide. Large numbers of Kurds fled their homes; some went to Iran, the rest to the barren mountainsides of Turkey, where CNN found them.

Because he was an avid CNN watcher, President Bush found them as well. When Secretary of State James Baker took a hastily arranged and conducted visit to the camps (he was on the ground for about ten minutes) and reported that the scenes on television were only too real, something had to be done.

The options were restricted. The Kurds could not simply be left where they were; large numbers would die (as they were doing), and it would all be chronicled on global television. The connection between Bush's calls to arms and the Kurdish situation was being made, implying that the United States was at least partially to blame. Moreover, the Turkish government, with a Kurdish problem of its own (a secessionary movement led by the Kurdish Communist Party, or PKK), did not want the refugees to stay and worsen their problem, a sentiment that the United States, as a NATO ally, could not ignore.

But what to do? To alleviate the disease and starvation that was killing mounting numbers of Kurds daily, the Security Council passed Resolution 688, which empowered the provision of "humanitarian assistance" to the Kurds by member states and forbade Iraqi interference with relief efforts. The American response was to send military forces and relief supplies in support of the resolution; Operation Provide Comfort was born.

Alleviating suffering, however, was only a Band-Aid for the deeper problem of what to do with the Kurds. They could not live on the inhospitable mountain sides forever and survive, and the Turks demanded that they leave. At the same time, the Kurds refused to go back into Iraq for fear of the wrath of Saddam Hussein that had sent them fleeing in the first place.

The answer was entirely tactical: move them back into Iraq under the protection of American and other allied forces. The method was to create the exclusion zone from which Iraqi military forces are barred and which is enforced by allied, principally American, military forces. The zone, which remains in effect, was a necessary action to entice wary Kurds off the mountainsides, thereby alleviating the dual tactical problems of the relief effort and Turkish demands. Behind its protection, an increasingly autonomous Kurdistan that says it does not want full independence as a state but acts increasingly like one has emerged. In the summer of 1992, the principle was extended to the skies over southern Iraq, excluding the Iraqi air force from attacking Shiite rebels (Operation Southern Watch). As noted earlier, this arrangement was temporarily challenged in 1996 when the Iraqis made an incursion into the area in support of the activities of the Kurdish Democratic Party (KDP) and withdrew after U.S. objections.

The importance of the two exclusion zones in Iraq is the precedent they represent. Both were erected for arguably admirable humanitarian purposes: to relieve suffering and oppression. There is little indication in either situation that much thinking beyond the immediate effect took place at the time. The geopolitical, systemic effects, however, are not inconsequential: the continuation of the zones *are in direct violation of Iraqi sovereignty* defined in Westphalian terms, and as such, implicitly champion the controversial notion that when states act in an unacceptable manner towards parts of their populations, the primacy of state sovereignty gives way to a "higher" principle. The United States, as the chief guarantor in both cases, has never indicated that it considers the areas as anything other than sovereign Iraqi territory or that its actions represent an advocacy of the rights of individuals and groups over the rights of states. Rather, the United States more modestly maintains that the government of Iraq cannot *exercise* its sovereign authority as long the operations remain in force.

The situation in Bosnia offers parallels applied in the opposite direction: sovereignty provided an excuse not to intervene. The problem began with the long-anticipated breakup of Yugoslavia in the summer of 1991. Yugoslavia, which came into being in 1929, was a multinational state that was held together after World War II by the charisma and iron hand of its President, Josip Broz Tito. On his death in 1980, many predicted a rapid disintegration, but that was temporarily forestalled. The underlying problem, however, was the absence of shared nationality among Yugoslavs. Conscious Titoist population migration policies had caused the intermixing of nationalities throughout the six "republics;" the phenomenon was most pronounced in Bosnia and Herzegovina, where the three major nationalities (Roman Catholic Croatians, Greek Orthodox Serbians, and Muslim Bosnians) were most thoroughly intermixed and, hence, where the potential for violence was greatest.

As the process of disintegration began, attention focused quickly on Bosnia. Croatia's declaration of independence, rapidly recognized (some argue, inappropriately) by Germany, set off violence there as Serbian enclaves sought autonomy or to attach themselves to what was left of the Yugoslav state (mostly Serbia and Montenegro). The UN commissioned a peacekeeping mission, UNPROFOR (UN Protection Force), to supervise a cease-fire that proved little more than a lull in the fighting.

The fighting quickly spread across the border into Bosnia. The Muslim plurality (about 44 percent of the population) declared the independence of Bosnia and Herzegovina, and Serbs and Croats there viewed it as a Muslim state where their rights might not be honored. Serbian and Croatian "militias" moved to grab as much of Bosnia as they could, presumably for annexation to either Yugoslavia/Serbia or Croatia; the Muslims were left to fight for as much of a Bosnian state as they could keep.

The subsequent tragedy must be seen in this light. The Titoist policy of national migration and integration had created an ethnically integrated, checkerboard pattern, not unlike Lebanon, held together by the slimmest threads of intercommunal cooperation. When that began to break down, it created a scramble for territory, claims on which could most strongly be based on the ethnic purity or clear majority of one faction or another. "Ethnic cleansing" for Serbs meant forcing Croats or

Muslims out of territories they wanted to control; the Croats and the Muslims attempted to do the same, with varying success.

Siege warfare against Muslim-controlled towns and cities near the boundary of what Serbs feel to be Serbian soil became the most visible symbol of the policy of the "ethnic cleansing," specifically condemned in UN Security Council Resolution 771. The formerly intercommunal city of Sarajevo, where the Austrian Archduke was assassinated to start World War I and where the 1988 Winter Olympics were held, captured the tragedy.

Sarajevo evoked multiple images. The most vivid are of the siege itself. Like all other sieges in history, this one was not pretty. The Bosnian Serbs (and occasionally Croatian militias and regulars) surrounding the city sought to terrorize or starve and reduce the will of the civilian population to the point that they would surrender and leave. The methods, including random attacks on civilians, were cruel and nasty. Unlike other sieges in history, this one (and parallel sieges in a number of other towns) were shown on television, where it was impossible to ignore the carnage and the suffering; the most vivid image was of an open-air market attacked by mortar fire that killed more than sixty Sarajevans.

The other image, which reflected international frustration with the entire enterprise, was that of an impotent United Nations peacekeeping force hunkered down in Sarajevo, unable visibly to affect the situation. The problem was that neither was UNPROFOR designed for the kind of war zone in which it was entrapped for over three years nor did it have the mandate to do any more than it did, which was to try to distribute humanitarian aid when it could. In context, UNPROFOR was formed for the limited task of supervising a transient cease-fire; it wandered into Sarajevo almost by accident (it was looking for someplace to locate its headquarters) and found itself in the middle of the siege.

The crisis in Somalia has both similarities and differences. The immediate precipitant was public awareness of the enormous starvation that began occurring in the late summer of 1992, when negotiations between rival clans to form a government broke down and the country fell into communal violence and anarchy. A combination of drought and the withholding of food for political purposes created a human problem of enormous dimensions: by the time the United States reestablished the food distribution system, an estimated 100,000 Somalis had already died; without the humanitarian effort, projected deaths approached 1.5 million, about one-quarter of the entire Somali population.

Deputized by UN Security Council Resolution 794 on December 4, 1992, the United States launched a massive relief effort under the banner of Operation Restore Hope. The purpose, not unlike that in Turkey, was to reduce human suffering, and nearly 28,000 American troops were dispatched in the name of saving Somalis.

The Somali adventure must be seen in terms of two levels and at least three stages. The first, and most visible, level of the crisis was the humanitarian disaster, which cried out for intervention. That crisis, however, was both transitory and only a symptom of Somalia's real, underlying problem. It was transitory because the drought ended in 1993 and harvests returned to sustainable levels. It was symptomatic because it arose from the other, deeper level of the crisis, anarchy.

Somalian anarchy is nothing new; Somali politics is the struggle between rival clans. When one clan is powerful enough, it seizes power; when none is, the result is disorder. In the 1992 context, the crisis was part of a cyclical power play. In 1991 the various factions had overthrown the dictatorial Siad Barre, but were incapable of forming a successful governmental coalition. The country plunged into anarchy, as the factions and their "armies" (notably those loyal to Generals Mohammed Farah Aidid or Ali Mahdi Mohamed). The weapon of choice in this war, not unlike that employed in Bosnia, was food.

The conflict went through three distinct phases. In the first, the United States restored the distribution of food on a humanitarian basis. In the process, it implicitly altered the balance of power, since the withholding of food was a weapon presumably benefitting some clans at the expense of others (although there is no indication of an awareness of that impact). With order restored, the operation was then handed over to direct UN supervision, as American forces largely withdrew and were replaced by other national forces. In this phase, violence broke out as various factions attacked UN forces, presumably to get them to leave so that the civil war could recommence without outside interference. This situation, in turn, prompted the United States to return later in 1993 to help reestablish order, starting a third phase in which the objective quickly moved to brokering a political settlement to end the chaos.

What do these experiences share? The cases of Iraq and Somalia share both the tactical and the intrusive natures of involvement. In neither case was there apparently great concern about the long-term or precedential effects of what was done. In Iraq, the absence of Iraqi opposition has made both Operation Provide Comfort and Operation Southern Watch successful; what will happen either if Iraq seeks to reassert its sovereignty or if Kurdistan declares independence is less certain. At any rate, the U.S. involvement is open-ended, since the withdrawal of U.S. (as well as British and French) forces would almost certainly result in a brutal reassertion of Iraqi rule. Such a turn of events would leave the United States with the equally unpalatable options of going back to war with Iraq or of abandoning the Kurds. In Somalia, the lack of early strategic planning was even worse. As the *New York Times* suggested at the time the Security Council Resolution was being passed, "Thousands of American troops are about to be committed to a distant land, for ill-defined purposes, without real consultation with Congress or President-elect Clinton, without serious debate or even a semblance of executive leadership." Those words sounded like sour grapes when they were written; by latter 1993, they sounded prophetic when U.S. troops returned for a second time, equally undecided on what they were doing.

What was different in Bosnia was that the tactical stage passed without any international response, leading to the much more difficult underlying problems of what territorial outcomes would occur. Had Saddam Hussein resisted the exclusion zones, we might have faced a similar problem in Iraq; we may still, possibly in the form of environmental warfare reminiscent of the oilfield burning in the Persian Gulf War. In Somalia, help arrived, but it was assistance that did not address the underlying problem until late in 1993, when negotiations resumed in Mogadishu against the background clamor of Congressional demands for withdrawal. The Bosnian difference was that the problem became very serious before any action at all was taken.

What are the long-term effects? Iraq and Somalia seem to reinforce the assault on state sovereignty; the international inaction in Bosnia seems to suggest the opposite by implicitly endorsing the alteration of political boundaries by force. The effect on the United States and its view of Second Tier conflict is also ambivalent. Americans were both embarrassed at inaction in Bosnia and reluctant to send American forces there. In Somalia, we were proud of saving lives but repelled by being in the middle of bloody civil strife. The lack of challenge of our Iraqi efforts leave that situation in precedential limbo.

These three instances were harbingers of things to come. In 1994, the United States sent troops into Haiti to reinstall President Jean-Bertrand Aristide to power and, not coincidentally, in the hope that doing so would stop the embarassing flow of Haitian immigrants to south Florida. Also in 1994, the United States joined the rest of the world in standing by and watching the rampage in Rwanda. Chaotic new internal wars rumble across central Africa, in parts of the former Soviet Union, and in Asia.

We have adopted no consistent pattern of reaction to these occurrences, for at least three related reasons. First, we have not decided whether or how our interests are sufficiently engaged in these situations to decide on a common course of action. Second, the outbreaks of violence appear ideosyncratic enough to defy generalization. Third, the whole phenomenon is new and unique to the point that we are still struggling to understand it.

HUMANITARIAN INTERVENTION
AND SOVEREIGN RIGHTS

Two additional characteristics are shared by the three cases and extend to other new internal wars. The first is that, as internal wars where the problem of outside intervention by the United Nations or anybody else is roughly akin to that of counterinsurgency, it is not clear that outside interference can be positively conclusive. The ability to rectify the situation in Bosnia is similar physically and politically to Lebanon, where efforts have been notably ineffective over the years; the roots of conflict are simply too deep to be quelled by outsiders whose presence and interference inevitably is resented. Somalia is the same, and the de facto secession of Kurdistan engineered by the American command on the ground in Turkey could face a similar fate if the Iraqis decide to contest the situation.

This suggests that, at least in two of the possible sites for American involvement, the restraints on using American forces first articulated as the Weinberger Doctrine in 1984 (which Colin Powell apparently had a hand in drafting) and going through Powell to Anthony Lake's four rules of engagement may be violated by involvement. In opposing the interposition of American forces into Bosnia in the Winter 1992/93 *Foreign Affairs*, Powell argued that "the use of force should be restricted to occasions where it can do some good and where the good will outweigh the loss of lives and other costs that will surely ensue." This statement closely parallels Lake's second and third rules ("Can force actually do any good?" "Is the cost acceptable?"). Lake's fourth rule ("Is there a way out?") was added when the Clinton administration announced and subsequently met a withdrawal date from Somalia.

The other commonality among the situations is the absence of concrete American interests in any of these situations or their potential outcomes (a concern raised in Lake's first rule). Given the depth and abject nature of suffering in all three situations, it appears—and is—hard-hearted to suggest that the United States is not affected by what happens in Bosnia, Iraq, or Somalia. In the kind of traditional calculus of interests discussed in Chapter 7, few, if any, American interests are involved. No matter how these conflicts come out, Americans will not be adversely affected in any measurable manner. The same is true in subsequent instances, with the limited exception of Liberia, where some symbolic interests arise from the fact that the country was founded by liberated African-American slaves and from the need to send forces to protect the evacuation of American and other states' citizens when fighting broke out.

The only way to justify the use of outside force in these situations is to expand both what constitutes interests and to extend that definition to incorporate a different standard and base for sovereignty. The expansion of the definition of interests incorporates something variously called "humanitarian interests" or even "humanitarian *vital* interests," conditions of humankind that, when violated, are worth going to war over. When these occur within states as the result of intergroup fighting (including the government versus part of its population), the notion of state sovereignty gives way to something called *universal* or *popular* sovereignty, which suggests the supremacy of individual or group rights over the rights of states.

Both of these controversial assertions have roots that go back to the formation of the modern state system in the seventeenth century. When Jean Bodin first devised the idea of sovereignty as a way to foster strong central government to bring order to a chaotic sixteenth century France, he included the notion that sovereignty was "supreme power over citizens and subjects, unrestrained by law." The sovereign within his or her realm, in other words, held absolute sway over the citizenry (then subjects). The English philosopher John Locke, on whose thoughts so much of the American system is grounded, disagreed, arguing that sovereignty resides in the people, thereby creating the notion of a popular sovereignty that overrides the authority of the sovereign (a notion endorsed by Jean Jacques Rousseau).

There has been a disagreement on this point ever since these views were articulated over two hundred years ago. For the most part, the idea of state sovereignty is the "supreme power of the state, exercised within its boundaries, free from external interference." (See *The American Political Dictionary*, 1993 edition.) The problem is that this notion of absolute, impenetrable sovereignty creates a veil behind which unprincipled rulers or governments can hide to suppress, even terrorize, their populations; sovereignty thus becomes, to paraphrase Samuel Johnson's famous depiction of patriotism, the "last refuge of the scoundrels."

Both the notion of humanitarian interests and popular sovereignty are controversial. They have their roots in the ideas of natural law and just war developed in the seventeenth century by Hugo Grotius, who asserted that there are basic human conditions that are universal and that justify the recourse to force. Hardly anyone as a matter of principle argues against human rights, although a number of Second Tier nations—principally human rights violators—tried to argue the relativity of such rights in cultural terms at the 1993 UN conference on human rights in Vienna. Western notions about how individuals and groups should be treated are moving toward universal acceptance, a phenomenon that is a spinoff both of the fall of communism and the more universal adoption of a desire for both political and economic freedom.

What is controversial is the assertion that protecting those rights is both a *vital* interest (thereby justifying the use of force for its rectification) and a *right and obligation of the international system* to enforce, including the use of international force. The two elements are closely related to one another in practice. If the international system, deputized by the United Nations or some other organization, is to take action in rectifying governmental horrors against its population, then there must be some good reason to do so: the interests involved must be vital. At the same time, there must be a legal justification for doing so. Since intervention in civil affairs has traditionally been viewed as an infringement on national sovereignty and, thus, illegal under traditional, Westphalian concepts of international law, some superior legal principle such as universal sovereignty must be embraced to justify action. If one controversial element is embraced, they both must be. If one is rejected, they both must be, as well.

The notion of humanitarian vital interests has been a particular shibboleth of Boutros-Ghali, who espouses both expansion of definitions of what is worth fighting for and elimination of the confines of older, more restrictive notions of sovereignty, which he feels are outmoded in a new international order in which ideological division no longer provides a barrier to the effective enforcement of human rights standards.

The two "principles" are sequential. In the kind of traditional view of interests, humanitarian interests fall toward the lower end of both the importance and intensity scales: major or even peripheral in importance, and world order or value promotion in intensity. In either case, they clearly fall outside the bounds for which force would be used. To include these situations in the realm of national security concerns for which force might be employed requires either moving them on both scales—from major to vital and from world order to economic well-being or survival—or redefining what is, indeed, vital.

The first justification lacks plausibility. No matter what happened in Somalia, for instance, American well-being was not endangered: the United States has essentially no economic interests in the region, and it is not clear that any political outcome would endanger our access to the Suez Canal or remove the Horn of Africa from the roster of staging areas for the Persian Gulf (the two closest approximations of traditional American interest in the region). The same calculation would apply to American involvement in almost every other potential Second Tier conflict, except where petroleum is involved.

This raises, once again, the question of whether the Cold War realist paradigm is applicable to these situations, and whether the criteria of that paradigm leads to distorted, inappropriate responses. If humanitarian intervention is to be justified, as the *National Security Strategy of the United States* suggests, the definition of vitality must be expanded to encompass situations of enormous human suffering like that befalling the Kurds, the Somalis, and the Bosnians. This expansion, however, has five hurdles to overcome.

The first is finding a *suitable definition* to designate those circumstances that include or exclude the activation of vitality of interests. Historical precedent does not help much. An obvious instance would seem to be attempted genocide, as was apparently the case in Somalia, where a quarter of the population was at risk; the system tolerated a greater death toll in Cambodia inflicted by the murderous Khmer Rouge. One could counter that Cold War concerns made international intrusion into Cambodia impossible while Pol Pot and his gang of cutthroats were inflicting their horror; however, the 1993 rampage against the Hutu in Burundi by the Tutsi and the Hutu against the Tutsi in Rwanda in 1994, in which international action was conspicuously absent, did not have Cold War overtones. The simple fact of the matter may be that the connection between human rights values and vital interests extends no further than which atrocities are publicized by global television.

The second problem flows from the first: what *criteria* will determine when international action will or will not be contemplated, and what kind of situation will warrant different forms of action. Once again, precedent is not very helpful. Humanitarian violations during 1993 in

Bosnia and Haiti (over the installation of President Jean-Batiste Aristide) were hardly parallel, and the responses varied; troops were sent to Haiti in 1994, but not to Bosnia until the end of 1995.

It has been suggested both inside the military and outside that intervention should occur when the prospects for success (Lake's second rule) are good but not when they are poor. This criterion of "doability" has the twin drawbacks of being potentially very cynical (the saw about Kuwait and Bosnia, that "the U.S. Army does deserts, but it doesn't do mountains") or of encouraging villains who happen to live in militarily difficult terrain or operate in intractable political situations.

The question of criteria is important because of another hurdle, the *sheer volume* of candidate situations for humanitarian intervention. The UN found out through its flurry of actions in 1992 that there are very real limits to its own resources and to the additional resources its members are willing or able to commit to these kinds of situations. Boutros-Ghali, for instance, announced in April 1996 that the UN had exhausted its general operating funds for the year in the *first quarter* and would have to rely on voluntary contributions for the remainder of 1996. Boutros-Ghali's activism suggests that the international community has an obligation to become involved essentially wherever wrongdoing occurs, but that is a very long list of places. It can be argued that the more restrictive the definition and criteria are, the more likely it is that the criteria will be upheld. Conversely, restrictive definitions and criteria mean that some grisly villainy will be tolerated.

The fourth hurdle is *public support*, primarily but not exclusively in those First Tier states that would have to bear the brunt of the expense and sacrifice of international activism in this area. For the United States, the legacy of Vietnam suggests that public opinion will turn against actions that are not clearly worthy of sacrifice, in the traditionally defined American interest, and reasonably short and bloodless. In those instances where one or more of the criteria have been violated, the American people have turned on the operations. Somalia is the obvious example; Americans were delighted when the humanitarian mission of opening up the food distribution system was the object and could be accomplished in a straightforward manner (television images of cheering Somalis did not hurt). When the United States returned and took casualties in the midst of the clan-based civil war, opinion changed. By contrast, the absence of casualties in Haiti meant public opposition never arose.

The question of public support returns us to the Clausewitzian and Napoleonic underpinnings of the realist paradigm and its effect of leading to absolute judgments about interests and justifying only large-scale purposes for intervening. In the chaos of new internal wars, sweeping purposes of stabilizing systems and "restoring" democracy may be unattainable, but more limited forms of assistance—providing a lull in the fighting in Bosnia to give peace a chance or ministering to Rwandan refugees—may be possible. These, however, are modest goals with limited impact. Will the American public allow the placement of its forces in harm's way for such modest ends?

The fifth problem is that of *sovereignty*. Traditional norms of international law are quite clear about when a state can intervene in the sovereign affairs of other states: there is no such right. That does not mean, of course, that states do not interfere in the internal affairs of other states. The history of American policy toward Central America and the Caribbean has largely been one of military imposition. Operation Just Cause in Panama in 1989 was one recent instance; what was called the "intervasion" of Haiti (part intervention, part invasion) was an even more recent example.

Until recently, the assaults on state sovereignty have been practical, not publicly based on matters of fundamental principle. The American government, as the guarantor of the exclusions in Iraq, has never justified them on any but the practical grounds of, for instance, providing adequate incentive to get the Kurds to leave Turkey. Similarly, the principle underlying the UN operation in Somalia has never been explicitly defined in terms of sovereignty.

The implicit challenge to sovereignty is, indeed, occurring and even became fashionable for a time during 1992 and 1993. A prominent champion of this cause of universal sovereignty (otherwise called the rights of individuals and groups) has, unsurprisingly, been Boutros-Ghali, whose organization and, by extension, its Secretary-General, become more central in a world where state sovereignty is diminished. He stated in a 1992 *Foreign Affairs* article that the assault has already begun, maintaining that "the centuries-old doctrine of absolute and exclusive sovereignty no longer stands." In his continuing advocacy of American involvement in Bosnia, even conservative columnist and former Richard Nixon speechwriter William Safire joined the parade, extolling the "new sovereignty" (a term borrowed with acknowledgement from former Secretary of State George Shultz) and asking, "When do the world's responsible leaders have a right to intrude on what used to be impenetrable sovereignty?"

The answer is not abundantly clear, nor have those leaders jumped enthusiastically on the universal sovereignty bandwagon. There are clearly more opportunities to intervene in these kinds of affairs than resources, including popular will, can support, and there is the conviction among many that these kinds of things are none of our collective business. More fundamentally, however, if states hew to the notion that there is an international right to intervene in other countries' affairs when there are perceived or real violations of the rights of individuals or groups, then governments of those states leave themselves open to be intervened against—to have their own sovereign territory and authority compromised. The matter of who decides when violations have occurred becomes critical. Matters of broad principle give way to the practical concerns such as, "Will I be next?"

There is, moreover, some precedent for humanitarian intervention, although its precedential nature is suspect. The Crimean War, for instance, was provoked by the Russian assertion of 1853 of the right to protect Christians from persecution by the Sultan of the Ottoman Empire. More recently, the same claim was made by Japan in 1931 to justify its invasion of Manchuria and by Hitlerian Germany when it invaded the Czech Sudetenland in 1938. Contemporary justifications, of course, lack the imperial motive—at least, from the viewpoint of First Tier interveners.

More broadly, the assertion of a right, duty, or obligation to protect individuals and groups from the atrocious behavior of their own governments, particularly in the midst of internal (civil) wars, redefines the purposes for which the international community will use force in the future. Specifically, the role of internationally derived force moves from the relatively passive role of peacekeeping to the very arduous role of peace enforcement. This raises a policy question with which the Clinton administration is wrestling and which was raised by Thomas L. Friedman in the *New York Times* as American forces moved into Somalia: "If halting starvation or upholding human rights are now legitimate criteria for American intervention abroad, as compelling as protecting traditional strategic interests, where does President-elect Clinton draw the new red line?" A sizable part of the answer requires understanding the political and military natures and dynamics of the various kinds of actions proposed.

PEACEKEEPING, PEACE ENFORCEMENT, AND PEACE IMPOSITION

The systematic involvement of the international system in the internal affairs of Second Tier states, absent the motivation of Cold War concerns, is a relatively new and unique phenomenon for which the Cold War experience offers little guidance. In the Cold War system, the motive for becoming involved was geopolitical: promoting one ideology or thwarting the promotion of the other. With that set of criteria removed, the rationale has become humanitarian and altruistic: saving people from their governments, or even from themselves. This problem is most acute in the so-called "failed states," where ethnic and other animosities have devolved to especially bloody warfare.

There is little precedent for dealing with these situations. Propelled by the Persian Gulf War experience, the United Nations has become the prominent institution by which the major countries have chosen to activate their concern and their action. The UN, after all, is the one organization that has had great credibility within the Second Tier, and it has a track record in dealing with Second Tier matters through its peacekeeping efforts.

Lacking a better framework or institution to organize international efforts, the UN Security Council authorized Secretary-General Boutros-Ghali to survey the problem and to recommend ways to deal with it. His response was a monograph entitled *An Agenda for Peace: Preventive Diplomacy, Peacemaking, and Peace-Keeping*, published by the United Nations in 1992. The distinctions he made have, unfortunately, become the standards by which discussions on the topic are framed.

Defining Terms

Boutros-Ghali proposed a fivefold set of strategies by which to organize international efforts for dealing with violence and instability in the Second Tier. These are summarized in Table 10.1, along with notation of the stage of a conflict in which each occurs. Some of the designations are intuitively obvious and straightforward; others contribute to a distortion of the real problems that contribute to the unfortunate preemption of the conceptual high ground by the secretary-general. It should further be noted that the term "peace enforcement" is not a separate category in *An Agenda for Peace*, but a subdivision of peacemaking that refers to peace enforcement *units* that are available to enforce peacemaking efforts. The term has been adopted as a separate activity by the United States military, hence its listing as a discreet category.

Three of the distinctions are uncontroversial, representing traditional UN roles. Preventive diplomacy is one of these: "action to prevent existing disputes from arising between parties, to prevent existing disputes from escalating into conflicts, and to limit the spread of the latter when they occur." Peacekeeping, similarly, refers to the traditional UN role of interposing United Nations forces between formerly warring parties who have agreed to a cease-fire in order to facilitate maintenance of the cease-fire and, hence, to facilitate the peace process. Peacebuilding refers to "action to identify and support structures which will tend to strengthen and solidify peace in order to avoid a relapse into conflict."

Each of these roles is difficult, if not conceptually controversial. Preventive diplomacy works some of the time, but not always. Such efforts during the summer of 1992 did not, for instance, prevent the disaster in Somalia. Peacekeeping efforts are often strained, as in Lebanon, by the restiveness of the parties, and they may even prolong the tensions by creating a calm that seems to make difficult negotiations unnecessary, as in Cyprus. Peacebuilding, akin to traditional ideas of statebuilding, often sounds better than its results. Attempts to negotiate a political order in Somalia are exemplary of this difficulty.

The real controversy surrounds the wartime activities, peacemaking and peace enforcement. Peacemaking refers to "peaceful means" of bringing warring parties to cease fighting in accord with Chapter VI of the Charter, which authorizes sanctions that may be imposed. The Lord Owens-Cyrus Vance mission to Bosnia is an example. Peace enforcement refers to efforts by deputized forces under UN control to *reestablish a lapsed peace*. Presumably, this is what UN forces in Somalia were doing in 1993.

These designations are unfortunate for three reasons. The first is that they distort the normal meaning of language. Peacemaking suggests a condition of war that is to be ceased, and there are more ways than diplomatic efforts to bring this about; the range of instruments of power can be employed to make peace. Peace enforcement, similarly, suggests, in common use of language, that there is a peace to be enforced; at a minimum,

TABLE 10.1   **Conflict Stages and Means of Resolution**

Conflict Stage	Policy Tool
Prewar	Preventive diplomacy
Wartime	Peacemaking
	Peace enforcement
Postwar	Peacekeeping
	Peacebuilding

the need to reestablish peace suggests that war, not peace, exists at the time peace enforcement units are deployed.

Second, the classification is not exhaustive. In the real world of Second Tier conflict, the operative condition is warfare from which one or more of the contending parties is benefitting and which at least those benefitting prefer to continue. Diplomatic efforts ("peacemaking" narrowly defined) proved irrelevant in Bosnia until the breakthrough in Dayton in December 1995 (after more than three years of fighting and killing). In a country like Liberia, it is not clear that putative political leaders have enough control over the forces they pretensively lead—let alone those of opposition groups—for a negotiated settlement to mean much. Peace enforcement implies a will to reassert peace that may be missing. The classification thereby leaves out the most stressful activity that may be necessary to stop these conflicts, the violent employment of military force to *create* peace—what we will call *peace imposition*.

The third problem is that the categories, by omitting the most important category, suggests a continuity of activity that is, in fact, missing. Boutros-Ghali's scheme posits a neat progression that ignores the possible need for active military intervention—peace imposition. Conceptualized as it is, the only form of military action necessary is peacekeeping or peace enforcement, neither of which are militarily arduous and which suggest militarily easy tasks. The problem is that real solutions require the employment of active forces into hostile environments, a problem we will detail later. Exclusive reference to the Boutros-Ghali categories simply distorts the realities involved and leads to the misapplication of force, notably the placing of peacekeepers in an environment where peace imposition is actually the task at hand. The UNPROFOR mission is the clearest case of sending the wrong forces into the situation.

If the Boutros-Ghali categories are unfortunate, they are understandable because they reflect the unique perspective of the United Nations in at least three ways. First, all the activities the UN proposes for itself are relatively inexpensive, a reflection of the limited resources of the world organization. Peace imposition, by contrast, is relatively costly and probably beyond UN means. (The basic UN budget is roughly $2.5 billion per year; additional resources must be obtained through assessment of the members. The lack of prompt payment—especially by the United States—

has hampered UN efforts.) The United Nations, in other words, cannot afford to be a peace imposer.

Second, the attitude of most UN officials is hostile toward the kind of active military engagement that peace imposition entails. As an example, the UN does not collect "intelligence," a basic military need; instead, it provides "public information" about situations. Most, if not all, officials who join the UN staff are dedicated to doing away with, not waging, war. The UN culture is, in other words, basically antimilitary—dedicated to peace, not war.

Third, the UN's experience is skewed away from military applications. Peacekeeping, a primarily defensive, passive form of military action, is where the UN has experience. Prior to the engagements in Bosnia and Somalia, the only proactive military engagement that was truly a UN operation was in the former Belgian Congo (Zaire), where UN forces became engaged in the civil war, and that operation is generally considered a failure. The Korean and Persian Gulf Wars were technically UN operations, but were, in fact, U.S. operations under UN auspices. The UN, in other words, lacks practical experience at peace imposition.

This inexperience frustrates those national forces that perform UN missions. In the early days of UNPROFOR, for instance, the Canadian commander, Gen. Lewis McKenzie, was routinely denied defensive weapons necessary to protect his forces by UN officials who thought such armament would be unnecessarily provocative. For well into its mission, UNPROFOR was similarly handicapped by the fact that the office in New York that authorized its activities was only open from 9:00 A.M. to 5:00 P.M., Eastern time, from Monday to Friday.

There is a fundamental qualitative difference between the kind of activity proposed by Boutros-Ghali and peace imposition. The categories of preventive diplomacy and peacebuilding can be thought of as a continuum of essentially nonmilitary activity, where the prevailing circumstance is peace or its proximity. Peace imposition, by contrast, is an option of an entirely different order that applies when war is ongoing and is desired by some or all parties; in some cases, peace imposition may be prefatory to engaging the UN framework, or it may be considered if that process fails.

It is important to make the distinction for four reasons. The first is to avoid mistaking situations and, thus, conceptualizing and responding inappropriately. UNPROFOR, for instance, was a peacekeeping response to a peace imposition situation and, hence, had no realistic chance of carrying out its mission; it was the wrong kind of force for the problem. Second, peace imposition "opportunities" are much more widespread in the current environment than are peacekeeping chances. Third, peace imposition situations are much more difficult to deal with, because they involve outside interference in internal wars. As such, they are akin to counterinsurgency situations; the post–World War II record of successful outside interventions in internal wars is sufficiently dismal to give cause for caution in the future. Fourth, it is not at all clear that the United Nations has either the resources or expertise to direct or meaningfully participate in peace imposition operations. If these are conducted by anyone, it will be one of the major First Tier countries, including the United States, or by a collective organization, such as NATO.

Fundamental Distinctions

Understanding the differences between peacekeeping and peace imposition is thus an important American defense policy problem, since there will be times when the United States feels tempted or impelled to become involved, as it did in the case of Somalia. These differences can be placed into three admittedly overlapping categories: environment, context, and mission challenges.

ENVIRONMENT.   The environmental factor refers to an assessment of the situation in the target country at the point at which action is being contemplated. Two factors, both shockingly obvious but fundamental in their impact, stand out by means of contrast when thinking about peacekeeping or peace imposition operations.

First, one must know whether peace or war exists. In a peacekeeping situation, peace (or at least the absence of active hostilities) has already been established; a cease-fire is in place, leaving the peacekeepers with the task of maintaining that peace. By contrast, a peace imposer enters an arena of actual ongoing combat—war. The task of the peace imposer is to create peace by causing combat to cease.

The second environmental factor is related to the first: in a peace imposition situation, some—or possibly both, or all—of the combatants prefer the continuation of hostilities to their cessation. Were this not the case, it would be virtually true by definition that a cease-fire would exist that required only monitoring—that is, a peacekeeping environment. By contrast, peacekeepers enter a situation only when all parties have agreed to a cease-fire and where, implicitly or explicitly, all sides have agreed that they prefer the absence of hostilities to their presence. What this means is that peace imposers face a more arduous and difficult environment than do peacekeepers.

It is also possible, as in Bosnia, to encounter a hybrid situation. When IFOR arrived, there was a peace in place, and the IFOR was purposely intimidating enough that no one would challenge their enforcement of it. The settlement, however, disadvantaged some, notably some Serbs, who hardly supported the structure of the peace.

CONTEXT.   The context in which outside force is inserted refers to the attitudes and conditions of the host groups or countries where one form of force or the other may be inserted. Three related conditions stand out most prominently in this regard.

The first is whether the outside forces are invited and, if so, by whom they are invited. Peacekeepers operate on the concept of explicit invitation by both parties to facilitate maintenance of a cease-fire. The normal pre-condition for accepting a peacekeeping role is that peace has been restored and that both or all parties want that situation to continue. Thus, universal invitation is prerequisite to forming a peacekeeping force. By contrast, a situation where peace imposition is contemplated is one where some or all parties to the combat prefer the continuation of war (presumably because they are either winning or because a cease-fire would leave them disadvantaged). Generally, those who are losing and fear losing more will want to see peace imposed; those who have more to win will not.

This leads to a second contextual point: peacekeepers are welcome in the country (or between the countries) where they are interposed; peace imposers will almost certainly be unwelcome by some partisans and may, depending on how the imposer acts, become unwelcome to all. Once again, this is a virtual tautology: universal welcome is one of the conditions for forming a peacekeeping mission. By contrast, the peace imposer is being asked to break up a fight that at least someone is enjoying. As when a policeman breaks up a barroom brawl, imposing a peace may be for the greater good, but it is hardly likely to seem that way to the brawlers at the time. Moreover, the kind of peace that is imposed will almost certainly favor one side over the other, thereby earning the enmity of whoever comes out the loser.

The third condition deals with the receptiveness of the parties to a peaceful settlement of their differences. In a potential peacekeeping situation, such a settlement either exists already or is preferred by the parties to the continuation of war. The peacekeepers then have the primary role of keeping the former combatants apart.

Peace imposers face an altogether different situation. The continuing existence of warfare is clear evidence that at least one side prefers to continue pursuing military rather than political solutions to the differences that caused them to go to war in the first place. As long as that is the case, the outside peace imposer is rather more likely to be an irritant than a lubricant for the peace process.

The contextual elements define the receptivity of the contestants to outside intervention. For peacekeepers, the context is comparatively benign; for peace imposers, that situation is almost certain to contain large measures of hostility. This distinction is important to note, because the peace imposer is likely to experience the ingratitude of some or all of the parties to the war it interrupts. In Somalia, for instance, the United States broke up a war; when the peace it imposed disfavored the aspirations of some elements—notably, General Aidid—he expressed his displeasure violently. Americans were initially shocked at the ingratitude of the Somalis; we should not have been.

The dynamics in Bosnia are potentially similar to those in Somalia. Although the leaders of two of the factions (the Bosnian Serbs were indirectly represented by Serbia) agreed to the Dayton solution, clearly not all of their followers concurred (especially the Bosnian Serbs). IFOR was thus in a sort of limbo, fully supported by some but not by all. Those who did not support the peace went along as long as IFOR did not become an active part of implementing the statebuilding aspects of the mission.

MISSION CHALLENGES. The specific problems that a military force inserts into a peacekeeping or peace imposition setting must be dealt with and overcome. All flow from the fact of being sent into an active, or formerly active, war zone. Four major differences stand out for peacekeepers or peace imposers.

The first difference, to which allusion has already been made, is the neutral or partisan role of the forces. Strict neutrality is a hallmark of the peacekeeper and a quality that must be maintained if both sides are to respect the restraining role played by the peacekeeper. Both sides must believe that they are being treated fairly by the peacekeeper; otherwise, the peace will become fragile, and anyone perceiving unfairness will likely disinvite the peacekeepers. To insure neutrality, peacekeepers are typically drawn from neutral, disinterested states and from countries such as Norway or Canada that have longstanding peacekeeping traditions and are, hence, generally viewed as trustworthy.

Peace imposition missions most likely begin with the *intention* of neutrality and nonpartisanship, as well, but imposers find it impossible to remain nonpartisan in their *effect* on the situation. The initial perception of neutrality is likely to have one of three sources. The humanitarian motivation of the peace imposer ("our purpose is to alleviate human suffering") is above partisan reproach or, at least, will seem so unless, as in Somalia, partisan politics underlies suffering (the withholding of food as a weapon of war). Second, the confusion of the Boutros-Ghali categories of actions, notably peacekeeping and peace imposition, suggests a parallel between a peacekeeping and a peace imposing attitude: peacekeepers are neutral, so peace imposers are too. Third, the inability of imposers to remain neutral may arise from simple ignorance of the situation. There is, once again, little reason based in the public record to believe that the United States understood the nature of the clan war in Somalia and the geopolitical implications within Somalia of U.S. humanitarian efforts.

The different dynamics of what peacekeepers, on the one hand, and peace imposers, on the other, do, make nonpartisanship possible for one and unlikely for the other. Peacekeepers enforce a status quo to which the parties have agreed; peace enforcers, implicitly or explicitly, change a status quo that was being altered by violence. The purpose of peace imposers is to alter an existing situation by causing an end to combat: that, in and of itself, changes things to the advantage of some and to the disadvantage of others. Moreover, the mere presence of heavily armed peace imposers will almost inevitably become an irritant; someone will throw a rock, a nervous soldier will overreact, and the incident will cause resentment.

This dynamic difference is critical in contemplating the use of American forces in a peace imposition role because of the need for public support for military involvement. The United States entered Somalia as peacekeepers with a lofty humanitarian goal and little appreciation of the internal political situation with which we were interfering. Our intervention interfered with the war between Generals Aidid and Mohamed Ali Mahdi, and General Aidid eventually came to believe we were undercutting him. When the United Nations temporarily replaced the United States, it was viewed as even more of a barrier. Incidents occurred between soldiers and civilians. In the end, some Somalis became disenchanted with the United States, and many Americans became disenchanted with Somalia. This dynamic was so obvious that one wonders now why anyone was surprised by it; that it will recur in future peace imposition situations is equally obvious.

Bosnia once again points to the anomaly of mission requirements. Since there was in fact no consensual basis for peace, IFOR could maintain its neutrality (and hence acceptability) only by remaining passive. That demeanor, however, meant that IFOR had to stand idly by as violations occurred, such as the burning down of former Serb suburbs around Sarajevo that were supposed to be turned over intact to Bosnian authorities by departing residents.

A second difference has to do with the difficulty of accomplishing the military mission. Assuming that a peacekeeping force is inserted into a true peacekeeping situation, its mission is rather simple and straightforward. It is there for the well-defined mission of enforcing a cease-fire line, and it has the general support of the contending parties to carry out that mission (although there are always incidents that mar the smooth accomplishment of the task). Peacekeeping becomes difficult or untenable only when a peacekeeping force is inserted into a situation that really requires peace imposers.

As previously explained, peace imposition is more difficult. To reiterate, the underlying internal situations into which the peace imposers are likely to be thrust resemble insurgency-counterinsurgency disputes, where the history of outside interference is unimpressive. Such situations are intensely political, and the politics is likely to be poorly understood by decision makers, much less by the military forces themselves. Employing force to suppress the lethal activities of one group may have political and military consequences whose nature is unknown to the forces doing the suppressing. Most of the fighting in these situations is done by small units—company-size infantry units or below in some situations—with the result that effective decisions about who to fight and why may occur at a very low point in the chain of command. In the worst of cases, the violence is random and uncontrolled, often conducted by fighters who are little more than children, as in parts of Africa.

A third difference has to do with the uniqueness of and controversy about a mission. Peacekeeping is not a problem on either count: it is a traditional, accepted practice, and the role of the "blue berets" has been well established over time. The fact that, as noted earlier, seventeen peace-keeping missions (or at least missions designated as peacekeeping) were in place in 1993 provides evidence in support of their legitimacy.

Such is hardly the case with peace imposition. Part of the difference comes from the fact that peace imposition in other than the context of Cold War competition is, itself, new; when American and Soviet surrogates came into conflict, one or the other side interposed itself out of openly partisan motives. The closest the United Nations came to peace imposition during the Cold War was the ONUC (United Nations Operation Congo), where peacekeepers became embroiled in thwarting the attempted secession of Katanga (now Shaba) province from the newly declared state of Zaire. That action was not one of the UN's great moments, as its neutrality was temporarily shattered and it became involved in heavy fighting for which the peacekeepers were not well prepared. The idea of nonpartisan, humanitarian intervention in internal conflicts is simply so new that its principles and consequences have not been thought through thoroughly.

The fourth difference deals with the obviously different kinds of forces needed to conduct one or another kind of operation. For peace-keepers, the model is well defined. The forces can be rather small, lightly armed (nothing larger than hand-held weapons for the most part), passive and defensive in nature, and equipped only for personal self-defense, not for combat. (It is a standing joke among peacekeepers that an ample supply of suntan lotion is a basic part of their equipment.) The peacekeeper is essentially a physical barrier between two adversaries, and his role is to ensure that the parties cannot resume hostilities without first attacking the United Nations in the form of the peacekeepers.

Peace imposers have to be quite different. Given the environment into which they are placed and the roles they play, they have to be combat troops, equipped and prepared to participate in combat. As such, they have to be offensive-oriented and be authorized to engage in combat. Peace imposition forces therefore have to be larger, more heavily armed, and more fully supported than their peacekeeping counterparts.

This difference in force types and requirements is also fundamental, and confusing the types of forces with the different missions can have disastrous results. For one thing, peace imposition is considerably more expensive than peacekeeping; as noted, peacekeeping fits within the means of the UN; probably only the major First Tier states can physically afford to be peace imposers. At the same time, however, the dynamics of peace imposition mean that these missions will be more controversial within both the host state and in the states that provide the peace imposers. Any state that volunteers peace imposers and expects to be thanked for the effort is engaging in an act of sheer fantasy.

The new system—and especially the United Nations—has so far ignored these realities. The failure to distinguish between peacekeeping and peace imposition forces and missions can lead to misunderstanding both situations and requirements. UNPROFOR, for instance, is a classic peacekeeping force that was sent into a peace imposition situation; as such, it was a sitting duck since its inception, with no realistic opportunity to influence the situation. Similarly, it is possible to imagine circumstances in which peace imposition will give way to peacekeeping. In the case of IFOR, a force configured for peace imposition was sent to peacekeep. The UN could not have afforded such a configuration; NATO, conscious of the effect that sustaining casualties might have at home, hedged its bets by sending a force that was unlikely to be challenged and clearly capable of a devastating response if it was.

This last point is important: peacekeepers and peace imposers are different kinds of forces, and misusing them is detrimental to situations and to the forces themselves. Fighting forces prepared to impose peace are trained to shoot first and ask questions later (permissive rules of engagement); peacekeepers are trained never to fire first except in the case of imminent personal danger (restrictive rules of engagement). Peacekeepers are not trained for offensive combat, and using combat soldiers as peacekeepers will either erode their combat readiness or result in instances in which they take inappropriate actions, such as overreacting to domestic incitation.

THE CALCULATION OF INVOLVEMENT

For the United States, both peacekeeping and peace imposition represent reasonably novel missions. American forces have some limited experience in peacekeeping, notably in monitoring those provisions of the Camp David accords dealing with the Sinai Peninsula and, in a more limited way, acting as observers in the UNIFIL mission in southern Lebanon and in Macedonia. Unlike militaries that routinely assign forces to UN peacekeeping, the American armed forces lack the special training and indoctrination necessary to produce soldiers with specific peacekeeping skills. The U.S. training that most closely approximates what is needed is that for military police, but the fit is imperfect, and few receive the training. The U.S. Army War College's Strategic Studies Institute established a peacekeeping institute in mid-1993, but it remains an embryonic enterprise mostly dedicated to producing doctrine. The most active service in confronting these problems is the U.S. Marines, largely through their annual Emerald Express symposium series.

The situation is somewhat different for peace imposition. In one sense, peace imposition is akin to any combat, and it thus is within the purview of normal fighting units. At the same time, however, the style of encounter is more like counterinsurgency warfare, about which the U.S. military has never shown much enthusiasm or skill. As part of reducing the size of the armed forces, the Army has sharply curtailed the Foreign

Area Officer (FAO) program, from which it gains its formal expertise on different parts of the world—a strange action if peace imposition in multiple Second Tier cultures is envisioned.

Aside from the question of preparedness for these kinds of missions is their compatibility with defense policy. That policy, of course, is now in transition, and either or both peacekeeping and peace imposition could be incorporated into it. The question of whether these missions, especially the more controversial peace imposition role, should be added thus becomes a defense policy agenda item.

The polar positions reflect the modern version of the realist-idealist debate in foreign policy generally. The idealists have, by and large, adopted the humanitarian interests position that the United States, as the remaining superpower, has both a right and an obligation to provide the leadership—if not always the physical forces—necessary to relieve human suffering wherever practicable. Steeped in the Wilsonian tradition, interventionists see the present absence of major power conflict as a historic opportunity to enact the idealist agenda of freedom and human rights.

The realists' most articulate spokesperson was (until his retirement from active service) General Colin Powell. He does not so much deny the desirability of embracing human rights as the practical matter of whether the goals are attainable. As he put it in a 1992 *Foreign Affairs* article: "Is the political objective we seek to achieve important, clearly defined and understood? Have all other nonviolent means failed? Will military force achieve the objective? At what cost? Have the gains and risks been analyzed? How might the situation that we seek to alter, once it is altered by force, develop further, and what might be the consequences?"

This is a daunting set of questions, nearly impossible to answer positively in any highly fluid, uncertain situation such as those where peace imposition is an option. A not-so-hidden purpose for raising them is to inhibit the kind of rapid commitment seen in Operation Provide Comfort and later in Somalia. On this overall question, President Clinton was apparently initially drawn toward the idealist, interventionist position during the early days of his presidency; by the fall of 1993, however, he had moved noticeably toward the realist position, no doubt partly because of the influence of General Powell.

This leads to a second policy and strategy concern, the question of interests in and outcomes of peace imposition. Peace imposition opportunities will mostly occur outside the realm of traditional American vital interests in places like Somalia, where interests are oblique, at best, and where it is hard to see how any outcome would affect those interests in a visible way. Moreover, guaranteeing favorable outcomes, where they can be defined in a coherent manner, may remain an elusive target.

The inability either to define interests or to specify the accomplishment of clearly articulated goals will inevitably lead to confusion over missions, and that will be reflected in diminished public support for actions. Somalia, again, is an example. Operation Restore Hope was initially very popular because it seemed bounded in time and highly successful. The euphoria began to dissipate, however, with the reinsertion of American forces, and then public support waned.

This result leads to a third question about intervention: how is the agenda set? Who decides when and when not to become involved in peace imposition missions? In the early days of the post–Cold War environment, the answer seemed to be global television: instances where violence and atrocity were publicized (the Kurds in Turkey and starving children in Somalia) received great public attention and moved to the top of the policy list for action, whereas those that were unpublicized (in the Sudan and Angola) were not placed in the policy "in basket."

An agenda influenced by the media—particularly global television—has become part of the policymaking process. In all likelihood, the public will be bombarded even more in the future by images of world events—including the most horrible ones—as new global television systems come into existence and technology makes the flow of accounts even easier. How this imagery will affect the agenda is less certain. A few peace imposition failures may sour the public on the whole idea. It is also entirely possible that constant footage of violence and atrocity will desensitize us to the horrors; the bloated bodies of victims of massacre in Burundi floating down the river dividing Burundi from Rwanda or the carnage in Liberia did not evoke any great outcry in late 1993, for instance, nor did the slaughter in Rwanda in 1994.

A fourth point has to do with the question of who will provide forces for peace imposition actions. As noted, the kinds and sizes of forces necessary suggest that the pool of peacekeepers will not be adequate, in terms of either the quantity or the quality of forces needed. In this circumstance, the major powers will almost certainly have to be called upon, possibly in conjunction with forces from some of the largest and most powerful regional powers, when such forces are politically acceptable in the host countries. (For example, would Indian forces be acceptable in the Islamic countries of the Persian Gulf area?)

Who will supply these forces? The United States is in the unique position of possessing the logistical and support capabilities to make it an ideal instrument for moving forces to any theater, supplying them, and providing them with such necessities as satellite reconnaisance and intelligence (services that it has traditionally provided for peacekeepers, as well). The United States has sent forces to places such as Somalia, and the French, British, and Italians have similarly been willing to provide forces, especially in areas where they once had colonial interests, but is this a large enough base, or is further burden sharing necessary?

The answer probably depends on how extensive peace imposition becomes. If our assessment of the difficulties involved is at all accurate, public opinion will become a factor in the major industrial democracies, the use of the 8,500-man French Foreign Legion (part of the French contribution to UNPROFOR) being a partial exception. A large-scale commitment would heavily tax the traditional contributors and leave open the need for others. But who? The Russians will remain fixated on problems in the former Soviet Union for the foreseeable future, the Germans are struggling with the practical and constitutional consequences of overseas deployment (a problem shared by Japan, as already noted), the Japanese are culturally unwelcome in the Far East, and China has shown no interest. This situation leaves few alternatives and suggests that peace imposition efforts may be limited by available forces.

The final question has to do with strategy and tactics. As noted, peacekeeping and peace imposition are relatively new concepts for the United States, and the American military is only beginning to discuss them. In the wake of Vietnam, the armed forces did a great deal of work in the area of low-intensity conflict, which resembles the strife in many Second Tier states that are candidates for peace imposition. Much of the effort, however, was negative in its assessments, suggesting criteria that would keep the United States out of such frays rather than producing doctrinal and strategic guidance for involvement. Moreover, most of these investigations began with the assumption the United States would participate on one side or the other of the contending forces rather than as a putative neutral, a factor that must change the calculation.

The most important strategic decision is the point at which the mission will be deemed accomplished—the so-called end game. If merely quelling the immediate symptom—ending starvation in Somalia, for instance—is the goal, it can reasonably be accomplished by the imposition of maximum force to intimidate the contestants, as was done in Haiti and Bosnia. If the strategic goal is to ensure a more stable political situation where regression is unlikely—statebuilding—then a more arduous and potentially frustrating process is the object. That military and civilian leaders have not fully appreciated the fundamentally different nature of the two is indicated by designation of the change as "mission creep," an idea challenged in the Amplification box "Mission Creep versus Mission Leap."

No standard sources of guidance directly apply to peace imposition missions. The Army's basic doctrinal statement *(Field Manual [FM] 100-5)* is not, and its statement on low-intensity conflict *(FM 100-20)* is only partially relevant. Guidance for peacekeepers, such as *The Peacekeeper's Handbook*, is mostly about how to avoid fighting. Until some positive form of guidance can be provided, those called upon to involve themselves as peace imposers—Americans and others, alike—will be disadvantaged and will probably make mistakes that more adequate strategic and tactical preparation might avoid.

The Clinton administration announced its policy on these matters under the vehicle of Presidential Decision Directive (PDD) 25, as mentioned earlier. The policy distinguishes between three levels of involvement in UN missions, which presumably can be extended to non-UN missions as well. All are extensions of the Lake rules and Weinberger/Powell doctrines.

AMPLIFICATION

Mission Creep versus Mission Leap

Peacekeepers or peace enforcers can have two distinct roles: peacekeeping and statebuilding. The former role is appropriate when and where peace is clearly desired by all parties, in which case the parties can reasonably be expected to accomplish on their own any statebuilding functions that are necessary.

Statebuilding when there is an absence of agreement is entirely more difficult, especially for outsiders. In essence, it consists of a whole range of political and military activities, the purpose of which is to create the basis for a stable peace. Disarming rival forces, as was done in Somalia, is a form of statebuilding; helping to identify and bring to justice war criminals, as was flirted with in Bosnia, is another.

The two activities are fundamentally different and must be recognized as such. When one moves from peacekeeping to statebuilding, the mission has radically changed and must be accepted as such. In Somalia, the movement to statebuilding was described as a case of mission creep to be avoided in the future. The analogy is terribly misleading, because the movement from one form of activity is fundamental in its impact on the mission. The gap between the two is a chasm; the impact is more correctly a mission *leap*, not creep. Conceptualizing such a radical change with an incremental term like *creep* simply distorts thinking about the mission.

The least restrictive set of criteria apply to *U.S. support of UN peacekeeping missions to which the United States does not contribute forces.* In these situations, American involvement is limited to pledging to pay assessments to support the mission and, possibly, to providing logistical support. The criteria are that (1) the operations must further American interests, (2) respond to a real threat to the peace (defined as international aggression, humanitarian disaster, or gross violations of human rights or democracy), (3) have clear objectives, and (4) possess adequate resources.

Situations where there is *direct American participation in a peacekeeping mission* are more restrictive. In addition to the original criteria, American participation must be shown to be necessary for the mission to succeed, support of the public and Congress must be clear, and command and control arrangements must be satisfactory (American forces must operate only under U.S. command). These limitations presumably apply to U.S. participation both in UN operations and others—such as the Sinai—that do not fall under UN auspices (the stationing of American and other forces between Israel and Egypt in the Sinai was part of the Camp David accords of 1978).

The final situation is where *significant American participation in a peace enforcement mission* is suggested. Once again, three additional criteria are added: commitment of adequate forces to accomplish the mission, a clear plan to achieve the objective decisively, and a commitment to adjust the operation as necessary and a mechanism for doing so.

THE ROLE OF THE UNITED NATIONS

While its momentum as the agency of choice for solving the world's problems has slowed somewhat, the United Nations remains a central institution for dealing with violence and instability in the Second Tier. The UN is the only major intergovernmental organization with a broad political mandate in its charter and something close to universal membership. It has always had great legitimacy in much of the Second Tier, which has used it as a forum for asserting the discontent that Second Tier states feel toward the First Tier-dominated system. With the automaticity of the veto in the Security Council removed as a routine barrier to action, it is now a viable arena for the organization of effective action.

The question is whether the UN will now begin to fulfill the central international role its founders envisaged in a world of major power accord. The veto was included in the Charter to disable the organization in the event that the most important powers (notably the United States and the then Soviet Union) could not agree on action. Without that provision, the UN would have been torn apart over the numerous Cold War confrontations; instead, it was temporarily rendered inoperative—some would say irrelevant.

The UN is now relevant, and its role in the future is the subject of much interest and advocacy. The Charter mandates the central role for maintaining peace and security to the organization. Chapter VII of the Charter provides for standing forces drawn from the permanent members, with coordination from the highest military staff levels of those members, while the rest of the world stands by in a supporting role, largely disarmed.

None of these provisions has ever been activated, but calls for a much broader UN role abound. The apparent success of UN-sponsored collective security in the Persian Gulf War, combined with successes in peacekeeping in places such as Cambodia, have whetted appetites. Desert Storm, however, was neither really a UN operation nor collective security as envisaged in the Charter. The military operation was American, and the commander reported directly to the Pentagon, not the glass house on the East River in New York (UN headquarters). The form of collective security was that of the League of Nations—passing authorizing resolutions and calling for volunteers to enforce them—not the provisions of the Charter. The success of peacekeeping in Cambodia is balanced by stalemate in Lebanon and Cyprus.

The question of a UN future role has centered around two questions: what kinds of forces should be available, and on what terms? And who should control those forces if established? A range of possibilities has been put forward on each dimension of the problem.

The question of available forces arises out of concern about the ability of the organization to act quickly and decisively in crisis situations, hopefully precluding situations from deteriorating to larger proportions that become progressively more difficult to contain. The prototype often cited is Bosnia, where it is alleged that the insertion of adequate forces early in 1992 could have precluded the tragedy that ensued.

A range of four options has arisen in public discourse. The first is *to make no provision at all for a standing force*, relying instead on the hue-and-cry method used in Desert Storm and Somalia. This method requires the least commitment from states that are suspicious of the United Nations, that want to maintain absolute control of their forces, that fear an intrusion on their sovereignty by subordinating forces to the UN, and that may have political difficulty in designating troops to a "foreign" command. As such, it is a very attractive position for the United States to take.

A second alternative is to *use the UN as a deputizer*, designating a state or states to take the lead in organizing responses to situations identified by the Security Council. This is the concept implicitly undertaken in Desert Storm and Restore Hope, in both of which cases the United States was given the de facto mandate to organize the international response but in which it retained operational control of forces. This concept is similar to the "lead agency" concept employed in areas such as antiterrorism in the American federal government, where one interested agency is identified to coordinate the efforts of a series of other interested agencies spread through the government. If one assumes that most of the "lead countries" from the First Tier would come from NATO (a reasonable assumption), there would be a reasonable prospect of military coordination as well. Obviously, IFOR is the prototype of this form.

A third possibility is the *designation of units from the major powers for potential use in UN-sponsored peace imposition actions*. This is, of course, not a new idea; national units from a number of member states have been earmarked for peacekeeping duty for some years, and countries such as Norway have special career tracks and training regimens for designated peacekeepers. The resources available are not, however, adequate to the more ambitious task of peace imposition. Such a scheme could exist within the confines of a deputizing system in which the appointed lead country would know that certain kinds of forces would be available from designating countries. The designation could allow coordination and, possibly, even training of these units during peacetime to increase their efficiency in much the same way that NATO countries conduct joint training exercises. American air transport and AWACS surveillance aircraft would be obvious candidates for such designation. It has never been entirely clear how this option is preferable to the deputizing option.

The fourth option is *a standing UN armed force, with units assigned from national armed forces.* A force in the range of 50,000 to 60,000 has been suggested in the United States Congress as the optimal size for a UN "rapid reaction" force that could be called quickly to the scene when breaches of the peace threaten to upset the system. The chief advantages of such a force are that it would be available in a timely fashion and that it could be integrated into a single, cohesive force, thereby overcoming the logistical and other problems associated with internationally assembled forces.

Because these options would gradually increase the empowerment of the United Nations itself, the question of control becomes progressively more important, especially if some form of permanent UN force is considered. Control is also an important factor because the United Nations currently has no real structure for commanding and controlling armed forces. Technically, such forces report to the Security Council, but an international committee is inadequate for dealing with operational matters. There is no real day-to-day staff structure to advise commanders; indeed, until very recently, the reporting contact for commanders in the field was available to answer the telephone only during regular Monday to Friday working hours, as noted earlier. Further, the antimilitary cultural bias of the organization means that it would be difficult to create a structure with current resources.

The development of any kind of force that is attached to the UN would therefore require the parallel devising of a command structure, unless the deputizing option is chosen. There are three candidates: the Security Council, the Military Staff Committee, and the Secretary-General. All, of course, have standing in the Charter that make them reasonable candidates.

The first would be an expansion of the role of the Security Council, creating a military command structure directly under it that would parallel the Secretariat but report directly to the Council itself and take direct orders from the Council. One might argue that creating a new bureaucracy in an already heavily bureaucratized organization is hardly a good idea, but it would have some advantages. If it were composed of military officers assigned to the command, through a system parallel to that of the U.S. Joint Chiefs of Staff, and civilians with a military background or interests, it could overcome the antimilitary bias of the organization more generally and would also likely have greater credibility among national military establishments (notably, the American) than a structure composed of existing UN personnel.

A second possibility that would avoid the creation of a new organization would be to activate and expand the Military Staff Committee. The Charter envisages a broad role for this body, but it has heretofore been manned at a low level because of its inactivity. The Charter provides for military representation at the highest level and the rotation of chairmanships among the permanent members. This procedure would ensure that each permanent member participated and also maintained an effective veto on the use of its own forces in particular situations. The Committee could also be the agent to appoint lead countries in particular cases. For it to have credibility, a high-ranking officer would have to be appointed from each country—for example, the vice chairman of the U.S. Joint Chiefs of Staff.

The third possibility is the designation of the Secretary-General as the military reporting channel. Boutros-Ghali suggested this role for himself when he was the leading administrative officer of the United Nations. His argument is that such designation would be appropriate because he is an agent of the Security Council and because he heads the already institutionalized bureaucracy of the UN. Opponents of this option fear it would place too much authority, including day-to-day jurisdiction over national troops, in the hands of one individual.

CONCLUSIONS

How these issues are resolved will largely define the role of the United Nations and, possibly, the international community as a whole in dealing with the violence and disorder of the Second Tier. The current system, as manifested in Somalia, does not work especially well; the absence of a military coordinating structure, for instance, was largely to blame for the number of casualties incurred by American Rangers in an attempted raid in Mogadishu in October 1993. (Armored units that could have come to their aid were nearby, but there was no effective way to order them to the rescue.)

Given the inherent difficulty of carrying out peace imposition missions and the likelihood of their arising, it is urgent that the most efficient kind of mechanism and structures be devised. Piecemeal efforts hastily conceptualized and devised will clearly not be sufficient in light of the problems of the new order.

Suggested Reading

Boutros-Ghali, Boutros. *An Agenda for Peace: Preventive Diplomacy, Peacemaking, and Peace-Keeping.* New York: United Nations, 1992.
———. "Empowering the United Nations," *Foreign Affairs* 72, 5 (Winter 1992/93):89–102.
The Clinton Administration's Policy on Reforming Multilateral Peace Operations. Washington, D.C.: U.S. Department of State, May 1994.
Helman, Gerald B., and Steven R. Ratner. "Saving Failed States," *Foreign Policy* 89 (Winter 1992/93):3–20.

Kober, Stanley. "Revolutions Gone Bad," *Foreign Policy* 91 (Summer 1993):63–84.

Lefever, Ernest W. "Reining in the U.N.," *Foreign Affairs* 72, 3 (Summer 1993): 17–21.

Luck, Edward C., and Toby Trister-Gati. "Whose Collective Security?" *Washington Quarterly* 15, 2 (Spring 1992), 43–56.

Metz, Steven. *Special Report: The Future of the United Nations: Implications for Peace Operations.* Carlisle Barracks, Pa.: Strategic Studies Institute, 1993.

Pickering, Thomas R. "The U.N. Contribution to Future International Security," *Naval War College Review* 46, 1 (Winter 1993):94–104.

Snow, Donald M. *Peacekeeping, Peacemaking, and Peace Enforcement: The U.S. Role in the New International Order.* Carlisle Barracks, Pa.: Strategic Studies Institute, 1993.

Stevenson, Jonathan. "Hope Restored in Somalia?" *Foreign Policy* 91 (Summer 1993):138–154.

Weiss, Thomas G. "New Challenges for UN Military Operations: Implementing an Agenda for Peace," *Washington Quarterly* 16, 1 (Winter 1993):51–66.

Chapter 11

Implications for American Forces and Missions

The American military establishment is being asked to engage in a reassessment of its contribution to the country's security at a time when the defense environment has been fundamentally altered and former rationales have been overcome by events. It is a wrenching experience for all involved. There is a lack of consensus about what threatens the United States, either physically or psychologically, and an administration initially more interested in domestic politics and international economics has only begun to address the problem seriously in the past couple of years.

Examples of the dilemma abound. In early November 1993, for instance, the Russian Republic formally abandoned its policy of "no first use" of nuclear weapons, stating that under limited circumstances of attack against Russia, the Russians might, indeed, initiate nuclear weapons use to ward off the attack.

During the Cold War, such a statement would have produced an absolute torrent of analysis and concern. Newspaper columns and scholarly and popular journals, to say nothing of television interview shows, would have been filled with somber, even dire, assessments of the announcement and its implications for American security. In the climate of the post–Cold War world, however, the announcement warranted only a brief, one-day story in the major newspapers, as if it lacked importance. The Russians, as successors to the Soviets, are no longer a menace, so why worry? Moreover, no one really took "no first use" to be more than a propaganda statement that would not have been honored in war anyway. So what? When the Russians and Americans announced later that they would no longer target one another with their weapons, hardly anyone noticed.

The flurry of activity within the defense establishment about American participation in United Nations–sponsored military actions offers another example. Throughout its existence, the UN has been anathema to the American military, the epitome of what is wrong in the world and the epitome of soft-headed thinking. Yet, in 1993, the armed forces embraced the world body. At a small, largely unpublicized conference at the U.S. Army War College in October 1993, career officers waxed positively rhapsodic at the prospect of UN-sponsored missions as they prepared for a larger meeting with a similar focus later in the year at the National Defense University in Washington.

The spring of 1992 offered a similar instance. A Pentagon employee (whose identity has never been revealed) leaked to the press a draft of the Illustrative Planning Scenario, a classified Defense Department document that serves as a source of guidance for sizing and planning American forces. The worst-case scenario (the most stressful set of problems the military might have to handle) was a combined operation in which the United States would simultaneously be required to fend off another Iraqi invasion in the Persian Gulf and a North Korean invasion of the Republic of Korea. The report set off howls of derision, even when the Defense Department sheepishly explained that these were not predictions of likely activity but, rather, kinds and sizes of operations that might occur anywhere in the world. Despite the criticism the scenario received, it reappeared as the basis for sizing force in September 1993 under the late Secretary Les Aspin's "bottom-up" review (a discussion follows).

All these examples demonstrate a common thread that permeates the defense intellectual community: the search—to this point largely unsuccessful—for an organizational alternative to the Cold War. When the political scientist John Mearsheimer titled a 1990 article, "Why We Shall Soon Miss the Cold War," he referred to the likely chaos that might ensue in the former Soviet bloc and the dangers that situation might produce for world peace and stability. His lament clearly extends to those who think about and plan for future uses of American military force.

Rethinking the rationale for American forces is pervasive, affecting all levels of strategy and policy. The collapse of the traditional threat has produced uncertainty as the major foe. On one hand, the argument is made that in an atmosphere of extreme uncertainty about where the need may arise for application of force, high levels of flexibility and capability are needed. That is essentially the argument former Chairman of the Joint Chiefs of Staff, Colin S. Powell, made in defense of his "base force" concept (the minimum force structure necessary to deal with foreseeable contingencies) in the latter stages of the Bush administration. The element of uncertainty, however, makes planning difficult both to achieve and to defend before a Congress potentially casting a hungry eye on defense budgets.

The Clinton national security team has done relatively little to produce a distinctive vision that might serve as an alternative to the current confusion. With the exception of former Defense Secretary Aspin, who served as chair of the House Armed Services Committee (HASC) prior to assuming his position, the national security team—particularly, after Powell was replaced by non-Washington insider, General John

Shalikashvili, and Aspin by Perry—lacks substantial experience. The Clinton administration has thus been plagued by the same charge often levelled against the Bush administration it replaced—that it lacks a strategic vision of the end of the century.

The administration has acted at the margins. It cancelled further production of the B-2 bomber on the grounds that there was no real future mission for such a sophisticated but expensive airplane, and Aspin announced a broad review of strategic nuclear weapons policy at the end of October 1993. In addition, cutbacks in the overall size of the armed forces were announced in September 1993. There was great anticipation in early 1997 that the Quadrennial Defense Review (QDR)—an exersise mandated by Congress and due later that year—would answer some of the questions.

Several fundamental questions that require new answers will be addressed in the pages that follow. We will begin by looking at the future role of nuclear forces and their control, a concern raised earlier. Next, we will turn to conventional, or nonnuclear, forces and examine how they may need to be restructured for a new environment. This will lead to the question of resources available for defense: the budget. In view of likely budgetary constraints, we will examine future roles and missions—that is, where should the United States be prepared to fight? who should do the fighting? and how should they be organized to meet new challenges?

THE CONTINUING ROLE OF NUCLEAR FORCES

As noted in Chapter 6, the thermonuclear arsenals of the United States and the Soviet Union were the most striking symbols of the Cold War international system and national security apparatus it spawned. At its pinnacle, both countries confronted one another with around 12,000 nuclear warheads, deliverable against each other's territory using rockets and other forms of missilry against which defense remained only theoretical. Additionally, each side maintained over 30,000 nuclear warheads of shorter range for possible use in a war between them. Before the weight of these arsenals helped lead to the conclusion by both superpowers that war was inconceivable, nuclear weapons spawned a whole area of inquiry: the study of nuclear deterrence, with derivative concerns such as arms control, disarmament, and proliferation.

This situation has changed dramatically in some respects, and not at all in others. The dramatic change is the end of the geopolitical rivalry that enlivened the concern over possible nuclear war. Nuclear calculations always began from the dual criteria of capability (what arsenals were physically capable of doing) and intention (what those possessing them would, in fact, be willing to do). The weapons (capability) were always known; intention was a matter of speculation, but the general hostility of the relationship made hostile intent a plausible motivation that required dissuading. What is clearly different now is that hostile intention has evaporated, at least for the foreseeable future. Americans no longer worry about the Russian military threat, nor do they feel the need to take heroic measures to assure the containment of hostility. Even the resurgence of the Russian Communist Party has not significantly changed this perception.

But, whereas intent has disappeared, capability has not. The START (Strategic Arms Reduction Talks) I agreement reduced the number of strategic warheads to around 7,000 apiece, and a follow-on START II could lower that number to 3,000 or so for each once it is ratified by both the appropriate legislative bodies in the two countries. The Intermediate Nuclear Forces (INF) Treaty began the process by which most of the shorter-range weapons have been dismantled. Still, even projected arsenal sizes are adequate to do great—even mortal—harm to any country against which they might be unleashed.

Thus, in a sense, nothing has changed. Russia, while lacking visible hostile intent, still possesses a nuclear capability that merits attention, particularly in light of instabilities within and conflicts between several of the successor states. The problem of proliferation remains, highlighted by horror scenarios surrounding the possible acquisition of nuclear weapons by unstable Second Tier states. Arms control has seemed less pressing as adversarial fires have cooled. The result has been a policy review to understand what continuing place nuclear weapons have in American national security policy.

The Soviet Successor States

The simple fact that Russia still possesses nuclear weapons makes some concern unavoidable. That concern is heightened by political uncertainty in Russia itself and in several other republics, as well as ongoing civil wars and conflicts between successor states into which a nuclear-armed Russia might be drawn.

In the early days after the breakup of the Soviet Union, there was concern that former Soviet strategic and theater weapons were located outside Russia and, hence, outside Russian control. Strategic weapons were stationed in Belarus, Ukraine, and Kazakhstan as well as Russia, and theater weapons were located in the successor states along the Sino-Soviet border. Through a series of negotiations that included significant American participation, all came under Russian control.

This problem of so-called "loose nukes" has been supplanted by a newer concern, the security of fissionable materials in former Soviet research and power reactors. Soviet accounting and security procedures for monitoring these supplies were notoriously—and uncharacteristically—lax, and the records do not account for a good deal of weapons-grade material. This became an active concern when Russian mafia nearly succeeded in selling a quantity of weapons-grade material to an officially unnamed Middle Eastern customer believed to be Iran. The prospect of

Middle Eastern terrorists gaining nuclear bomb material in this way has spawned active Russian-American cooperation to devise ways to plug the leak.

A second concern is about the political stability of a number of the successor states, especially Russia. In a number of states, such as Ukraine, the ruling elite has not changed much; although they no longer call themselves communists, basically the same people rule in much the way they did before.

It is Russia, itself, that raises the most concern. In an atmosphere of economic chaos and rampant crime and corruption, Russian democracy seems increasingly tenuous. The "war" between Russian President Yeltsin and the Congress of People's Deputies (a *Soviet* legislature set up by Mikhail Gorbachev and composed almost exclusively of members of the old Communist Party of the Soviet Union) in the fall of 1993, complete with elite Russian tank forces opening fire on the parliament building before the television cameras, reminded the First Tier that things could change politically for the worse within Russia at almost any time. The worst case would propel a new authoritarian regime opposed to the West into power—armed with those several thousands of nuclear weapons.

In one sense, a continuing nuclear balance between Russia and the United States serves as a hedge against a political downturn in Russia. Even an antagonistic regime would be forced to conclude, as did its communist predecessor, that war between Russia and the United States is unthinkable and, hence, that rivalry cannot be allowed to become so intense as to raise the meaningful possibility of war. Until Russia becomes a fully stable political democracy—if it ever achieves that status—nuclear capability acts as a floor below which relations cannot be allowed to fall.

A related concern is the instability in several of the other republics. As noted, a civil war of secession has been going on for sometime in Georgia; Armenia and Azerbaijan continue to contest enclaves; and war could easily spread from Tajikistan to other central Asian locations. While these conflicts pose no direct threat to Russia or to Russian-American relations, their expansion could. A result of the Stalinist policy of migration is that there are Russian nationals in every successor republic, and at some point they may become targets of xenophobic nationalism. If they do, the Russians will come to their aid if Russians follow their own military doctrine (including first use of nuclear weapons). Should the Russians choose the unlikely response of teaching a nuclear lesson to those who would suppress emigre Russians, the consequences are unknown. As already noted, the exploitation of the Caspian oil and gas fields by, among others, American oil companies will create a level of U.S. interest in the area that has not previously been evident.

A final concern is that, unlike the United States, Russia is proximate to a number of states that are potential possessors of nuclear weapons sometime in the near future. The worst problems are where the central Asian and Middle Eastern states are contiguous to Russia. The Russians will be physically vulnerable to nuclear attack much sooner than the

United States, making the control of proliferation and, where that fails, deterrence a much more pressing matter for them. In that circumstance, retention of a nuclear arsenal far in excess of that possessed by any potential Second Tier nuclear power remains a matter of prudence.

The Problem of Proliferation

During the Cold War, it was commonplace to talk of two forms of nuclear weapons proliferation: *vertical* proliferation, increases in the size of the arsenals of current possessors, notably the Soviet Union and the United States; and *horizontal* proliferation, increases in the number of states that possess nuclear weapons. Over time, the superpowers came to be in essential accord about limiting both forms of proliferation, if for different reasons. Although the problem of vertical proliferation is a shadow of its former status, horizontal proliferation remains a highly visible concern in the new order.

As noted in Chapter 6, the stockpiling of nuclear weapons to levels for which they could not be matched to any political purpose (vertical proliferation) provided part of the dynamic for ending the Cold War, and arms control processes aimed at limiting nuclear arsenals became the cutting edge of East-West relations under the general heading of detente. With the Cold War over, the remaining question is: what size of arsenals do the major powers need to maintain as a hedge against a deterioration in their relations and to ensure that third parties from the Second Tier are not tempted to attack them with nuclear or other weapons of mass destruction?

The superpowers also came to believe that stunting horizontal proliferation was in their mutual interests. The dynamic underlying this agreement has been depicted as the *N + 1 problem*, where *N* refers to the states currently possessing nuclear weapons and *+ 1* refers to the additional problems that these states believe will be created by an additional state gaining the capability. Typically, the *N* states believe that the status quo (with their possession) is stable, but that additional nuclear club members will destabilize the situation. Unfortunately, states that contemplate obtaining the weapons do not believe that *their* obtaining the weapons would be destabilizing, and they only come to oppose further proliferation when they have become part of *N*.

The most obvious problem that horizontal proliferation causes is that it increases the number of countries that have their "finger on the nuclear button," thereby mathematically increasing the number of states that can initiate the first explosion of a nuclear device in anger when more than one party possesses the weapons. This aspect of the problem arguably becomes more serious when opposing countries in regional conflicts—India and Pakistan, for instance—both possess the weapons.

The spread of nuclear weapons to the Second Tier (then the Third World) was a particular Cold War concern that led the superpowers into agreement about limitation. In most developing world scenarios where one could imagine a nuclear confrontation if weapons spread were not halted, one opponent was related to the United States while the Soviets had a close relationship with the other. In the event of hostilities that might turn nuclear, would the superpowers be sucked into the conflict, directly confronting one another because of the actions of their associates? Given the absence of any experience, no one knew; the best way to avoid finding out was to avoid the occurrence of new nuclear weapons states.

The problem is different now. The removal of the Cold War overlay makes less likely an escalatory process in which the countries of the First Tier or Russia are inexorably drawn into a Second Tier nuclear war. The problem from a First Tier vantage point thus changes to a two-sided concern. On the one hand, there is the residual possibility that even a very small nuclear war between Second Tier states (none of which has many nuclear weapons) might escalate through dynamics that our lack of experience has caused us not to anticipate. On the other hand—and currently considered as more important—there is the possibility that some Second Tier state will acquire the capacity to attack a First Tier state with nuclear weapons.

A cautionary note about proliferation is necessary here. Discussion and concern over the prospects has been lively since the late 1950s and early 1960s, with the emergence of a reasonably large literature predicting that by the 1970s or 1980s, 20 to 30 nuclear powers would exist. But this has not happened; as shown in Table 11.1, the list today is about what it was then.

The list in the table requires some explanation. The admitted members category contains all those states that publicly acknowledge their possession of nuclear weapons. They are listed in order of acquisition, with China the most recent (joining in 1964). South Africa never admitted possession until the F. W. de Klerk government announced destruction of the weapons.

The other categories represent the problems. The unadmitted list refers to those states that generally are believed to possess nuclear weapons but that do not admit possession. The Israeli stockpile at Dimona has long been fairly public knowledge. (A former employee created a scandal by publicly stating its existence.) India detonated a "peaceful nuclear explosive" in 1974 and, although it maintains it has no weapons, it is known to have all the components needed to facilitate fabrication. This capability has, in turn, spurred Pakistan's development of the "Islamic bomb." The likelihood of a North Korean bomb fueled a cycle of speculation in the summer of 1993 that lasted through 1995 until the North Koreans agreed to reactor inspection by the International Atomic Energy Agency (IAEA).

The third column, active aspirants, lists those states widely known (or believed) to have ongoing research and development programs at one stage or another. The list is conservative; some analysts would expand it.

TABLE 11.1   Nuclear Weapons States

Admitted Possessors	Unadmitted Possessors	Active Aspirants
United States	India	Libya
Russia	Israel	Iran
Great Britain	Pakistan	Iraq
France		North Korea
China		South Korea
South Africa*		Taiwan

*Has destroyed all weapons.

SOURCE: John McCain, "Controlling Arms Sales to the Third World," *Washington Quarterly* 14, 2 (Spring 1991):84.

It is worth noting that a pair of historic rivals, Iran and Iraq, appear on the list. Democratization, however tentative, of South America has reduced concern about Argentina and Brazil, former members of this group, but there has been nothing to cause a similar reduction in concern about the Iraqi-Iranian relationship.

The point is that proliferation has occurred more slowly than many had predicted thirty years ago. This is partly the result of aggressive arms control efforts headed by the United States and the Soviet Union, beginning in the 1960s; the status of those efforts is part of the general policy review regarding American nuclear weapons policy.

Arms Control and Proliferation

Efforts at nuclear arms control began in the wake of the Cuban missile crisis, as already noted in Chapter 4. Although the earliest efforts were primarily directed at the Soviet-American relationship, repressing horizontal proliferation was an important secondary concern.

The first major arms control regime, the *Limited Test Ban Treaty* (LTBT) signed in 1963, illustrates this point. Its major purpose was to ban the testing of nuclear weapons in the atmosphere, a ban that was gradually expanded, through subsequent agreements, to prohibit testing everywhere except underground. There was particular pressure to reach such an accord from those places downwind of test sites, notably Japan and the central United States, which experienced high radiation levels after tests were conducted in the atmosphere. Moreover, both countries had experimented sufficiently with atmospheric testing that they had little left to learn from more tests; thus they gave up little by ending atmospheric testing.

There was a horizontal proliferation dynamic involved, as well. While the Americans and the Soviets had learned all they needed to know from testing in the atmosphere, others had not. France, which was just beginning its testing program, refused to sign for that reason, as did

China. More importantly, the level of nuclear science at the time suggested that no state developing nuclear weapons would have confidence that they worked unless they engaged in atmospheric testing. To the extent that potential weapons states could be drawn into the LTBT, therefore, the cause of nonproliferation was served.

The most explicit attempt to control nuclear arms spread was the complicated and controversial *Nuclear Nonproliferation Treaty* (NPT). Based in the idea that all proliferation is undesirable (a notion challenged in the Amplification box "Is Proliferation Always Bad?") it was negotiated in 1968 and entered into force in March 1970. This enduring treaty received its twenty-five-year renewal in 1995—an event designed to exert pressure toward universal adherence to it. Once again, the primary sponsors were the United States, the Soviet Union, and Great Britain; their mutual interest was to avoid the spread of weapons to Third World states.

NPT thus creates two distinct classes of states, with different and— some argue—unequal obligations. The first category of states are the nuclear weapons possessors, which agree to do two things: not to share nuclear weapons technology or materials with non-nuclear states, and to engage in activities leading to nuclear disarmament. The other category encompasses those that do not possess nuclear weapons; these states agree neither to seek help in acquiring nor to acquire them. The result is a kind of caste system, separating those that have the weapons and those that eschew any right to develop them in the future.

There have always been several problems with NPT, the first of which is membership. Among the nonpossessors, there have always been two categories of state: signatories and nonsignatories. Most states, including many troublesome ones (Iraq, for example), are signatories that signed either because they had no plans to develop the weapons at the time or felt they were giving up little by signing. At the same time, a number of states did not wish to place themselves in the position of giving away an option they might someday like to exercise or of being placed in the position of reneging on an international agreement; hence, they did not join NPT. Israel is a notable example.

A second problem has been enforcement, a matter that achieved great publicity in the wake of the Persian Gulf War. The NPT authorizes inspection of suspected violations by the IAEA, a specialized agency of the UN, and signatory states agree to inspection on demand by IAEA inspectors. The problem has always been a shortage of IAEA inspectors; this shortage allowed Iraq to come close to nuclear weapon fabrication. When Iraqi violations became obvious, a Security Council Resolution (No. 687) reiterated Iraqi willingness to accept inspectors as part of the cease-fire ending the Persian Gulf War. In a similar vein, many nonpossessing signatories—notably, India—complain that the possessing states have done virtually nothing to live up to their obligations to engage in disarmament.

A third problem has been that it is technically easy for a country to remove itself from the regime; the only requirement is to provide a six-

AMPLIFICATION

Is Proliferation Always Bad?

While there is general agreement with the proposition that non-proliferation is more desirable than the spread of nuclear weapons capability, the position is not universally endorsed. The general proposition that proliferation is bad begins with the assertion that the more states that have nuclear weapons, the more chances there are that someone will start a nuclear war. This, of course, is the base of the N + 1 problem already discussed. Moreover, the additional states that might acquire nuclear weapons are mostly in the Second Tier, where, it is alleged, regimes are more volatile and subject to radical change; hence, nuclear weapons might fall into the hands of irresponsible leaders who might be less inhibited than more judicious leaders (this assertion is particularly insulting to many Second Tier leaders). The image of Iran's Ayotollah Ruhollah Khomeini and Iraq's Saddam Hussein in possession of nuclear weapons is often raised in support of this position.

It is, however, possible to argue that, in at least some cases, proliferation may actually *stabilize* the relationships between states. It is a fact, after all, that no states mutually possessing nuclear weapons have gone to war, and in cases such as the competitions between the old Soviet Union and China and between China and India, mutual possession may actually have calmed relations as leaders came to fear that a confrontation could escalate to a nuclear exchange. This certainly may have been the case in 1991, as already noted, when opaque deterrence may have helped quell a conflict between India and Pakistan. Similarly, the practical (if unacknowledged) possession of nuclear weapons by Israel is a powerful part of the war-and-peace relationship between Israel and the neighboring Islamic states. This is not to suggest that proliferation is always *good*, by any means, but rather to suggest that it is not always necessarily bad.

months notice of intention to withdraw. Although no state has renounced its adherence to NPT, a threatened renunciation by North Korea during the summer of 1993 added fuel to fears that the North Koreans had decided to exercise the nuclear option.

More contemporary efforts center around the *Missile Technology Control Regime* (MTCR). This agreement is the first explicit First Tier effort to control activity in the Second Tier by banning the export of missile technology by those who adhere to MTCR. Significantly, MTCR is a product of the Group of Seven (G-7), the economic summit of the world's most powerful industrial democracies. Russia has also agreed to honor its intent, as have more than twenty-five states as of 1994. The problem is that MTCR is an informal agreement, not a treaty, and that a number of Second Tier states that are in the missile business have yet to come under its provisions. There are, however, hopes that the MTCR process may become something of a nonproliferation model for the future.

The American Nuclear Policy Review

At a news conference on October 29, 1993, Secretary of Defense Aspin announced a fundamental review of American national policy regarding the place of nuclear weapons in the national security structure, the first such comprehensive review, he maintained, in forty-five years.

Like many other observers, Aspin was almost wistful about the passage of the Soviet threat that had formed the underpinning for policy and strategy. "The old Soviet threat, while very dangerous, had developed a certain comfort level," he said. "We developed kinds of rules of the road. We developed theories of deterrence. We developed arms control theories." All those theories translated into a force structure and targeting plans against the Soviet Union, some of which are still in place, even if the Soviet Union is not. (Both countries had agreed not to target one another.)

As presented, there appeared to be three assumptions that underlay the review process. The first is that the nuclear problem remains central to defense planning: "The post–Cold War world is decidedly not post-nuclear." Thus, nuclear weapons have an ongoing, if altered, role to play. Second, the nuclear threat no longer comes from a unified Soviet enemy, but has been replaced by a multitude—upwards of ten to twenty—of "terrorist and rogue states" with limited nuclear weapons capability "to destroy a few cities each." Aspin referred to the threat as "a multiheaded monster."

The third assumption is that traditional calculations of how to deter nuclear attacks may be ineffective against this new breed of Second Tier nuclear powers, that they "may not be deterrable." This is a familiar theme in much of the proliferation literature and is often voiced in terms of fanaticism (the new actors are not "rational" in a Western sense) or cultural difference (some cultures do not respect human life to the extent the West does). This supposition, it should be noted, is no more than a hypothesis for which there is no direct empirical evidence: Second Tier states have, in fact, attacked others with nuclear weapons with the same regularity as have First Tier states—that is to say, not at all. The same arguments were also used to describe a Soviet leadership indifferent to the loss of its citizens' lives.

This review was hampered by the fact that almost all the thinking about nuclear weapons—especially deterrence—during the Cold War occurred within the specific context of bilateral Soviet-American relations, with only a smattering of concern for escalatory potential in the event of a Second Tier nuclear war, nuclear terrorism, proliferation, and the like. The extent to which those theories can be extended to the new context is an open and interesting question.

Some of the most fascinating implications have to do with hardware and targeting. Given that the "rogue" states will have very small arsenals—most of which they will be unable to deliver against the United States for the foreseeable future—the size and nature of American forces are in question. The MX (Peacekeeper) missile, with its ten 500-kiloton warheads, was designed for use against "target rich environments" in the Soviet Union (areas with multiple strategically important targets). It is hard to imagine a rogue Second Tier state against which even a single MX payload would not constitute overkill. At the same time, a primary objection to MX was its theoretical vulnerability to a Soviet strike; no Second Tier state could conceivably attack an MX. The missile is a scheduled victim of the START process because its supposed vulnerability contributed to instability; so what is the rationale for retiring MX now?

MX is not alone in the conceptual limbo. The B-1B and B-2 bombers were designed to penetrate extremely sophisticated Soviet air defenses that exist nowhere in the Second Tier. Moreover, against what kind of Second Tier nation does one put a billion-dollar aircraft at risk? For that matter, how many highly sophisticated Ohio class (Trident) submarines, difficult to locate and destroy, does one need against a series of potential foes that have no navies at all?

The Bottom-Up Review, released on September 1, 1993, under Secretary Aspin's authorship, provided—without particular justification—the administration's projections for offensive nuclear forces, based upon two assumptions. The first is that the successor states that had not already agreed to do so (Ukraine and Kazakhstan) would turn over the nuclear weapons under their control to Russia and join the NPT as non-nuclear states, which they have done. The second assumption is the ratification of START II limits, which the proposed force structure would implement.

The proposed structure mirrors the old TRIAD of aircraft-launched, intercontinental, and submarine-launched ballistic missiles, although it tilts the total force more heavily toward highly secure sea-based missiles. Under its provisions, the United States would maintain eighteen Trident submarines, equipped with the highly accurate C-4 and D-5 missiles (the most advanced MIRVed missiles that were being fitted into the submarines as the Cold War ended); an air wing consisting of up to ninty-four B-52 H bombers (the least aged of the B-52s), equipped with air-launched cruise missiles (ALCMs), and twenty B-2 bombers; and 500 Minuteman III missiles armed with single warheads.

This construction represents some notable change. First, it removes two highly controversial weapons developed during the 1970s and partially fielded during the 1980s: the B-1B bomber and the MX/Peacekeeper missile. The B-1B was cancelled in 1977 by President Carter and resuscitated by President Reagan. Its career was marked by cost over-runs, performance shortfalls, and upkeep difficulties. The report does not discuss whether B-1s will be retained for conventional duties. Cancelling MX and removing MIRVs from Minuteman III similarly shuts the book on land-based MIRVed ICBMs, which, as noted, have always been the subject of controversy and charges of destabilization.

One weapons system whose time may come under the review is GPALS, or a designated successor (all services have ongoing programs) the defensive system against small, limited nuclear launches. This missile defense was difficult to justify when the Soviets were the primary concern, since any Soviet attack would overwhelm it. The threat has now been sized to the weapon's capability. The QDR is expected to speak to missile defense programs, as well as other nuclear programs.

Targeting is the other intriguing problem. The Soviets presented the designers of the Single Integrated Operational Plan (SIOP) with a concrete, coherent set of targets against which to program American warheads. In the absence of any possible intention to incinerate cities or missile silos in the former Soviet Union, they are currently aimed at remote ocean locations. How many are needed to cover a "target set" that has not even been designated? How does one convey to potential adversaries the news they may be on the list (to deter them) when they are only potential, rather than actual, adversaries?

These are difficult questions, and it is probably fortunate that they are also neither critical nor immediate matters. Certainly for the remainder of the century and probably well beyond, the only country that will have any meaningful capacity to attack the United States with nuclear weapons is a Russia utterly lacking in motive to do so unless things go terribly wrong there. This absence of a system-threatening problem allows planners the relative luxury of planning against the highly improbable.

CONVENTIONAL FORCES: HOW MANY? WHAT KINDS?

Changes in nuclear forces pale by comparison to projections for conventional forces. The basic absence of roles and missions for the nuclear forces in the foreseeable future—until such a time as Second Tier states may pose a problem that nuclear force might address—makes strategy and policy less pressing for the administration in that area. Moreover, the maintenance of nuclear forces is relatively inexpensive, and reducing the force to 3,000 warheads would save about $10 billion a year—hardly a drop in the bucket of the $261 billion budget for fiscal year 1996.

Reductions in conventional forces, however, will be both extensive and traumatic. Under the Clinton administration, the active duty force has fallen from its 1993 strength of about 1.7 million to around 1.4 million by 1995; the QDR is expected to exact a further total force reduction (active, reserve, and civilian) of 140,000. By contrast, the authorized active duty force was about 2.15 million on the eve of the revolutions of 1989 that marked the beginning of the end of the Cold War. Although the services will absorb different levels of reductions, all will be affected.

Two motives underly these reductions. The first and most obvious is budgetary; the defense budget is a veritable cornucopia of controllable funds that can be sacrificed to other priorities—notably, budget deficit reduction. The second is the shrinking threat and, thus, less apparent need for capability and readiness than that dictated by the necessity to confront and repel a short-warning, massive Soviet thrust into Germany. The two threads come together on the need to procure additional military capabilities and reach sharpest focus over so-called "big ticket" weapons systems (or "platforms" in Pentagon jargon) such as main battle tanks, aircraft carriers, and new fighter and bomber aircraft.

The Conventional Debate

Although it is not entirely clear that the moment will be seized, the current environment of relative threat tranquillity offers an opportunity for a basic examination of the tenets of defense policy and military posture that derive from that policy and the strategies that implement it. The current structure was developed piecemeal in an atmosphere which, until recently, did not require the great coordination among the forces mandated by the Goldwater-Nichols Defense Reorganization Act of 1986. The structure was also largely dictated by the Soviet threat and individual responses to that threat as manifested in Soviet capabilities.

Aspin's bottom-up review, which has been criticized as neither bottom-up nor comprehensive, offered a first, tentative rationale for conducting this reassessment. It used a simultaneous Iraqi invasion of Kuwait and Saudi Arabia and North Korean invasion of South Korea as its standard, arguing that the United States must be prepared to fight and win both encounters at the same time (the "win-win" strategy). Force structure was then estimated for that task. Given that these scenarios and, in all likelihood, the details of force structure were products of the Bush Pentagon, these estimates probably represent no more than an interim solution that awaits the thorough review the QDR is to produce.

There are impediments to a truly comprehensive review of the armed services. One is the sheer size and complexity of the task, dealing with three separate services—the Army, the Navy (including the Marines), and the Air Force—in addition to the quasi-military Coast Guard, which is administratively housed in the Department of Transportation. Each is a multifunctional force with overlapping capabilities, and each is itself a complex organization.

Second is bureaucratic inertia: the defense bureaucracy is the largest within government. In addition to the active uniformed services, there are reserve components for each service, a permanent civilian bureauc-

racy, and a layer of politically appointed top Defense Department officials. Each group has its own perceived interests, which are at some odds
with those of others. This inertia is compounded by the extreme conservatism and resistance to change of these groups, especially the individual
services, which can be counted on to view any attempts at reform with
suspicion. Their success at resistance was most recently demonstrated by
the so-called White Commission on roles and missions (named after its
chair, the Deputy Secretary of Defense designate John P. White). The
commission, the staff of which was dominated by retired military officers, recommended essentially no basic changes for the services from
Cold War roles and missions, although it did make some important recommendations in areas such as jointness.

Third is the fact that any decisions to alter the structure occur in a
highly politicized environment. A reduction in forces, for instance,
causes a realignment in the base structure (where different forces are
based), and those changes occur within the constituencies of individual
members of Congress. The political fight created by the 1991 and 1993
rounds of base closures was repeated in 1995, and will be accompanied
by similar dynamics in communities where weapons systems contracts
are no longer let or where production lines come to a halt as contracts are
cancelled, to cite two obvious examples.

The debate is further complicated by interbranch concerns within
the government itself. In the Bush years, the relations between Congress
and the executive about defense budgets had a partisan character, since
the Democrats controlled both houses and the armed services committees
were chaired by two powerful and influential members, Nunn of SASC
and Aspin of HASC. The partisan role was reversed in 1994, as the
Republican-controlled houses of Congress presented President Clinton
with defense budgets larger than he requested.

Remaining tensions include that of leadership; will the Congress or
the president take the lead? As a general rule, Congress is more likely to
wield the budget cutter's axe, despite its recent performance. President
Clinton shows little sustained enthusiasm for these matters, and Secretary Perry did not articulate a strategic vision. The relations between
Congress and one of its former colleagues, Secretary Cohen, remains con-
jectural. The president must shore up relations with the professional military, which were harmed by initial mistakes such as his handling of the
gays in the military issue at the beginning of his term. Budget reductions
are not the way to heal those relations. Reform will take a further batter-
ing because Senator Nunn, who has some very strong and well-
organized ideas about reform that are more detailed than those presented by the administration, retired from the Senate in 1996.

Three overarching concerns will likely dominate discussions of reform. The first is the size and nature of the force, a matter somewhat dependent on questions of future roles and missions. The second is the
question of force redundancy and the degree to which it can be tolerated

in the future. The third is the relative balance between the active component (AC) of the force and the reserve component (RC), always a political football in interbranch dealings.

The first concern is about what the force will look like at the end of the process. An initial review occurred under the Bush administration and resulted in Powell's base force concept: the minimum size the armed forces could be and still retain their operational cohesion across a range of missions. That force was composed of an AC force of 1.6 million and did not represent a substantial realignment of missions or structures; critics referred to it as the old force "times .75," meaning that it was the Cold War force reduced by one-quarter.

The Clinton program further reduces force size to about two-thirds of its Cold War size. Military professionals and many analysts are not sure that the bottom has been reached. In fact, many expected the bottom line to be about one-half the original strength, although there has been no public talk about such deep reductions by Clinton officials. The more basic questions concern what this force will look like. A force two-thirds its former size clearly cannot do all the things the old force could, but it may not be called upon to do as much.

Early discussions have not been entirely encouraging. Shortly after Aspin entered office, the Defense Department began to tout a new strategy by which the United States worst-case scenario would be two simultaneous Second Tier conflicts, each up to Desert Storm in size. The debate was about whether the strategy and accompanying forces should be configured to "win-win" (conduct conclusive offensive campaigns at the same time) or "win-hold-win" (engage in decisive actions in one theater while holding in the other, then win the second after the first is completed). A major problem with this approach was that it was premised on what many view as the unrealistic Iraq–North Korea scenario. Moreover, raising this scenario leads to the conclusion that retention of a force dominated by "heavy" weaponry is needed, a conclusion with which many disagree (see the following discussion).

The second concern has to do with redundancy, a particular fixation of Senator Nunn that has been a major agenda item because of his concern. There is disagreement about redundancy on several grounds. Some argue (Powell, in particular) that force redundancies are actually beneficial, while others argue they are an unaffordable luxury. The argument also focuses on realigning roles and missions and on whether a given force should be solely responsible for a particular activity.

No one denies that redundancy exists. The Navy possesses an army (the Marines) and both a carrier-based and a land-based air force (the latter largely for reconnaisance and antisubmarine warfare near the coast). The Air Force has a small navy to patrol around air bases and a small army for base security. The Army, not to be outdone, maintains riverine patrol boats and an air arm composed mainly of helicopters. The Marines, in addition to being the Navy's army, also has its own air force for close air support of its land operations. Each service has its own separate special forces.

Proponents of this redundancy—largely, but not exclusively, within the armed forces themselves—argue that it results in a more effective force than a less redundant force would be. Having several armies, for instance, gives the leadership the options of, say, using Marines or light infantry, such as the 82nd Airborne, for rapid deployment missions like Somalia or, more recently, Liberia. Moreover, the result is more specialized forces; the Marine air corps, for instance, is more enthused and thus more adept at close air support of land operations than is the Air Force, which would much rather save its fighter aircraft for air-to-air combat. An unspoken further virtue is that retention of redundant capabilities maintains the military operational specialties (MOS) and career paths of many high-ranking officers.

The opponents counter that this redundancy is inefficient and unaffordable under current budget constraints. Specialized missions have meant an expensive lack of standardization of equipment. The Air Force, Navy, and Marines each buy different fighter aircraft rather than a similar design modified for their unique problems (such as landing on aircraft carriers). This lack of standardization has occasionally been very embarrassing. During the Grenada operation, for example, an Army artillery spotter could not communicate with a Naval ship off the coast because their radios did not work on the same frequency. (The soldier had to place a credit-card phone call to Ft. Bragg, which relayed the coordinates to the ship.) A major purpose of creating the "procurement czar" as part of the Goldwater-Nichols act was to reduce this problem; service resistance has made the effort less than a stunning success. Ironically, this criticism has resulted in plans for a joint strike fighter—an advanced aircraft for use by all air services which critics say none of them need.

In addition, missions for which none of the forces has particular enthusiasm can be ignored or underrepresented in current conditions. For instance, the lowest operational order of priority for both the Air Force and the Navy has always been troop and supply transport, which they consider to be running an "airline" or a "cruise ship" operation for the Army. In a particularly embarrassing part of the Desert Storm operation, the shortage of adequate troop ships was evident. The Pentagon initially blamed this shortage on a penurious Congress, only to find out that Congress had, indeed, appropriated funds for additional transports; the Navy had not spent the money. Failure to rectify the airlift and sealift incapacity are particularly problematical given the de facto role of the United States as the transporter and supplier of international efforts to far-flung combat zones.

The third concern is the mix in size and mission of the active and reserve components of the forces. In the wake of the Vietnam experience, then Army Chief of Staff Creighton Abrams took the lead in assigning important military functions to the reserve component. His purpose, borne out especially forcefully in the Persian Gulf War, was to ensure that any major engagement of American forces would require calling up at least some reserves. His reason was political: activating reserves required an implicit approval of military actions by the public that did not occur before Vietnam. In the future, the American people would have to approve action in advance by endorsing the call-up of reserves.

Major noncombat elements are now assigned to the reserves. In the Army, which has done more of this than the other services, activities such as psychological operations (psy-ops), civic action, and a good bit of transportation support are exclusively reserve assignments, and the medical operation during wartime relies heavily on reserves.

The future role of reserves is a matter of ongoing contention. Within the active component, there is opposition to an expanded role on the dual grounds of military effectiveness (reserves are alleged not to be as capable as active members, particularly in combat) and relative claims on budget. Reservists argue that they are discriminated against in equipment, training, and resources: for example, they get the oldest and worst equipment and least access to modern weapons systems.

The AC-RC mix, as it is known within the military, is a particular bone of contention between DOD and the Congress. The reserves are the darlings of Congress, which consistently tries to expand the reserves over the objections of the Pentagon. The reason for Congressional support of the reserves is political: reserve units mean armories within congressional districts, and support of the reserves translates into political support among constituents. In addition, since reservists are part-time soldiers ("weekend warriors"), they are considerably less expensive to maintain than active duty personnel. To the military professionals, the gap in performance between active and reserve components is so great as to make the investment a waste of money better spent on the active force. The result is a perpetual disagreement, wherein the Congress proposes a greater parity between active and reserve components (as high as a 1:1 ratio) and the Pentagon fights to stave off this political intrusion, preferring something more like a 2:1 active-reserve ratio.

One incident from the Persian Gulf war illustrates with particular clarity the operational level of controversy. The 24th Georgia National Guard armor brigade, a combat unit, was among those activated as a round-out brigade for the war. As was the case with all three activated reserve combat units, it was sent to the National Training Center (NTC) in the California desert for specialized training for the desert conditions of Kuwait. (Active forces regularly train at NTC.) The problem was that the 24th Georgia never left NTC, sitting out the war there; like the other two units, it remained on active duty throughout the war but never left the continental United States. The Army maintained that they were not fit for combat and that their insertion into the war would have resulted in unnecessary casualties. The members of the unit were furious, charging their active duty counterparts with open discrimination.

None of these issues is easily resolvable. They are complicated problems that reside in a very real environment of uncertainty about where and when force will be necessary. The existing structure provides an inertial drag that makes reform and change more difficult; any reform steps on someone's toes, either in the Pentagon or in the Congress.

The Proposed Structure

During the 1992 campaign, candidate Clinton promised to cut the defense budget by more than $88 billion more than President Bush had proposed for the period between 1995 and 1999. The end result would be a $1.2 trillion budget for those years, considerably less in terms of both real (actual) and constant (buying power adjusted for inflation) dollars than had been projected during the Cold War. To accomplish these goals, each of the services was to face reductions in both personnel and equipment, the two largest controllable elements of service budgets. In each case, projected reductions reflect at least implicit assessments about future roles and missions. The proposed force was outlined in Aspin's *The Bottom-Up Review*, as captured in Table 11.2. These figures represent only the barest outline of what the force will look like, and will undoubtedly be further reduced as a result of the QDR. It takes on meaning when placed in the context of the individual services and the relative impact on each.

The Army has experienced major reductions in manpower. From a peak during the 1980s of eighteen divisions, the Army has downsized to ten divisions. In active manpower terms, this means that it will shrink from its 1990 level of around 746,220 to about a half million (according to Defense Department figures, active duty strength stood at 521,036 in May 1995). In addition, the Army has had to defer some modernization spending, such as for a new main battle tank.

Two Army issues stand out for the future. The first is the AC-RC debate, which affects the Army more than the other forces because Army reserve forces are both larger and their roles more central than in the other services. Using Congressional Research Service figures for 1990, for instance, reserves and the National Guard represented about 48 percent of total active and reserve Army strength. (The equivalent was 19 percent for the Navy, 18 percent for the Marines, and 23 percent for the Air Force.) The Army Reserve and the National Guard are, after all, the descendents of the militia tradition in American society. The battle lines in this debate will be between the professional military, which would prefer a ratio of about two active component members for every reservist, and Congress, which would prefer something approximating the 1:1 ratio mentioned earlier. Although Aspin's *Review* comes down on the side of the professional military, a lively debate in Congress will persist whenever the issue is raised.

The other major Army issue is the balance between light and heavy forces. The traditional, NATO-oriented Army emphasized heavy forces:

TABLE 11.2   Proposed Force Structure

Army	10	active divisions
	5+	reserve divisions
Navy	11	active aircraft carriers
	1	reserve training carrier
	45–55	attack submarines
	346	ships (total)
Marines	3	marine expeditionary forces
	174,000	active duty personnel
	42,000	reserve personnel
Air Force	13	active duty fighter wings
	7	reserve fighter wings
	Up to 184	bombers

SOURCE: Les Aspin, *The Bottom-Up Review: Forces for a New Era*. Washington: Department of Defense, September 1, 1993.

tanks, heavy artillery, and mechanized infantry, for example, all of which were necessary to combat a similarly equipped Soviet force. Light forces, by contrast, are more lightly armed and mobile: airborne infantry and ranger and special forces (as well as Marines) fit into this category. No one proposes eliminating either category; rather, the issue is whether as much heavy force is necessary in a world where there are relatively few heavy armies that one might confront and where the requirement for rapid insertion into volatile situations suggests the need for more mobile, hence light, forces. The Army, like the other armed forces, is dominated at the highest ranks with leaders from the heavy MOSs, who are reluctant to downgrade the importance of their specialties.

The Navy was the favored force of the Reagan years, when it was projected to grow to a force of 600 ships. The centerpiece of the surface Navy was fifteen or sixteen carrier battle groups that would form the basis for global naval presence and dominance and that could execute the forward maritime strategy in the event of war.

The end of the Cold War leaves the Navy vulnerable, because one victim was the Soviet Navy, which has been divided among the successor republics, notably Russia and the Ukraine. There simply no longer exists a major naval challenger to the American Navy, raising questions about the need for such a large, expensive force. The same is true for the Navy's submarine force of hunter-killer submarines and ballistic-missile-launching submarines; the absence of a viable opponent raises questions about the continuing need for large numbers of vessels. An area of greater emphasis may be power projection aimed at countries on the littorals of major bodies of water that are of concern (such as the Arabian Gulf or the Straits of Taiwan).

The answer has been force reduction. The fifteen-carrier-group Navy was premised on seven groups on station in the world's major oceans (the Atlantic, Pacific, and Indian Oceans and the Mediterranean) at any point in time, seven in home port, and one for training. Under the Clinton plan, that total will be reduced to twelve groups, thereby restricting the number on patrol to five. Attack submarines will decline from a 1990 level of ninety-nine to fifty-five. The total Navy is projected to decline from 546 to 346 ships, with obvious implications for manpower numbers. In terms of personnel, it went from an active duty strength of about 604,500 in 1990 to roughly 464,000 in 1995. Further QDR-driven reductions are likely.

The Marines fare somewhat better. Because of their high mobility, they can be made available in crisis situations by placing a Marine Expeditionary Force (MEF) off a coast for rapid insertion. They have become, in a sense, the instrument of choice in situations such as Somalia, and they will clearly be in much demand if the United States follows an active policy of intervention in Second Tier conflicts. Because of their highly visible successes in places like Somalia, their strength in 1995 was at 172,000—down from 197,000 in 1990 but significantly higher than the 159,000 projected by the Bush administration had it won a second term. Their visible commitment to unconventional missions like peacekeeping (which it calls complex emergency operations or CEOs) has enhanced its relative position among force elements.

The Air Force faces a problem similar to that of the Navy: the disappearance of a viable opponent. In the past, the Air Force has been structured for two primary missions: strategic nuclear engagement with the Soviet Union and engagement in the European theater. The strategic mission encompassed land-based ICBMs that are largely phased out under arms control agreements and strategic bombers intended to penetrate Soviet air defenses that no longer exist and to destroy Soviet targets that we no longer have any reason to destroy. These presumptions are reflected in the reduction of ICBMs to 500 (from around 1,700) and of bombers to 184 (from 1990 levels of 366). The European theater mission consisted of establishing air superiority by knocking the Soviet air force out of the air and then providing close air support of ground operations. Both missions evaporated with the demise of the opponent.

The highly publicized brilliant performance of the Air Force during the Persian Gulf War makes cutbacks harder to accept than they might otherwise be, but cutbacks have occurred—for instance, in tactical fighter wings from twenty-four to twenty. The Air Force did win the battle to keep the distribution of those wings at thirteen in the active component and seven in the reserves, rather than the 10-to-10 ratio suggested by some members of Congress—another likely point of future debate. Active duty strength shrank from 535,000 to 400,000 between 1990 and 1995, and the Air Force will take additional QDR-mandated cuts.

FUTURE MISSIONS

It is reasonable to ask whether these proposed reductions produce reduced capabilities that endanger the national security. Clearly, the force that will survive the downsizing will not be capable of doing all the things that the 2.15-million-man force could do. Whether a less-capable armed force makes a difference in American national security depends critically on the missions it is likely to be called upon to perform.

The discussion of missions can be framed in terms of five loosely related conditioning factors. These are the changed international environment, the technological superiority of American and other First Tier forces, the absence of a likely major opponent in the operative environment, the likelihood of longer lead time to prepare for any major engagement than was possible during the Cold War, and the emergence of a new category of quasi-military missions.

The changed international environment, of course, is the emergence of a world of two distinct tiers. The first tier contains all the major system actors, all of which are political democracies with intertwined market economies. As they grow ever more similar, there are essentially no conflicts among them that have the potential to devolve to war. As a result of this reality, intra–First Tier relations have a minimal national security content and place hardly any demands on military forces for the United States.

This fact of commonality does not mean that there are no differences among First Tier states. As the states of the First Tier reconfigure into economic regions—the EU, NAFTA/FTAA, and APEC, for instance—there will be economic disagreements between them over matters such as terms of trade, but these divisions are unlikely to degenerate into violence or even a significant possibility thereof. At the same time, geographic and historical factors will cause them to disagree among themselves where their interests are affected in Second Tier conflicts and, hence, where different kinds of responses can be made. In all likelihood, however, this phenomenon will be manifested in no more than verbal disagreement or in some First Tier states becoming involved in some, but not other, systemic responses to Second Tier problems. As noted, mature political democracies do not fight one another, and military threats among them would be decidedly hollow.

The Second Tier, of course, is entirely different. Composed of the rest of the world, it is incredibly diverse, both politically and economically. Essentially all of the violence and instability in the world will occur within the Second Tier and, occasionally, in isolated interactions between the tiers in areas such as terrorist attacks. The major question for the United States and its national security apparatus is where or whether it wants to become involved in lessening Second Tier violence and suffering. Such a determination has not yet been made in any systematic way, but it is not a critical matter in the sense that responding to the Soviet threat was a generation ago. Some criteria by which to form a policy will be suggested in the concluding chapter.

The second factor is the obvious technological superiority of the United States and its principal First Tier allies. The technological gap, expressed in passage into the third industrial revolution, cleaves the First and Second Tiers economically; except for those states that are near entrance into the First Tier—Pacific Rim countries, for example—the dynamics of technologically driven change are likely to widen that gap rather than narrow it. This is, of course, the phenomenon previously identified as the Revolution in Military Affairs. At the same time, sharing technologically derived advances with cooperative Second Tier countries can provide a long-term impetus to the widening of President Clinton's ring of market democracies and, hence, to lowering the level of violence and instability.

This technological gap is evident in military matters, as well. The Persian Gulf War, to repeat, is a harbinger of future military interactions between the tiers. Its obvious implication is that Second Tier states have little chance to defeat First Tier states in war, even if they possess numerically superior armed forces. A lesson of the coalition in the Kuwaiti theater of operations (KTO) was that there were many more troops there than were needed to defeat Iraq. For the United States, that fact means that a smaller armed force can still be potent and decisive.

The third factor is the absence of a realistic large-scale opponent for the United States in the foreseeable future for which a massive standing force would be necessary. This is, of course, an entirely different circumstance than the problem posed by the Cold War confrontation with the Soviets. Why did the United States need a standing, ready force of over two million with a reserve of another million or so? The answer is that the Soviet standing armed forces presented a concrete, plausible enemy that had to be countered.

There is nothing remotely equivalent to that problem in the contemporary environment. Certainly, there are large armed forces in the world. Russia still maintains a large proportion of the former Soviet Union's armed forces, but they have been weakened morally and physically and have reoriented themselves doctrinally to a defensive posture. For the foreseeable future, they will pose no particular threat outside the borders of the old Soviet Union. Their performance against Chechen rebels raises questions about how potent a force they are within Russia. China has a very large standing force, but it is also largely defensive, technologically backward, and directed by a political leadership that could scarcely be called aggressive. Similarly, India has a very large army, but it is difficult to imagine circumstances where the United States would find itself at war with India. The North Koreans, especially armed with nuclear weapons, pose a problem, but South Korean preparedness is such that massive American ground combat assistance would probably not be needed in another Korean War scenario. The need to create the joint Korean-Iraqi scenario to produce a plausible large war is indirect testimony to the absence of realistic prospects.

The fourth factor is that the United States would likely have considerable lead time before it was forced into another major conflict. Once again, this situation is quite unlike the Cold War, where the warning time of a Soviet attack was measured in days, meaning that the armed force that would have to stop the invasion had to be constantly in place—a so-called force in being. A major purpose of that force would have been to slow the attack sufficiently to allow reinforcement from the United States. Since the initial invasion was envisaged as a very large attack, a large—and very expensive—forward deployed force was necessary in Europe.

That situation has changed. The worst case that one can imagine is a Russia reverted to an expansionist authoritarian regime seeking to reestablish its empire either within the boundaries of the old Soviet Union or beyond into Eastern Europe. In order to build a force adequate for such a task, the Russians would have to engage in a very large rebuilding process that would be quite visible and would allow adequate time for the United States and its allies to reconstitute their forces.

The fifth factor is the emergence of a series of new missions that are unlike the traditional war-fighting, and even peacekeeping, roles the military has undertaken. These are situations, exemplified by places such as Somalia, Bosnia, and Haiti, where the situation is one of war or its potential but where the purpose of introducing American (and likely other First Tier) forces is not for physical combat, but to provide other services that will facilitate the settlement of disputes.

Falling somewhere between war fighting and statebuilding, these new missions are novel for the U.S. military, which recognizes—or at least suspects—that some of them fall beyond their expertise or solution. The result is a kind of ambivalence. On one hand, these roles are better than nothing at all; on the other hand, they do not provide the kinds of expectations and actions that soldiers undertake. This ambivalence is well reflected in the kinds of names they are given: "peace operations," "military operations other than war," "humanitarian relief operations," or "complex emergency operations."

Much of the difficulty comes from trying to fit these missions into the Clausewitzian-Napoleonic mold. Generally, they involve the measured application of military force to achieve very limited, even reversible results. The American mission to Haiti did not result in "victory" in a "war"; rather, it provided temporary stability in which the Haitians could try to produce order. But there were no guarantees. In Rwanda, American relief efforts did not "save the day" for suffering Rwandans; but it did provide potable water and rudimentary sanitation for the war's refugees. Similarly, IFOR did not guarantee a peaceful Bosnia after its removal; but it did stop the war for a time and provide some opportunity for a healing process to begin.

Embracing these kinds of operations requires a change in the mindset by which the United States views the application of military force. We may be entering, in Edward Luttwak's phrase, a period of "post-heroic warfare" where the Clausewitzian-Napoleonic framework does not always apply and where, at least from time to time, more modest actions must be tied to more modest ends.

CONCLUSIONS

These conditioning factors affect the preparations for likely uses of military force, but they do not provide absolute boundaries, because circumstances can change. The least likely area of change is within the First Tier itself; serious horror scenarios are difficult to conjure. Saddam Hussein's invasion of Kuwait, on the other hand, demonstrated that the other three conditions may not always hold. Iraq ignored—if, indeed, it recognized—the effect of the technological gap; it employed a large armed force, and it attacked with little warning. Had the Iraqis not stopped their aggression with Kuwait and gone on and occupied the Saudi oil fields—which was far from impossible for them in the early days—the military problem would have been much more severe for the United States and its allies.

The most likely occasions for the United States to be called upon to use armed force in the foreseeable future are in the Second Tier. In the absence of a threat to something as basic as American access to Persian Gulf petroleum, these instances will arise in the absence of sizable American geopolitical interests, and they will, in most cases, call for measured involvement.

Two planning contingencies—beyond the Iraq-Korea scenario—appear likely candidates for concern. The first is the involvement of American forces in future UN-directed or UN-sponsored peacekeeping/peace imposition operations, for which the IFOR mission in Bosnia may prove to have been a prototype of sorts. Participation in these peace operations provides some vision of likely future involvements. First, it assumes that "in most cases," American efforts would be as part of a multilateral effort, probably under UN or other auspices. Second, it envisages more active military action than reestablishing cease fires (the UN definition). Rather, it suggests activities such as "forced entry" into host facilities, controlling foreign and host country military movement, and establishing and defending civilian protection zones (the intervasion of Haiti is an example). Third, it suggests the devotion of primarily light military units to these tasks, such as light infantry, airborne units, Marine expeditionary brigades, and special operations forces.

The other, and more difficult, planning case is based in uncertainty. The United States has done, and continues to do, a good job of preparing for—and in the process, deterring—situations that it anticipates. For example, a reason that North Korea is inhibited from attacking South Korea is their knowledge of our response. It is the unpredicted and, in some cases, unpredictable future crises for which planning mission requirements is most difficult.

Suggested Reading

Abshire, David. "Strategic Challenge: Force Structures, Deterrence," *Washington Quarterly* 15, 2 (Spring 1992):33–42.

Blodgett, John Q. "The Future of U.N. Peacekeeping," *Washington Quarterly* 14, 1 (Winter 1991): 207–220.

Crocker, Chester A., Fen Osler Hampson, with Pamela Aall (eds.). *Managing Global Chaos: Sources and Responses to International Conflict*. Herndon, Va.: United States Institute of Peace Press, 1996.

Durch, William J. (ed.). *The Evolution of U.N. Peacekeeping*. New York: St. Martin's Press, 1992.

Guertner, Gary L. *The Armed Forces in a New Political Environment*. Carlisle Barracks, Pa.: Strategic Studies Institute, 1992.

Haffa, Robert Jr., and George Quester. *Conventional Forces and the Future of Deterrence*. Carlisle Barracks, Pa.: Strategic Studies Institute, 1992.

Kampelman, Max M. "Secession and the Right of Self-Determination: An Urgent Need to Harmonize Principle with Pragmatism," *Washington Quarterly* 16, 3 (Summer 1993):5–12.

Layne, Christopher, and Benjamin Schwartz. "American Hegemony—Without an Enemy," *Foreign Policy* 92 (Fall 1993):5–23.

Luttwak, Edward N. "A Post-Heroic Military Policy," *Foreign Affairs* 75, 4 (July/August 1996), 33–44.

Mahnken, Thomas G. "America's Next War," *Washington Quarterly* 16, 3 (Summer 1993):171–188.

Mazarr, Michael J. "Nuclear Weapons after the Cold War," *Washington Quarterly* 15, 3 (Summer 1992):185–201.

Renner, Michael. *Critical Juncture: The Future of Peacekeeping*. Washington, D.C.: Worldwatch Institute, 1993.

Rosenau, James N. *The United Nations in a Turbulent World*. Boulder, Colo.: Lynne Reiner, 1992.

Schlesinger, James. "The Impact of Nuclear Weapons on History," *Washington Quarterly* 16, 4 (Autumn 1993):5–16.

Chapter 12

Defense Policy in a Changed International Order

The tremors unleashed by the events of 1989 continue to rumble through the international system, as it adapts to the end of the bipolar Cold War and the emergence of a successor order. As a principal byproduct of that systemic change, the structure of the national security subsystem has changed as well, reacting to and attempting to anticipate changes in the overall system and their implications for the American defense establishment.

Part of the problem is the apparent absence of an analogous historical system. Academic constructs based in theoretical analyses of past systems—bipolar, multipolar, even unipolar—seem inadequate to encompass the evolving reality. The reason for this probably is that all these constructs were devised to describe an essentially Eurocentric world, in which most of the globe could be ignored because it was not an effective part of the system—Asia during the eighteenth and early nineteenth centuries, for instance. Possibly the analogy that best fits is the clash of civilizations when Asia and Europe encountered one another via the Mongol and Arab incursions into Europe, for which we have no systematic organizing devices.

Modern analogies do not help much, either. Analysts who are pessimistic suggest that the current incoherence may resemble the periods between the world wars, when no dominant state or coalition of states could organize the peace and where a weak system could not stop the spiral into chaos and war. Optimists look backward toward the general peace and tranquillity of an eighteenth century marked by a convergence of political ideology in Europe and the general desire to avoid war. The pessimists tend to ignore the calming effect of the general agreement among the emerging First Tier and the existence of a remaining superpower, the United States, as its natural leader. The optimists ignore a chaotic Second Tier that had no equivalent in the Euro-centered system of the eighteenth century.

The solution to dealing with the concurrent existence of great order and stability and of disorder and instability is to recognize that there are, in fact, two distinct subsystems in the current system. Whether one calls them zones of peace and zones of turmoil, as Singer and Wildawsky do, or a World of Tiers, as the current analysis does, the distinction allows one both to provide a framework in which to understand the dynamics of the current system and to define more precisely the security problem, as it affects both the overall system and the national security of its members.

The idea of conceptualizing the new international order as a World of Tiers, introduced in Chapter 1, has been employed as a building block in those chapters dealing with the contemporary situation. We can now formalize that discussion and, in the process, hopefully provide a framework within which to think of the national security problem.

The World of Tiers is portrayed in Figure 12.1. Any physical depiction of an intellectual construct runs some risk of distorting the idea to create a picture, but it can be worth the attempt to better describe the idea. In the figure, the familiar two tiers have been drawn with a unitary vision of the First Tier as a kind of roof over a regionally divided Second Tier. The United States is pictured at the apex of the First Tier roof because it is the remaining superpower in the sense of possessing the widest array of instruments of power (as described in Chapter 7) and because the appeal of American values (soft power) means the other members of the system increasingly look to the United States for leadership. The division of the Second Tier into a series of subtiers further suggests

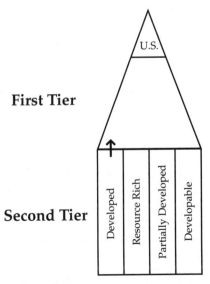

FIGURE **12.1**   **World of Tiers**

that this tier is by no means a unity and that different regions have distinct problems. The arrows from the Second Tier to the First Tier indicate those subtiers from which one can most reasonably expect states to rise and join the Clintonian "ring of market democracies."

The First Tier (or Singer and Wildawsky's zone of peace), of course, encompasses in essence the advanced market democracies who were part of the anticommunist coalition of the Cold War system. Due to a shared belief in the intertwined ideas of political democracy and market-based economy (the political and economic manifestations of free choice), they have become remarkably alike, a situation reinforced and even furthered by their increased contacts within a truly global economy, which they collectively dominate.

The degree of similarity that has emerged, as well as the common interests that have been part of that similarity, has been generally underplayed in discussions of the evolving system. Constructs such as Huntington's "clash of civilizations" (that appeared in a 1993 edition of *Foreign Affairs*) imply underlying cultural differences that create a conflict that undermines, at least in part, their commonality. Certainly there are differences between traditional Japanese culture and the European culture, for instance. As a practical matter, however, the bonds are more important than the differences. The countries of the First Tier may not march to the sound of the same drummer on all matters; on the important questions, however, their similarities are greater than their differences.

On most issues, one of the values they share is an acknowledgement of American primacy among the equal partners of the First Tier. Despite rejoinders about American relative decline and charges of American inconstancy and inconsistency, the United States remains the only country in the world with a global reach economically and, especially, militarily. The latter is of particular salience in security issues: the U.S. military was designed for global competition with a globally ambitious Soviet Union. The Russians no longer have that ability to project forces worldwide; the degree to which the United States retains that ability will be a matter of American budgetary decisions. The degree to which the First Tier can order chaos around the world will be a function of the size of the American shoulders on which the world must ride. The performance of the United States to this point suggests a high level of future activism.

This premise does not suggest anything like American hegemony or the need for American leadership on all matters; the U.S. superiority is *relative*, not absolute. The analogy of a senior partner or big brother, not of an overarching hegemon, describes the American place in the First Tier. (This is why, among other reasons, the notion of unipolarity or what some analysts prefer to call unipolycentrism to describe the international system or the American place within the First Tier is misleading.) Moreover, the First Tier contains essentially all the major powers that colonized the Second Tier. The result is a residue of interest that will encourage those powers (notably France and Great Britain) to provide the leadership—to act as the lead country—in some cases, while the United States merely acquiesces or limits its role to such actions as providing logistical support.

Discussing the Second Tier in a unified manner is also misleading, and the division of it into regional subtiers is only a partially satisfactory way to sharpen distinctions. Asia and the Pacific—defined as that part of the Asian landmass minus the Middle East (the Persian Gulf and Diaspora)—contains at least four discernible subregions having different structures and problems: the Pacific Rim countries, Southeast Asia, South Asia, and the Pacific. North Africa and sub–Saharan Africa are distinctive subregions; the problems of the Persian Gulf and of the Diaspora (the historic Arab-Israeli conflict area) differ; Latin America is composed of South America, Central America, and the Caribbean, each with different problems; and there is a good bit of difference both between the former Soviet Union and eastern Europe and within each.

These differences are manifested in various ways, one of which is differential probabilities of subregions joining the First Tier. In Asia, a number of the Pacific Rim countries (South Korea, Singapore, Taiwan, and Malaysia, for instance) are more or less poised for membership. In Latin America, a number of South American states, notably Argentina, Brazil, and Chile, are near-members; NAFTA will bring Mexico into the fold; and a second NAFTA round could enhance the chances of Argentina and Chile. Similarly, some of the successor states of the Soviet Union (such as the Baltic states) may become eligible in time, as may eastern European states such as Poland, Hungary, and the Czech Republic. Economic underdevelopment stands in the way of early entrance by African countries, and the absence of political democracy outside Israel in the Middle East similarly restricts entrance.

NATIONAL SECURITY IN A WORLD OF TIERS

In structural terms, the major difference between the Cold War system and that of the present is the disappearance of the old Second World and the adversarial relationship between the First and Second Worlds that was its principal dynamic and the driver of the national security system. Indeed, one reason to redesignate the system into two tiers is to remove the ordinal gap created by having to go directly from the first to the third worlds. That the notion of ordinality and, thus, implicit rank remains is an unavoidable limitation of language; zones of peace and turmoil, despite the absence of overt ordinality, still retain the core value (peace is better than turmoil).

The disappearance of the Second World has more impact on the national security structure than on any other aspect of the dynamics of the international system. The reason, simply enough, is that the East-West confrontation, while both political and military in nature, was basically a military competition; if one side or the other fell perilously vulnerable on the military dimension, nothing else was of great consequence.

It is because of this centrality that thinking about national security is more affected in the new order than thinking about other issues such as economic development or the environment. Lifting the veil of East-West confrontation allows clarification of other issues; development, for instance, can now be argued on its own merits, shorn of Marxist-market or anticommunist-communist political arguments. Lifting the Cold War veil from the national security structure leaves a decidedly intellectually naked emperor; there is very little intellectual structure left. This may especially be the case for the inadequacy of the Clausewitzian framework of the Cold War for organizing thinking about the present and future.

How does the end of the Cold War affect the remaining structures? It can be argued that it simply clarifies relations that were blurred by the Cold War obsession. The countries of the First Tier, for instance, have been growing more alike for well over a decade. Now that the Cold War has disappeared, we simply have the time to concentrate on the implications of that similarity. The dynamics of the Second Tier also are different from what they were during the Cold War, but only to the extent that existing differences are no longer caught up in the chess game between East and West. There was conflict and instability within and among Second Tier states then, and there still is now. The perspective through which we view those problems is different, however, and we have yet to come entirely to grips with what that new perspective means in national security terms.

National Security in the First Tier

The relations among the states of the First Tier remain in a state of basic tranquillity, what some term the democratic peace. The key word here is *remain*. The national security problem of opposing Soviet communism and its expansion was part of the glue that bound together the countries that composed the First Tier; the transformation of Japan and Germany into market democracies was originally largely motivated in terms of geopolitics, for instance. However, as time has passed and the countries of the First Tier have become more economically and politically similar, their common bonds have come to transcend the military competition. We no longer need the negative glue of common opposition to remain in harmony.

Some argue that this is too optimistic an assessment, that the collapse of the common enemy will allow us to turn upon one another and to invigorate old differences suppressed in the name of a united front before the enemy. Thus, for instance, Japan no longer needs the United States to form a shield against Soviet expansionism in the Far East, and it can now act more independently—specifically, in terms of the economic competition between the two countries. Similarly, the European members of NATO no longer need American protection from the Red Army;

differences about questions such as terms of trade can now become more prominent, driving wedges between First Tier states.

All of this may indeed, be true, but the central point is that the countries of the First Tier have become so much more alike that disputes among them are disagreements between friends that may cause occasional acrimony but do not threaten the basic friendship. Japan and the United States, for instance, have too much involvement in one another's economies for either to take action that would threaten the other, and the same is largely true of Europe and the United States. To project "the coming war with Japan" (the title of a sensational book about likely trade wars) is to miss the point. The Clinton administration's 1995 threat (quickly withdrawn) to place huge surcharges on imported Japanese luxury cars is about as "hot" as conflicts get.

The standard rejoinder to this kind of optimism is to go back to the period leading to World War I, when it was widely argued that the economies of Europe were so interdependent that general war was impossible. That analogy, however, is flawed: the governments of that time were not uniformly democratic, and the narrower horizons of people then allowed a demonization of other peoples that is quite unlikely today. To suggest that the popularly elected government of Japan could make the case to its citizens to go to war with the "demon Americans, the white hordes" (or vice versa) is absolutely fanciful.

The countries of the First Tier share four basic characteristics with overwhelming national security implications. First, there is a general structure of peace among them that is likely to endure. Second, there is general agreement among them about the kind of overall international system and national security environment they prefer. Third, their economic superiority to the Second Tier states extends to military might; the First Tier has the bulk of the political, economic, *and* military power in the international system. Fourth, the natural leader of the First Tier is the United States, and the rest of the First Tier will turn to it for leadership whenever such leadership is forthcoming or needed.

In a sense, none of these characteristics is new; only the environment in which they are pursued is different. The countries of the First Tier have been at peace with one another since 1945; they have generally preferred a peaceful world and have looked to American leadership. The only thing different is that Soviet power made the superiority of Western military power arguable during the Cold War.

The general peace, to repeat, has two basic elements. The first is the existence of the shared values of political democracy and the capitalist, market economics among First Tier members. The second is economic interdependence among the members. Each of these characteristics reinforces the general pacificity among them. Political democracies rarely engage in physical violence with one another, because free people do not choose to initiate war, especially with other peoples who share their basic political values. Interdependence adds to this general predilection in two ways. It promotes greater interchange among the economic elite, who get to know one another and thus become impervious to appeals based in their differences. It also makes war more difficult because of mutual dependence on one another for production.

The result is to create a condition within the First Tier roughly analogous to that in eighteenth century Europe, where the elites of the major countries shared a common ideology and freely circulated among the capitals of Europe that effectively comprised the international system. The series of economic summits (G-7) in which the major economic powers engage likewise provides an ongoing forum for interchange. The successful conclusion of the Uruguay Round of GATT shows that problems can be overcome through patience and compromise, and the emergence of truly international corporations—especially the so-called stateless corporations—provides a circulation of economic elites similar to that in the eighteenth century.

The bottom line is that there are no significant national security problems among members of the First Tier. Time, effort, and resources do not need to be devoted to military preparations to deter or defend against military attacks from other First Tier states. Since these states, by virtue of their superior technological bases, possess the greatest military power, the result is a situation where there are no military threats that threaten the integrity of the international order which the First Tier dominates.

This simple difference is the greatest contrast between the current order and the Cold War system. That system was necessarily obsessed with avoiding a nuclear confrontation between the major protagonists, and there is simply no analogous problem in the current environment.

This revelation does not mean that the milennium is upon us. The eighteenth century analogy may be instructive: it was the emergence of diverse political ideologies spawned by the American and French Revolutions that reintroduced divergent political ideology to the European continent and divided states along political lines worth fighting over. It is not apparent what parallel division might create the same effect in the contemporary world, but it would be foolhardy not to admit the possibility.

The second shared characteristic of the First Tier states is their general preference for an orderly, peaceful world. Expanding the pacific nature of First Tier relations to the Second Tier via expansion of the ring of market democracies is a shared preference, even if it is recognized that such a process will be difficult and, in some cases, impossible. It is, nonetheless, a preference both because a peaceful world would be one where First Tier states would not be drawn into Second Tier conflict and where the climate for expanding the global economy more broadly would be enhanced. Mechanisms like the APEC, the Free Trade Area of the Americas, and the EU may provide the structure for such an expansion.

There is nothing Pollyannish in this preference, and the First Tier is under no illusions about the prospects. Faced with very certain breaches in worldwide tranquillity, this preference suggests that collective efforts to enforce the peace are preferred to unilateral efforts. This tendency arises both from the recognition that there are more disturbances of the peace than any one, or handful, of states, can deal with and from their general agreement on the world they prefer.

There will, nevertheless, remain special circumstances in which individual First Tier states will feel the need to act individually in pursuit of their particular interests. A general breakdown in the Philippines, for instance, might evoke a strong American response because of the historic colonial relationship. The Russians, although not admitted members of the First Tier, have already demonstrated in Georgia that they will take a strong hand in unrest in the former Soviet Union, and former colonial rulers will be more prone to act where they once held power and authority.

The third characteristic of the First Tier is their preponderance of military power. The source of this strength is not numbers: only about one-seventh of the people on earth, according to Singer and Wildawsky, live in the zone of peace. Rather, the source of preponderance lies in technological superiority that allows smaller but more sophisticated military forces to overwhelm and defeat much larger but less-sophisticated forces, the result of the RMA. This advantage holds even when Second Tier forces possess some of the advanced weaponry associated with the First Tier because of differences in training and competence.

This advantage is reinforced because most of the First Tier militaries have practice in coordinating the application of military force as members of NATO. While NATO is an organization with a questionable future due to the disappearance of its enemy, it has allowed the militaries of the major powers to learn how to deal with one another in detailed ways. This coordination, for example, contributed to the ability of the British and French to interact with the United States in Operation Desert Storm (despite the fact that France was not at the time technically a member of the military command of NATO) and in IFOR.

This military advantage is not without limitations. There have been, and will continue to be, situations where there will not be consensus that even a coordinated effort will bring about a favorable outcome. Bosnia was the obvious example. As well, the major self-limitation for all First Tier states will be public opinion, which generally opposes the application of military force except in very measured ways or where overwhelming interests are clearly involved—neither of which characteristics are clearly present in most Second Tier conflicts.

Fourth and finally, there is general, if in some cases grudgingly admitted, agreement that the United States must provide the significant leadership in First Tier security matters. This is so partially because of its status as the remaining superpower, which includes the fact that it is the only country that still retains global military reach. It also reflects the fact that the United States retains more military punch than other First Tier states.

The American leadership role is bounded. The rest of the First Tier may look to the United States to lead, but it increasingly does so through the United Nations. The United States is in a push-and-shove match with the United Nations about the relations between the world body and its most powerful member. The issue is basically about leadership: is the UN the vehicle for carrying out First Tier wishes, or does the UN set the agenda? President Clinton's September 1993 entreaty that the UN must learn to say no in some cases of possible actions before the United States says yes defines that relationship. The ongoing controversy about the creation of a permanent UN force creates a continuing debate. Resolution of this critical question of leadership is made more difficult because the United States has yet to articulate a coherent set of policies and strategies for dealing with Second Tier unrest.

National Security in the Second Tier

The tranquillity within the First Tier is clearly not matched in the Second Tier, the locus of almost all of the world's instability and unrest. Much of the violence in the Second Tier can be traced back to the pattern of decolonization that began after World War II. States unprepared by their colonial masters for political independence inherited situations of great poverty, imperfect political boundaries, and a host of other conditions that would have made stable governance difficult for the best prepared. For those lacking the skills and experience of self-rule, the task was overwhelming. The last spate of decolonization is currently at work in the successor states of the Soviet Union and, sadly enough, the same pattern is appearing selectively in places like Chechnya.

It oversimplifies matters to talk of a single Second Tier. Rather, we can identify four characteristics that make up the national security problem of the Second Tier, noting its differential application in specific regions. The first characteristic is, indeed, that very lack of uniformity: some parts of the Second Tier are more unstable than others. Next, the Second Tier lacks a set of common values that would enable it to approach the First Tier in any monolithic sense. Third, the splintered nature of the Second Tier leads to a preference to view military matters in terms of collective defense rather than collective security, which has great import for the United Nations. Finally, the military capabilities of the Second Tier limit the kind and extent of goals that can be pursued by military means.

The pattern of instability in various regions of the Second Tier is depicted by conflict type in Table 12.1. As the table shows, the potential for internal conflict resides in all regions, although it is most prevalent in specific subregions. Sub–Saharan Africa, notably central Africa, has shown the most internal violence, and places such as Zaire were almost certain to experience this form of violence sometime. Latin American internal violence is mostly found in Central America and the poorest regions of the Caribbean, such as Haiti. There is potential for internal unrest in Iraq and the most politically backward of the oil-rich states, such as Saudi Arabia. South and Southeast Asia have simmering internal

TABLE 12.1   Instability in the Second Tier

Form	Africa	Latin America	Middle East	Asia	Second World
Internal	X	X	X	X	X
Regional			X	X	X

problems, and the Balkans and the southern successor states to the Soviet Union show considerable violence potential. Major regional conflicts are concentrated in the Persian Gulf, South and Southeast Asia, and in Korea. As noted earlier, the majority of the new internal wars occur in the poorest parts of the world in countries that are outside the globalizing economy and that have scant prospects of future inclusion.

One striking note is that the potential for violence is least pronounced in those parts of the Second Tier that are closest to joining the First Tier. In the past decade or so, large-scale democratization has occurred in South America that, while still in its infancy, has nonetheless stabilized politics on the continent. Regional conflict between the two major South American states, Brazil and Argentina, seems considerably more unlikely than it did ten years ago. The Pacific Rim countries, with the exception of divided Korea, has likewise achieved considerable tranquillity. Regional conflicts, indeed, seem to be on the ebb.

This diversity is also manifested in the absence of common bonds between and among Second Tier regions. There is a common cry and appeal for developmental assistance from the First Tier, but it is largely drowned out by particularism and attempts to gain special status. There is some commonality on aspirations to attainment of First Tier status, but on specific attributes of First Tier characteristics such as human rights, there is less than accord, as was clearly manifest in the 1993 UN Conference on Human Rights and Development and subsequent forums, such as the UN-sponsored conference on women in Beijing in 1995. At those conferences, mostly authoritarian Second Tier regimes tried, without success, to argue that the meaning of human rights was cultural rather than universal, largely a way to cover up what are human rights abuses by western standards. The inability to articulate common values and thereby present a united front compromises any leverage the Second Tier has with the First.

The third characteristic is that the Second Tier will likely look increasingly toward individual, rather than collective, solutions to their problems. The collective security, multilateral approach to problem solving evolving in the First Tier will likely be unmatched in the Second Tier, for the simple reason that collective efforts will be organized *against* Second Tier states, including possible intervention in internal conflicts that entails violation of the state sovereignty of select Second Tier states. Since there will be far fewer cases where individual First Tier states will act unilaterally in Second Tier conflicts, the best strategy for noninterference is to avoid the principle of collective action. As noted in the last chapter, this preference will make Second Tier interaction with the United Nations more adversarial than it has been in the past.

Fourth and finally, the absence of advanced military capability will limit the kinds of military involvement of Second Tier states. While those states possessing NBC capabilities are a partial exception, this has two direct consequences. The first is that internal wars are likely to continue to be fought in the manner of low-intensity conflicts, for the simple reason that insurgents will have little alternative and that governments will be militarily incapable of anything but counterinsurgency, at least in those cases where the violence is coherent enough to be described in those terms. The second is that regional conflicts will also be self-limited in terms of ambition by the absence of physical capacity for greater ambition. The possible exceptions to this rule are South Asia (India and Pakistan) and the Persian Gulf (Iran and Iraq).

NATIONAL SECURITY AT THE INTERSECTION OF THE TIERS

For the countries of the First Tier generally, and for the United States specifically, the implications of this analysis for national security are clear. Shorn of the old Cold War rivalry, the national security problem now moves to the intersection between the First and Second Tiers (including parts of the old Second World that became part of the Second Tier). The reason is equally clear: the occasions for employing military force are in the Second Tier, not the First.

Once again, there is nothing terribly new about this scenario. Since World War II, the United States has been involved in a series of military activities which, with the exception of the Berlin Airlift of 1948, have been in areas that are part of the Second Tier: Korea, Quemoy and Matsu (islands off the Chinese coast that are part of Taiwan), the Dominican Republic, Vietnam, Lebanon, Grenada, Iran, Panama, and Iraq, to name the most prominent.

The common thread in all but the most recent of these involvements was the Cold War confrontation. Communist North Korea invaded anticommunist South Korea, Communist China threatened the Republic of China, communists were purportedly posed to take over the Dominican Republic and later Grenada, and the Republic of Vietnam was menaced by the communist North Vietnamese.

The Cold War provided criteria to guide possible involvement that are absent in the wake of communism's effective disappearance. Instead, we can begin to think about where we will likely become involved by asking a series of four questions, the answers to which we will then try to convert into possible priorities in the final section of this chapter. The first question is: What is the nature of the First Tier–Second Tier relationship? Do we care what happens in large parts of the Second Tier? The second has to do with connecting interests and threats: How do we resolve the interest-threat mismatch? The third is a matter of First Tier/American role in the Second Tier: How much do we wish to impose? Finally, there is the question of self-limitation: How much involvement will democratic publics allow?

The kind of relationship the First Tier has to the Second is likely to depend on situation-specific circumstances. The question, in essence, is what—if any—basis for involvement in the Second Tier exists in the absence of a Cold War motivation. For former colonial powers, the answer may be residual interests in former colonies: economic investments or colonial settler populations that need protection in the event of hostilities, for instance. Geographic proximity may also provide motivation in some cases.

These kinds of motivations will not activate American concern except in limited ways: the United States might feel the need for involvement should the New People's Army be on the verge of taking over power in the Philippines, and it has historically shown an interest in quelling anti-American unrest in Central America and in protecting American access to vital petroleum reserves, as in the Persian Gulf.

But what of involvement where those criteria are not met? It is difficult to imagine any overwhelming sense of kindredness or traditional American interest that would involve the United States in internal violence and atrocity on the African continent. As noted, we have ignored very brutal, atrocious wars in places like Mozambique, Burundi, Rwanda, and the Sudan within the last few years; the same is true of the Asian subcontinent. At the same time, the United States became involved in the longest war in its history in Vietnam, where no discernible American interests existed, and it threw its military might into the fray in Somalia. The answer to the question, "Do we care?" appears to be, "Sometimes."

The second question returns the discussion to the matter of national interests and the interest-threat mismatch. In traditional terms, the situation can be restated: the threats in the new environment are not particularly interesting, and American interests are not particularly threatened by the pattern of Second Tier instability and violence. A traditional analysis would suggest that the United States would hardly ever involve itself physically in the violent affairs of most of the Second Tier.

There are two polar responses to the mismatch. One is simply to acknowledge it, argue that the mismatch is irreconcilable, and conclude that the United States has little business getting involved in internal wars and regional conflicts where demonstrable American vital interests are not affected adversely by worst outcomes. This position is the classic realist argument. Had it been applied, for instance, to Somalia, the United States would have stayed home; the only demonstrable American interests in the Horn of Africa are access to the Suez Canal and as a staging area to move into the Persian Gulf. The level of those interests is questionable, and it is unclear how any outcome in Somalia would affect those interests adversely. Moreover, the intractability of the situation did not match up with the implicit guideline that U.S. force be used only for large purposes; the possibilities for change were always modest at best.

The other polar response is to realign interests to match the threat. The mechanism for doing so may be to expand those situations deemed of national vital interest. The specific instrument is the adoption of humanitarian vital interests to justify intervention in the internal affairs of states that act atrociously toward their populations. The accompanying precept of this expansion of interest is to adopt the notion of universal sovereignty, thereby making it both an interest and an obligation to aid the beleaguered. This has become the position of the idealists; their agency of choice to carry out the mission is the United Nations. An adjunct to that line of reasoning is to adopt the position that there are many Second Tier situations where U.S. force cannot decisively change things but can make matters somewhat better and, therefore, to decide that such limited actions are worthy.

This debate about interests turns the traditional realist-idealist debate on its head. In the Cold War, realists were more likely to advocate the use of American force out of geopolitical necessity: countering communist expansion was the definition of vitality of interest. Idealists, on the other hand, generally counselled the husbanding of force, preferring nonmilitary solutions and downplaying the vital importance of unfavorable worst-case outcomes. The debate over what to do about the Sandinistas in Nicaragua during the early 1980s captures this traditional debate nicely: the possibility of a hostile Marxist regime in Central America aroused realists to call for action to overthrow the Sandinistas, while idealists argued that vital interests were not involved and that force was thus not justified.

In the post–Cold War system, positions on the use of force are nearly reversed. The realist analysis suggests a very limited role for American force in the world, because traditional vital interests are generally unaffected by Second Tier violence. The idealist position embraces the expansion of what constitutes a vital interest and thus concludes that the use of American force is justified in nontraditional situations. Thus, idealists favor a more expanded use of force than do realists.

The third question has to do with the kind of role that the United States and other First Tier states will acquire in dealing with Second Tier problems. Recognizing that there are more candidate situations for involvement—particularly if involvement in internal wars is part of the list—than there are available resources, the question has two parts.

The first part is the extent of involvement. Is the First Tier to intervene only in select cases and for the limited objectives of peacekeeping as outlined by Boutros-Ghali and discussed in Chapter 10? Or is the purpose to impose an order wherever violence and atrocity occur, and to act as a collective hegemon over the Second Tier? The latter is clearly a much more involved, expensive, and demanding task and leads to the second part of the question: Who will do the work? If either goal is to be pursued, U.S. leadership will have to be evident, but it is also clear that the United States cannot physically lead in all instances for reasons of resources and will. That being the case, what mechanisms will exist for choosing those who will lead specific missions? Assuming that something like the lead country concept would be in place, who will choose the leader?

This topic leads to the fourth question, which is about the extent to which First Tier publics will support military actions in the Second Tier. The concern arises because the chief military limitation on democratic states of the First Tier is public support. This is nothing new; over a century and a half ago, Carl von Clausewitz articulated the "holy trinity" of linkage between the government, the army, and the people. If any element in the trinity fails to support the use of military force, it will likely fail.

This problem is not only American, because the First Tier countries that possess the military might to intervene into the Second Tier are all democracies. A corollary to the proposition that democracies do not initiate wars against other democracies is that democracies do not accept casualties—body bags coming home—unless there is some compelling justification that will often be difficult to make and sustain, especially if involvement becomes lengthy. The afterglow of Vietnam makes Americans particularly sensitive to this charge; depending on the eventual outcome, Somalia may provide a parallel caution for the future.

THE FOG OF PEACE?

Predicting the future is always much more treacherous than describing the past because, as this author pointed out in an earlier book, *The Shape of the Future*, the past has happened and the future has not. The future always entails occurrences that we are unable to predict—factors unforeseen and, in some cases, unforeseeable. The problem is particularly acute when the change in conditions is fundamental and the search for analogies proves difficult, as is clearly the case today. Who, for instance, would have predicted U.S. troops in Port au Prince, Haiti, in 1994? Or in Bosnia in 1995 and 1996?

The American national security apparatus is in the midst of a crisis about its future role and mission. Its predicament approaches the state of a dilemma. The professional community is, on the whole, conservative and realist in its orientation. It does not view lightly the idea of putting young American lives at risk unless there is some demonstrable threat to American interests. The dilemma is that the apparatus also faces severe reductions in resources that can only be staunched by embracing uses of force that contradict its own basic realist precepts. The strained attempt of the professional officer corps to find a way to embrace support for the

United Nations—an institution it has reflexively rejected for decades—captures the agony involved.

The early post–Cold War experience does not provide much guidance as to where and when the United States should use force in the future. The contrast between systemic reaction in Somalia and the long period of inaction in Bosnia provides little positive direction. Coming to grips with the possibility of using U.S. forces for less than Napoleonic ends is central to ordering policy: will the United States embrace, as a matter of policy, the use of its forces for less than decisive ends?

One can easily overstate the extent of uncertainty in the present circumstance, and we can suggest some guidelines for the United States in choosing when and where to apply force in the Second Tier. To this end, nine influences will be identified and presented, in no particular order of importance, on the assumption that some will be more important than others. The first three address the question of our level of awareness of situations. The next two concern what the United States is being asked to undertake. The last four influences reflect former National Security Advisor Anthony Lake's four rules on using force and suggest the likelihood of success. For clarity's sake, the factors are summarized in Table 12.2.

The first factor is the level of atrocity and horror of a given situation. As a general rule, the greater the horror and atrocity involved, the more likely some form of international action will be contemplated. In the first two post–Cold War situations in which the United States became involved, Operation Provide Comfort for the Kurds and Operation Restore Hope in Somalia, the term "genocide" was prominently mentioned. Kurdish fears (warranted or not) of genocidal attacks by Iraqi forces caused them to flee; similarly, genocidal levels of death predicted in Somalia from starvation partly motivated intervention. Fears of repression and retribution helped fuel the Haitian intervasion; genocide in Bosnia was literally unearthed as IFOR settled in.

Genocide represents a level of atrocity that could reasonably activate international efforts, including an American component, especially if such acts were committed by a country signatory to the UN Convention on Genocide (which includes most countries). Operationalizing genocide is, however, never easy in individual cases, and it leaves open the question of what actions short of genocide should create international intervention. The Bosnian and Rwandan war crimes trial outcomes will go a long way toward defining practical international standards.

A second and corollary factor is the level of publicity received by instances of Second Tier violence. This factor suggests the strong role of global television, which has the option of publicizing instances of great suffering and atrocity or ignoring them. In some cases, global television has been effectively prevented from covering the gory details of ethnic and other violence, as in the Sudan. There is also, as mentioned earlier, the possibility that the viewing public will eventually become desensitized to carnage, to the point that television pictures will not activate the

TABLE 12.2   **Involvement Factors**

WHAT WE KNOW:

1. Level of atrocity
2. Amount of publicity
3. Recognition factor

WHAT WE ARE ASKED TO DO:

4. Burden sharing/leadership
5. Time commitment

PROSPECTS OF SUCCESS:

6. Interests involved
7. Efficacy of force
8. Cost
9. End game

"do-something syndrome." Additionally, the effect of moderate levels of coverage—as in Burundi in 1993 or in Azerbaijan and Armenia—on world opinion is still an open question.

A third factor, influenced by the first two, is the average American's low degree of recognition of distant places and the people involved. The well-chronicled American lack of interest and knowledge about foreign affairs is especially great in matters dealing with the countries of the Second Tier, and it will be hard to gain widespread public support for sending forces to places and/or over issues of which the average citizen has never heard. Stimulating sufficient public interest—especially where threats are not particularly compelling—will require a good deal of citizen education, a process in which the global media will play a major role.

The next two factors on the list deal with what the American people, through their armed forces, are being asked to do in specific situations. Who will authorize and participate in the actions? The United States has shown willingness to act unilaterally where its interests are clearly engaged or where it simply feels that it must. We would, for instance, have conducted Operation Desert Storm on our own had others not volunteered. The same was true of early efforts in Somalia, and the U.S. action in Haiti was essentially unilateral, if with an OAS imprimatur.

Burden sharing, however, will be a hallmark of American willingness in the future, especially if the roster of actions expands. Spreading the lead-country role widely will be necessary for the American people, who instinctively shrink from being designated the world's "globo-cop." Moreover, it remains to be seen how long the "honeymoon" between American military forces and the United Nations will last. If the UN bureaucracy insists on an aggressive, inclusive presence wherever violence breaks out—that is, if it fails to learn to say no, in President Clinton's terms—that relationship will likely sour. These questions largely created U.S. veto of the reappointment of Boutros-Ghali, the leading advocate of an expanded UN leadership role, for a second term as secretary-general in 1996.

The fifth factor is the duration of the operations. It is virtually an axiom in democratic societies that they tolerate best military actions that are quick, decisive, and generally as bloodless as possible. Lengthy involvements are tolerated only when the aims are so overwhelmingly important as to justify greater sacrifice, an idea elaborated in Snow and Drew, *From Lexington to Desert Storm*, or when American forces do not incur significant casualties, as in Haiti and Bosnia. Second Tier actions will hardly ever meet this criterion. Recent evidence of this truism is found in Somalia: the first time in was short, decisive, bloodless, and overwhelmingly popular. When the Americans returned for an apparently open-ended stay and incurred human losses, the public debate quickly turned to a congressional–White House debate on setting a time limit to get the troops out and forced their withdrawal.

The last four factors, borrowed with acknowledgment from Lake, address the likelihood of achieving goals to which the American people can subscribe. Item six raises the question of what American interests are involved. This is important both as a guiding criterion and as the basis for rationalizing action to the American people. The statement of what American interests are engaged in some unfavorable outcome are, in effect, a statement of why the country is asking some Americans to sacrifice, up to and including their lives.

This will, in my view, be the central question in determining American participation in the Second Tier. Those favoring broad involvement argue that the forces are, after all, well-paid professionals who volunteered to be placed in harm's way: they go wherever they are sent. Those hastening caution retort that those professionals are also the sons and daughters of voters who will take out their displeasure on officials who put their children in physical danger for less than truly vital reasons. The interventionist argument is better cocktail party talk than good politics, unless the United States weds itself to small, discrete involvements that are less than Napoleonic in their impact but that do some good *and* involve few casualties.

The seventh item turns on whether the insertion of American forces can actually do any good. Despite the high combat effectiveness of American forces, the answer is not always obvious. As was argued in Chapter 10, a number of the potential roles will be in peace imposition, and it is not at all clear that military force can solve those situations, especially where state building is required. Once again, there are relatively few available situations where grand objectives may be achievable; there is no shortage of small conflicts where limited ends may be attainable. Haiti and Bosnia represent one vision of the future.

The eighth factor is cost and its acceptability. If potential engagements are short and decisive, cost is less likely to be a problem. But if commitments become extensive and individual involvements are extended, then cost—including the sacrifices entailed in other areas—will have to become part of the calculation.

Finally, there is the necessity of finding a way to end commitment—the endgame. The United Nations record is not encouraging here: peacekeeping missions develop a life of their own and, in places such as Cyprus, become solutions of their own. The United States, upon returning to Somalia, was faced with the question of how to know when its purpose had been accomplished and it was time to go home. Setting and implementing an arbitrary date for withdrawal answered the second part of that question, but not the first. Involvements are likely to be inversely attractive to their open-endedness, and this is especially true in nondecisive situations like Bosnia where imposing permanent solutions is probably impossible.

It has become fashionable to describe the post–Cold War era as particularly chaotic, unpredictable, and even dangerous. Such depictions overstate reality and make deciding about how to deal with the new environment appear more difficult than is really the case, in at least two ways. First, the absence of a central, system-threatening conflict such as the U.S.-Soviet nuclear confrontation means the world is in much less danger of self-immolation than it was before; the language of dangerousness is misleading. Second, that the locus of violence and instability in the world is in the Second Tier does not represent any great change; that is where the fighting and dying occurred during the Cold War. What is principally different is that the old Cold War criteria no longer order how we view these conflicts.

All this suggests is that the new international order is not so incomprehensible as is frequently advertised. The question is not so much what the nature of the national security environment is as it is about how the United States (and others in the First Tier) want to influence that order. Lifting the fog of peace, which is the more general condition of the United States today, is not so much a matter of what the system is like as it is a policy question of how we want the system to be.

Suggested Reading

Barnet, Richard J. "Reflections (the Age of Globalization)," *New Yorker* (June 16, 1990):46–60.

Cullen, Robert. "Human Rights Quandary," *Foreign Affairs* 72, 5 (Winter 1992/93):79–88.

Carter, Ashton G., William J. Perry, and John D. Steinbruner. *A New Concept of Co-operative Security.* Washington, D.C.: Brookings Institution, 1992.

Diebel, Terry L. "Internal Affairs and International Relations in the Post–Cold War World," *Washington Quarterly* 16, 3 (Summer 1993):13–36.

Fromkin, David. "The Coming Milennium: World Politics in the Twenty-First Century," *World Policy Journal* 10, 1 (Spring 1993):1–7.

Huntington, Samuel P. "Clash of Civilizations?" *Foreign Affairs* 72, 3 (Summer 1993):22–49.

Klare, Michael T., and Daniel C. Thomas (eds.). *World Security: Challenges for a New Century*. New York: St. Martin's Press, 1994.

Neumann, Robert G. "This Next Disorderly Half Century: Some Proposed Remedies," *Washington Quarterly* 16, 1 (Winter 1993):33–50.

Schlesinger, James. "Quest for a Post–Cold War Foreign Policy," *Foreign Affairs* 72, 1 (1992/93):17–28.

Snider, Don M. *The National Security Strategy: Documenting Strategic Vision*. Carlisle Barracks, Pa.: Strategic Studies Institute, 1992.

Sullivan, John D. "Democracy and Global Economic Growth," *Washington Quarterly* 15, 2 (Spring 1992):175–186.

Index